The Next Chapter

Javier A. Robayo

Cover Art Work
Floral Bouquet by Smiths-The Main Street Florist Butler, PA
www.smithsmainstreetfloral.com
Photograph by Bob Napoletan
Napoletan Photography Butler, PA
www.napoletanphotography.com
Final Design by Jaime O. Robayo
Robayo Designs Ansonia, CT

DEDICATION

This book is dedicated to every courageous human being who is not afraid to embrace change in order to be who they are meant to be.

ACKNOWLEDGMENTS

Jaime O. Robayo, for the enthusiastic support and the sage advice on every aspect of life. I love you, Dad.

Sheri Robayo, my pretty wife, once again for her patience, and sharp eye for typos. But most of all, for her honest reactions at every turn of the story.

Dr. Kimberly Miller, my editor, for pushing me into that elusive next level.

Christina Fifield-Winn, for her brutal honesty, unconditional friendship, and invaluable help.

Beth Warheit BSN, RN, CMSRN, for all the insightful information on Atrial Fibrillation and AIDS, your patients are fortunate to have you.

Diego Gavilanez, one of the most courageous persons I've ever known, for one of the most inspiring conversations I've ever had.

Jennifer Belisle, for her support, and unequaled humor.

Kendra and Amber Robayo, my inspiring daughters, for always showing me there's more to life than work.

Any and all errors are mine.

Nothing takes more courage than being yourself. - T.L. Tate

To be nobody-but-yourself -- in a world which is doing its best, night and day, to make you everybody else -- means to fight the hardest battle which any human being can fight; and never stop fighting .- E. E. Cummings

The Next Chapter

Prologue

London, July 2011

Bad idea, Lewis…

I can't bloody believe how many people are jammed in this place. It's barely after six and still hotter than blazes. There shouldn't be this many people until closer to midnight. It's almost fascinating how a thousand people or more can quickly reduce a warehouse to phone booth status. To make matters worse, this DJ is apparently a firm believer in maximum volume. The laser beams bounce against mirrored surfaces and sting the eye. As I look around, I think I'm the only one feeling uncomfortable.

Next to me, my rave friend, Audrey Burton, notorious London artist, bounces in place to each sonic boom pulsing out of the gigantic subwoofers.

I give her a pleading look that she ignores as she hugs some bloke, dressed head to toe in leather. How can he stand it in this heat? The sun's still blasting us through the dirty windows, making me feel like an ant under a magnifying glass, the amplified heat reducing me to a crisp.

I leave Audrey to her socializing and make my way to the makeshift bar. I don't want a drink as much as I want to get away from the sound system.

The bartender, a pretty lass done up in psychedelic makeup with an emphasis on glitter, sways up to me.

"Water!"

Her eyes widen out of their black and metallic purple eyelids in confusion. She cocks her head to one side and stares at me curiously.

"Just water!" I shout over the monstrous din.

The creature shrugs and turns to fill a tall glass with ice and water out of the tap then slams the glass in front of me.

"She's rude, that one," shouts a tenor voice at my ear.

I turn to face a startling set of grey eyes twinkling with amusement. My eyes follow the delicate lines of his nose and down to a remarkable smile.

"Brandon," he says, extending his right hand. "I didn't mean to give you a fright," he shouts the apology.

"Lewis."

The grin widens. Brandon has a chiseled jaw, lean cheeks and a creamy complexion, but his eyes are his most commanding feature and he seems to know it.

"I've seen you at other raves," he says in my ear. "I promised myself to talk to you if I saw you again."

I draw back and he leans closer, offering me his diamond studded ear. When I lean in, I inhale a cloud of warm cologne fumes emanating from his skin. It's not altogether unpleasant, but it makes me grimace. The reaction surprises me, but I don't know why exactly.

I forget what I was going to say to the bloke.

Sensing my hesitation, he turns to face me and smiles as he takes me by the elbow and leads me away from the bar. We navigate our way through a throng of dancing bodies into an adjoining large space.

The air is damp, scented of wet concrete, but it's cool on my neck. Sound registers as though I'm underwater. I don't want to think of the damage I inflicted upon my hearing.

"It's a bit quieter out here," Brandon observes needlessly.

I'm not about to affirm the obvious. "I don't remember ever seeing you."

His smile turns shy. "You were Terry Dougherty's partner, weren't you?"

I suddenly feel uneasy. "Do you know Terence?"

He nods. "I knew him quite well for a time."

I feel a strange wave of heat at the implication.

"Not what you think. We were just casual friends, but he often talked about you." A slight shake of his head. "I always hoped to meet someone like you."

Flattery, one of my favorite ice breakers. "Tell me about yourself, Brandon."

He proceeds to give me an entertaining account of his life as though he's rehearsed the entire diatribe. He's attractive, and given his evident intellect, perhaps a good match for me, but I'm not getting an urge to spend more time with this lad.

"Lewis, why don't we go to Bow Ties?"

He's forward, this one.

I glance at the back door to the club, realizing raves are for kids. A quiet setting for what may be an enjoyable conversation sounds perfect. Audrey may box my ears for leaving her, but we often go our own way unless we have Samantha, although that won't be an issue. There won't be another rave for Samantha.

I turn back to Brandon, who's fidgeting as he waits for my reply. "You know, that's a good idea, Brandon."

"I left my car near the station."

I nod. "I'll meet you at Bow Ties," I promise.

An initial meeting doesn't warrant sharing a ride to an intimate setting and he seems to understand that.

"I'll see you in a bit," Brandon smiles and fixes me with a penetrating gaze.

His hand squeezes my forearm and he's about to say something, but then changes his mind. He smiles and strolls off in the direction of the station.

I walk down the alley and turn up the street as I text Audrey about my plans. Her reply is instantaneous,

It's about bloody time you get some action, chap. If you don't take him, I will, lms

I grin at her use of Samantha's Textish for *laughing myself silly*.

I start replying that I might keep Brandon all to myself when the cry of a child startles me.

"Oh, little darling, forgive Momma," a soft voice cries. "I have it right here, baby."

The woman is shuffling towards her car, which is parked behind my BMW. She has an infant in a carrier in one hand while perilously balancing a bag, an accordion folder ready to burst, and a shopping sack, which is about to dislodge its contents. I quicken my pace when I see her stumble. She's wearing sandals, what Samantha calls flip-flops. I never liked the bloody things, but women have a major disregard for safe footing when it comes to footwear. Her big toe is practically off the foam platform with each step she takes, and the thin stem between the toes must be cutting in painfully though she doesn't seem to notice. I reach her right before she drops everything, including her baby, to break her fall.

"It's alright, It's alright, I'm just trying to help," I say soothingly when she tenses at my touch as I manage to keep the sack from turning over.

Satisfied that I'm not dangerous, she sags tiredly against the side of her car, her right hand still gripping the carrier. Her baby starts wailing, her piercing cry echoing on the empty street.

She looks at me with wide eyes and I try to give her my most harmless smile. "I can help you load your bags, Madame. It sounds like someone needs you," I say, nodding at the little one.

The woman parts her brown hair, revealing an oval shaped face with startling blue eyes that judiciously gauge my intentions. After a moment, she gives me a tired smile that jolts me as an image of Gwen Amaya appears in my mind.

"Thank you, ever so much. It's been one of those bloody days," she says ruefully.

I open the door and situate her stuff in the back seat while she's trying to soothe her baby.

I'm about to bid her good night and leave, but there's something about her that sets off a strange buzzing in my head. My eyes go to the baby. She's a beautiful, tiny girl with barely a wisp of hair.

"She's quite lovely," I say in an attempt to dispel any sense of threat the mother might still feel.

She kisses the top of her baby's head and turns to me. "Would you mind?"

I barely get my arms ready to receive the crying little girl. The woman rummages through a bag and emerges with a bottle in hand. She mixes purified water and the contents of a can of formula.

"I should've fed her before we left," she says remorsefully.

The baby has stopped crying in my arms while I subconsciously rocked her gently. Her round little head rests over my shoulder and her tiny fist is tight around the fabric of my shirt.

My heart seems bent on knocking my ribs out of the way in order to get out, and my eyes sting.

What in the bloody hell…

"Oh, she likes you," Momma says with a beatific smile. "You must have the daddy gene," she says knowingly.

I smile back, suddenly accosted by an emotional storm of unknown origin.

"May I?"

I blink back to the moment. She's waiting for me to hand her baby back. I gently transfer the little girl to her mother's arms. Baby's eyes flutter open and stay on me the entire time.

"This is Lanie," the woman offers. "Lanie, say hi, sweetie."

Lanie's eyes fix on the nipple of the bottle as her little arms reach for it. No more than a few seconds later, her eyes close while she drinks with evident contentment.

I'm smiling.

I'm smiling even though something is churning up my insides.

The woman gently rocks her baby in her arms and finally looks up at me. There is no trace of weariness like when I first saw her.

"Thank you so much, Mister…"

"L-Lewis," I stammer, surprised at the choked tone of my voice. I clear my throat hoping she didn't notice.

Her smile falters for just a second. "Lewis, you're very kind."

Something about the sight of the infant makes me feel like crying.

Get it bloody together!

"Have you any children?"

I shake my head.

"Oh well, when you do, they're just going to love you."

I say nothing for a moment. "Can I help you with anything else?"

"Oh no, you've done enough."

Lanie's asleep. Her mother places her back in the carrier then gently locks it in place on the car seat. After shutting the door, she shocks me by giving me an affectionate hug.

"You tell your wife, she's got a real gentleman in her hands."

Without another word, she climbs behind the wheel, waves, and maneuvers out of the spot. I watch her drive away as tears roll down my face while images of two girls from Pennsylvania fill the landscape of my thoughts.

I never make my meeting with Brandon.

1

London, October 2011

My feet are killing me.

The bloody kicks I decided to wear this morning are turning into unendurable torture and the pain sours my mood. Hopefully Samantha doesn't notice. She's gotten me waiting on her once more, longest wait so far. Is she sewing the bloody gown?

"You'll like this one!" She calls from the changing room.

I smile at the young little trollop from the shop, who's fetched yet another bloody gown.

"If I say I love this one, can we call it a day?" I ask her, but it sounded more jovial in my head.

"Impatient, are you? That's ironic, coming from the chap who tried on every bloody button-down at Hendricks'. Longest day of my existence," she gripes.

I can only sit back and cross my legs. I can tell my feet are swollen. Why do I have to be so bloody formal? The groom is anything but. I'm willing to wager he'll go to the altar in combat boots.

"Ready?"

I put my foot down, fighting the urge to grimace, and try to paste an eager look on my face.

When I hear the latch slide open I sit up straight, trying to come up with another scathing remark. Samantha's tried on so many gowns I'm actually running out of ideas.

I hear a gasp from the shop woman as a vision of pure, ethereal beauty walks up to a platform to stand in front of a large, triple-paned, full-length mirror. A corona blurs the ceiling lights, reminding me to breathe. I actually feel lightheaded.

My baby is all grown up...

"Alright. Let's hear it," Sam says defiantly.

I can't find my voice.

Samantha stands tall, her chestnut hair gathered into a long tail over her bare shoulder. Her gaze is boring into me, the unique beauty of her flecked grey eyes, piercing me in place. She could be a stand in for Kate Beckinsale, given the saucy little lips and her thin upturned nose.

"Well?"

I find myself standing, twirling a finger in the air, not so much for her to turn in a full circle, but for me to buy just enough time to compose the right words.

Samantha rolls her gorgeous eyes and twirls slowly.

I have to admire her toned back and slim arms. The bodice shows off a wonderful hour glass figure that she keeps with a daily regimen of exercise.

A wedding gown is meant to make a princess out of the bride and its power defies logic. I've seen women of epic proportions become beautiful upon donning the gown. In Samantha's case, she easily enhances its beauty, rather than the other way around.

"Will you open up your gob today or what?"

I start saying something but I can't. A lump of emotion has sealed my throat shut. I see the skinny little lass my best friend once was, and I can't reconcile that image in my mind with the stunning beauty before me. The frown of her perfectly sculpted brows softens, and a shy little smile curls her lips.

I love to see her smile. I love that she graces this wretched planet with it more often than before. I'd missed that sight for several years.

"Lewis?"

I can't talk now. I can't trust my bloody voice. To make matters worse, I can't even hide my expression under the pretense of a congratulatory embrace, or some other gesture. I feel like a bloody fool when my eyes begin to sting. "I don't have the words," I finally consent. "You make Cinderella ordinary."

Samantha's eyes widen before she bursts out laughing. For whatever reason, I wonder whether she has any clue as to how strong she really is. Must be her laughter. After all she's been through...

"I guess I'll say it's sweet of you to find me topping some cartoon lass. What a compliment." She curtsies, the gesture making her look even more regal.

I quickly wipe my eyes while she's not looking and find a way to give her an approving smile.

"Very well," she says, standing a bit straighter.

I notice she has yet to look in the mirror as though waiting for my opinion to allow her a glance.

"You had me going. Now, what do you really think?"

I take a closer look. The bodice flatters the lines of her torso and manages to make her breasts look femininely demure by showing only a tasteful hint of cleavage. The thin straps over her shoulders make her swanlike neck look long and graceful. Unlike traditional gowns with the straight line between the bodice and the train, this dress contours to the flare of her hips and makes a V over her flat stomach, and the small of her back. "I think you've found your gown, luv."

"You don't think it's too much?"

"Too much what?"

"Seems a bit racy," she says, still not looking in the mirror. "Too silvery white perhaps? I should try on the candlelight—"

"Sam," I say patiently.

"—the off-white perhaps. I—"

"Sam."

"—I just had to see what that pretty—"

"SAM!"

"What?" The startled look on her face is priceless.

"Shut your bloody gob and look in the blasted mirror!"

She stares at me, her eyes pleading.

I nod. "Go on."

She shakes her head and bites her lip.

I'm about to try reasoning with her but I know better. This requires a bit of action. I sigh and roll my eyes skyward as I climb the first step of the platform, careful not to step on the hem of the gown.

"Lewis..."

I take her shoulders and turn her ninety degrees, but the clever drama queen she is, shuts her eyes tight. "Open them," I say softly.

"No."

"Samantha, open your eyes."

I'm standing right behind her, my face over her shoulder, when she finally opens her eyes. I see shock in them, then the familiar giddiness of a little girl who always thought herself beautiful in a Sunday dress, before her eyes fill with tears.

"Don't cry, lass. It won't do for you to think so highly of yourself."

"It's not that."

I gather her hair and pull it up to simulate a French twist, her favorite updo. The transformation is subtle, but the result no less stunning. "You actually look quite elegant, luv."

"I look just like..." Tears spill over her long lashes.

"Yes, well. Your mother was a fox too."

There's a sad smile on her face as she turns. Her head comes to rest on my shoulder.

"If you get weepy mascara on this, I'm dragging your bony arse back to Hendricks' and you'll buy me another bloody shirt. And if you think I took a long time choosing this little number..."

She sniffles loudly. "I'll buy you ten."

I give her the most delicate embrace, terrified of wrinkling the fine material of her gown. "You look the way a fairy tale princess should look," I say sincerely.

Somewhere behind us, someone blows their nose. The honking rudely cuts into the tenderness of the moment. When Samantha and I look back, the young shop employee gives us a sheepish smile as she dabs at her eyes with a tissue.

"Pardon me," she says in a small voice. "But I must say you will know nothing but happiness."

Her assumption brings a smile to Samantha's face but knowing me as well as she does, she's quick to caution me with her eyes.

"You're very kind," I nod at the girl.

We watch her gather four other gowns, and give her a smile of gratitude.

I turn back to Samantha. "Is this your gown, luv?"

She looks into the mirror again, her eyes searching the eyes of her reflection. My breath catches as she does this, but her smile only widens before nodding happily. "This is the one."

I let go of her hair and mouth a *Thank You* that she doesn't miss.

"Was it really that bad?"

I go still and look into her eyes. "Do you want the bloody truth, or do you want me to be a friend?"

"Geez! I'm sorry. This is very important."

"I'm glad you found 'The One'. Now, what will you do to return to me those seven hours of my life I'll never get back?"

"Dinner?"

"Sold."

"Can you help me get out of this?"

"I think that's Lancelot's job." I love the look she gives me when I call her fiancé anything other than Jason Stephen.

"Not tonight, it isn't."

"Stop right there," I warn her. "I don't need to hear about what goes on behind the bloody bedroom door."

Samantha gives me her wicked grin. I've seen quite a few men bewitched by it, but it has no effect on me and I know—and relish—how much it bothers her.

The elaborate bodice of the dress has more clasps and hidden buttons than I think necessary. My fingers are almost too thick to handle the delicate hardware. "Can I just rip it off you? There's enough time to repair the bloody thing."

"Funny."

"How'd you get this on?"

"With a lot of patience," she muses.

Now I understand why it took so bloody long before she finally stepped out of the fitting room.

Finally the last little clasp gives up its maddening hold and I hear Samantha taking a deep breath. "Too tight?"

"No!" She barks indignantly, holding the bodice over her chest and carefully starting down off the platform. "I was afraid your clumsy hands would ruin it."

"Of course you were."

When she shuts the door of the fitting room, I wave at the shop employee. She walks quickly, her brown bob bouncing with each step. I finally get a good look at her tag without squinting when she's near. Like bloody hell I'll ever wear the blasted eyeglasses I need.

"Maggie, dear. Would you be a luv and take care of this?" I hand her my credit card. "Make sure this covers any alterations and any supplemental costs, accessories and whatever else."

"Yes, Sir."

"Oh, and Maggie?" She looks up with a disposition that says she's ready for anything. "No mention of my name."

She answers my wink with one of her own, and then she quickly turns the corner past a display and disappears.

"When's pretty Gwen flying in?" I call to Sam, referring to her best friend from the US.

"Not sure yet. God! What am I going to say when I see her?"

"Um… How about 'Welcome to the Queen's Land'?"

"You know what I mean!" She snaps.

I do. Gwen and Samantha share quite the peculiar friendship. Distance, old feelings, infidelity, a murder attempt, nothing's ruined it. In fact, they are probably closer than ever. Gwen is to be the matron of honor after all.

Samantha knew how to pick them. I got to know Gwen and her husband Tony personally, and I found them both to be great people. I look forward to seeing them again.

I suddenly remember something from a letter she wrote to Gwen. "Did you mean it?"

"Did I mean what, luv?"

"You told Gwen she could punch you in the eye. Did you mean it?"

The latch clicks open and the door is pulled inward. Samantha emerges in an orange tank and faded jeans frayed at the cuffs. Her dainty feet somehow keep her flimsy sandals in place.

"Do you think she will?" There's real anxiety in her voice.

"Someone claiming to be your friend sleeps with your husband and then nearly gets him killed. What would you do?"

Color rises to her face and her eyes look wounded and uncertain. "She will punch me in the eye."

"Probably both eyes." There's fear in her widened stare. "Don't be daft. Gwen is a class act. Honestly, the fact that she continues to write to you defies logic."

Samantha's eyes have taken a faraway look. "She's a better woman than I'll ever be."

I silently agree. "Don't be so hard on yourself, Sam. I don't think Gwen makes a habit of looking back."

Her eyes turn hopeful.

"I mean, so long as you don't allow your sordid impulses to bed her husband again, you'll be just peachy, luv."

Her knuckles crack when her fist hits my shoulder.

2

Samantha talks me into heading back to Kensington so she can change. Nathan Jeffries' mansion is too much of a temptation so I oblige without fuss.

"Let me see if I understand this correctly, Gwen is your gal of honor," I say, stretching my feet on the couch of the luxurious formal living room. "But I have to do all the heavy lifting for your little soiree?"

Samantha's fingers are a blur over the keyboard of her laptop. I know no one else who can type as fast. "Gwen won't be here until next week and we've got to get things accomplished."

"Very well, she has a valid excuse," I concede. "But what about Lancelot?"

Samantha stops typing and shuts her eyes tight. "He has a name, you know."

I can't hide the smirk. "He's got two. So annoying! Why do you have to address him by Jason Stephen?"

A dreamy little smile appears on her pretty face. "Because it sounds hot."

"Spare me," I plead, rolling my eyes.

"You asked!"

"The point is," I give her a serious look, hoping to wipe off that lovesick little grin. "Shouldn't he be helping you with some of the details?"

Samantha avoids my eyes, a sign that I struck a nerve.

"That's what Lorna is paid to do," she says in a flat voice.

Lorna Matthews is an overly optimistic pain in the bloody rear, but she's worth her considerable weight in gold when it comes to planning a wedding. "Oh, that's right, your wedding planner extraordinaire. Where's she been?"

Samantha considers this. "She has flowers, invitations, and a whole other set of details that she's diligently overseeing." She scowls. "If you don't want to help me, you can just leave."

She's too easy to ruffle. "I don't mind helping you, Sam. I love being here for you. I just wanted you to keep an eye on the big picture."

Sam stands off her chair and practically jumps on my lap. Her chin comes to rest on my shoulder.

"He's working so much," she says in a shaky voice. "I haven't seen him in an entire week, Lewis."

"When did you talk to him last?"

"Two nights ago. He's on assignment in Turkmenistan. Nathan didn't want him to go, but Jason insisted. It had something to do with a friend of his from the service."

Since Jason Stephen and Samantha officially got together, they haven't been apart any more than mere hours. He just wouldn't leave her side, and I didn't want him to. At first, it took a group effort to keep Samantha from falling off her precarious perch of sobriety. I felt more than a little remorse for suggesting that they were spending far too much time together.

I hope her anxiety doesn't land her at the bottom of a bottle of vodka. With this in mind, I figure I'd better put some of her fears to rest. "The Stans aren't known for good communications of any kind, luv."

"The Stans?"

"You know, Afghanistan, Pakistan, Uzbekistan, Turkmenistan, the 'Stans."

"Oh."

Me and my big gob...

I mentally berate myself when her eyes fill with sadness. Samantha didn't intend to drag me through each bridal shop in the Greater London area just to find a gown, I realize. She was trying to keep her mind occupied so she wouldn't think about Jason Stephen.

He works as a specialist for Lions Securities. His duties normally include training and logistics. At least that's the way things have been since I brought Samantha back from the US. Jason Stephen gave up field work to get Samantha the right help to break free from her lifelong alcohol dependency.

When Samantha successfully completed her therapy, Jason Stephen vowed to never leave her side, and up until a week ago, he made good on his word. I wonder what took him away from her, especially while planning their wedding.

"Why didn't you tell me, luv?"

Samantha shakes her head and wipes tears from her eyes. "He told me not to worry. He said it was a routine escort assignment for a geological excursion."

"Like I told you, those areas aren't known for great communications. When's he due back?"

"Tomorrow."

I glance at the ornate grandfather's clock in the foyer. "It's still quite early, five hours ahead in Turkmenistan. I'm sure he'll call you as soon as he gets an opportunity."

Sam nods. "I'm acting like an idiot, I know."

"Samantha Kay Reddick, you may be many things, but an idiot is not one of them. Just take a deep breath and chin up. Everything is fine."

She does as she's told then gets up and goes back to her chair. I know I've got to get her focused on something else. "Did you finalize the guest list?"

She shakes her head.

"Don't tell me you forgot, Miss Perfect Memory. Didn't you give me a few pages worth of names?"

"Just because I remember them doesn't mean they remember me."

"Are you worried about a low turnout?"

She doesn't know how to respond to this.

"You realize that day is meant for you and Jason Stephen, don't you?"

She nods. "I know but I kind of want the big crowd."

"So what's the problem?"

"I have some acquaintances I'd love to see, but they're in New York, and I just don't see them wanting to hop the pond to come to the wedding of a friend who's all but forgotten them."

"Let me handle the RSVPs."

Suspicion flickers in her eyes. "Why? What're you up to?"

I ignore the question. "The list?"

"It's in my laptop." She turns the screen to me and pushes the Apple across the table.

I attach the list, and a few other interesting files, and send them to my private inbox. I don't need Samantha fretting over every little move I make. "I'll take care of it."

She looks dubious. "What're you going to do?"

"I'm going to take care of your RSVPs. Did we not just go over that?"

"You're up to something."

I give her my most innocent smile. "Sam, come now, luv. Have a little faith. Your lack of confidence deeply wounds me. Besides, when have I ever let you down?"

Her eyes narrow, but I know she's on the fence.

"I can always ask Audrey or Molly to do it," I offer in an aloof voice, knowing full well she'd never trust our two rowdy friends with an important task.

Samantha shakes her head. "I just know you're up to something, but I'm going to go against my better judgment because I don't know what else to do."

"You shan't regret it, luv."

"It's settled then."

"Now, I don't have your superb memory, but I do believe there was mention of dinner at some point in time today."

"A late dinner? Sounds perfect. I'm starved!"

As am I. I try to think of a decent place without a tempting bar, but I can't think of one. I'd hate to submit Samantha to temptation, but I could really go for a nice glass of red wine. "Anything in particular?"

She purses her lips in thought. "Italian?"

"Agreed."

***

Samantha seemed to regret the night coming to an end. In the past, whenever she gave me those sad, opaline eyes, I'd cave and stay the night with her. I don't think that's an appropriate activity between us now. Her fiancé wouldn't be happy about it, even though he knows bloody well nothing would happen between her and me.

For some reason, a fond memory of her grandmother floats in my mind.

I spent a summer in Rhode Island with Samantha, a year after her parents were killed in a traffic accident. Grandmum Reddick kept a vigilant eye on us, especially at nighttime. I let the lovable, old bird do her night watch for four nights before coming out to her to let her know she was wasting her time.

Her biggest disappointment was being wrong about Samantha and I getting married one day. In fact, several people share that disappointment, my own mother included. Samantha is my best friend, my little sister, my blessing, my curse, my partner in crime, my gleeful enabler, all rolled into one.

I miss Grandmum.

Although set in her ways, she accepted me for everything I am, and never showed me anything less than the affection one might reserve for their own grandkid.

I actually like to think about myself back then. I was so young, so bloody ignorant, and yet so sure of myself. I miss that certainty.

I stop at a red light and take advantage of the pause to switch playlists in the sound system. I'm not finding anything I'm willing to listen to despite the fact that I have over 10,000 songs at my disposal. Music is one of my favorite escapes, but my mind seems to have sprung a new trap.

I drive home to the sound of the engine. It does little to quiet the cacophony my mind has become as of late. I feel unsettled and I don't know why. Ironically, times like these send me running to Samantha, not so much to spill my guts, but to immerse myself in her dramas and therefore escape my own issues. However, the lass has too much upon her right now, and I don't feel I should be exploiting her company.

I drive past Hyde Park, its allure lost on me. I'm not one to sulk or make myself a palette of different hues of suffering. At least, that's not the person I've been for a very long time.

Something is changing within me. It makes no sense, really. I'm thirty-four by George!

I've heard plenty of wise people say that in order to know where you're going, you need to understand where you came from. Therein lies the problem. I don't want to understand where I come from, and yet, my mind inevitably takes me back to a time I don't care to remember.

Blimey, I don't want to do what Samantha's done for years. I don't want to rehash the past.

The sound system's dashboard display lights up with an incoming call. I groan when I read the name of the caller and debate whether to answer for a long moment. Bracing myself, I tap on the connect key and answer the call.

"You've reached the voice mail of Lewis Bettford. Please leave a—"

"Oh don't even try that with me, young man!" My mother says in a scathing voice.

"Mum, where are your manners? My recording is all upset now."

"You want to lecture me about manners, do you?"

I can only laugh as I picture her face tightened with annoyance. "It's a bit late for you, Mum," I say affectionately. "What's keeping you up, luv?"

"I just received an invitation from Sammie Kay," she says in a giddy voice. "I can't bloody believe it!"

"I take it this means you will come."

"But of course! At least I get to see one wedding in my lifetime."

I roll my eyes and fight the urge to snap. "I'm not taking the bait, Mum."

"Oh, pish posh, tell me all about it. Actually, why didn't you call me about it? Why is your mother the last to know these things?"

"One question at a time, old girl."

"Who's she marrying?"

"Didn't you read the invitation?"

"Must you be so bloody thickheaded, son? I don't want a name. I want an impression. It pains me that it's not your name in it."

Heavenly Father... "Must we go through this every time we talk?"

I expect her to ignore me and she doesn't disappoint.

"Who is he, Lewis?"

"You don't know him."

"Now, why do you think I'm asking you who he is?"

"His name is—"

"Jason S. McElroy, yes I can read. Now, who is he?"

I bite my fist and count to ten before answering. "He's one of Nathan Jeffries' men at his security firm."

"Oh! He's a spy!"

I frown at the display screen. "No he's not a bloody spy, Mum!"

Her laughter is rich. Is it any wonder I'm considered such a wiseass? My gene pool must be full of them.

"Ah! I couldn't resist. Lighten up, my boy. Don't be so bloody serious all the time."

"May I answer your question now?"

"By all means, dear."

"Thank you. As I was saying before your juvenile interruption, Jason Stephen is a security agent. He and Sam met a few years ago."

"Why'd you call him Jason Stephen?"

"That's his name."

"Why both names?"

I grit my teeth. "That's what Sam calls him, alright?"

"Don't you bite my head off, darling! I was just curious. Is he a good man?"

"Is he a good...? Bloody hell! What's your definition of a good man?"

"Does he love her? Would he die for her? Is there nothing in his eyes but her gaze? Is he a good man?"

Jason McElroy saved my best friend's life at least once. In many ways, he also saved her heart. "Yes, Mum. He's a good man. As good as they come."

"I'm happy to hear that, my boy. Sammie Kay deserves nothing less."

"I think you're right."

"I guess it'll do since she couldn't have you."

"Mum! I'm ending this call."

She laughs. "Ta ta, my boy. I'll see you in London."

"What will you wear?"

Static crackles in the silence. "Why?"

"So I know how to match your dress."

"That'd make it look like we are going to the wedding together, dear."

I blink several times, feeling utterly lost. "I imagine I'll be escorting you."

"Why, Lewis Jonathan. You assume too much," she says in a bemused voice.

"Whatever do you mean?"

"I've got my date, son. You'd best find your own."

3

I sit back in my comfortable leather chair and rub my eyes. It feels like I have a pound of sand in each. I've been staring at the screen for far too long.

I stand and go to the side bar only to remember there are no spirits there, or anywhere in my flat. Samantha has a habit of dropping by unannounced and the last time she came, I caught her staring at my bottle of Chase vodka.

I fear the day she gives in and falls off the wagon. Something tells me it's bound to happen, but I'm sure as hell not about to facilitate that event. I'll just have to content myself with a cup of tea.

The clock in my kitchenette reads 11:47 P.M., which means I put in about five hours emailing and responding to the long list of potential guests Samantha had on her list.

She'd been right. No one seems inclined to fly to London for her wedding. There are a few that make a tentative promise that I'm not about to rely on. Four of her former colleagues from Tennenby Publishing House responded they'd come. It might have to be enough.

After brewing the tea, I fill a mug and go relax in front of the TV set. I wanted to watch the Manchester United match I'd recorded while Samantha dragged me from one bridal shop to another.

I'm about to shut down the laptop, when a message icon appears. I click it open.

Lewis,

I was delighted to receive Samantha's invitation and I'm responding with an affirmative. It'll be great to see my Sigma Chi Rho sister! I don't mean to overstep my bounds but if possible, I'd love nothing more than to spread the word to the rest of the sisters. I'm sure Samantha would love to see them as well. Please let me know as soon as possible.

Yours Truly,
Quinn McDermont

"Sigma Chi Rho."

As far as I know Samantha was seldom sober at school and she wasn't known to be very social. In any case, I can't remember if she has ever mentioned anything about her sorority sisters.

The only way this email gets to me is if Quinn McDermont's name is on the list. When I scroll through the list, I find her name and a year next to her, 2000.

I scald my mouth with the bloody tea and let out a litany of curses that turn the air blue. Feeling the beginnings of a blister on my tongue, I open a browser window and run a search for Sigma Chi Rho in the Columbia University website.

Sigma Chi Rho is an honorary sorority and membership is extended solely to students with extraordinary marks. Something called grade point average, that's the system they use in America. As I recall, despite Sam's daily inebriation, she was never below a perfect 4.0.

I feel a slight pang of envy. I had to work extra hard during my academic career. I have a terrible memory and my language skills are in a perpetual state more apt for a third grader.

I entertain the thought of giving Quinn a green light as far as inviting the rest of the sisters, but since Samantha's never mentioned any of them, I decide to wait.

I shut off the laptop without replying to this Quinn and decide to go to bed.

Alone, my mind echoes with Mum's voice from her earlier phone call. It takes a long time before it recedes from my thoughts enough for me to sleep.

***

Light filters in through the blinds of my windows. I know this only because I feel a stinging discomfort on my eyelids. I roll, choosing suffocation by pillow over facing the bloody light.

"Has anyone spoken to you about sleep apnea?"

I nearly jump out of my skin. "Is this payback for walking in on you?"

Samantha dazzles me with her grin and twinkling eyes. "At least you weren't in the loo."

"You nearly saved me the trouble, luv."

"Gross!"

"How long have you been here?"

"Long enough to wonder whether you were being attacked by a bear or snoring."

"I have a deviated septum," I croak.

"Something's definitely out of line in there."

I sit up in bed, trying to clear the cobwebs from my eyes. Everything seems too bright. "Is Lancelot with you?"

By the way her face falls, I know he isn't.

"No. But we talked last night. It's going to be another five days. The expedition or whatever the group is, found some fossils and decided to stay and study them."

"But he's well. That's all that matters, right?"

She nods happily but her smile is fleeting. "There's only one problem."

"What is it?"

She starts to talk but then changes her mind. "I'd rather show you."

"I must get a good shower, luv, before I do anything. I feel quite offensive." I rub my cheeks, feeling the coarse stubble I wish I could eradicate.

Samantha is staring at me strangely. Her eyes seem to be fixed upon a spot on my chest. I pull the sheet up to cover my naked torso, belatedly realizing how comical I must look. "What are you staring at?"

She blinks fast as though she's trying to come out of a daze. "Forgive me, luv. I just… It's nothing. Sorry."

"What were you looking at?"

She huffs a breath, blowing a strand of hair from her face, revealing a shamed expression.

"Sam?"

"I just forgot about that." She points at my chest.

I look down wondering if she's losing her mind. "Do I have something on me?"

"You most certainly do."

"What is it?" I push the sheet down and try to figure out just what the devil caught her eye.

She reaches and tugs on several chest hairs.

"Hey!"

Samantha giggles. "You're so fuzzy!"

I scowl at her as I cover myself with the sheet.

"Do you have the fuzzy arse to match?"

Heat travels up my spine and into my face. A wave of humiliation crushes over me, leaving me speechless.

"Uh oh, I know that look," she says, sidling off the bed, careful to place herself within reach of my hand.

"You're a tart," I growl.

"Get in the shower, fuzzy."

I reach for a slipper and fling it at her, but she's already out the door, squealing as it flies over her head. "I don't think I like you this bloody happy!"

***

I don't feel like wearing my presumptuous garb today. I slip into a pair of jeans and throw on a navy blue cotton t-shirt. The shapeless garment is surprisingly comfortable.

I'm about to walk out of the room when I think back on all those times I've had to endure interminable waiting epochs, while Samantha puts on her face and wages war with her hair.

With a wicked little grin of pure satisfaction, I go back in the bathroom to work on my hair. I'm not usually fastidious about much, except when it comes to my hair. It's not a gay thing, or I guess it could be. It's more of a personal thing. I can't feel good if I don't look properly groomed.

The face staring back from the mirror is a bit on the long side. I see a nick on my square chin and plenty of razor burn over my neck.

I find that the aftershave balm makes a false promise of soothing comfort when the stinging burn almost makes me scream, like the little kid from the *Home Alone* movies.

From the medicine cabinet, I extract a tin of pomade that I rub on my hands before running them through my sandy brown hair. The widow's peak gives me a perfect point of reference to evenly distribute the strands back. I committed the grave mistake of attempting self-styling and botched up more than a few layers of hair that now sweep down over my forehead. I let it go. It could be worse.

Feeling mildly satisfied, I grab a pair of leather sandals and slip them on. I think of donning a wool hat as a recent photo of Brat Pitt floats through my mind, but I don't want to mess up all the work I just did.

When I make my way down the narrow hallway from the bedroom, I hear furious typing. Samantha laughs in between bouts of mercilessly tapping the keys. I wonder if she's chatting online with Gwen. And here I hoped to find her bored to pieces, impatiently awaiting my reemergence. There's no way for a lad to beat a lass at her games.

"Is it Gwen?"

Samantha smiles and lets her eyes roll towards me for a quick second. "You look different, but I guess I can be seen with you."

I watch her eyes roam over the screen. She laughs and types something else in record time.

Resisting the urge to stand over her shoulder, I prepare tea for two. I add low calorie sweetener and a few drops of lime juice for Samantha and do the same for myself.

Sensing my approach, Samantha's fingers fly over the keys then she closes the screen just as I set the tea cup in front of her.

"Ah, you're a luv!" She exclaims.

"What's the big secret?"

She sips the brew, makes a face then looks at me. "Did you use sugar?"

Typical stalling tactic. "No."

She sips at her tea once again. "Lime juice?"

I scowl at her. "Of course."

Another sip. "Then I think it's perfect."

"Bollocks! Who were you talking to?"

"I wasn't talking, I was chatting."

One...Two...Three...Four...

"Alright, alright, don't get your knickers in a twist," she says, palms up in surrender as she registers the sour look on my face. "I was chatting with Gwen about girlish stuff."

"What girlish stuff?"

"Wedding night stuff."

"Spare me."

She sticks her tongue out at me before sipping more tea.

"What did you want to show me?"

"A photo." She puts the cup down on the table, and opens the screen of the laptop. Her fingers peck at the keys sporadically. "Here it is. Look."

I turn the laptop and look at the screen. Jason McElroy is crouching down before the camera. He's dressed in black cargo pants, combat boots, and a heavy parka. "Horrid ensemble. Is that the crime?"

"Take a closer look at the background," Samantha points.

The background consists of an imposing mountain, but I know that's not what concerns her. It's the group of people standing just behind Jason. I see three faces. One belongs to Justin Lombardi, another of Nathan's field agents, good chap. The second face belongs to an older gentleman who bears all the attributes of a professor. The last face is a striking rendition in brunette prettiness. Although her features are a bit blurry, she's nonetheless attractive. She seems to be staring at Jason's crouched form in the foreground. "The girl?"

"The girl," Samantha confirms.

"What about her?"

"She's got her eye on Jason Stephen. My Jason Stephen."

I tamp the urge to laugh. "That's who Lombardi and Lancelot are guarding?"

"Some of them. He told me it was a group of twelve."

"And you think this lass is getting friendly with your fiancé?"

"I have an odd feeling."

"An odd feeling," I echo. "Let me guess. This is another one of those women's intuition things, isn't it?"

Samantha looks put off. "Yes."

I close the screen and fight the urge to burst out laughing. "Sam, he's about to marry you. Doesn't that mean anything to you?

"Of course it does. But he's out there with her. Do you understand?"

"Not one bit," I confess.

"She's totally his type. You don't think I ought to be worried?"

"No."

She crosses her arms. "A picture is worth a thousand words."

I give her a sideways glance. "Yes, but this one only says, 'hi Sam, I'm in the bloody mountains!'"

She looks away.

"Don't be such a girl. Jason Stephen has eyes for no one but you."

"Tony had eyes for no one but Gwen, and look what happened," she snaps.

I don't even want to add to this line of dialogue. "Do you really want to reopen that can of worms?"

She shakes her head, her eyes clouded with remorse. "I'm just getting uneasy about him being gone so long. I miss him like crazy. I miss him holding me, because when he does, I don't want to be anywhere else."

"Well, I'd like to use one of your expressions here, if you'd allow me."

"What expression?"

"Cut the shit!"

She stares at me, feigning shock. A second later we're both laughing.

"The sun rises and sets in your eyes, according to Jason. Don't ever believe otherwise, okay?"

She nods, a smile curling her lips and her eyes taking on a loving shine. "When did he tell you that?"

"We talk more than you think, luv."

"What else have you talked about?"

"Man stuff of no concern to you."

"What did he say?"

"Demanding answers won't get you any. You have to answer a few questions for me."

"Fine. But I'm going to ask him and I have fun ways of getting him to talk." She winks.

"I want you to tell me about Sigma Chi Rho."

Samantha's cup of tea is halfway to her mouth when she freezes at the mention of her sorority. "Why?"

"Because one of your sisters is eager to, not only come to your nuptials, but also tell the rest of the sorority."

"Which one?"

I'm not sure I like her apprehensive demeanor. "Quinn—"

"—McDermont!" She covers her mouth with her hand, like a little kid caught muttering a curse. "Quinn? Are you kidding me?"

"Why do you, girls, have to do that squealing act? She responded to your invitation with an email. She sounds like a sweetheart."

Her brow furrows. "Quinn McDermont a sweetheart?"

"Isn't she?"

Samantha bites her lip. "Let me see the email."

I comply and soon she's reading the message. I remember it consisting of only a few lines, but Samantha's probably dissecting every word, as though she's trying to make sense of a lost scroll written in an alien script. I'm about to begin questioning her, but she'd only use the suspense to mercilessly torture me. I adopt a bored expression and leave her in silent communion with the message of the mysterious Quinn McDermont.

I finally have an opportunity to watch my football match. I turn on the TV and select my recorded programs from my digital recordings menu. I hope Tottenham trounced Manchester United.

Samantha comes around the couch, picks up my feet and drops them on the floor before sitting down next to me. "I can't believe I was such a lush," she says.

"Feel free to elaborate when you're ready, luv. I'm done asking questions."

"Cranky today, aren't you?"

I put a finger to my lips. "Shhh."

She crosses her arms and leans back, sinking into the couch. She kicks off her sandals and props her feet on my Benotti coffee table. I'm about to complain about it, but I change my mind. At least she's quiet. Of course, Samantha is quiet the way a heavily clouded sky is quiet before unleashing a storm. I sense she's ready to talk but I give her no encouragement.

"Is this the match from Sunday?"

I nod.

"Hotspurs by two. Sorry, luv," she feigns contrition after blatantly spoiling the score.

"Bloody hell, Sam!" I complain, stabbing the controller and shutting off the TV.

The annoyance on my face is lost on her.

"Okay, now that you're done watching your match, we can talk, right?"

I shut my eyes tight and wave in a "whatever" fashion.

"Quinn was a horrid despot who tormented me throughout my entire pledge period."

"Okay. I'll reject her as politely as I know how," I mutter, still smarting from her spoiling the football match for me.

"No. You can't do that!"

I glance at her. "You just said—"

"Quinn's my big sister."

The look in those iridescent grey eyes of hers fills me with foreboding, despite Samantha's dazzling smile. I take a deep breath and release it slowly. "There's a whole lot of drama there. Isn't there?"

She shrugs. "Just one of those typical rollercoasters."

I can only stare at her as possibilities run wild in my head.

Here we go…

4

"You've never mentioned this big sister of yours."

Samantha shrugs. "I haven't spoken to her since before I left Brooks. She was going to be my maid of honor."

"What happened?"

Samantha mumbles something under her breath. "...but hopefully we can recover our friendship."

"Wait," I stop her. "What was the first thing you said?"

Her eyes dart around. "It's not important."

I give her a pointed look. "I'm out that bloody door in three seconds if you keep playing cloak and dagger. Do you understand me?"

"Fine."

"What is it with you? Normally your gob runs off to the ends of the world around me."

"I know, it's just..." She looks me up and down, back up. "You look so different."

I give her an incredulous look. "How am I supposed to look?"

"You know," she says, giving me a once over.

"I know what?"

"You know, like, shirt and tie or... slacks and a button down Oxford, a turtle neck. You know?"

"I wasn't aware I had to dress up for you to talk to me."

"It's not that. Don't be irritated, okay? You've just been quite different since we got back from Pennsylvania."

"Different how?"

"I don't know how to say it, okay?"

"Just bloody say it," I command.

A look of resignation comes over her lovely face.

Since when do you find her face so lovely, Lewis?

"You've been looking and acting…"

"Spit it out," I order.

"Um…manlier?"

I can feel my eyebrows climbing high on my forehead. I'm surprised at the sudden defensiveness sharpening my tongue, but I manage to fight off the urge to bite her pretty little bonk clean off. Instead, I give her a wry grin and decide to deflect the issue. "Are you trying to shag me?"

"NO!" she shouts indignantly.

I grin at her. "Come now, you think I'm hot. There's no shame in admitting it, luv. Say it."

"Stop it!"

"You want me. Say it."

"Shut your gob! That'd be so incestuous!"

I laugh. "Don't fret. I know you have needs and all, but I'd much rather take you back to Soho than let you have your way with me."

She narrows her eyes. "Lewis, I'm warning you."

I sit up just in case she decides to bruise my shoulders with her fists. "Where'd all this come from?"

"You've been a little different. Can we leave it at that?"

I'm actually disappointed that she's not extracting these thoughts out of me. "Okay, okay." I'd better let her cool off before I speak, but of course, I don't. "Would you like me to change so you can talk to me?"

Her bony knuckles strike my right shoulder, sending a jolt of pain down my entire arm. Despite the sting, I laugh at her.

"I was trying to give you a compliment!" she cries.

I think of a smart retort but her hand is still fisted at her side. "Let's backtrack. I asked you what happened with Quinn. You mumbled something and then tried to brush it off. Now, what did you mumble?"

"I kissed Quinn's husband."

I say nothing but give her a piercing look.

"Shit," she curses softly. "I slept with him, alright?"

"Is there a friend you have left whose husband you haven't slept with?"

The reaction is instantaneous. Her fist finds the meatiest part of my shoulder with a resounding smack. The agony is overwhelming. "Alright! I'm sorry! Too soon?"

She gives me a dark look. "It was Brooks' idea, okay? I don't believe I have anything more to say about it."

This is something I don't care to even think about. Brooks Waldenberg, Samantha's ex-fiancé used her as bait in a blackmailing scheme to further his business ventures. I can't have her thinking of that dark time in her life. "At least all your friends seem to forgive you... Wait!" I put my good arm up to ward off another blow. "I meant Quinn is being friendly. Or are you going to tell me that she's only trying to set you up?"

She shakes her right hand and finally puts it down on her lap. "It's obvious she must have divorced him."

"Is your assessment based on that female telepathy deal?"

She nods. "I have to make her a bridesmaid."

"What about the other sisters?"

She purses her lips in thought. "I don't want to make them bridesmaids."

I give her an impatient glare.

"It'd be great to see Gina and Lynn," she muses. "Grace, Ann, and Leah too. Oh, can't forget Ashley."

"Wouldn't dream of it." I can see her mind still crunching through years, and names, and events of her past. "One question. Any enemies?"

Samantha gets up and begins pacing.

"I'd say Kayla Mason and probably Sarah. But I can't invite Keri without those other two."

"Why not?"

She looks at me as though the answer should be obvious. "They're sisters."

"Wow, you people take this sorority business far too seriously."

"No, I meant they're sisters in the biological sense. They're triplets."

"Oh. Are they pretty?"

"You bet your ass."

Whenever she gets lost in memories of her other life, as I like to think of her life in New York, she has a tendency to bend her speech into a more American dialect. It's quite sweet, except for the array of unfamiliar expressions that roll off her tongue. "Keri is good, but you don't get along with the other two?"

"Correct."

"May I ask why you don't get along with the other two?"

"No, you may not."

"She slept with their men too," I mutter silently.

"Pardon me?"

"I said they're adults, Sam. I'm sure Keri is allowed to come by herself, if she's so inclined to come, that is."

Samantha thinks for a moment. "It makes sense."

"Well, what do you want me to tell Quinn?"

She lets out a frustrated breath. "I'd love to see them but I couldn't expect them to spend all that money on airfare, and I couldn't possibly fly them in. If Quinn can make it, that'd be absolutely terrific. She could afford it."

"If there was a way to make that a non-issue, would you want them all here?"

She stops pacing and looks at me with undivided attention. "What are you saying exactly?"

"I'll fly them in."

She shakes her head. "You're insane. Do you how much money you're talking about?"

It's my turn to exhale in frustration. "I'd love to make you privy to my financial records, but I don't like to see you cry. I'll take care of it."

"I'll pay you back," she offers.

"I don't want your bloody money. If you're so willing to pay me back, the last thing I want is cash," I give her a wry grin.

She crosses her arms. "You're going to make me do something humiliating, aren't you?"

"The thought has merit," I tell her, just to watch her squirm. "Let's call it my wedding gift to you, luv."

She scrutinizes my eyes for a sign of deceit but finds none, and her eyes widen. "You're so sweet! Throw in a Lamborghini and we have a deal."

"Don't push it, lass." I could've bought her a new car with what I paid for her wedding gown, but she doesn't need to know that. I took great care in hiding the price tag from her.

"You're the best," she says, shaking her head and gracing me with one of her best smiles.

I love to see her happy.

"What would I do without you?"

I look at her, holding back a sudden lump of emotion. "May we never have to find out, Sam."

We sit in comfortable silence for a long moment, allowing me to reflect on our close friendship. I often like to think email was created because of Samantha and me. After she left for America, I saw her only during her school breaks, sometimes three times a year, but of course it wasn't enough. We wrote to each other at least once a week and when *America Online* came about, we nearly forced our parents into bankruptcy by emailing each other so much.

Email, I think in wonder. It definitely cemented our bond for eternity. I'm quite fortunate to have her friendship. It hadn't been an easy treasure to keep, for Sam knew how to push people away, particularly when she felt she was being judged. Over the years, I've had to accept quite a few disturbing things about her, but she's also had to accept some of my own disturbing traits.

I openly wept from joy the day she told me she was coming to live in London. I'll never admit that to her, of course. But I did.

When I think of those first months of her life here, I find it ironic that I nearly lost her more times during those days than when we lived an entire ocean apart. I reflect on how much she had to change since then. I wonder if she is aware of how much I've been changing as well.

Change…

It had all started once she returned, but I don't feel like thinking about that right now. "My old woman sends her regards."

Samantha frowns. "I don't like it when you call your mum 'old woman'. First of all she's not old. She's younger than Nathan. How is she?"

"She's concerned about the kind of chap you're marrying."

She gives me a knowing look. "Why? Because it's not you?"

I groan. "In essence."

Samantha has an array of expressive smiles and the one curling her lips right now is sad, but she recovers quickly. "I can't wait to see her," she says. "Does she still teach dance?"

"She's got three instructors. She does more one on one coaching now. It gives her more time to herself."

"Oh! Will you dance that waltz you two always dance?"

"If her date allows."

Samantha's smile fades and a look of anticipation widens her pretty eyes. "What date?"

"I'm sure I don't know. She told me to get my own date."

"Do you have anyone?"

"No."

She flutters back to the couch. "Who's her date?"

"She never revealed much more than what I already told you."

"You have to find out!"

"That old bird's love affairs are no concern of mine."

"You're hot when you lie."

I give her a sideways glance and stand off the couch. "Alright, back to Quinn. What do you want me to tell her?"

She bites her lip in thought. "Tell her I'd love to see her, and the Moppins."

"Moppins?" I asked perplexed.

Samantha nods grinning like a little girl. "We were the Sigma Chi Rho Moppins."

"What's a Moppin?"

"It's just something we made up, I really don't know."

"Moppin."

Samantha pats her legs and stands. "I have to meet with Kristen. Would you like to do dinner again?"

I look at her up and down until she shifts nervously.

"What?"

"Do you still want to fit in that pretty princess gown?"

"That's not nice," she accuses. "Jason Stephen thinks me perfect. That's all that matters."

"Love is definitely blind," I mutter just under my breath.

"What?"

"Saladin and Joel, five o'clock."

She makes a face of pure distaste. "Fine."

"Salads are good for you."

She makes a sour face at me before grabbing her keys and her purse off the table. "What will you do while I'm gone?"

"Well, I'm certainly not going to sit here sulking and lamenting your leave. I have the Reds' match to watch."

"From Saturday?"

"Get thee hence!" I shout.

Samantha puts her hands up in surrender, blows me a kiss and leaves, laughing.

Ten minutes later, I'm navigating through the screen menus when my mobile chimes. I select the football match and retrieve the text.

Liverpool by one. GO REDS! =)

"TART!"

5

"Hello?" answers a smoky, yet delicate, voice.

"Hullo, my name is Lewis Bettford, I'm a friend of Samantha—"

"Oh my God! I've heard so much about you!"

I'm taken aback by the exuberance. "Is this Quinn?"

"Yes, it is! What a surprise!"

"I imagine you know what I'm calling about."

"Absolutely! Red's getting married. It's about freaking time!"

"I suppose it is," I say tentatively.

"You received my message?"

I always cringe when an American states a question. "Yes, I did. I talked to Sam and she's keen on the idea of passing along an invitation to the rest of your Moppin group."

"Aw, Moppin! That brings back so much…"

I hear nostalgia in her voice. "Quinn, I'll need to know how many people will be coming, and where they'll be flying from. I'm taking care of airfare and hotel costs. There's no maximum amount," I say, trying not to sound too pompous.

"Why would you do something like that, Lewis?"

"It would mean quite a bit for Samantha to have you ladies here. I didn't want the expenses to be an issue for her guests."

"Lewis, you make me wish I'd seen you first." She laughs provocatively. "But there's no need for any of that. I'll get back to you and let you know the details."

"You do realize I need to make reservations, don't you?"

"No need. Tell Red it's going to be a Moppin invasion."

I smile. "You're one intriguing lass, Quinn."

"And you're a sweetheart, just like Samantha's always described you. We'll be in touch."

Several questions buzz around in my head about Quinn McDermont. The most prominent one: why didn't Samantha ever talk about her?

I look at the clock, but I realize she's probably not done with her therapist. Knowing her the way I do, Samantha will clam up if I launch an interrogation on her Moppin sister.

I stare forlornly at the flat screen and curse my best friend for spoiling the football matches I've been looking forward to watching. I'm trying to think of a way to get her back, aside of forcing her into some healthy eating. Nothing comes to me, but come to me it will, I vow.

On a whim, I decide to Google Quinn McDermont. I could access Lions Securities' search engines but I don't feel right about abusing my access to their servers, despite the fact that I coded ninety percent of them.

As expected, the screen fills with a myriad of diverse article titles, newspaper matches, and irrelevant links. I scroll down each line until a promising hit catches my eye.

Tabitha DiNario breaks record for most wins held by Quinn McDermont, the former Columbia University tennis star.

I click on the article and the screen opens a window with a photo showing a young skinny girl holding a tennis racket, wearing an intense look on her face. Opposite Tabitha DiNario is a photo of a decidedly beautiful blonde with a winning smile, arms raised in victory. The caption beneath the photo identifies her as Quinn McDermont.

While Tabitha is wrapped in some atrocious little black number splashed with loud purple and phlegm green stripes, Quinn wears a more traditional white top and tennis skirt that bespeaks of class.

The article is from a summer ago and goes on to describe DiNario's accomplishments. The last two paragraphs are devoted entirely to Quinn. By the time I scan the first paragraph I decide the reporter is madly in love with her, given the litany of superlatives. The last few lines offer the most promising tidbit.

"...recently divorced Andrew Fischer after a five year marriage," I read aloud.

I know the name well. Andrew Fischer is one of the founders of Quantumview, a company that gave its customers access to any television programming in the world. I'm a subscriber myself. Quantumview is satellite television on steroids.

I try another search with Fischer's name and Google returns another list of matches. The second hyperlink shows a series of photographs and I click on the images.

Andrew Fischer looks rather dashing in a well cut tuxedo at an award ceremony. The photo captured him while delivering an acceptance speech, perhaps. I scroll down to older photographs and find what I'm looking for.

Fischer smiles at the camera next to a stunning blonde with scintillating blue eyes and the second most perfect smile I'd ever laid eyes on. Her hair is almost platinum blonde and it spills around her shoulders. It's none other than his former wife, Quinn McDermont, and unless her husband is about seven feet tall, she's quite short.

I admire beauty in all its forms. I love well-depicted paintings, I love sad, haunting songs, I love magnificently written poems, and I love to look at beautiful women, a major contradiction to most given my lifestyle, but who couldn't react with a racing heartbeat before such devastating beauty?

"Oh, chap, how could you possibly let that one go?" I say to the grinning Fischer.

If there's one thing I've found throughout my life is that beautiful women are often all looks and no substance. I've met some exceptions, but a great majority tends to view their own looks as a justification of entitlement of all things in life. They expect the world to be handed to them without offering much more than a dazzling smile, and a little flash of skin in exchange.

It's human nature to be drawn to beauty. Everyone will do for beautiful people what they'll never even consider doing for less than pretty faces. I learned to accept that particular way of the world early on. It was one of the things that made me turn my back on complicated relationships, so to speak. From that very first—and only—wound in my tender youth, I've wanted no part of such heartbreak evermore.

From what I gather, Quinn is the antithesis to my theories. I force myself to dial down my reaction to her evident beauty by keeping in mind that the stylists and cosmetologists of today work absolute miracles. I'd like to see how beautiful Quinn would look if either caught in the rain, or just recovering from a flu.

I can't deny she has substance, however. Not only is she a tennis star as reported in the article, but she graduated at the top of her class with a PhD in Biomechanics. She is also an accomplished photographer. According to the bio, some of her work has graced the fabulous pages of *National Geographic,* and some travel publications. "Impressive. Another overachiever like Samantha," I muse.

I wouldn't be surprised if I do a search on the famous Moppins and come to find they're all type A personalities, beautiful and successful, just like my best friend.

The thought of Samantha reminds me about our dinner "date". When I look at the clock at the corner of the screen, I see I have plenty of time. I navigate back to the results of my search and click on another article.

I frown at the pop-up window offering me a subscription to *Famous*, a fairly well-known, scandalous American tabloid. I decline the offer and I'm taken to another index. Quinn's names are hyperlinked to several recent articles. I take a moment to read some of the headlines, which are only weeks old.

Trouble in Paradise
The Other Women
When Ice Castles Crumble
Quinn McDermont-Fischer's Ultimatum to her Husband
101 Women (Or Ways) To Lose Your Wife
Andrew and Quinn: Sleeping In Separate Homes
Quinn: "It's Over"

"By George…"

It never ceases to amaze me how quickly the bloody tabloids exploit someone's tragedies. I don't even get into the articles themselves. I'm positive they're filled with sensationalistic lies and fabricated testaments from anonymous "close friends of the couple".

I think back on the sound of her voice and conclude that it's clear Quinn McDermont is one tough lass to have gotten through this onslaught.

***

By the time I walk inside Saladin and Joel, I have a blister the size of a Sovereign from the sandal strap on my right foot and the burning agony makes my mood go downhill fast. I curse the bloody fool who designed these summer fashions, though I ought to curse myself for wearing them, trying to keep up with the ever changing trends.

I scan the booths and tables, but it's clear Samantha is late as usual. I check my mobile for a message and find one missed call though it's not from her.

A perky brunette saunters over to my table and gives me a pretty smile. I put her at around twenty. Her eyes are easily her best feature, big and dark. The olive skin and thick, dark hair make me think of the Mediterranean. I wish I could speak Italian like Samantha.

"I'm Milena. I'll be taking care of you," she says in a childlike voice that actually adds to the initial charm.

"Hullo, Milena. I'm waiting on a friend. We'll both take tea, I'm sure."

"Yes, of course."

Two cups of tea later, my stomach is growling and there's no sign of Samantha. I try her mobile, but the call goes into voicemail and she hasn't returned any of my text messages. I even engage on a flirtatious chat with my server, Milena, until she mentions her husband and the fact that they are expecting their first child in eight months. She looks so happy I think she'll burst.

As I congratulate her, it occurs to me that she's bound to make some beautiful children, provided the father is just as good looking, of course. The image of two particular little ladies floats in my mind, putting a smile on my face.

My mobile rings out a generic ringtone that tells me I don't know the caller. When I look at the London number, I recognize it as the missed call from earlier in the day. I hit send and connect the call. "Hullo."

"Hi, Lewis."

I recognize Quinn McDermont's voice instantly. I have to take one quick look at the mobile, which shows me a London number instead of an international code with an American area code. "Hullo, Ms. McDermont, either you have an excellent relay service or you're calling me from the old city."

"Actually, you called my cell phone, my American cell phone that is, just before I disconnected it. I'm calling you from my London *mobile*. I wanted to make sure you had this number in case you needed to reach me."

This bit of news takes me aback. "Are you already in London?"

"Yes. I've been here for a few days already."

I don't believe in coincidences. I'm so stunned I don't know what to say. What are the bloody chances?

"Lewis, I mentioned I'd call you with some details about potential guests."

"Yes, of course."

There's a pause on the line. "You're wondering what I'm doing already in London, aren't you?"

"Actually, I'm wondering why you didn't mention you were in London when we first spoke."

"I'm so sorry. I can explain." She clears her throat. "I'm afraid my cell phone conversations are not exactly private these days, not back home, anyway. I didn't want to say much until I obtained a cell phone here, where no one knows me. You don't know anything about this, but I had to get away from home. I've been the flavor of the month for every tabloid in America for the last few months. I had to get away, and I don't want anyone to know where I am."

I can still see the headlines in my mind. "I can understand that."

"I don't feel right about asking this, but I must. Would you be a dear and refrain from telling Sam I'm here, just for a few days?"

"May I ask why?"

Another pause. "It's not something I care to talk about over the phone."

"What do you suggest?"

"Well, as a matter of fact, I'd like to meet with you at your office."

"My office?"

"I need some solutions, Lewis."

I suppose she may have done a search on me, the way I did on her. "How do you know about my company?"

"Are you kidding? Solutions did the security systems for Bionics, about two years ago?"

I jot my memory. Bionics is a British company that does research on artificial limbs and joint implants. They contracted Solutions to secure their servers some time ago.

I suddenly remember Quinn is a Biomechanical Engineer. It stands to reason she's had some dealings with Bionics. "Yes, actually I'm the one who oversaw the project."

"Does the name Fitzgerald sound familiar? Dr. Fitzgerald?"

The image of a florid, well-fed sexagenarian with a booming voice comes to mind. "Actually, it does indeed."

"He highly recommended you."

"I'm quite flattered. How can I be of service?"

"I'd like you to call me, preferably soon. My schedule is open for the next couple of months. I have to go for now. As I said, I just wanted to provide you with a number where you can reach me."

"Yes, of course."

"Please keep me a secret from Samantha for just a few days. I promise I'm eager to see her."

"I won't say a word," I agree with a pang of guilt. I owe no loyalty to Quinn McDermont, but my instincts tell me to meet her first, before bringing her up to Samantha.

"Thank you, Lewis. I really appreciate it."

Once the call ends, I thumb my contact list and add Quinn to my contacts. I'm trying to figure what she wants from me when the mobile buzzes in my hand, alerting me to a text message.

Almost there

In Samantha time, "almost there" means at least a half-hour. She always takes for granted that I'll forgive her, which I do. I made her wait fifteen minutes once and to this day I doubt she's ever forgiven me.

Without another text, the screen on my mobile reverts to the home page. In the background, the two little faces I was just smiling about while Milena expressed her joy at the prospect of motherhood, peer out through curious eyes; Brooke and little Emily Amaya, Tony and Gwen's daughters.

It's bothered me to no end that I didn't get a parting word to the little cuties. It's bothered me I didn't get a parting word to Gwen and Tony, though everyone understands the strange circumstances that forced me to stay with Samantha as she battled through her emotional breakdown after Tony ended up fighting for his life. I've held more than a few calls with them to at least explain my side of things, and they've been incredibly understanding.

I think about the Amayas often.

Strange that just when you think you know yourself as well as you ever will, something happens that shows you otherwise. I never once felt I'd missed out on not being part of a whole family until being around the Amaya's showed me what it's like.

My mother raised me all on her own. There was never another man in the house besides me. Mum had me at a young age, and she's quite the dish to this day. I'm sure she caught more than a passing glance from several chaps in her twenties and thirties, but she never dated anyone for very long. In a way, I feel responsible for that. Perhaps I was far too needy when I was a child.

I've often wondered if Mum felt obligated to devote all of her time to me since we had no other family. The closest thing to family we had were the Reddicks.

I had an uncle and aunt in Samantha's parents, but lost them in a horrific traffic accident when we were fifteen. I had a grandmother in the very lovely Lady Reddick, who passed on just before Samantha moved back to London. And now I only have Mum and Samantha, although technically, I'm about to lose my best friend to her soon to be husband.

I know I won't, but once she's married, things won't be the same and in my mind, that only equates a loss.

Samantha was supposed to leave for Germany for six months, but when the engagement took place, Nathan Jeffries, her boss and father, for all intents and purposes, insisted for her to start her career at Lions in London as an interpreter after she returned from her honeymoon. In retrospect, it was a good decision. Samantha needed to be around family for a while longer. It also did much to mend whatever fissures were still in the fabric of her relationship with Jason.

I'm also well aware that time waits for no one and my mother will not live forever, despite her vociferous promises to do just that.

I don't relish the thought of growing old alone and therein lies the basis of this sudden change within me.

It started subtly, nearly unnoticed, at first. I might've eventually come to face this reality, but having met Tony and Gwen certainly has added a new perspective to my entire life. I might have been able to brush that off as well, but I certainly couldn't brush off the whirlwind of new emotions that surged through me when I saw my reflection in those little girls' eyes.

Now, each time I think of reading *Green Eggs and Ham* to them, I have to fight the urge to break down and cry. Even now my eyes sting. It's out of my control. It's an overpowering assault on my very soul that I don't presume to understand.

I resist an irrational wave of resentment towards Samantha. I don't hold it against her that she should've noticed something by now. I know she was in no condition to delve into the depth of my psyche as she's done in the past. After she healed enough, she was riding a high with Jason Stephen and I didn't want anything to bring her down from her soaring joy. She deserved it. Not because she's an angel. Blyme, far from it!

I thought she deserved it because for most of her life, since the death of her parents actually, Sam knew nothing but self-recrimination and guilt that she tried to escape with alcohol. It dominated her for most of her life.

But she is stronger now. Delicate, but strong. She's still as fragile as a mended porcelain doll, but she's stronger than she's ever been.

She's certainly noticing things now. I'll have to do a superb job of heeding Quinn's request and keep her a secret. It may prove nearly impossible not to bring that up.

Just as I'm about to get up and leave, I catch the bounce of a chestnut colored ponytail on the window. A minute later, Samantha walks in and navigates through chairs and tables to reach my booth. She slides several shopping sacks emblazoned with the logos of different stores, before sitting across from me.

Noticing my disapproving glare on the evidence of her shopping, she shrugs and offers no apology as she reaches for my water glass.

"Is it safe?"

I nod and watch as she drinks the entire contents in one gulp.

She closes her eyes and exhales in delight. "This is admittedly, the best water in Westminster."

"You were fashionably late an hour ago."

A sheepish look comes over her face. She starts to talk, thinks better of it, starts to talk again, but nothing comes out of her gob. She hangs her head, the picture of remorse. "I made the mistake of stopping at Athena's."

"Well, we could all use some wisdom, some more than others." I hide my smirk behind the menu.

Athena's is a fashion line that caters to "hot thirty-somethings", and if Samantha felt the need to do some retail-healing, she must have had a tough session with her therapist.

"Nice," she says with a sarcastic scowl.

We settle on garden salads and I request a dressing sampler tray. Samantha tells Milena, our server, not to add the bits of bacon or cheese. She also asks for virgin oil and vinegar in lieu of one of the dozen creamy dressing possibilities I'm getting in the sampler.

"Don't look at me like that," she warns.

"Are you feeling well?"

"Peachy."

I know her too well. Whatever is bothering her is sure to come out in the next few minutes. The best strategy is to let her stew in whatever issue *du jour* until she can't take it anymore. It usually takes less than three minutes.

Milena brings our salads. The wooden bowls are large and the bed of greens is thick and succulent. Appetizing if you're a rabbit. That it tastes like brittle water wafers without the dressing is beside the point.

I know I'll still be starved after this, but knowing how much Samantha detests healthy food, I figure it's the best way to punish her for ruining my football matches earlier.

When I take that first bite of the insipid roughage, it takes everything in me not to make a face. It occurs to me at that moment that I should probably find ways to get Samantha back that will affect only her.

"Are you enjoying this?" She asks.

I force the chewed up weeds down my throat. "Yum."

She rolls her eyes as she mixes the oil and the vinegar before adding more than a dash of salt and pepper.

"I'm surprised you didn't go for the bacon and the creamy French."

She stabs at a slice of tomato and glares at it malevolently. "Gwen told me she's lost fifteen pounds."

I wait until I've mashed up the next bite before saying anything. "So?"

"So?" She puts the pierced tomato back in the bowl. "I'm going to look like a bloody cow next to her!"

It's my turn to roll my eyes. "Whatever makes you think that? You exercise like a bloody Olympian. What are you talking about?"

Unlike me, Samantha's face undergoes a series of expressions of pure displeasure as she chews on a forkful of salad. "I need to get thinner," she says around a mouthful.

I grimace as I push a napkin towards her. I hate some of her habits. Samantha has some of the worst table manners I've ever seen. "You still look great. Your muscle tone is better than it was when you first got here. You're fine."

She smiles. There's a piece of lettuce stuck between her front teeth.

"You've got something…" I point in the general direction of her mouth.

She quickly puts her head down and picks at her teeth with her fork. I resist the urge to run out of the place.

"Do I have anything in my teeth now?"

I know she's peeled back her lips to show me her teeth, but I don't even look. "Seriously, luv?"

"You're the one that wanted to go the way of the bloody rabbit today."

"Well, it appears I'm helping you reach your goals," I counter.

"Since when do you take notice of someone's muscle tone?"

"Doesn't everyone?"

"No."

I shrug. I want to tell her Quinn is in London, but there is something in the way her Moppin sister asked me not to tell Samantha that I decide to feel the situation out first. "I spoke with your sister, Quinn."

She looks anxious. "And?"

I dab at my lips with the napkin, letting the anticipation build. "She said to tell you it will be a Moppin invasion."

Her eyes widen. "Are they coming?"

"Quinn said she'd message me with the details. She actually declined my offer to take care of their expenses. What do you make of that?"

"Interesting. I'm sure I don't know. She's bloody loaded, so perhaps she's willing to fly them in herself." She fixes me with one of her penetrating stares. "Did you speak with her over the phone?"

I try not to swallow hard, a reaction evoked by her narrowed gaze. "Emails. Are you going to summarize your meeting with Dr. Kingman?" I ask, hoping it's a good deflection.

Her eyes go flat. "I wasn't planning on it. Why?"

"Never mind. How about Lancelot, where is he?"

She shrugs like she could care less. "He'll be back in two days. Truthfully, I don't think he even knows."

I study the gleam of anxiety in her eyes and the tight jaw. "That lass on the photo is still bothering you."

She gives me an exasperated look. "I just have this odd feeling about it all, and I can't wait to bloody see my baby."

"Sam, he loves you. You'll do well to trust him, luv."

She stretches her arm on the table and opens her hand palm up. I take her hand and squeeze it.

"I know. I just have too many things running through my head."

This worries me.

In the past, when Samantha felt her mind was cluttered, she inevitably became a nervous wreck and in order to function, she'd drink vodka like a Russian peasant. I know when I feel cluttered I drink a glass of wine that often relaxes me. But for her, one drink may be the first step off a ledge into a familiar abyss. "Sam, talk to me, luv."

She stares into space for a full minute. I have this vivid memory of similar times when she'd get that look on her face right before she shook herself to pieces with the need for alcohol.

I hold my breath and my heart stutters, but at long last she gives me a comforting smile and looks into my eyes with a clear gaze.

"We're always talking about me. Why don't you tell me something about you?"

"Sam."

"Come now, Lewis. The best thing you can do for me is distract me from my issues. Please?"

"Stay strong."

"Like steel," she promises.

"Steel rusts."

"Titanium then."

I hope so.

6

My stomach makes a horrid rumbling that's too loud for Samantha not to hear. I give her a dark look before she says anything, but she ignores it and subjects me to one of her knowing grins. Despite the levity, I sense something is on her mind. It's best I keep her talking, and I know just what subject to bring up. "So why did you never mention your Moppin sisters?"

She shrugs. "I don't know. You know me. I was drunk ninety percent of the time I was in school. I was fairly popular because of that. Other than that, I didn't really have much to do with the sorority."

"What did the sorority do?"

She squints, turning back the hands of time, I think.

"There were some community events but, I don't think I ever helped with a single one of those." She takes a sip of water. "We bitched. That's what we did. We bitched and we fought and some stole other's boyfriends. That kind of thing. We partied a lot and we sucked up to the faculty. "

"Sucked up?"

She sees my lascivious grin and jabs a perfectly manicured forefinger at me in mock warning. "We kissed up to the professors and the deans, we didn't shag them… Well, not always."

"Oh, I get it. You partied so much your marks were suffering."

Samantha laughs. "Hardly. Our collective GPA was four point two. Our marks were excellent. You couldn't join unless you had at least a three point eight. We prided ourselves in being not only the prettiest women on campus, but also the brightest."

"So were you the charity case?"

She gives me a dark look. "Why am I friends with you, again?"

I laugh, but I know better. I couldn't possibly dispute either point when it comes to Samantha. "Sounds like elitist rubbish."

She nods thoughtfully. "It was."

"That's not the Samantha I know."

She gives me a sad smile. "I was a different fool back then. I was recruited after topping the Dean's list over Kayla Mason after my first semester at Columbia. Kayla was in the same Lit program."

Seeing the blank look on my face, she decides to elaborate.

"There was another honors society recruiting top students but the Sigs didn't want to lose me to them so they practically dragged me into their fold."

"How'd they lure you?"

She pokes at a crouton with her fork. "I was a little compulsively competitive."

"A little?"

She waves her hand dismissively. "Word was the Sigs were the best and I wanted to be the best Sig. In retrospect, I don't really know why. I wasn't really in control of myself. The Sigs partied and back then I went where the alcohol was. I didn't think I'd fit in otherwise. I preferred to be alone most of the time."

"Where does Quinn McDermont fit through all this?"

"Quinn was a year ahead of me. She was the vice-president of the sorority and appointed herself my big sister. She was also in charge of our hell week."

"Hell week?"

She nods. "It was actually ten days of hazing."

I see something like fear flicker in her eyes. "In other words, it was a chance for the sisters to humiliate the newbies."

"Exactly. Quinn was the worst."

I shake my head at the foolishness. "Why even bother?"

Samantha thinks for a long moment before answering. "Youth demands pseudo-values."

"Meaning?"

"We wanted to be more than everyone else. We wanted to be special."

"You weren't kids. You were in your early twenties by then," I point out.

"I was still a stupid kid."

I don't disagree. "So, Quinn puts you through hell and all, but you still seem to think fondly of her. I don't understand, luv."

"Once I got through all the idiotic initiation rites, she began acting more like a big sister. I don't remember opening up to her much though, except for one time." She shrugs. "I think we just finally grew up."

"Well, with you, that's up for debate," I say deadpan as I turn my head, looking for the waitress to refill my drink.

"What do you mean?" She grins.

"What do you expect out of her when you see her?"

"I'm sure I don't know. You'll like her. She's incredibly smart. I remember envying her parents something terrible."

"You met them?"

She nods. "They live in a farm in Connecticut. Big on horses. Her dad is a total DILF, and a real sweetheart. Her mum was a little weary of me, and her little brother is a lot like you."

"DILF?"

Samantha swallows audibly, making me wince. She taps her sternum a couple of times before taking my glass of water and drinking it all. "You've never heard of DILF?"

"Enlighten me."

"You know, Dad I'd Love to… Shag." She grins.

"That'd be DILS."

"Well, yes, but I know how you feel about my horrid American cursing."

I shake my head at her. "Shagging her dad… You're incorrigible."

"He's like a Viking god! I'm only human."

"And you have needs, right."

"Exactly. We had a bit too much fun that weekend, polished off a fifth of good Irish whiskey. I wonder if Quinn remembers that."

I have a sudden, horrid vision of Samantha and her old college sister carrying on like American spring breakers on a drinking binge within the week, girls gone wild London style. I decide to appoint myself chaperone just in case.

"I know what you're thinking," she says.

"I'm not thinking anything."

She narrows her eyes. "I'm not going back to that again, Lewis. I'm not. My drinking days are behind me and that's exactly where they'll stay."

I let out a long breath of pure relief. The determination in her eyes is incredibly reassuring. "I'm happy to hear you say that."

She shrugs. "I don't think I'll ever stop feeling so ashamed of the way I was."

"Don't look back, luv. This new you is light years away from that lost little lass."

"You're sweet."

I want to tell her that guilt and remorse won't get her anywhere, but I can't. Lately I've been dealing with my own sleepless nights on account of the way I was. There's so much I could've done for Samantha. Instead, I was one of her greatest facilitators. I was responsible for putting her in danger more than a few times.

My gut twists painfully when I think of walking into her closet and finding the half-empty case of vodka. A real friend would've seen the problem right then and there, and done something about it. Instead, I let her drink herself into oblivion, virtually on a daily basis, under the excuse that she needed to escape her torturous mind rather than confronting it.

"What's the matter?"

I give her a tremulous smile. "Just thinking I should join your inevitable girls' night out when your friends get here."

"Absolutely," she surprisingly agrees. "I used to brag about you. It would be great to show you off!"

We leave Saladin and Joel, vowing to never again step through its doors. I walk her to her Mini Cooper and she does all she can to stall. I'm about to give in and keep her company for the night but fortunately Alicia calls her.

"Alicia wants me to meet her for dessert."

"Where are we going?"

She shakes her head. "No boys allowed. Girls only."

"Oh, please," I scoff.

"Don't you have a football match to watch?"

"Funny. Give Alicia my best and be smart and don't go overboard on the ice cream. You've got a gown to fit into."

She frowns at me, her mouth agape for a moment. "Remind me why we're friends again," she laments.

"Because, who else could possibly put up with the likes of you?"

She steps up, hugs me tight and kisses my cheek. Whatever shampoo she's using lately is positively intoxicating.

Three blokes walk by, their eyes dancing over her curves before giving me a congratulatory nod.

"They were looking at my arse, weren't they?" Samantha whispers.

"You wish. They were looking at mine."

She glances at the men and makes a face. "Ew, so not your type."

I laugh.

After Samantha leaves, I limp an entire block to my BMW. As soon as I shut the door, I pull the evil little leather confection off my foot and resist the urge to throw it out the window.

Traffic is light through the narrow streets, an unusual fact given the time of day. I drive past Hyde Park when it hits me that I'm driving in silence. It may seem a small thing, but it's quite uncharacteristic for me. I glance at the screen on the dashboard, but I feel no inclination to power the sound system.

Samantha always talked about silent moments of introspection. She'd spend an unhealthy amount of time revisiting the past and reliving some not so pleasant moments. I've always told her she was wasting her time, so it's ironic that I'm now engaging in the same activity. I can't help it though.

Something is nagging at me all the way to my flat. When I pull into Cadogan Square I notice the lights are on. I park on the street and walk up to the quaint brick edifice I call home when I'm in London. I might as well think about making this a permanent arrangement.

There's a slick-looking, silver Peugeot sedan parked where I'd normally park. I groan, recognizing the peace sign sticker Mum has used to decorate every mode of transportation available to her over the years.

Entering the building I wonder why I don't simply ask Mum to move into the ground floor of the building, but I know better. Madeline Bettford cherishes her independence.

For now, I have the unit rented to a Scottish couple who are hardly ever home. They run a printing business and seem to always be traveling, which is great for me. I don't particularly enjoy sharing a living space with anyone. When I bought the building, it was divided into four apartments and there was quite a bit of work to be done.

It stands on the corner of Cadogan Square, just off Pont Street. The realtor went on and on about character, pointing out the graceful arches, decorative bass relief brick work, and the tall chimney, boasting a dozen smoke pots. A black wrought iron fenced gallery on the second floor is the perfect people watching spot. Each apartment had about 1200 square feet of living space.

I left the ground floor alone and hired a meticulous contractor to unify the other three apartments, plus the attic. The second story alone was turned into a large office, my own gigantic studio. The third story was partitioned into a tiny kitchen and a large living room where I love to unwind by watching films, or football matches. The rest of it was turned into three good sized bedrooms, each with its own bathroom. Climbing the steps, agonizing over the bloody blister on my foot, I berate myself for not having the foresight to install an elevator when I had the chance.

I can already hear Dido singing in her trademark haunting voice from inside the door. Mum's quite the hipster when it comes to music. She loves few things more than perusing my vast collection.

I close the door and remove my other sandal, making a mental note to throw the bloody things away.

A mouthwatering aroma wafts from the kitchenette, something with chicken broth, I think.

My mother sits on the couch, reading through a magazine. A half-empty goblet of wine rests on the end table. She looks up and gives me one of her dazzling smiles. I try to look past the new wrinkles on her once porcelain skin and smile back.

"Why, Lewis," she gushes. "Don't you look handsome!" She stands and opens her arms to me.

I stand a good foot taller than her. I kiss her cheek and hug her svelte frame. "You're looking quite lovely, as always."

"Yes, I know, dear." She glances over my shoulders. "Where's Sammie?"

"She and Alicia had plans."

"Oh, the soon-to-be Mrs. Jeffries. Nathan is too good for her," she muses.

"Now, don't start that. They're perfect intellectual matches."

"Don't be daft, my boy. There is more to life than brains."

Mum's strong opinions about everyone and everything are written in stone. There's no point in arguing. "I wasn't expecting you until tomorrow, Mum."

"Richard thought it best for me to stay here until he gets back from his business trip."

"Tell me all about Richard."

She pats my chest and sits back down. "He's a good chap." Without another word, she goes back to the magazine.

"Mum?"

"Yes, luv?"

I've learned over the years that the women in my life have a tendency to reveal things at their own pace. Why they should feel the need to create a sense of anticipation is beyond me. I actually find it quite tiresome, but I figured out what the countermeasure is. I simply stop asking questions and the silence eventually breaks them. "Nothing."

Growing up without a father lends to a close relationship with your mum. I never had a chance to sit back and wonder what I was missing mainly because Mum did a fantastic job of filling the gap. But after seeing what a whole family is, like the Amayas, I've not only started thinking of growing without a father. I've started thinking what it's been like for my mother to be so alone all these years, and the guilt is almost more than I can bear. I don't even know whether she didn't date solely because of me. What has life really been for my mother without a man to care for her?

Mum opened her own dance school soon after I was born. By the time I started walking, she was pretty well sought after by aspiring dancers. She's a patient, yet demanding instructor. A couple of ballerinas who headlined London productions took their first steps at the Bettford School of Dance.

The studio in Liverpool doubled as our home. My earliest memories play a montage of dancing figures of all ages to a classical piano soundtrack. There is something magical about ballet, even more so when you watch someone as talented as the incomparable Madeline Bettford perform.

"Oh, I hope you're hungry, my boy." She stands and quickly walks to the kitchenette.

"What'd you make?" I ask as I follow her.

The kitchenette is no more than a glorified galley. Everything is within reach, practically at arm's length, and there's very little counter space. For a bachelor like me, it's the perfect size. The new appliances are wasted on me. I'm on a first name basis with most of the restaurants in the Greater London Area.

"I have a bone to pick with you," she says as she opens and shuts drawers and cabinet doors. "I can't believe you've never used the set of knives I gave you five years ago."

I laugh. "You know I don't cook."

She smacks her lips in disapproval. "You'd save a fortune if you did."

I tamp down my retort. Mum grew up in lean times and she's conservative to a fault. I've wanted to get her a housekeeper, but she's fought me every step of the way. I lost the fight to get her a brand new house several years ago. She says there's nothing wrong with the old building. I had to lure her away on a cruise just to get some renovation work done. I endured a daily lecture on saving money during each meal at sea. By the fourth day, I was having gleeful dreams about pushing her into the blue waters of the Mediterranean.

"So what'd you make?"

I try to take a look but she blocks me. There isn't enough room for me to go around her.

"Guess," she challenges.

She removes the pot's lid and the scent of Rosemary turns my mouth to water, and prompts my stomach to growl loudly. "Scouse stew," I say in a shaky voice.

Mum smiles at me over her shoulder. "A little taste of home."

With an effort, I turn away from the stove and quickly set up two settings on the round, glass top table. By the time I set the silverware, my hands are shaking I'm so famished.

Mum brings the pot out to the table and sets it down in the middle on a folded dishtowel. I have some gadget that's supposed to do the same thing, but I don't remember where it could be.

"Be a dear and get the wine, boy."

"You cooked *and* brought wine," I quip. "And it's not even my birthday!"

"The wine," Mum points to the table while I chuckle.

I quickly pour a bottle of Bordeaux into two goblets and set them on the table before sitting down. Mum already has her plate full. I grab the ladle and gather up the biggest chunks of lamb. It's a just reward for enduring the insipid weeds I forced down my throat at Saladin and Joel earlier.

"Don't forget the leeks and potatoes. Get some carrots too," she orders.

The broth is impossibly thick and I can't wait to soak it up on a chunk of crusty bread. "You're the absolute best!"

"I certainly am," she says. "Well, let's hear the verdict. Go on."

I take a bite of lamb that is so succulent it brings tears to my eyes. I can't utter a word so I let her have a long moan.

"That's what I thought," she says with satisfaction.

I polish off three bowls of stew before I remember I have a whole glass of wine to deal with. I actually have to fight the urge to eat more. Mum's made enough to feed a small army.

Grateful for the food, I invite Mum to sit and relax while I clean up. She agrees, but not before launching into a lecture about the evils of using a dishwasher. I humor her by washing the two bowls, two sets of silverware and one goblet, by hand. I don't want to admit that she makes perfect sense. I've run the bloody machine with as little as one single dish and a cup.

I'm just about done cleaning the counters when my mobile chimes. It's Samantha.

"Don't call me pathetic, but I'm bored and lonesome," she says when I connect the call.

"I won't call you pathetic. Download a book."

"Arse!"

"I'd love to provide you with my superior company, but I'm not allowed to leave the house."

"Oh..."

She sounds so crestfallen I bite my tongue before I call her pathetic. I could make a habit out of playing with her emotions. "Get your skinny little arse over here. I've a surprise for you, anyway."

"You're a luv!"

I end the call, finish up wiping the counter and grab my goblet on my way to joining Mum when there's a knock on the door. I limp down the wooden steps, wondering if my tenants are home after all. Whoever's behind the door, raps more insistently. I can only shake my head when I open it. "Sam. Blimey, what a surprise."

7

"Where did you call me from? Just outside the door?"

"You wish! I was home. My Mini can fly."

"Right," I murmur, unable to resist the urge to look down the street from the window. Sure enough, Samantha's white Cooper is parked right behind Mum's sedan.

She brazenly walks in without removing her sandals. I begin to follow, but she stops in her tracks and turns towards me.

"Is that Scouse stew I smell?"

I give her a grin as I nod. Samantha turns around and flies up the steps after kicking her sandals off clear across the floor.

"Mum!" Her voice carries such unabashed joy in that one word.

When I make it to the top and look into the living room, I see a sight that nearly breaks me. I stand back and allow them to have their warm moment. My mother's been crazy about Samantha Reddick since the day she was born.

The women begin chatting animatedly as though they forgot my very existence. Mum's holding Samantha's left hand, her keen eye on the diamond of the engagement ring.

When I rejoin them, both look up at me. Samantha's eyes grin as much as her saucy little mouth. Mum's eyes flash something akin to disappointment that I have no trouble interpreting. Can't a man and a woman simply be friends without the whole world around them wanting them at the bloody altar?

Mum returns her gaze to Samantha. "Tell me everything."

"Only if you promise to tell me everything about Richard," Samantha counters.

Mum's face turns almost childlike as she looks skyward and sighs exaggeratedly. Whatever the meaning is lost on me but Samantha giggles, her whole body shaking with excitement.

I'm about to sit down when both women turn with a flat look on their face, clearly demanding privacy. I resist the urge to point out that this is my place and relent. "I have to check on a few things for work, ladies," I say, getting up.

They both grace me with a thankful smile and are careful to utter a single word until I finally limp down the steps back into my studio.

It's good to have everyone home…

I'm not sure where the thought comes from, but I find it more than apt. I imagine Mum is living out her fantasy of visiting Samantha and me at *our* home. I'd laugh out loud but the laugh never quite makes it out of me. I'm once again accosted by a notion of change.

"It's all Sam's fault," I say to no one. "She's turned you into a bloody sentimental mess."

I know Samantha is blameless, but I feel better after condemning someone else.

I rub my hands and slap at my face lightly, the way I've seen half-asleep students do when the teacher is a bore. The three screens before me come to life at the push of the space bar. First thing I do is cue up a random playlist and in seconds, I'm listening to the angelic voice of Mazzy Star. I follow the slow beat by bobbing my head as I scan my emails. There's a message from Quinn McDermont.

Lewis,

There will be four other girls accompanying me to see Red's nuptials. I'm also bringing a date along. As for the others, they're far too busy with babies or divorces, etc.

I have an apartment in London, near Chelsea Harbour, where they'll be staying, and I have access to a private flight, so you won't have to worry about them.

I'd like to meet with you because I need your capable services. My privacy has been invaded on every front back home, and I have several articles and research data that I want secured.

Please call me as soon as you have a chance.
Looking forward to our meeting.
Quinn

"Interesting," I muse.

I wonder how I'm going to keep from Samantha the fact that I'll be doing a job for Quinn or that she's been in London all this time. I stand and go to the side bar to pour a glass of wine when it hits me I don't have any, even as I savor the aftertaste of the Bordeaux.

"Bloody hell!" I just now remember the wine Mum and I were drinking.

I feel my heart in my throat, expecting to find Samantha drinking from a full goblet. When I peek into the living room, Samantha has her hands around a tall glass of ice water, which does little to allay my fears. Samantha used to fill water bottles with vodka all the time.

Mum's saying something about Richard's beautiful blue eyes when Samantha looks over at me and Mum stops talking.

"Pardon me. I just wanted to offer you something to drink, Sam."

She gives me a suspicious look as she rattles the ice in her glass. "Since when do you ever wait on me when I visit you?"

Mum looks on with interest, aware that something is amiss, given my demeanor.

Understanding dawns in Samantha's eyes and she shakes her glass at me again. "Just water, luv."

I breathe a sigh of relief.

"Lewis Jonathan Bettford," Mum says in an imperious voice. "How about giving Sammie Kay a little credit?" She puts a protective arm around Samantha's shoulders.

"I thought…" the words die in my throat.

Samantha smiles warmly at me. "I'm alright, promise."

I feel only slightly vindicated, but Mum's scowl is withering. "Good."

They both stare at me. Their expressions are the opposite extremes in the spectrum of affection. Samantha looks at me adoringly while Mum looks like she's contemplating flaying me alive.

"Well, then," I stammer. "Carry on."

I return to the studio awash in shame. If Samantha sees a lack of belief in her, she may lose belief in herself, and that's the last thing I want for her. I'll have to explain myself to her at some point. Preferably without Mum glaring at me while I do so.

I get back to the screens and when I read Quinn's message again, I try to recall the names Samantha threw at me, but I don't have her perfect memory. I wonder which four are coming.

I check my digital calendar for the month of October then I glance at the folders on my desk. I had originally cleared the entire month but some emergencies arose, leaving me no choice but to work. I have a staff of three capable techs, but they work out of Liverpool.

Since Terence left, I've been the only London representative of Solutions, a situation that will need to change soon. I originally hoped that in this age of wireless communications, I could efficiently run Solutions' operations from a virtual office, but many clients preferred meetings in person, which forced me to stay in London. I think it's time to accept that I can't do it all on my own, and organize a reliable staff.

It was much easier when Terence and I were together. He knew how to delegate efficiently and my skills, although enviable by most, are no match to his. Where I have to buckle down and study new defense coding and understanding the never-ending rush of new viruses and other cyber-attacks, Terence seemed to always be a step ahead of everyone else.

I may be too hard on myself. It can't be an accident that Solutions is second only to Terence's firm, Ancile Incorporated, named after the shield of the Roman god of war, Mars.

If it weren't for Nathan Jeffries, charging Solutions with handling the cyber security of his company, I'm not sure I would've survived the dissolving of my partnership with Terence.

My eyes find a photograph of him and me, stuck in the corner of a framed William Blake poem, *Love's Secret.*

God help me, I don't want to miss those days, but I miss that closeness Terence and I once had. I miss knowing I wasn't alone.

"Focus on today, lad," I tell myself, taking my eyes off the frame, fighting the onslaught of the loneliness I've felt since he and I parted ways.

I try to refocus my attention on the calendar. The wedding is set for Saturday, the 22nd. I type a note into my mobile to remind me to get in touch with Lorna Matthews, the wedding planner, and although I'm positive the woman has everything under control, some reassurances would go a long way to make me feel better.

Samantha gave me the impression that the allotted time was not going to be enough and she told me as much. I didn't know what she had to fret about and made the mistake of ridiculing her concern once. After she chewed me down to a nub, I know I will not to make that mistake again.

In order to better understand Samantha's worrying, I took the advantage of calling Gwen just to vent. In her melodious voice, she painted quite the picture about what a girl envisions when it comes to weddings. I promised to be more understanding from that point on.

The calendar on my right screen shows Gwen arriving exactly a week from today, on the 12th. I can't wait to see her and her husband Tony. Gwen told me that despite having to attend a few promotional events for his book on a wheelchair, he was recovering pretty well.

I can't even imagine what that reencounter will be like. Tony was shot by Samantha's ex-fiancé in an attempt on her life. He spent three weeks recovering at the hospital from the wound.

I endlessly berated Samantha for sneaking away the way she did in the aftermath of the shooting. I still see that broken look on her face in my dreams as I subjected her to the most torturous lectures I could muster at 30,000 feet over the Atlantic. I've come to care a great deal for Gwen and Tony after all.

For her part, Samantha took it all in stride, head down, tearfully enduring things that she needed to hear. As she withdrew into herself more and more, I realized I might have been pushing her into drinking herself to death once we arrived home. But she actually shut my gob for good when she pleaded I take her to rehab as soon as we landed in Heathrow.

Seeing her gripped by such turmoil, I made two calls and took her to the most reputable detoxification clinic in the UK. I drove her myself.

I spent many nights agonizing over her. Samantha was cut off from her world and I didn't get a word from her for months, until she successfully completed the first two phases of her treatment.

The day I was going to pick her up from the clinic, Jason McElroy showed up at my flat.

I won't soon forget that conversation…

I planned on rewarding Samantha with the biggest, most epic shopping trip. I wanted to take her to Ellesmere Port and spoil her for an entire week. I was actually in the process of gathering a few things for her, since she left her luggage in my car, when there was a knock on the door.

I checked the security displays and saw Jason McElroy standing at my front door. Lions was often visited by vendors of security equipment and we'd test their products by installing them in our own residencies.

I opened the door, wondering if there was an emergency at Lions but as soon as I took one look at Jason, I knew it involved Samantha.

I thought of telling him to leave after the little selfish rows he had with her, but the utter remorse in his pale blue eyes gave me second thoughts. "Jason, come in, chap."

"I would've called, but…"

"It's quite alright. What's happened?"

He shook his head. "I'm a bloody imbecile… I don't deserve her, Lewis… not that she'd want anything to do with me now…"

Alarmed by his demeanor, I quickly fixed him a glass of brandy and offered it to him.

"I gave up drinking," he said with a sad, apologetic smile. "For her."

I took the glass back to the side bar.

"I miss her, Lewis. Her face dominates my thoughts and I'm going mad. I want her to know I regret everything I said to her before she left. Would you please tell her that when you see her? Nathan mentioned she'd leave the clinic today. So when you see her…"

He stood to go to the door, his stride uneven like that of a wounded soldier, which ironically, he was.

"Jason, wait."

He hung his head as he spoke. "You and I have had our differences, haven't we?"

I said nothing, sensing there was more.

"I admit I've just been jealous of you."

I don't know why I always associated violence whenever I looked at Jason, but at that moment, there was nothing hostile about the defeated way he spoke. "Samantha is more like my sister, Jason. She's always been that to me."

Jason nodded. "It's just the way she can talk to you. I envy that more than you could possibly know. I envy the way she opens herself up to you."

I had nothing to say to that. It had taken a lifetime to attain such closeness with Samantha and often there was more give than take on my part.

"I apologize for everything, Lewis. I deeply regret not being there for you and her. When I realized what was happening, I lost it. Can you believe that? I survived one of the worst ambushes of the bloody war with a cool head, but the thought of Samantha getting killed undid me. I should've been there for her, for you. I'm..." He shook his head and turned back to the door.

"Jason. I think you need to be there."

There was an eager, hopeful look on his face. "Do you want me to go with you?"

"No. I think you have a lot to talk about and I know her, Jason. She's quite fond of you whether you believe it or not. She knows she wasn't fully in control of herself back then. Perhaps you can begin anew. It should be you up there anyway."

He looked at me, bewilderment in those wounded eyes. "You're her best friend, and a much better man to her than I'll ever be."

I smiled. "I won't argue with you, chap. But you're the one in love with her, and I believe she knows that."

"She's in love with someone else."

"She's in love with a bloody ghost. All she needs is to be shown something real, and she'll respond. Show her what you feel for her. Perhaps it'll be a risk for you because right now, there are no guarantees. But I have a feeling that if you show her what you feel for her, without expecting anything in return, she might just surprise you. You two belong together."

"How can you say that?"

I approached him and placed my hand on his shoulder. "You and Samantha together make a whole. There's no telling where you will grow from there." I saw understanding in his eyes. "She needs you to help her heal as much as you need her."

"I will protect her with my life if she'll have me," he said in a resolute voice.

"She'll have you and I'll hold you to that."

Jason nodded once, firmly. I could see something change in his eyes. "What should I say?"

I sighed. "Whatever is in your heart for our girl. Pour it all out and then let her make up her mind. But let me warn you, she may need time."

He nodded thoughtfully. "It doesn't feel right. You're the one who saved her."

"I brought her back, Jason. It's up to you to save her heart, and you'd better be ready to give it your all. Samantha's heart has been in tatters for a long time."

Jason Stephen McElroy, former commando of Her Majesty's SAS, looked me in the eye as tears rolled down the chiseled planes of his face. "I love her, Lewis. I love her more than anyone knows, and I don't want a life without her."

I was a bit surprised at his frankness. I'd never known that side of him, but I knew right there and then that I was right to send him in my place. Perhaps this new version of Jason was meant for the new version of Samantha.

It was awkward to lay a reassuring hand on his big shoulder. I was once quite attracted to him physically, but I realized how much I liked him for my best friend after a while. "Jason, if there's any chance for you to have a future with Samantha you need to be determined to look ahead, from this point on. I believe you both need that."

I watched him square his shoulders, a broken lad on the mend. "I will. I'm forever in your debt, Lewis."

To this day, our little talk has remained a secret from Samantha.

I click on the 17th and type in *Moppins' arrival 3:00 P.M.*

"Are you cross with us?"

I hit the sleep key at the sound of Samantha's voice and the screens go black. "Not at all, luv. Mum asked of you as soon as I got home."

She smiles. "She's sweet. She told me to say good night for her. She was tired from driving."

"If I knew she'd be here today, I would've gotten the guest rooms ready."

"I took care of it."

"You did?"

She nods. "I needed something to do while we were talking."

I frown. "Why?"

She looks a little uncertain. "Call me a liar, but I could smell the wine as soon as I walked in."

I try to suppress a look of genuine worry. "Impossible. The air was saturated with Scouse stew."

She smiles thinly. "You know what I mean."

"You're doing terrific, Sam. You're strong."

Her eyes glitter. "Thank you."

"I promise to get rid of every drop of spirits in this place."

She frowns. "I love you for that, but you don't have to. I can't very well ask the entire world to get rid of alcohol for me."

I walk over and embrace her. "I'm so proud of you, luv."

"It is getting easier." She squeezes me and pats my back.

Now I really don't want Quinn and her friends to take Samantha out on the town.

Samantha squeezes me once more before pulling back. "I love this song! Is that Tori Amos?"

I clear my head enough to register the song. "Yes, some sort of fairy tale song." We listen to the song for a full minute. I can tell Samantha is anxious about something. "Have you talked to Jason?"

She nods with a smile that lights up her face. "He messaged me before I got here. He'll be home Friday. John Howard is taking his place."

"Great, so I can cancel our little trip into Soho then."

She grins. "You're never going to let me live that one down. Are you?"

"Not on your life. What are you so anxious about?"

She looks surprised. "How'd you—"

"Sam, your pretty face might as well be a computer screen with very large font letters."

"I don't do so well on my own anymore."

"Are you still having the nightmares?"

She nods slowly.

I think her perfect memory is more of a curse than a blessing. Samantha got through things any lesser woman would have lost her mind over at the hands of her ex-fiancé. She's entitled to have a lot more of an effect than mere nightmares. "Go get your bag. You can stay."

Her smile rivals that of a child's on Christmas morning. She gives me a quick, grateful hug and runs out to get her bag out of the boot of her car.

After we both change into sleeping attire, I leave her in my room and go back to the studio. I open the futon and retrieve a pillow and a blanket out of a small closet. I'm slowly falling asleep to the beautiful voice of Norah Jones in the darkness, heeding her words to go away with her when the futon shifts.

"Ah, you're such a needy lass," I tell Samantha in mock disapproval.

She silently gets under the cover and is asleep in minutes. Her hair is cascading away from her face and her arm is wrapped around me as I lie on my back. It occurs to me then that once she's married to Jason, she won't need me to keep her company anymore. She shouldn't need me now, I think with a bit of alarm.

Perhaps that's the change I've been sensing.

Samantha has been a part of my life ever since I can remember. She was barely three years old when her mother brought her to the studio for her first *petite danseuse* class. Over thirty years ago, I think in awe.

I was hanging off the *barre,* just playing around before class when Kathleen Reddick brought her little girl in. Samantha had a confident, little lopsided grin. She wore a light pink body wrapper tutu over white tights.

While Mum talked to Kathleen Reddick, little Samantha walked right up to me and began copying my movements. Later, after the lesson, I asked Mum if that little girl was an angel, for I'd never seen a prettier creature. Mum smiled and said, "No more than you are."

That's my first recollection of Samantha in my life. But in truth, our friendship goes back further than that.

Samantha's grandmother, Victoria Reddick, helped Mum take care of me when I was an infant. I can still recall Grandmum fondly telling us what a lovely little pair we made sharing a crib. With Samantha's father, Jack, still serving in the Royal Navy, Kathleen relied on her mother-in-law to look after Samantha.

The Reddicks lived right next door until Kathleen was offered a position in the faculty at the University of Rhode Island as a professor in Literature. I was too young to properly process what that meant and I missed Samantha terribly once she left for the US.

Our friendship survived because of Grandmum allowing me to call Samantha on the telephone, and their frequent trips back to Liverpool during school breaks. By the time we turned the corner from childhood into adolescence, the families were so close that the Reddicks would send her to spend her entire summers with Grandmum and subsequently with Mum and me. For those wonderful weeks, my world was complete.

I think everyone had us married from the time we were first graders. I can't say I blame them.

When that horrid period of sexual confusion set in for me, I felt such remorse over dashing those expectations more than anyone knows, but there was nothing I could do about it.

I glance at the top of Samantha's head as the memories float around in my head.

I never thought this much about anything before, especially events from the past. This is her arena. She's the introvert, the tortured soul, how did our roles reverse so drastically?

It has to be the wedding.

My best friend is about to move further down on the road of life, and she'll go on without me. Things will inevitably change and up until now, I didn't want to admit just how much I fear it. I'm also thinking Samantha shares my fear. It may explain the reason she's anxious to the point that she needs to sleep beside me, the way we did when we were kids; too afraid to sleep alone during a storm, each looking for comfort in the other and never failing to find it.

I close my eyes and will my mind to shut off for the night. I'm happy to be a comfort to my best friend. I'm honored that she's found some relative safety in my company.

She'll never know how much of a comfort she is to me at this moment or how much of a comfort she's really been throughout my entire life.

8

As full as I was last night after inhaling most of the Scouse stew, the smell of frying bacon wafting from the kitchen makes me tremble with hunger. I sit up on the futon and stretch only to yelp when I feel a stabbing pain behind my neck. The dull aches in my knees make me not happy about this aging business.

Mum is at the stove, pushing eggs around on a hot skillet. I can't remember ever buying a skillet, but apparently I must have.

"Good morning, luv," she says over her shoulder.

"More so when you're near," I quip.

Mum gives me a smile and rolls her eyes theatrically. "Get some tea brewing, please."

She wears her hair boyishly short, yet no one could possibly question her femininity. Her features are delicate, hazel eyes upturned at the corners, a Patrician nose in the middle of a perfect oval face adorned with full lips. Although she's short of stature, barely over five feet, her limbs are long and toned. She still maintains a dancer's physique that makes her look forty rather than fifty-three. She wears a casual ensemble, dark slacks, a charcoal blouse and a black wool vest. I wonder where she's going.

I set about to brew the tea as requested then go to my front window, expecting to find Samantha's Mini Cooper on the street but she's gone. "When did Sam leave?"

"I tried to keep her for breakfast, but she insisted she needed to run because you," she stabs a finger at me, "told her she needs to watch her weight." Her gaze turns scornful and her hands are at her waist. "Are you blind or something, son? Sammie Kay looks as perfect as a woman can look."

I smile. "You should've seen her at McDonald's in Philadelphia."

"No wonder she runs so much." Mum's bemusement fades. "How foolish of me was it to drink all that wine in front of her?"

The change in the mood of our conversation nearly gives me whiplash. "She's fine. What made you say that?"

"I noticed her eyes kept going to the bloody goblet I was holding." She gives me an intense look. "How's she?"

"She's strong," I pronounce with conviction.

Mum nods slowly, clearly unconvinced. "Well. I'm glad you were there for her. I know Kath and Jack adore you for it."

"And Grandmum," I say softly, unnerved by the quiver in my voice.

Mum rubs my shoulder and sighs. "They can't make them any better than Lady Reddick. I'm terribly sorry I didn't make it to the service."

"Mum, we've been over this. You were in France at the time. Sam understands that."

"I certainly hope so. That woman was one of the best people I knew."

I feel tears in my eyes but I know if I let go, we'll both turn into a sobbing mess. "What did you and Sam talk about?"

Mum blinks back a wave of emotion and gives me a pointed look. "Lady business."

"Oh, you gave her The Talk for her honeymoon night."

Mum looks stunned. "I don't want to know. Let's just pretend our little Sammie Kay is as pure as glacial water."

There's nothing I can do about the onslaught of laughter that shakes me from the inside out. If Samantha is pure, then I'm the bloody Queen of England.

"Eat your breakfast!"

I jump out of the way of her swatting hand but once I sit down, I don't dare take a bite until I can get control of myself.

Mum heaps a plate for herself and sits across from me with a scowl. "Eat," she commands.

When my plate is clean I look for the skillet on the stove, eager to get some more. I don't see it on the stove, but I see its shining handle sticking up from the sink.

"What's the matter?"

I keep my eyes on her plate. "Are you really going to eat all that?"

Mum pulls her plate closer to her. "Since when did you become a bottomless barrel? Boy, you had more than enough."

I content myself with two tall glasses of orange juice.

"I need to talk to you, Mum."

She stops chewing to look at me. Unlike Samantha, her table manners are impeccable and only when she's ready to respond does she encourage me to elaborate.

"Talk to me."

"Lately I feel strange. I'm uncomfortable in my own skin. Every time I think I have the answer more possibilities pop up. I can't stop thinking."

There's concern in her eyes. "Thinking of what?"

"Everything. Nothing. I don't know."

I can sense she wants to lecture me on the value of clear and concise conversation, but she must see something in my face that censures her.

"Are you afraid of losing Sammie Kay?"

I have the distinct feeling Samantha already gave Mum the gist of my plight. "I am. But whatever else this is goes back further."

She nods in understanding. "Despite her growing up in America, Sammie Kay is the biggest part of your life, my boy. Nothing will get in the way of your friendship. Believe that."

Her words are a soothing balm. "So, did you finally give up on the idea of her and I doing the couple thing?"

Mum pats my cheek affectionately. "Sammie's presence in your life has been my own vindication, my boy. I can't help it if I wanted a more permanent arrangement between you two."

The truth of her words is confounding. "How so?"

She sighs. "Nothing pained me more than to see you growing up all by yourself. Nothing."

Sometimes, my mother loves to torture herself with such notions. "I didn't grow up by myself. I had you."

"Yes. You did indeed. And I turned you into a bloody ballerina." She shakes her head sadly.

I know there's some deep meaning to the way she's speaking, but I can't afford to face this right now. "You turned me into the best there was."

She smiles. "That's not so difficult when there's practically no competition. But you're sweet for making me feel better."

Time to change tactics. I suddenly sense Mum's dealing with her own feelings concerning Samantha's wedding.

"There are a few things that I'd like to discuss with you, but I have to go into Lambeth to meet with Richard. Unless of course, you need me."

I thought I had this huge long discussion in me, but suddenly I don't. "We can talk whenever you want, Mum. What time do we have to leave?"

She gives me a bemused smile. "*I* have to leave in a few minutes. What are *you* going to do?"

I shake my head at her. "Being this secretive doesn't become you, dear."

"Mystery is my middle name. You're on your own for dinner. Don't wait up, luv."

"Mysterious, alright."

Her gaze is soft upon me. "Sammie Kay will always be part of your life, Lewis. Don't be afraid of change. Embrace it, okay?"

I nod.

She kisses the top of my head and turns for the door.

"Thanks for cooking, Mum," I call as she leaves.

When I hear her car speed down the street, I feel a pang of separation anxiety. Perhaps it's time I find what to do when I'm by myself. Despite Mum's assurances, I know that soon Samantha won't be so readily available to keep me company.

***

It seems foolish to stow an umbrella in the car before I drive, especially on a bright, sunny morning but in London, everyone knows to take sunglasses and umbrellas wherever we go. October is normally dry, but the London climate is famous for its unpredictability.

The anxiety that sent me running out of my flat abates only when I cross the Thames on the Battersea Bridge, windows down, stereo blaring. The sight of Clapham Park also brings me some peace of mind.

Winslade Road is empty of parked cars and I easily find a spot right by the door of the quaint little row house where Audrey Burton lives. Audrey's house is a rather drab, two-story block building with a tiny, fenced front patio. The little iron door squeaks in protest when I push through.

Audrey could easily afford an estate in Kensington or a place like mine near Hyde Park, but living from hand to mouth while in art school has changed her perspective on life drastically. She's not foolish though. The proximity to Brixton prison prompted her to make her place as secure as possible. Unfounded fears perhaps, but she did keep some valuable art pieces.

I lift the brass knocker, which is shaped like a lion's paw, and strike the plate.

"I reserve the right to shoot Hooligans upon sight. Come in at your own risk!" Audrey's throaty voice is muffled, but clear enough from behind the heavy metal door.

"Hullo Sweetie," I offer in way of greeting once I enter.

"Well, if it isn't the bloody Queen of England herself coming to see how the little people trod along."

Audrey peers at me from behind a large canvas. A utility cart sits next to her. The upper shelf holds an array of mason jars with different brushes in them. Several different tools, whose names I can only guess, crowd the top. A small bucket on the lower shelf of the cart is full of tubes of oils.

"Blimey, lass. You are the busy one," I remark as I take stock of the different easels containing pieces in all sorts of stages. Some are penciled in, while others look halfway done.

"I'm a victim of my own bloody success."

I take a few steps into the studio, my eyes dancing over several finished paintings, each one more stunning than the next.

"That's far enough Lew! I don't want anyone seeing this one."

"I just wanted to give you a proper hello."

She scoffs. "I know you want this," she strikes a pose, tracing her thick curves with one hand, giving me a lustful grin, "but you'll just have to take a number and stand in line."

"You wish!"

She pulls on a sheet hanging on a wire to cover the canvas without letting it touch its surface. Satisfied with the concealment of her work, she walks over to me and crushes me in a bear hug.

"I wasn't joking about the blue bloods coming to check on the downtrodden. What's going on?" She draws back in gives me the once over. "What are you wearing?"

"Questions the lass wearing the kilt, fishnet stockings, and combat boots," I shoot back. "Surely you see the irony, luv."

Audrey frowns at this. "In those faded denims and that raggedy shirt, you just look very unLewis-like, luv. And I always look like this."

Good point. "Have you been talking to Sam?"

She shakes her head.

I'm suddenly unsure what I came to see Audrey about.

Audrey Burton is the third member of our Liverpool trio. The Burtons lived a few houses down from the Reddicks, and naturally, Audrey and Samantha were friends. Even back then, Audrey would refer to me as "one of the girls". In the brief time we shared in school, when our all-boy prep school invited her all-girl school to participate in academic contests, she was the one chasing bullies away, defending the "ballerina boy".

I learned early on that school children are the cruelest people in existence. It seemed bullying was just something we all had to endure, and much more so when you're a sexually confused kid.

"The last time you came to visit, you were having man troubles," Audrey remarks. "What's his name? Do you need it to look like an accident? Or can I indulge in some creative torture?"

Audrey and I have always had a tendency to play off each other and have seldom had a frank discussion about anything. That usually fell on Samantha's shoulders, but for the first time in my life, I don't think I can unburden myself to my best friend, which essentially makes Audrey next in line. "I don't have anyone at the moment."

Audrey nods. "You've been going solo since Terence. Again, not like you, luv. You're usually in high demand, and move like a little butterfly, flittering from flower to flower sampling their goods. You had that bloke eating out of your hand at that last rave we went to, which was…" Her eyes roll around in thought. "Blimey! Back in bloody July! As I recall you left me high and bloody dry, at the mercy of those beasts." She grins.

I appreciate her attempt at levity, but I can't fight the wave of revulsion that hits me at that moment. "I haven't felt up to much of anything these days."

Audrey cocks her head in thought. "Besides the new look and the gloomy disposition, what else is new with you?

I can't seem to gather my thoughts. I'm usually the one extricating information out of my friends in order to provide some piece of advice. I'm usually the one cracking the jokes and making the snide observations. "I don't feel like myself today."

She studies me for a moment. "Come, sit." She pats the seat of an upholstered stool.

I do as she says. She offers me tea and before I can answer, she quickly fills two mugs and hands me one. "What is it? Normally you go to Sam when you're blue. Since you came to me, I'm to assume it's something to do with her. Isn't it?"

I sip at the bitter brew and scald my lips, aggravating the blister from the other day. "Perhaps."

"Is it the wedding?"

"Yes and no."

"Wonderful," Audrey sighs and drinks the tea without flinching. "What's worrying you? Is Jason back yet?"

"She said he'll be here Friday."

"Will you explain to me this yes and no business?"

"I need to ask you something first." Unable to sit still, I stand and pace back and forth in front of her.

"Well, the bloody suspense is killing me. Just talk, Lewis."

"What made you adopt Goth?"

Audrey purses her lips and I patiently sit quietly as she formulates her reply.

Audrey's mother, Dr. Joyce Burton, wanted nothing more than to have her only daughter follow in her footsteps as a cardiac surgeon. Audrey had other plans, however. Her parents punished her for disappointing them by cutting her off, leaving her entirely on her own. The once pampered little princess, who got anything she wanted at the pout of her lips, was forced to become a survivor. When she found herself able to stand on her own two feet upon becoming a famous artist, she shunned her parents for life, her father for his cruelty and her mother for her single minded expectations. She loved to brag that one of her paintings brought in more money than her mother made in five years.

I recall few conversations from that time. Audrey expressed her rebellion by transforming herself into a ghoul. She adopted the Goth counterculture, which served her well in the London underground of art where most people praised her originality. In reality, it was a slap in the face of her parents and everything they represented.

"I don't know that I adopted it. I think it was the other way around. My parents made me a cast off, so I figured I ought to look the part."

"Yes, but you're not as into it as you once were."

"No. It's more of a style now, rather than a lifestyle."

This gives me pause. "What's the difference?"

She looks confused. "I'm surprised you, of all people, would ask that question. A style is how you look. A lifestyle is how you live."

"Oh, no more Satan worshipping for you then."

"Nope, no more live sacrifices. Pity…"

I laugh. "Does that mean you're eventually going to join the mainstream?"

She shrugs as though she couldn't care less. "I'm not sure. Perhaps given the right circumstances, sure."

"You would change?"

She nods. "Absolutely. Lewis, no day is the same as any other day. That fact alone ought to prompt change within all of us. I think of that more and more now. I mean, I don't want to be fifty and still dress this way."

"But a style is easier to change than a lifestyle."

She looks at me with renewed interest. "It all depends on what you're doing it for. Take Sam, for instance. She changed her entire lifestyle. Whether it was for herself or for Jason Stephen is up for debate. I honestly think she changed because she didn't want to find herself alone anymore."

I want to point out that she would never have been alone with me around, but suddenly an image of Gwen, Tony, and their little girls floats in my mind. "I think I understand."

"At some point, you've got to grow up, luv."

There are a million different thoughts flying through my head. The source of this sudden introspection eludes me. It's a lurking presence just at the periphery of my mind, and it knows how to hide when I shift my focus, only to tease me with an ephemeral appearance. "Do you think I've been different?"

Her greenish gaze narrows. "As much as I've seen you?"

A pang of guilt makes me look at the floor. "I've been busy with work, and Samantha. She's had me in tow to every bridal shop in the city."

I casually walk by the counter in her corner kitchenette and pull a stool. There's a small box on the seat, pink with blue letters advertising its use. I pick it up and frown at the small package. It's a home pregnancy test. "Audrey?"

"Oh, by George. Give me the bloody thing!"

I let her snatch the package out of my hand. "It's so not what you think, luv. I'm not about to add a distended belly to this marvelous physique you see before you."

I'm still in shock, despite her joking. "Are you…?"

"For fuck's sakes!" She glares at me. "It's a bloody sample. The Welford wankers wanted a special graphic on their bloody piddle sticks. It's not mine."

"Why is it open?"

"Well, I bloody tried it. What?" She demands, registering the questioning look on my face. "Haven't you ever wanted to piddle on a bloody preggo-stick?"

There's no deceit in her eyes. "Alright, I believe you, luv. I do."

"Bloody hell, Lewis." She shakes her head in exasperation. "I'm bloody allergic to little imps. Do you really think I'd go mess around to end up with child?"

"Okay. Forgive me, honest mistake. It just took me by surprise, that's all."

"Men, squeamish as convent nuns getting flashed for the first time." She smacks my shoulder with the package. "Now, where were we? Oh, yes. The bloody bridal shops and your busy life, blah, blah, bloody blah."

"I was trying to apologize for not being around."

"Don't be daft. I'm not talking about that. When was the last time you went to a rave? That's right. You haven't, because I usually get an invite when you go. Unless you're cheating on me."

"No. I didn't feel like going."

"What have you been doing then? I don't know you to be a workaholic."

"Working," I tell her, at once thinking how sad that it's all I've been doing as of late.

"I'm not trying to make you feel guilty, luv. I've been quite occupied with different projects. Which reminds me. I need your infinite wisdom concerning internet matters."

"You couldn't afford me," I tease.

"Afford you? That's why I'm not hiring your avaricious arse. I'm requesting a favor from a friend."

I grin. She could easily afford a team of programmers. Audrey Burton is wealthy the way small diamond mining countries are wealthy, but you'd never know by her frugal ways. She drives a '68 Volkswagen Bus. I had the misfortune of driving the bloody clunker once. No power steering, no power breaks, and no bloody stereo. The experience nearly drove me to kiss the bonnet of my Beamer each time I drove it.

"I'd like my own website. All the cool artists are doing it. My adoring fans actually demand it."

"Only if you show me your mystery piece." I point at the covered canvas.

Audrey looks at the easel then turns to me with a scowl. "You are a worse haggler than an Arab merchant."

She goes to the far wall and hits a few switches that pour light into the converted studio. After buying the little house, Audrey hired the same chap who did the work in my flat and, after much haggling, she had him tear down the partitions to create a large work space. She also requested an impressive array of track lighting that mimics a blazing sun at full capacity.

She has me stand before the old sheet that covers the canvas then pulls it away revealing a sight that takes my breath away.

"Bloody hell…"

"That's exactly the reaction I want," Audrey says in a laugh as she comes to stand beside me. "Do you think she'll like it?"

"I know she'll love it," I say in a properly awed tone. "It's absolutely beautiful, luv."

Audrey looks at her own work with a critical eye. "Of course the lighting is a bit embellished, considering the water through the windows is behind the main subject, and his pose actually looks a bit too dominant. But I like the illusion of space between them. It could've been better."

I backhand her shoulder. "Shut your gob! It's perfect."

"Don't tell her a thing. I want to unveil it at the wedding."

"I give you my word."

She gives me a satisfied nod. "Now, unless you have some more soul bearing to do, let's talk about my website."

9

Three hours later, I'm driving back to my flat after settling on the design content for Audrey's website. I tried convincing her to hire a professional photographer for the website images, but she scoffed at the idea. She's planning on taking the photos herself.

When she brought an old 35mm model out of a cabinet, I told her I'd let her borrow my Cannon digital. Something tells me that's exactly what she was counting on. I'm not worried about the photos. Audrey has been called a Master of Light in several art circles.

Feeling less burdened than earlier, I'm thoroughly enjoying the vocal prowess of the lovely Colbie Caillat when the buzzing of my mobile rudely interrupts. "Yes?"

"Mr. Bettford? This is Lorna Matthews."

"Yes, of course. How are you Ms. Matthews?"

"Quite alright. Can you make it down to Rosenthal Gardens?"

I think about it for a second. Rosenthal Gardens is the wedding venue. I couldn't go with Samantha and Jason the day she toured it, but she told me it was exactly what she dreamed. "On High Street?"

"Yes."

"Is something the matter?"

After a slight hesitation, Lorna says, "Not something that can't be handled. I was told to consult with you in case any issues arose."

"Me?"

"Yes, that's what the lovely Miss Reddick said."

Thanks, Sam... "I'm just leaving Lambeth. I'll be there in about fifteen minutes."

"Terrific."

Following the Chelsea Embankment, I drive west along the Thames before turning north on the A220 all the way to High Street. I pull into the drive of Rosenthal Gardens and feel as though I'm driving into a bloody post card.

The grounds are beautifully manicured. The drive is a graceful, winding path of paver blocks that leads to a large fountain that marks the very center of the grounds. The building itself has a bit of a Greek revival air to it. It's all large windows and Ionic columns, boasting an ornate cupola made entirely of glass over the main hall. A pair of auxiliary halls bookends the structure, giving it an elegant symmetry. The bride is going to look right at home in her resplendent gown, a princess in a castle.

Samantha's initial plan consisted of having the wedding at Nathan Jeffries' Kensington mansion but his fiancée Alicia wouldn't hear of it, and she quickly hired Lorna Matthews. Together, with a hesitant bride, the women made the necessary reservations and organized the entire affair in record time.

Rosenthal Gardens is only a few minutes away from St. Mary Magdalene Abbots Church where the wedding is to take place.

I find Lorna's large frame swiftly moving from end to end. Her short assistant follows her around, quickly jotting notes on a clipboard. I watch the assistant free her writing hand to shake off the cramps in her fingers and huff a breath skyward. When she sees me, she taps on Lorna's shoulder and points at me.

Lorna is a large woman in her late forties. Her dark eyes miss nothing. She has a broad smile that makes her eyes pinch nearly shut. After quickly firing a set of instructions to her flustered assistant, she walks up to me, hands extended before her.

I meet her halfway and she takes both my hands in greeting.

"I'm so glad you could make it."

I look around at the beehive-like activity. "A little early for Sam's wedding. Isn't it?"

Lorna releases my hands and gestures to a nearby table. "This isn't for the lovely Miss Reddick. This for the Crisswell and Barnes wedding."

I shake my head in awe. "How do you do this week in and week out?"

"It's my life," she proudly proclaims. "All this work is so worth it in the end, you'll see. Every couple gets to be king and queen for the day."

Considering her gargantuan fees, I'd expect nothing less. "What can I do for you, Madame?"

"Stacy!" Lorna calls for her assistant.

Stacy shuffles quickly over.

"McElroy-Reddick," Lorna says.

Stacy nods and shuffles away. Lorna is silent until Stacy returns with a thick folder. I notice an array of color tabs separating its contents. Lorna opens up to a blue tab and turns the folder around to show me the photos of the bridesmaids' gowns.

"Lovely," I comment.

"I agree. But the only problem is that this gorgeous color is better suited for a December, or a January wedding."

I recall Alicia being quite adamant about the wedding color complementing the silvery hues of Samantha's eyes. Knowing what I know of my best friend, I didn't think it was a good idea, but Samantha actually liked it.

"October is the last of the warmer months and it would be far lovelier to theme the wedding in a more vibrant pallet."

I wonder why she hasn't asked Samantha about this. "So, what do you suggest?"

Lorna's smile makes me nervous. She raises a hand, palm open and her assistant quickly places a manila folder that Lorna swiftly brings down to the table and opens it before me.

"Blimey... That's vibrant, alright."

Lorna extricates a piece of fabric and hands it to me. "This is a fairly new color, tangerine tango."

"It's overly orange."

Her pudgy cheek twitches in distaste. I think "overly orange" is the last thing she wanted to hear.

"That's the beauty of it."

Lorna shifts through some sheets and produces a large photograph of a bridal bouquet. The combination of tiger lilies, orchids, daisies, blood red rosebuds, a touch of whimsy, and thin dark fillers is stunning in its beauty.

"Whatever happened to white roses?"

"White roses are reserved for funerals. This is much livelier and bursts with warmth and passion."

"So, fiery red is the color of passion," I muse.

"Absolutely," Lorna agrees, her eyes glittering. "But there's more to it than simple passion. Where I come from, a combination of orange and deep red are said to be the colors of change."

"Of course," I allow. "The way the foliage changes before the winter."

"Not exactly, Mr. Bettford. It's more of a change of our inner selves, a benign change. The starting point of new life."

I've never been one to accept New Age concepts, but something tells me that's not what this is.

"I've known Alicia for many years. She's told me enough about Miss Reddick to know that this wedding is the result of a major change in herself, a change in her soul. It seems apt."

"I'd have to agree with you."

Lorna smiles. "I make it a point to respect my client's choices, but I felt it necessary to add this new wrinkle."

"Augusta may not be happy. She'd be making new gowns," I tell her, worried about the cantankerous Augusta Flynn, one of the most sought after dressmakers in London.

"Madame Flynn has been quite agreeable once I explained everything."

"Anyone capable of getting that old bird to agree on anything has got my respect."

Lorna nods noncommittally. "Thank you. I understand you're a man who knows fashion. I wanted to run these designs by you," Lorna says, placing a photograph of a gown next to the bouquet photo.

The design is a gorgeous, full length, strapless piece of terrific allure. Its most commanding feature is a subdued bow at the abdomen that seems to cinch the material around the model's figure. I try to picture Gwen or Alicia wearing the gown. "Breathtaking" would fall miserably short of doing such an image any justice.

"Have you talked to Sam about these?"

Lorna looks uncertain. "I shouldn't be the one making the suggestion. You stand a better chance to convince her."

"What makes you think that?"

"Well, normally I rely on the maid of honor to iron out these last minute details. But she won't be here until next week and that may not be enough time to have all the alterations done."

"I'll run the idea by her," I offer.

"I need you to convince her."

This takes me by surprise a bit. "Doesn't the bride have the final say so on these matters?"

"Of course. But I wouldn't be doing my job if I didn't give the bride the best possible option."

Interesting. "What do you have against the silvery blue."

"Absolutely nothing. It is beautiful and it would go well with our bride's beautiful eyes. I've been after my people to develop that very color. In fact, I can't shut my gob about it."

"Then what's the problem?"

Lorna laces her fingers and gives me a curious glance. "No one has ever used this theme, and I'd like to make this a most unique wedding for a most unique bride."

I nod, though understanding eludes me.

"Mr. Bettford, I want this bride of ours to shine."

Her eyes are bright with passion. I'm sold.

"I just don't feel our bride is in love with the color of her eyes," Lorna adds.

When Samantha was fifteen, she lost her parents in a traffic accident. She's blamed herself for their death every single day since. To this day she believes that had she not run away, her parents wouldn't have been on that icy road on their way to find her. The crushing guilt was exacerbated when the police had her identify her mother's body. Kathleen Reddick's dead gaze has haunted Sam since. The beautiful, iridescent eyes she got from her mother became something Samantha couldn't face. I still expect her to avoid looking into mirrors for fear of suffering horrific panic attacks induced by the flashback.

She's broken out of that self-imposed prison of guilt thanks to the diligent work of her therapist, but I've always questioned just how well she actually is as far as dealing with the grief and the guilt.

That Lorna Matthews sees this conflict in Samantha despite knowing little about her, tells me how much she cares for the brides she works for. I gain a new appreciation for this fabulous wedding planner.

"I'll certainly give it a go. Thank you, for bringing this to my attention."

"Not at all. The goal of this business is to have the happiest bride at the end of the day."

I leave Rosenthal Gardens after treating Lorna to a verbal bath scented with plenty of flattery that leaves her giggling like a schoolgirl. I never once have to lie or embellish anything. Her work is impeccable, her style incomparable.

A style is how you look. A lifestyle is how you live...

Audrey's words stay in my head all the way to Kensington until I pull into the drive of Nathan Jeffries' magnificent mansion. I'd been here more than a few times before Samantha moved back to London, but I've been a virtual permanent resident since.

In the kitchen, Margaret, housekeeper extraordinaire, greets me with an affectionate kiss on the cheek. I love the old bird. We have a ritual of sorts in which I treat her like the royalty she is to me.

I tell her she looks especially ravishing tonight and she fans herself as she laughs. She tells me Samantha is upset and speculates on the reasons in her quick Southern Irish accent. I promise to make her a cup of tea that will leave her smacking her berry colored lips and she graces me with a trilling laugh.

Walking past the library, I can only deduce Samantha is upset over Jason. I wonder if the bloke changed the date of his arrival once more. I climb the spiral staircase and hear quiet sobbing before I even get to Samantha's bedroom door. When I go in, I see her lying face down, crying over her pillow.

"Sam?"

She sniffles and turns to look at me through puffy eyes. "Hi."

I try to subtly look around for an empty glass or a bottle of vodka, and sigh thankfully when I don't see either. "What's happened, luv?"

She sits up and wipes at her eyes. Her long chestnut hair falls over her face like theater curtains marking the end of a play.

"You're going to think I'm being utterly daft."

"Do you mean more than normal?" I expect her to look up with annoyance, but she keeps her eyes down.

As I've done more times than I can count, I pull her chair from the desk and roll it close to the bed so I can sit across from her. Once I sit, I take her hand in both of mine and wait until she gathers herself. When she finally meets my eyes, her expression is one of embarrassment.

"It's all too much," she cries.

She could be talking about a million different things. Her ambiguity only means she needs more time so I say nothing.

"I just wanted a small affair. I wanted to have it here. I'm not even going to know anyone coming to this bloody thing!"

I've been considering the same thing for some time now. Alicia might have gone overboard in the entire wedding planning bit. Strange, considering she has grand wedding plans of her own.

"Why don't we talk to Alicia about it?"

"I can't do that," Samantha says miserably. "She's been so wonderful about everything. I can't possibly be so ungrateful."

"Sam, it's your wedding, luv. It's supposed to be whatever you want it to be. You are queen of the land for one day and at the end of the day, nothing matters unless the bride is happy." I intentionally use Lorna's own words.

Samantha nods slowly, wipes off a few more tears, and exhales as though in relief. I don't presume to make up her mind for her at the moment. It's better to distract her with something else, let her flush out the emotions so more rational thinking takes place in her mind.

I know that she'd know exactly how to help me move past a similar issue. I have my own tides of emotion and reason, and no one knows those ebbs and flows better than my best friend. Is that something I will lose forever once she's married?

The anxiety that's taken all day for me to work off, returns with renewed force.

Think of something else!

"Quinn, her date, and four of your sisters are coming."

Samantha whips her head around to face me. "Which ones?"

"Has it ever occurred to you to actually talk to Quinn and find out from her?"

"You know me and telephone conversations."

I give her an incredulous look. "I do. It took me two hours to get rid of you the other day."

Her chin drops. "That's kind of mean."

I take care to soften my voice. Her skin is thinner than I thought at this moment. "Just call her. Right now."

It suddenly occurs to me that Samantha doesn't know Quinn is in London, but it's too late to retract my suggestion. I think furiously of a way to play off my mistake as sweat pebbles over my forehead. Then it hits me, a way out. "It's about..." I pretend to have some difficulty retrieving the time on my mobile. Thin, but it's all I have. I thumb a text to Quinn as discreetly as possible, turning away from Samantha under the pretense of searching a better signal.

Made a mistake, Sam is calling your "American" mobile

"...Eleven over there," I mutter, watching anxiously for a reply.

The damning chime from Quinn's reply nearly makes me drop the device.

Got it ;) turning it on

I slowly let out the pent up breath as I scroll down to the number.

"Are you alright?" Samantha asks suspiciously.

"Quite, quite. I'm just scrolling through emails to retrieve her number for you... ah! Here it is, elusive bugger."

I put my mobile in her hand, the number already keyed in.

Samantha's right eyebrow is high on her forehead as she waits for the call to connect. "You're acting strange."

"I've got to make Margaret some tea. Have a good chat, lass," I say, patting her thigh before getting up.

"When did you add her number to your contact list?" She asks pointedly.

"That supermobile automatically adds every piece of information into an email contact, luv. Moving at the speed of modern business," I reply quickly, quoting the slogan for my service carrier.

Quinn, answer the bloody call!

"Did it work?" I ask, hoping to tamp down the anxious note in my voice.

"You never tapped send."

Samantha has little understanding of communication technology. Most people do, and I take advantage to carry out the little lie. I'd better see Quinn soon. I don't like lying to my best friend. "Oh, well then..."

When I get to the door, I look back to see if Samantha is making the call yet. She's still holding the mobile away from her ear.

"Call her."

She nods, taps the screen and whips her hair out of the way. "Happy?"

"Quite." I stay put until their conversation ensues. At first they exchange hellos, but soon the chat is pointed by several one word exchanges like "really?"; "no!"; "yes!" and even a "shut up!"

"The gift of gab," I mutter as I make my way downstairs, my nerves frayed.

I can hear some activity in the kitchen.

"My sweet Margaret, allow me the privilege of serving you my best cup of tea, luv."

Seeing Margaret blush and giggle makes me feel like my usual self for the first time in a long while.

"How's Miss Samantha?"

"Darling, the female mind is a wondrous, yet mysterious cavern full of hidden strengths, particularly Samantha's."

I quickly prepare the tea and wait just a bit for the water to boil.

Age has wrinkled Margaret's kind visage with care. The old bird is in her sixties, late sixties come to think of it, but her pale blue eyes shine with a fierce intellect. She wears her silver hair short, much like the lovely Julie Andrews in *The Sound of Music*. They share a remarkable resemblance. Around strangers, Margaret carries herself with a dignity that's humbling. For anyone else, it takes some time to get past that veneer of professionalism. Margaret is quite fond of the people she works for. I've never heard her utter an unkind word in all the years I've known her.

When Samantha and I were kids, she treated us like her own. Much like the Maria from *The Sound of Music*, she was a governess of sorts. Many times, she made us help her clean our messes and if we got out of line, which was often the case, we ended up washing the dishes. Of course, when we behaved, Margaret rewarded us with succulent pastries made by her own, loving hands. Samantha and I have never looked at her as a servant. Come to think of it, no one in this majestic home ever has.

"I suppose it is, young Lewis. The little sweetheart might have a case of wedding nerves, is all."

"Are you saying she has cold feet?"

Margaret frowns. "Young Jason is quite taken by her, and that child loves him so. I can tell." She winks and takes a sip of her tea.

In Margaret's mind, Samantha's never ceased to be a child.

She closes her eyes and nods happily. "What is your secret, young Lewis? This tastes like heaven."

"It's all in the loving touch, m' Lady."

We both turn to the sound of tires rolling on the crushed stone of the drive. The tiny vehicle looks more like a toy. I can't imagine feeling safe in a car where I can simultaneously touch both windscreens by barely stretching my arms.

Alicia climbs out of the Smartcar and flips her sunglasses over her head. She's quite a sight, tall and svelte, in a well cut, dark suit. The closer she walks to the house, the higher my level of anxiety climbs. I don't enjoy confrontations. Alicia and I get along famously, but this wedding business has brought out some unfamiliar facets from the women involved.

Women, I think to myself, bundles of contradictions and estrogen imbalances, each and every one of them.

Margaret leisurely sips at her tea as Alicia enters the kitchen and smiles at her. "Hullo, Margaret. I see Lewis is spoiling you again."

"Would you care for a spot, luv?" I ask her.

Alicia grins at me. "Nothing better than your special tea, luv," she says, nodding.

I pour another cup of tea and serve it to Alicia with flair. "I hope it's to your liking."

Alicia sips from the cup, closes her eyes and moans with genuine pleasure. "I don't know how you do it."

I bow, grateful for the compliment.

"Seriously, what's the secret?"

I can't bring myself to tell her how I brew the tea with highly sugared water and a mix of orange and lemon extracts that I hide in one of the cupboards in their own home. Alicia's diet is strict the way commando training is strict. "The mysterious joys of life must be appreciated just as they are."

Alicia sips more of the tea. "Very well. It's just so sweet, like the nectar of the gods."

"Aren't you having any, young Lewis?"

"Not today, my dear Margaret. It's enough for me to see you enjoy it."

"Where's Sam?"

I turn back to Alicia. "She's talking to a sorority sister of hers."

She looks interested. "How many people are coming from America? Do you have an exact number?"

"All I can tell you is that there are five sisters coming. Samantha mentioned a handful of Tennenby people, but I forget the exact number."

Alicia recites a list of names, counting each with her fingers. There are eight of Samantha's former colleagues attending her wedding. If I asked, Alicia would easily recall every name on the guest list thanks to her eidetic memory.

"I feel a bit strange having only a handful of guests from her American life. I'm already close to two hundred guests, but they're mostly people from Lions Security and they've only known Samantha for a short time," Alicia says.

I couldn't have asked for a better opening to bring Samantha's concerns forth. "It's interesting you should say that, luv."

Alicia is still thinking aloud. "It isn't often that the groom's guests outnumber the bride's."

This gives me pause. Nathan Jeffries' security firm employs over four hundred people. I'm quite certain they've each received an invite. It makes perfect sense as both the bride and groom work at the firm now.

"What is it, Lewis?"

I pull a chair out and brace my elbows on the table when I sit. "I think that's why she initially wanted a small ceremony."

"I knew it," Alicia says as she lets her head hang. "What am I to do, Lewis? Everything is reserved!"

Sensing the sudden tension, Margaret stands and gathers the cups and saucers before quietly leaving the kitchen.

"Oh, how could I be so stupid?"

I take a hold of Alicia's perfectly manicured hand. "Fret not, luv. I can try to convince Sam to stick with the plan. Like you said, everything is already reserved."

Alicia squeezes my hand but shakes her head. "I'm perfectly fine with whatever Sam wants. I admit, I got carried away."

"Sam knows you have the best of intentions, luv," I tell her. "The important thing is that there's still time to edit the plans."

Alicia bites her lush lip, still anxious.

"Lorna wants nothing but a happy bride, and I have the feeling she will move heaven and earth to make that happen."

"She is the very best," Alicia agrees.

"I'm glad you have such confidence in her."

Alicia looks at me with concern. "What is it?"

"Have you ever heard of red and orange signifying change?"

Alicia shakes her head.

"If I may," Margaret says from the doorway. "I remember my grandmother talking about that."

I nod. "Lorna threw a little wrinkle into the planning. She suggested doing the wedding in warmer colors, the colors of change."

"Interesting," Alicia says thoughtfully.

"Margaret, dear, do you recall anything else?"

"Perhaps," she steps closer to the table. "I remember a story about a coldhearted princess who never laughed until the day a woodsman gave her a bouquet of fiery colors. The princess changed into a lovely woman, who went to rule her people with kindness, leading her kingdom into prosperity. The reds and oranges signify a good change within."

"Change…" Alicia says reverently.

"It's apt for Samantha," I tell her.

Alicia and Margaret smile in approval.

10

"…Are you kidding?" Samantha sees me, smiles, and pats the bed. "The gown? It's a Jean Gabrielle. Yup, Paris… I know, right?"

She is sitting with her back on the headboard, legs crossed in the lotus position, looking like a teenage little tart.

For someone who continually professes to abhor telephone conversations, Samantha's been talking for the better part of an hour.

"No! I'll wear it the day of the wedding. You shall only see it in my closet… No, I'm not going to let you bloody wear it!" She laughs.

Feeling suddenly weary, I stretch across the bed, my feet still on the floor. I put my hands beneath my head and close my eyes, enjoying the reprieve. I need to find a convincing argument for Samantha to go on with the wedding as planned, despite Alicia agreeing to have it any way Samantha wants, I realize that this late in the game, every small change will be monumentally magnified.

"Hell, yeah!"

I open my eyes at the expletive.

"Oh, you're such a sordid minx! When did you meet him?"

The tone of her voice makes me imagine the kind of shenanigans six young women reverting to college age are bound to spawn once they get together. I shudder at the possibilities.

"You leave me with a lot of questions, but I understand. I hope it all works out, luv."

I prop my head up to look at her, raising a curious eyebrow.

"Sounds yummy." Samantha laughs. "Very well... you too, luv."

She pulls the mobile away from her ear after ending the call then looks at me.

"Okay, that felt pretty good." She hands me my mobile. "Needs charged."

"You're quite welcome," I grumble, frowning at the flashing low battery warning.

"You told me to talk to her."

"Do I want to know?"

Her eyes fix on mine for a moment.

Uh oh... I imagine Quinn told her she's already in London, but I'll just have to wait until she confirms my suspicion, and so far she hasn't.

"She wants to take me on a night out on the town to celebrate her divorce."

"And you declined like the good little lass I know you to be, correct?"

She grins. "Of course not."

"What was the 'yummy' comment about?"

"Her new man. She had to get going or else I would've found out more."

"Promise to leave this one alone, okay?"

"I have my own man, thank you."

And that's never stopped you before... "Do you feel you've changed?"

Her brow furrows. "What kind of question is that?"

I decide it'll be better for me to deal with one issue at a time. "Sam, I talked Alicia into downsizing the scale of the wedding. She assured me that you have the final say so on any arrangement concerning your wedding, so you can now have a small ceremony. However—"

"Whatever for?"

I glance at her as I sit up on the bed. "Were you not just weeping over the size of the bloody wedding? Did you not just tell me you wanted something small?"

She rolls her eyes and folds her arms. "I was just having a moment."

My head spins. "What do you mean by having a moment?"

I see her eyes rolling right, which she usually does when scanning her memory for some incriminating line from me.

"I must have been having one of those estrogen imbalances."

Curse her blasted memory. "In other words, you were a bit stressed, and vented out the first thing that crossed your mind."

She gives me a broad smile. "You're so understanding, luv. Best girlfriend ever!"

"That's me, a regular Betty to your Wilma."

She chuckles. "Are you still in love with Betty Rubble?"

"Brunettes are foxy, and that little nasal voice would be like music in bed."

Samantha pinches her nose. "Oh, Barney! Take me! Oh! Oh!"

We laugh until tears sting our eyes and we run out of breath. We look at each other for a brief second and break into another fit of the giggles. When we were little we often watched *The Flintstones*. A wave of nostalgia eradicates my giggling.

"Alright," I take a deep breath and let it out slowly. "So, you're telling me you're agreeable about the size of your wedding."

She nods. "You're right, you know."

"Of course I'm right. I've always told you if you listen to me, you'll never shed a tear."

The look on her face is one of adoration and for the first time in my life, I find it somewhat unnerving. "Um… What am I right about this time?"

"I get to be queen of the land for one day. I might as well play the part."

I shake my head. "Gwen, please come soon," I plead silently.

"What?"

"Are you planning on having any more of these bloody moments of yours? Because if you are, I'd like to be better prepared to simply ignore you until your estrogen imbalance corrects itself, and you begin making sense once again."

"You know how hard it is to be a girl," she whines.

I do? This isn't the first time she uses such a line on me, but it's certainly the first time it makes me cross. The flash of anger is diminished slightly only because it surprises me so much. I try to mentally shake it off before Samantha notices. "Who's coming with Quinn?"

"Gina, Lynn, and Keri. Maybe Ashley… and Kayla."

Something sparks in my brain. "Kayla? Why does that sound important?"

Samantha only stares at me.

"Wait. Kayla Mason? Keri's sister? As in the Mason triplets, two of who don't much care for you?"

"Yes. Ironic, isn't it?"

"Are you alright about that?"

She shrugs. "I'd like to think that we'll be grown up about the shit we pulled on each other when we were kids."

I give her a piercing look she avoids by looking out the window. "That depends on what kind of shit *you* pulled."

Her sudden transformation into an ice sculpture tells me she's done with this particular path of conversation. I've found myself counting to ten in my head often, ever since Jason proposed to her. "Why can't the others come?"

Samantha's eyes seem to dance as she relates the "where are they now" version of her sorority sisters' lives.

I don't pretend to keep track of the names, but the events are a bit interesting. One girl is expecting twin boys anytime this month. Rumor has it her husband bragged about his virility to any willing ear, but it was her church pastor who'd held her hand at the initial doctor's appointment. For someone who abhors tabloids, Samantha relishes the gossip with glee.

Another of her sisters, Grace Edmonds, is on a mission trip in Ethiopia. Her rumor consists of leaving her husband and his two kids from a previous marriage, to run away with her new lover, a Frenchman who's talked her into joining Doctors Without Borders.

Grace has let herself go after a bitter divorce. Quinn told Samantha their poor sister used up more antidepressants than oxygen to go through life's motions.

Ashley Davis is happily married and Quinn doesn't think she'd do well without her husband, who is too tied up with work to attend. Samantha was happy at least one of her sisters had it right.

Sarah Mason is in jail for the second time after breaking her ex-husband's jaw, also for the second time.

"You Moppins are a scandalous lot," I remark when Samantha doesn't offer another name. "Anything I should know about the ones hopping the pond?"

The grin that Samantha gives me is bound to precede a nightmare when I go to sleep tonight.

"I'm sure they'll properly introduce themselves."

"Sounds ominous."

"Be afraid," Samantha says grimly. "Be very afraid." She cracks up at her own joke.

And then it hits me. "What'd you tell them about me?"

Samantha goes rigid, her expression tight. "Nothing at all."

"I know that look on your face. What did you tell them?"

"I said a lot of sweet things about you. They're all going to love you."

"Samantha?"

She rolls her eyes. "Fine. So I bragged about you. Hell, I always brag about you." She shows me a tiny gap between her thumb and forefinger. "A little."

"Bugger me…" In the old days, I might have started growling before chasing her like a rabid dog as she squealed through the house in juvenile glee. But those days are behind us now. "You don't know how to brag *a little*."

She grins. "No one I know has a friend remotely close to what you are to me. Of course I'm going to bloody brag."

I shake my head but her words are touching. "Are you excited about Lancelot coming back tomorrow?"

She nods.

"What about this whole friend-of-his business?"

She thinks for only a moment. "The girl from the expedition, Carol Higgins, is the sister of a former commando, who served alongside Jason Stephen. He's disabled now."

"War wound?"

Samantha shakes her head. "Training exercise mishap. He was worried about his little sister going on the expedition. He's the one who hired Lions on behalf of the university sponsoring the expedition."

"Say it with me. Lewis, you were absolutely right. I was overreacting like the fickle lass you so accurately know me to be," I say in a higher pitched voice, a woefully poor attempt to sound like her.

She rolls her eyes.

"Your female powers of extra sensory perception failed you miserably this time."

"Fine." She pouts.

"What time is Lancelot coming in?"

She nudges my hip with hers. "Stop calling him that. Around two or so."

"Good. You need some shagging."

"Hey!"

I laugh.

"Okay, true, but that's not the point. And F.Y.I. we're not shagging until the wedding night."

I burst out laughing. "Who are you kidding? You're so randy, furry little forest creatures run away from you, sensing your predatory needs."

Samantha wants to look indignant, and even cross, but she can't and soon we're both laughing.

"You're incorrigible," she chides.

"So, now that we fixed up your drama *du jour*, there's one more thing about your wedding."

"Oh?"

I give her the story of the significance of red and orange. She listens attentively. When I'm done, she opens up her laptop and does a quick search as though confirming my story.

"I love orange…"

I peek into her walk in closet where an entire section of orange tops hangs neatly. Her new sense of organization is another welcome change.

"Does that mean you agree with it?"

"You know me, I love things with significance."

I smile. "Excellent."

I quickly compose a text message for Lorna, letting her know the bride is in full agreement.

"Now that I've once again fixed your life, can we fix mine?"

"Of course. What's troubling you?"

"Tell me about Richard. I want to know how Mum sees him or what she sees in him."

She gives me a guarded look. "Richard who?"

"Richard, as in Mum's love interest."

"Oh, that Richard." She smiles. "What do you want to know, luv?"

"Where's he from? What does he do? How long has he been seeing Mum? Everything."

Her smirk tells me she's willing to torture me with this for an indefinite measure of time.

"Fine. I'll see you tomorrow," I snap as I get up.

"Lewis Jonathan Bettford, sit your arse back down," she orders in such an imperious voice, I actually sit.

"First off, don't you go messing things up for her."

"What's that supposed to mean?"

"It means," she stands to loom over me, "you will not snoop around under the guise of concerned son, to the point that you suffocate their relationship. Are we clear?"

"But I've never—"

"Are we clear?" she says in a louder voice.

I nod, never having seen Samantha this protective.

"Promise? I know what a bloody pain in the arse you can be."

I flash back to more than a few times when I inadvertently managed to spoil some bloke's interest in my mother. I've always rationalized my misdeeds with protecting her, but if Samantha's glare is any indication, Mum was clearly never happy about it.

"What all did she tell you?"

"You've always been overprotective of her," she says softly.

"She's my mother. I don't want her to get hurt by some wanker," I say lamely.

There's sympathy in Samantha's gaze as she takes my hands. "Mum wouldn't trade you for the world, you know that, right?"

There's something in her voice, something new that I don't recall hearing before in all the years we've been friends.

"Lewis, I won't presume to know what it's like to have parents at this age, but I know that if I did, I couldn't very well expect them to look after me my whole life."

A painful gash has suddenly opened in my heart. I don't like how close to the mark she is, but I seem to be unable to react.

"We grow up, luv. We have to make our own lives, create our own families, and our parents go back to being who they were before we entered their lives. Your mother is a beautiful woman with a heart of gold, and she has so much to offer to someone else. Moreover, she deserves to find love."

I can't look at her face anymore.

"I don't want to hurt you with this, okay? But you and I have always been brutally honest with each other. We'll never change."

I cut my eyes at her, feeling an unexpected bubbling of ire within. "We'll never change? We'll never change, you say. Sam, we're already changing. We're not going to be the same."

She looks wounded as she draws back. "Whatever do you mean, Lewis?"

"When the next storm hits, you'll have the comforting embrace of Jason's arms to allay your fears, darling. You'll have those deep conversations with him that you and I have been famous for since we were little." Something in me is desperately trying to regain the reins of this emotional runaway horse. "I'm not saying these things to make you feel guilty, Sam. Believe me. This is the way things should be and I want every happiness for you. I do. But I can't help feeling that I'm losing my best friend, or at least a great part of her. And I can't bear to lose my mother as well!"

Samantha might as well be a statue. She doesn't even blink.

"You are not losing anyone, Lewis." Her voice is unnervingly soft.

I try to pull my hands free but she holds on tighter. My nerves are sending mixed signals and I don't know whether to laugh, scream in rage, or cry. Sensing my turmoil, Samantha lets go of my hands and stands.

"I didn't expect you to snap at me this way." Her eyes fill with tears.

Now you've done it…

I want to apologize and claim temporary insanity. Now that I let my top blow, I feel suddenly better, much better than I have in days.

The sense of triumph is short lived. My tirade seems to have deeply hurt her, leaving me uncomfortable in my own skin. There's no taking back anything I said, not a single word.

"Sam," I say in a contrite voice.

She shakes her head and covers her face with her hands. I have no idea how to interpret that.

I have no words.

"This truly bothers you. Doesn't it?"

"Sam, don't."

"You mean more to me than you could possibly know, Lewis. You and I have been through a lot of shit. Like it or not, you shall always be a part of my life. It hurts me that you'd even question it. I'm always going to want you in my life. I'll tell you something else, and I hope you can forgive me for saying it."

Her words are like the well-placed strikes of an axe, skillfully chopping a wedge out of the trunk of a pine to weaken it, before striking the final blow that will send it toppling down. I'm exactly like that pine. I can't scream in pain as she cuts into me, but I hurt so much inside I actually want that final blow. And then it comes.

"You can't lay the blame on us for your loneliness, especially when you're not alone."

She takes my hands as I hang my head then she leans her forehead against the top of my head.

Despite what she says, I've a feeling I'm sharing some of the last meaningful moments of our friendship, moments like these.

11

"Blasted rain…"

The rain obliterates everything past six feet of the bonnet of the Beamer, but I mash the blasted accelerator and rocket down the motorway away from Kensington. I have no destination in mind.

It's beyond me how I lost it back in Samantha's room. I've seen her drink herself into a stupor or even tear her bedroom apart in a rage during some of these so called moments, and I've endured them all. I always thought she was blowing things out of proportion or being overdramatic. I'm always the one trying to understand her, trying to soothe her. I can't believe I had a moment like that. I didn't tear anything apart, but I spoke out of line and Samantha's right. But what's the answer?

We have to make our own lives, create our own families, and our parents go back to being who they were before we entered their lives.

How am I to think of Mum as anything other than my mother? Haven't I already made my life? And family? How exactly am I supposed to—

A fallen tree trunk suddenly materializes in front of me, prompting me to stand on the brakes in utter panic, all these convoluted avenues of thought disintegrate under the adrenaline onslaught.

Once everything stops and it becomes evident that I'm still in one piece, and so is my car, I crawl out from under my cloak of misplaced anger.

Perhaps I should've listened to Samantha and go stand by the pond, or sit by the carriage house with her. I shouldn't have left her alone.

The rain falls harder, treating me to a torturous percussion that drowns out all thought. Only when my heartbeat drops back to normal, I back out and drive around the fallen tree. At first I don't know where I am, but when I turn the corner I recognize the thoroughfare. It's quite the mystery how my brain managed to guide me to this particular spot. I make a left turn and find the neon sign that appeared in my mind only seconds before.

"The Bow Tie," I read aloud, thinking back on the many times I've been here.

The furious deluge slows to a more moderate shower that won't completely drench my clothes if I venture out. I reach back for a warm up top. The thin polyester is red with white tubing and a Liverpool Reds crest emblazoned over the heart. It'll have to do.

Thunder rumbles in the distance. I wonder if the storm is retreating or merely announcing its intentions. My hand reaches for the umbrella but I'm only fifty feet from the entrance.

I quickly open the door, jump out, and run for the long black awning. Despite the short distance, my hair is soaked and water trickles down past the collar of my shirt to the small of my back.

The Bow Tie lies on the high end of quality pubs in all of London. Most gay bars do. The stucco walls are a pristine white that makes me think of brand new paper. Every piece of trim is black with the exception of the red door. When I push it open, an unfamiliar Euro-techno song mercifully comes to an end in favor of a jazzy number more apt for the place. I climb down the eight steps to the main floor and walk all the way to the bar at the back of the large, dim space.

Even though it's early—barely eight o'clock— there's a pretty large crowd composed of well dressed, young professional types. A group in their twenties carries on loudly in the corner. I choose the farthest stool from anyone and order a glass of white wine from Old Ted, the bartender.

"Lewie, my boy. To what do I owe the honor of your visit?" Old Ted points each word with broad gestures of his arms and hands.

He looks sixty, though he's probably in his seventies. His bald pate gleams under the lights over the bar, and his dark eyes twinkle with merriment. Each time I see him, he looks thicker.

"Good to see you, chap."

"How's Terry? I haven't seen him much lately."

"You and me, both." The last time I saw Terence Dougherty, he told me he wasn't happy, and that he needed much more than I was willing to give. Thus, we parted ways and ended a partnership that lasted over ten years, which also almost meant the end of Solutions Incorporated.

Terence and I met during our university days, while working on a group project. There were five people in the group. Two lads who were hopelessly lost and quickly invited themselves into our group in order to save their grade, and Lisa Marietti, Terence's girlfriend.

Terence and I were hands down the best students all throughout our academic career at the University of Liverpool. We graduated at the top of our class. I was second to him by tenths of a point.

Up until that group project, we had only held a grudging respect for one another, but kept our distance.

It was while working together that we let the guards down and opened the door to a friendship.

"Are you two on the outs?" Old Ted asks with interest, rudely interrupting my reverie.

"We're old news, chap. Old news."

"Blimey, luv. I barely recognized you," he says, giving me an appraising look. "It's good to know it's not my wine driving my patrons away."

I smile at him. "Your wine *is* bad, but we all take pity on you, old fox."

"Whatever it takes, then. Where's that pretty little lass who's always with you?"

"Samantha?"

He nods. "Ah, that's it," he says with a dreamy smile.

"She's getting ready for her wedding."

"Oh, have her by for a congratulatory drink, laddie. She might put me out of business, but I'm willing to take that chance." He winks, shuffling over to tend to three blokes at the other end of the bar.

I take a sip of Old Ted's white, and savor it. It isn't as bad as everyone makes it sound. It's quite smooth and not so tart. The aftertaste is a different matter altogether. It is no 1955 Mont Caviziel, the wine Terence and I shared to toast our graduation. That same wine, we used to toast the start of our company, Solutions Incorporated, in a small room in Lisa's parents' house one year after graduating.

I can't recall the names of the two lazy blokes from the group. They were only there at the initial meeting and reappeared at the very end, expecting a great mark. Terence and I said nothing to the headmaster, but Lisa's Italian upbringing didn't allow her to let it go. After denouncing the two leeches, the headmaster used a simple test to gauge the involvement of each group member in the project. The two lads were promptly failed from the class. The two empty questionnaires were ample proof of their negligence.

When I first met Terence I couldn't help feeling a certain attraction. He came from a well to do family from Aigburth. He stood tall and wore his dark hair roguishly long. It fell over dark eyes that glinted with intelligence. He had the lean build of a midfielder and dressed impeccably well.

Rumors abounded of his sexual orientation until he put a stop to the debate when he started dating the Italian knockout, Lisa Marietti, and became the "It" couple at the University of Liverpool. By the time of the group study, Lisa was wearing a large diamond on her left hand.

A conversation of algorithms and quantum physics led to the deeper subjects of philosophy and theology. Terence's intellect was captivating. For his part, he'd never found a receptive audience to his genius and we each filled a void in the other's life. I may have been his equal when it came to integrating a network system, but his broad knowledge of other subjects made him more of a revered mentor to an awed pupil, particularly when it came to poetry.

Most people readily assume that a gay relationship is based solely on sex between two men. Unnatural sex is how the church and the more conservative lot refer to a gay relationship. Though it applies to a large number of cases, the assumption is inaccurate.

In the case of Terence and me, my admiration for his mind is what led to affection. I loved him like an older, wiser brother at first. In any case, lines were drawn, lines that I didn't dare cross that Terence hated to recognize.

Terence enjoyed the attentions of Lisa immensely, but other than in bed, they couldn't connect with each other.

Once they got married, the distance between them became more obvious, and he began spending more time with me. In retrospect, Terence needs constant praise and at the time, I was too awestruck to see clearly. I gave him exactly what he needed, unlimited praise. I didn't realize I was inadvertently driving a wedge between him and Lisa until she had enough, and ended up in another man's bed. Terence was devastated after the divorce.

He came to see me, barely able to stand, at the tiny flat I rented while attending school. I held him for hours on end while he cried over his lost love until exhaustion left us both asleep, only to wake in each other's arms. We laughed it all off and attributed the night to the empty bottle of whiskey lying on the floor.

The morning brought with it Terence's new reality, the loss of Lisa. Nursing a broken heart, he stayed the night at my flat for weeks. Eventually our conversations were less about Lisa and far more about each other. In our talks, I began feeling something similar to what I felt when Samantha spent her vacations in Liverpool, staying up entire nights catching up on our lives.

One particular night, Terence alluded to certain urges that assaulted him whenever he was around me, flattering me beyond belief. Our conversations became more intimate, and our friendship progressed into something more. It was tempting and exhilarating, but I held back out of fear I was no more than a distraction from his pain. I'm not one to be used.

The first time he went cold on me, I wasn't that surprised. But the change was so sudden I didn't understand what had happened at first. Thus began a vicious cycle that took place for years. Terence hopped the line back and forth whenever he either felt unfulfilled, or physically ignored.

The entire affair had proven incredibly confusing for me. But, like a complete imbecile, I gave in whenever Terence showed up at my doorstep in tears about his latest heartbreak.

He knew I was really taken with him. I was really taken with his incomparable mind, more than anything. I can't say I blame him for running off with a woman, or another man, when the mood struck him. I just accepted it for whatever it was, and knew to wait for his return, hoping against hope that he'd make up his mind about who he was and what he wanted. He liked to look into the future and while his plans always included me, I never understood why I couldn't see those same things.

When he finally did, I had to face the fact that I'd wasted a decade of my life I would never get back. I invested large sums of emotional capital only to have that most devastating crash that left me with nothing but memories, and awash in unrealized potential.

I hold myself responsible for that. My decisions put me in that situation and I had to live with it. But the pain...

Had it not been for Samantha being around when Terence got out of my life for good, I'm not sure what would have become of me. In the beginning I missed him more than I ever thought possible.

A bitter laugh escapes me as I stare at the amber contents of my glass. I was trying to keep Samantha out of my mind for the night by immersing myself in thoughts of Terence. I realize I'm making a poor attempt to wean myself from my best friend, the same way she'd try to wean herself off alcohol. I've been relying too much on her and soon I don't think I'll be able to do that. It's best if I find a way not to need her so much.

My mobile buzzes in my pocket. I expect to see Samantha's name on the screen, but it's not. It's Alicia's.

"Hullo?"

"Hi, luv. Is Sam with you by chance?"

"No. Is she not home? She could be running," I say in a hopeful voice even as I feel a rush of unease.

"Margaret just told me her car isn't here."

I set the glass down on the bar and look out the small window over the bar. It's still raining out. The thought of Samantha driving around in this weather is gnawing at my nerves.

"Did you try calling her?"

"Voice mail," Alicia says, her voice suddenly taut. "You don't think she..."

"Not at all," I cut in quickly.

The thought of Samantha drinking again is best left unconsidered.

"I'm a bit worried, Lewis. Usually she's writing or reading in her room."

"I'll find her, luv. She may have gone to my flat."

"Are you quite sure?"

I'm not. "She's been coming to see me when she gets lonesome."

"I suppose you're right." Her voice reflects a slight relief. "If she comes home I'll call you, and if you find her at your flat, call me."

"I will."

Alicia ends the call and I'm assaulted by foreboding. Our little discussion cannot possibly prompt her to take a drink. Could it?

No, I decide. I'm willing to wager she's down at the marina, or somewhere by the Thames. She often gravitates to bodies of water when she's nostalgic.

I key in a text. "Let me know you're safe. I'll come to you wherever you are."

I stare at the screen of my mobile until it goes dark, mentally commanding the bloody thing to light up with a message. It suddenly occurs to me that if I felt the need to go out for a drink, chances are rather high that it's exactly how Samantha feels and I curse myself for a bloody fool.

I have to find her before she does something stupid.

Old Ted walks up to me and sets a drink before me. "The lad on the end sends his regards," he says with a playful wink.

I turn to see a grinning face at the end. Dark, hungry eyes rove over me in a suggestive fashion.

I pull a ten pound note out of my wallet and drop it on the bar as I stand. "Nice gesture, but victim of bad timing," I say sarcastically.

Old Ted stares at me wide eyed for a second before taking the drink back.

"Ted, if Samantha comes in here, don't serve her a drop, got it? Not a bloody drop and call me right away."

Old Ted nods slowly, not understanding the request. He doesn't know Samantha is a recovered alcoholic.

Recovering... Recovering Alcoholic...

"I can ring you if she appears. Let me write down your number."

I recite the digits before going out the door. When I feel eyes on my back, I turn around to see Old Ted peering curiously at me. To his left, the grinning bloke is talking animatedly with a young, impressionable punk he'll more than likely bed tonight. A wave of nausea staggers me, making me quicken my pace to step outside, eager to feel the cold rain upon my face.

I tear down the street making a mental list of possibilities of where to find Samantha. After checking the first five pubs, I curse myself repeatedly for each time I took my best friend to some new watering hole, unknowingly providing her with a myriad of places where she can lose herself on a night like this one.

***

"Sam, where are you?" I ask the screen of my mobile for the hundredth time. In a city renowned for the abundance of compact vehicles, finding a white Mini Cooper brings a clear understanding of the needle in the haystack bit.

I leave five text messages that go unanswered. I call her three times, all unanswered. Finally, I call Kensington and Alicia tells me Sam's white Cooper is still not in the drive.

So, this is what getting an ulcer feels like.

I take a corner too fast out of the narrow street of the marina and the Beamer fishtails, sending my heart up to my throat. I fight with the wheel and regain control while berating myself hotly. Just then, my mobile buzzes in my hand.

"Sam!" I cry into the device.

"Try again," says a familiar voice.

"Mum?"

"No, it's the bloody Queen of England. Where are you?"

"Just left the marina. I'm trying to find Samantha."

She laughs softly. "What a tube. Drive yourself home. Sammie's been here having a nice little talk with this old bird."

The relief that washes through me overpowers my annoyance. "Why didn't she answer her mobile?"

"Because I wouldn't allow her, son."

This throws me. "Why?"

"Because we needed an uninterrupted conversation. Why else?"

I bring the mobile to my chest and turn the air blue, cursing like a drunken sailor.

"Lewis? Lewis?"

I hear her voice, growing shriller out of the tiny speaker. "I'm here. I'm on my way. Please tell Sam to stay there."

"How about I *ask* her if she would like to stay and wait for your cantankerous arse?"

One... Two...Three... Four...

"Lucky for you, Sammie is amenable to seeing you, despite your acting like a bloody fool."

"Mum, is she sober?"

There's an ominous pause at the other end of the line. "Drive safe, luv," she says, feigning sweetness before ending the call.

I quickly scroll through calls and tap on Alicia's. After reassuring her that Samantha is fine, Alicia sighs with relief and bids me good night. I feel a complete fool for not checking my flat first. I need to trust her more, I know I do.

Calm yourself down, lad...

I feel like Samantha and I actually argued, and I know that's just my wounded feelings talking. I can remember dozens of deeply philosophical lines I've dropped on Samantha during our arguments, like the final volley in a battle. She's always been a most gracious casualty, and she's always been able to listen to those words and eventually come to see reason. I can't think of a single philosophical gem to direct at myself.

Once again, I'm hit with the notion that we are not playing our usual roles.

...you can't lay the blame on us for your loneliness...

I've heard friends tell me stories about the ability of the women in their lives to utter some devastating line during arguments. One of the programmers I work with was full of such stories.

His wife is a little redhead, quick to laugh and quite shy, at first impression. I still have trouble reconciling that image with the fiery lass with the razor-sharp tongue from her husband's anecdotes. In short, he's deadly afraid of her temper. I've heard him remark he wished she'd throw a pan at his head, rather than verbally bash him.

Samantha's words were not delivered in anger. It was much worse than that. She stated them like a solid valediction, and I felt as though I'd been slapped by an iron hand. It's a new reaction for me.

Normally, I adopt an aloof demeanor, a thin veneer of indifference, and I carry on as though nothing could possibly bother me. It's something I learned to do in the face of a confrontation, early on.

You can't escape adolescence without building some sort of defenses against the verbal and psychological abuse we're all forced to endure, particularly when you are someone who lives a life that goes against the norm.

In all fairness, I kept my preferences to myself for as long as I could. It wasn't at all difficult. Unlike some blokes, I didn't announce to the world I preferred boys. I really didn't even know if that was the case, come to think of it.

The all-boys school I attended, St. Clement's Prep was one of the best in Liverpool, and one of the last schools to board the students for one trimester, as a way of teaching us self-reliance. Most boys relished the chance to live parents-free for a stretch, although the headmasters were exceedingly strict. But when you enclose a lot of pubescent boys and have no way of controlling every second of their lives, things happen. The restrictive environment seemed to only exacerbate the urges of sexual awakening, and more than a few boys engaged in activities meant to release some of those tensions. A good number grew out of the phase, but others found so much comfort, they wanted nothing else.

When I was fourteen, I befriended Marty Lavallette, a beautiful boy from Cannes, France. Marty was gay and so sure of himself that he didn't care who knew. Not only did he have all the overt mannerisms, and the irritating lisp "normal" society associates with gay behavior. He also dressed the part, employing pastel colors and silk scarves. The girls from our sister school, St. Mary of Mercy Prep flocked to him, which didn't sit well with the straight male crowd. One day after school, four lads beat Marty within an inch of his life.

It was quite the scandal, but despite the school proclaiming zero tolerance of bullying and persecution, the lesson was clear. People like Marty and me were on our own.

In the aftermath, I hid the fact I was gay, and Marty never forgave me.

There were other boys who took extreme precautions to hide their homosexuality, but weren't so successful and paid dearly in similar events. I'm ashamed to admit that I once took part in engaging in scornful belittlement of some of those boys, along with the other bigots, for fear of suffering a similar fate.

The blast of a horn makes me jump in the seat. I've slowed down to a crawl and didn't even know it, lost in a past I don't care to recall. An old bloke, driving a rickety lorry, glares malevolently as he passes me. In the spirit of good fellowship I nod and smile, but the man shakes his head and leaves in his wake a cloud of foul fumes that sting my eyes.

I'm forced to park an entire block away from my flat. When I catch the sight of Samantha's white Mini Cooper, I feel a simultaneous wave of relief and anger. When it abates, it leaves behind a hollow feeling as I think back on the things Samantha said to me, particularly concerning my mother.

When the rain comes down in heavier sheets, I don't quicken my pace. I simply shove my hands in the pockets of my trousers and take my time making my way to the portico of my home. I'd like to believe I'm holding my head down because of the rain, but inside, I know better.

It's shame.

12

The metallic scraping of the bolt sliding in place echoes through the studio. Other than the lamp on the desk, shadows rule the space. My hair is dripping on the wooden floor as I make my way up the steps. The muted conversation I first heard when I came in ceases, leaving only the haunting voice of Sarah McLachlan in lieu of a greeting.

Mum and Samantha are sitting on the sofa in mirrored poses, ankles crossed, hands on their laps, a look of expectancy on their faces that turns shocked as I enter the living room.

"Lewis Jonathan Bettford!" Mum says in a high pitched voice, getting to her feet.

Samantha also stands and runs up into the rooms, quickly coming back with a bath towel and a black t-shirt.

I take this concern for my well-being with a touch of apprehension. Even Russian interrogators allow their prisoners to heal before torturing them again.

"What were you trying to do, catch your death?" Mum berates me.

"It's just a little rain, Mum. It's fine."

She looks unconvinced.

"I tried calling you." I shrug, looking at Samantha.

"We were beginning to worry," she says with a remorseful look I know too well.

I want to blast her about not responding to my text messages, or my calls, but it'd be overkill. I can tell she feels badly about precisely that.

They fuss over me until I take the proffered dry t-shirt and excuse myself upstairs. After changing into dry jeans and socks, I rejoin them in the living room.

Mum folds her arms as she takes in my clothes with a disapproving eye. "Going somewhere?"

"That all depends," I reply, glancing at Samantha.

Mum's eyes bounce from Samantha to me then soften with understanding. "Perhaps we can have ourselves a little talk before you two leave." She goes to the coffee table, picks up a remote and shuts off the music.

Uh oh…

Mum takes a seat on my favorite recliner like a queen holding court, and gestures to us to sit.

Samantha and I share a smile as we sit on the sofa. I flash back to a few of these talks we've had over the years, one in particular that makes me blush fiercely.

"Son, what is it?"

I shake my head, suddenly accosted by a wave of giggling. "Nothing."

Mum pins me in place with a pointed look I know far too well. "Lewis?"

I try taking a deep breath, but one look at my best friend and I'm giggling again. The look of annoyance on both women only exacerbates my condition.

"Lewis, last time," Mum warns.

"This just feels a bit familiar. Forgive me."

Mum nods and looks at Samantha, who has gone rigid beside me. It's all I need to know she recalls that same particular scolding from when we were teens.

"Are you finished?"

I look at Mum and nod. "Forgive me, Mum."

She leans forward. "I think we each have much to say to one another. I'll start." She seems to settle in for a long talk. "His name is Richard Bergman. We've been dating for a few months now. He's a well to do lad from Wallasey."

"What's he do for a living?" I ask, unable to keep the parental tone out of my voice.

Mum's brow rides up her forehead. "You have a poor memory, my boy. You set up his company's intranet."

"I've done too many setups to remember them all. And I don't think I ever did work in Wallasey."

Mum smiles. "Medcourier, son. Richard works in London."

The name rings a bell. Medcourier is a company that handles the transport of human organs, a delicate endeavor if there ever was one.

Solutions was hired to optimize the software used to track their operations. The system was unsecure and prone to crashing. Terence and I advised the board of directors to employ the use of an entirely new intranet and we outlined a user-friendly set up that included the optimization of travel routes and other tools that greatly improved their services. Medcourier, much like many of Solutions' first customers, left to sign up with Terence after he and I parted ways earlier in the year.

Something flashes in my brain. An email lamenting the decision to leave Solutions floats in my mind. I can't remember the content verbatim, but I know how hard it was to read it. It was signed by the chairman of the board, one Richard Bergman. "Oh, bloody hell…"

Mum's face lines with anxiety. "That's why I didn't want to tell you about him, Lewis."

Once the initial shock recedes, I can only feel sympathy for my mother. "Small world."

Samantha reaches over and squeezes my wrist in warning.

"How'd you meet?" I ask.

Mum's eyes pierce mine for a long moment.

"Mum, I'm a big boy. I can handle it. I take full responsibility for what happened with my company. As you well know, I survived the setback and I learned much from it. I'm alright. I promise."

A little smile of contentment turns the corners of her lips. "Good. That's my boy," she says with a touch of pride.

"How did you meet?" Samantha asks, just as curious as me.

Mum sighs as her smile broadens. "His granddaughter was performing at Merseyside Dance and Drama Centre. I was called in by Karen to help with the performance. Richard's granddaughter, Jody, is quite talented. She's a lovely girl. She introduced me to her grandfather and that was that."

Karen White was once a student of Mum's. She was now the head instructor at Merseyside.

"Why, you sordid minx," I quip and Mum and Samantha giggle like a couple of little girls. "Sounds to me like there's more than that."

"I like him very much," Mum admits.

Judging by the broad smile on her face, I'd say it's far more than that. "So, let me guess. You've kept me a secret because of my business and the guilt is consuming your every thought."

"Despite your antics, no mother has been prouder of a son. I gushed about you, of course."

I can only smile.

"And fret not, luv. I made neither excuses, nor apologies for you. In fact, when the subject came up, I slyly deflected the entire affair. I will say that he regretted the board's decision to leave Solutions."

"He did?"

Mum nods. "No more business talk. This is supposed to be all about me."

Samantha laughs the way only the pretty ones can. "I can't wait to meet him!"

I faintly recall a tall, placid man in his sixties. The one thing that stands out the most to me is a deep basso voice. "I think I remember him."

Mum smiles. "Actually, he will refresh your memory soon enough."

"How soon?" I ask, feeling suddenly nervous.

Mum turns to Samantha. "Will you and your sweetheart join us, dear?"

"Absolutely," Samantha says.

"Lovely," I quip in a sarcastic tone. "I'll serve the *hors d'eouvres*, and pour the wine. Far be it from me to be a bloody fifth wheel."

Both women regard me with looks that contain not a single trace of amusement. Samantha is biting her tongue and I almost want to challenge her to speak, but the last words she said, with that same look on her face, still sting.

"If it makes you feel better, why don't you bring a date of your own, dear?" Mum challenges.

"That's what I was just going to suggest," Samantha adds.

I shrug. "I have no one in my sights."

"How come? Are you still pining over Terry?"

"Mum. What is it with you and baby names for adults?"

"What's wrong with that? I like it when Mum calls me Sammie."

I roll my eyes at her, which earns me a solid slap on the thigh.

"Mum!" I point at my leg.

"He bloody started it!" Samantha cries, pointing an accusing finger at me.

Mum shakes her head and laughs heartily. "I'm too old to put up with your shenanigans, but not too old to give you both a sound spanking. So don't tempt me."

Mum waits until we sober up.

"You've been more than best friends to each other for a long time now. Nothing will get in the way of that."

I drop my head when I feel her direct gaze on me.

"Lewis, my boy, in life everything changes and you need not be afraid of those changes because it's up to you to make them good or bad."

Mum's always had a way of realigning my thoughts in a way I can discern them. "I understand, Mum."

"Me too," Samantha adds.

"Lewis, keep this in mind. You're not losing your best friend and you're not losing your mother, luv. If you open up your heart, you may very well be gaining two new people in your life. Get to know them. Let them see the wonderful friend you can be."

There's nothing I can say to that. Samantha drapes her arm around me when I lean to prop my elbows on my thighs. The touch of her hand on my back is soothing.

"Remember, *you* control what you feel."

Taking our silence as studious agreement, Mum stands, satisfied with the effect of her lecture.

"This old woman is going to bed and you two have some things to discuss."

She embraces Samantha and kisses her forehead, then she messes my wet hair. "I love you both. Good night."

"Wait!" I call after her. "You never said when we're having this impromptu gathering."

Mum shakes her head at me. "Dinnertime tomorrow, son. I expect you to be on your best behavior. Good night."

Without another word, Mum goes upstairs.

"We don't have to talk if you don't want to. I'll just see you tomorrow."

The look of vulnerability in her eyes is almost more than I can take. "Tea?"

She nods, relieved she won't have to leave.

A few minutes later I hand her a steaming mug. No dainty cups for us, and no lumps of sugar.

"I'm sorry if I was a bitch," she says softly as she tears open a packet of low calorie sweetener.

"You put me in my place, luv. Won't be the last time. It certainly isn't the first."

"I didn't have to do it that way though."

She's holding onto the thick mug with both hands, head down. I lean forward and force her to meet my eyes. When she does, I smile at her. "I gave you no choice."

"So, does that mean I was right?"

I can't bloody believe her. "Gloating is an ugly thing to do, Sam."

She laughs.

We say nothing for a long moment, just two friends enjoying each other's company until the silence becomes deafening.

"Remember the last time Mum sat us down for a lecture?"

I can't help smiling. "Yes, I do. You got caught trying to take advantage of her innocent little boy."

Samantha barks a laugh. "Bollocks! We were thirteen!"

"Yes, but unlike you, I *was* innocent."

She laughs and shakes her head. "I was still innocent. I still can't believe we did that."

"I can't believe I'm still more innocent than you."

"Shut your gob!"

I laugh.

The summer before her freshman year in high school, Samantha went on and on about some Tommy chap who'd caught her eye. The attraction was mutual but there was only one problem. Tommy was involved with another girl and according to Samantha, it was serious.

One Friday night after a football game, Tommy and Samantha shared a kiss. But when she tried to steal another one, he politely declined. She figured he just didn't want to cheat on his girlfriend, and even liked him all the more for it. It was their little secret. But there's simply no possible way of keeping secrets when you're a teen. Secrets are the means for climbing the popularity ladder in most cases, the currency to buy a spot into the inner circles. I'd seen it all too often at St. Clement's Prep, and there was nothing to indicate that it was any different in American schools.

Tommy confided in a friend that he didn't want to kiss Samantha again because, despite her beauty, the girl was a terrible kisser.

In her American high school in Narragansett, Rhode Island, Samantha was automatically popular. She was beautiful, exceedingly intelligent, witty, British, and wealthy.

It's only human nature to draw pleasure from knocking someone like that off the top. Word got around that Samantha Reddick was a terrible kisser and she was devastated.

She couldn't wait to flee to Liverpool.

When she arrived, after licking her wounds, she had one thing in mind. She was determined to be the best kisser at Narragansett High.

When I asked how she planned on becoming the best kisser, she looked at me as though the answer should be quite obvious.

"You're going to help me practice, of course."

And so I did.

"Does Lancelot know where you learned to kiss?"

"Blimey, no!" she exclaims quickly.

"Will you ever tell him?" I press.

"No!"

I feign a wounded look. "Ashamed, are you, lass?"

"I just wouldn't want any weirdness between you two."

"Weirdness?"

"Do you really want to go there?"

I shake my head, flashing back to one of those moments that made the top ten of most humiliating experiences of my life. I made a pass at Jason Stephen only to find he had no interest. It was most mortifying.

"I can still see the look on Mum's face when we were sucking face behind the studio." Samantha says, laughing and nearly spilling her tea.

"Funny you should say 'sucking face'. That's pretty much how terrible you were at first."

"Hey!"

The memory plays vividly in my head.

We had gathered some of Mum's fashion magazines from the lobby where mothers patiently waited for their daughters to finish their lessons. *Cosmopolitan* was our favorite. Not only did it offer sage fashion advice, but it also contained several columns on sex and relationships. There were plenty of articles on the fine art of kissing. Samantha and I read every single one.

"I remember I almost had to tie you down so you'd kiss me," she complains.

"Perhaps you hadn't brushed your pearly whites," I muse.

She scowls. "Rubbish! I always had my spearmint gum at hand. Why am I friends with you again?"

I remember feeling so nervous I'd almost wet my pants at the prospect of kissing the girl whom I thought to be my little sister. When I voiced my concerns, Samantha threw her arguments at me like a drill sergeant. But it wasn't her vociferous threats that got me to lock lips with her. She used the one weapon powerful enough to reduce world leaders to wide-eyed, quivering fools walking on egg shells. She began crying.

"You do realize that my ego has yet to recover from that entire, sorry experience. Don't you?"

I can only laugh. "I remember you almost had it when Mum tapped your shoulder."

"Oh my God! Don't remind me!"

After agreeing to practice kissing with her, we went outside, behind the pool house. At my request, we kept the lights off. We took a clinical approach to breathing and tongue movement, following the guidelines so elaborately written on *Cosmopolitan*. Our first attempt was a little peck that left us rolling on the floor giggling. Once we calmed down a little, we sat across from each other and the kisses grew less timid, and less slobbery. I imagined any other hot blooded lad would've been thanking his lucky stars to be kissing Samantha's pretty little lips.

I won't say I didn't enjoy it, but I didn't have any overt reaction to the contact other than a slight tremor from nerves. Each time we stopped, we'd talk about what felt right and what didn't then we'd try again. For her part, when we were kissing, Samantha's breathing grew shallow, and her eyes were lightly closed, her lips soft and relaxed. We were in the middle of trying some kissing move called the double swirl. We must have been so focused on the kiss that we never heard Mum glide up to us.

Instead of calling our names, she simply tapped Samantha on the shoulder. She jumped up screaming, her teeth cutting my upper lip.

I remember there was something akin to relief in Mum's face. I remember resenting her for it.

After getting us back in the house, sitting on the couch before her, she tried talking to us about sex, but Samantha and I were too mortified to listen.

"I think I still have that scar," I say, prodding my lip with my tongue.

"Oh, whatever!"

We stare at each other and laugh for a full minute.

Samantha wasn't the only girl I've ever kissed. She certainly wasn't the first. I'd made that mistake a year before with... I dare not even recall her name.

"What's wrong?"

I glance back at Samantha, mentally tearing myself away from painful memories. "Nothing, luv. I'm right as rain."

She looks skeptical. "What's eating at you? And spare me the bluster and the I-could-care-less attitude. Something's been eating at you, so either you tell me or I'll just begin assuming, and you know what happens when I start assuming."

I take a deep, long breath. "I still feel like I'm losing you, Sam."

Her eyes immediately soften. "But you're not."

"Oh, but I am, luv. Everything is about to change."

"To tell you the truth, I am afraid of things changing. But if they do, it's not going to be because of me."

This surprises me. "You? You are afraid?"

"Of course I am. It's probably why I'm here." She looks away, embarrassed. "I'm afraid of being alone. Okay, afraid is too strong. I don't want to be alone at night. But once I get married, there will be no spending a lonely night with you. You're like a safety blanket I refuse to let go. I know I'm going to miss that. That's what makes me afraid."

"Perhaps, but you're strong, Sam. Gwen's right. You're stronger than you give yourself credit for, and you're only getting stronger every day." Her eyes fill with tears. "You never needed a safety blanket, but I've been honored to be that for you."

"I love you, you know that?"

I nod. "Of course you do. What's not to love about this?" I point at myself.

Samantha gets out of her chair to come and sit on my lap. Her arms wind around my neck and she lays her head on mine. "I'm serious. I wouldn't be here if it weren't for you. I wouldn't be this happy, this whole once again. You have no idea how much it kills me that you keep yourself from taking a chance letting someone into that huge heart of yours."

I say nothing.

"Grandmum said to me once that I deserved happiness. Me, Lewis. After all the things I've done, she felt I deserved to be happy."

I despise crying. Not because I hold some mistaken notion that it reveals weakness. Quite the opposite. I'm seldom strong enough to cry, and I just don't particularly enjoy that sense of vulnerability, but the mention of Grandmum never fails to evoke a tear or two.

"Lewis, you're the best person I know, and it stands to reason that if a tart like me deserves to be happy, by George, you're entitled to much, much more."

"I am happy."

"Shut your gob."

"I'm not happy?"

"I want to see someone in your heart."

"Come now, lass. Just because you're deluded in potion number nine, doesn't mean you need to match me up."

"Fine. Does it mean anything to you that your mother feels the same exact way?"

I shift just enough for her to know that she's struck a nerve. "Sam, I'm touched that you and Mum want me happy and all that, but perhaps you ought to consider I'm just not ready to open up to anyone."

She stands and walks over to the electronics cabinet and grabs a framed photograph. She looks at it for a moment before walking back and handing me the photo.

"I wasn't crazy about this bloody diva, but I know you were. You never told me what really happened."

The photo shows a large Solutions Inc. logo, navy blue lettering on a silver background. Terence and I are proudly posing for the cameras, both of us dressed in resplendent tuxedos for the opening of our headquarters in London.

"I told you, we grew apart."

"How?"

"That's a tough one to explain."

Samantha frowns in a way that tells me she will not simply drop this particular subject any time soon. "Do you still have feelings for him?"

I stare at the photo. Terence is grinning at the camera. His hair is dark and long enough to touch his shoulders. His eyes have a playful squint that matches the grin. "Not in the way you think."

"What way is that?"

"I don't love him. You can't love someone who doesn't love you back. At least I can't."

She cocks her head to the side and gives me a penetrating look. "Are you taking potshots at me?"

She's naturally assumed I'm referring to her days of chasing married men. "No, Sam. I promise, I'm not. We're not talking about you."

She looks slightly embarrassed.

"Terence was getting married. That's why we ended our partnership."

Samantha looks shocked. "Man or woman?"

"A woman. Sandy Cromwell."

"Is she pretty?"

"Does it matter?"

Samantha draws back in surprise at the bitterness in my voice.

"She worked for us years ago, nice girl." I shrug.

"Won't last," Samantha says with finality.

"That's not the impression I got when we last talked, and it doesn't matter now."

"So that's why you two parted ways," she muses.

It wasn't the sole reason, but I just wanted this conversation over. I can't say I was a full participant in that relationship. Terence wanted much more than I was ready to give, and that was that. He was excellent at the guilt trips.

Samantha stares at me for a long moment. "Fine. I guess you're not ready to let me in, yet."

"Forgive me, Sam."

"Mum and I may be moving on, but it's difficult to do if you feel abandoned."

I give her a sad smile. "That's my cross to bear, Sam. But I'll bear it better if I know you're both happy."

I can tell she's far from satisfied, but we've known each other long enough to know when to cease prying.

"Can we go to bed now?" Samantha feigns impatience.

"Do you promise not to sleep in the buff?"

She juts out her hip and gives me her best Marilyn Monroe impression. "Why darling, too tempting for you?"

I roll my eyes.

"I always have my trusty bag." She points at a dark grey backpack.

"Of course," I say and yawn. "Never know where you'll be spending the night."

"Hey!"

***

Sleep is slow in coming. Samantha lies curled up next to me, her safety blanket. I stare at the ceiling in the dark, wrestling with the upcoming changes I will be facing very soon.

It really comes down to one thing. I've got to let go of the two women who matter most in my life.

13

The scent of coffee permeates every breath I take. I open my eyes and find myself alone in my room.

"So this is what being a discarded teddy bear is like," I croak, wincing at the dryness of my throat.

I throw the covers back and catch the fragrance of Samantha's body lotion, mulberry something. I get up and walk into the master bathroom. After a long hot shower I dress in dark grey trousers, a cobalt blue shirt and a platinum tie. I'm wrestling my cufflinks in place when there's a knock on the door. "Come in."

"Why, Lewis! You look rather dashing, luv!"

"Good morning, Mum. Flattery will get you everywhere." I go to her and give her a light kiss on her cheek.

"Are you going into the office?"

"I am. I'm meeting with a new client."

"Oh, that's wonderful, son. Who is it?"

"It's a Scottish transportation firm."

"Great. I have this lovely place all to myself. What will I ever do?"

I glance curiously at her. "No shagging in my flat."

"Lewis Jonathan!"

I laugh.

"Sammie Kay and her fiancé will be here by five. I expect you to help me prepare things, so don't be later than four."

"No promises, Mum. I neglected quite a bit of work by helping Samantha these past few days."

She looks a bit put off. "Lovely," she says sarcastically. "It's quite alright. Richard will be happy to give me a hand."

"That'll be smashing, Mum. I'm looking forward to meeting him under different circumstances."

Mum's chin drops. "Do you mean that?"

I smile warmly at her. "Of course. He makes you happy, Mum."

"He does," she says softly.

"Why don't you do a bit of shopping? I see you in a lovely Versace that'll show off those long stilts of yours. Perhaps you can shag Richard into signing with me again."

The look on her face is absolutely priceless.

"You're incorrigible."

I shrug. "A wise woman once told me we all have needs."

She fists her hands at her waist and scowls. "And just what bloody tart would claim such rubbish?"

I grin. "Why, your Sammie Kay. Who else?"

There's no trace of indignation when I glance at her. Instead, she wears a wistful expression that I can't interpret. "It's so difficult to think of her as a grown woman. She'll always be that little dolly with the bouncy tail in the pink tutu and the lopsided grin."

I can easily recall that image.

"You once asked me whether she was an angel. I planned your wedding right then and there."

"Mum, not again!"

She puts her hands up, palms out, in surrender. "I know, I know."

"Did you see her before she left?"

"Yes. I was watching Mark Barton early this morning when she came out of your room. She sat with me for a bit."

There's no curiosity or accusation in her voice, as though sharing a bed with Samantha is the most natural thing in the world.

"You were watching Bloomberg?" I ask when the name registers in my head. Mark Barton is a fairly popular markets reporter. "When did you start investing?"

"Investing? Who cares about the bloody markets? The man is a fox!"

"I might have to speak to Richard about your philandering ways."

"Funny."

"Did Sam tell you what she was doing?"

Mum thinks for a few seconds. "She wanted to run before getting her hair done."

"Again?"

"Hush! She wants to look ravishing for Jason."

"She doesn't have to try very hard."

Mum steps up to me, and cinches the knot of my tie a bit tighter. Her direct gaze is a bit unnerving. "How was your talk last night?"

I grin. "Smashing!" Her stare doesn't waver. "You don't believe me? We ended up in bed after all." I bounce my brows over my eyes.

"Oh, be serious!"

I laugh.

"Isn't there some pretty face from the office you'd care to bring to dinner tonight?"

"I don't date anyone from work. Too risky."

"Oh, you can be such a stick in the mud," she grumbles. "What about Nadine?"

I'm perplexed. "Nadine who?"

"Nadine, the pretty blonde from Caffe Nero."

"I don't know Nadine from Caffe Nero, Mum."

"Don't be daft. Last time I visited, you and Nadine seemed to get along famously."

"Just being friendly."

"She was certainly being more than friendly."

I chuckle and shake my head as I start for the stairs.

"What about Marcel?"

"Marcel who?"

"Marcel, the strapping lad who dropped off your packages yesterday."

"You're unbelievable. The UPS man?"

"Oh, he was adorable!"

"Stop worrying about me, Mum."

"Lewis, how else will you find a date for Sammie's wedding?"

I want to give her a smart answer the way Samantha sometimes does. In this case, she would use something like 'one eight hundred escorts' or some other clever response preceded by the famous one eight hundred. The toll free code only worked in North America and the joke would be lost on Mum. In Europe, you simply call the direct number and pay the bloody toll.

"Fine, I won't meddle anymore."

"Thank you."

She follows me downstairs. I slide my feet into my new Black Label Calf Hopton Brogues and hope like hell they don't blister my feet any further than those bloody sandals I threw away. I would love to institute the American concept of casual Friday but London is still a bit too formal.

"You look dashing, luv."

"You taught me well."

I bend at the waist to kiss her cheek then open the door to a gloomy morning. I hope it isn't a bad sign.

***

By the time 4:00 P.M. rolls around, I'm still in the office preparing some of the groundwork for MacAchallies Transports. Meeting with the new clients was a joy.

Arthur, the senior partner, was an affable chap who complimented me at every turn. His assistant, a lovely lass by the name of Marney Ballach, shamelessly flirted with me while MacAchallies tended to several interrupting phone calls on his mobile.

I can easily engage my charming persona with pretty women, but in a work environment, I strive to be the consummate professional, so I ignored her signals. Unlike most women I've seen in that position, Marney showed no irritation. In fact, she wore a subtle little grin of bemusement throughout the appointment.

For whatever reason, some women tend to become alarmingly more flirtatious around gay men. I've always been confounded by this peculiar phenomenon. It's either comfort, or a sudden compulsion to challenge themselves perhaps. The former lies in the fact that they automatically assume a gay man will not engage in some pursuit to get into their knickers. The latter is different. It's almost as though women take up the challenge of changing a gay man out of his wrongful ideologies.

Personally, I do so enjoy a spirited bout of flirting. To me it's a test of wits, and it gives place to some enjoyable conversation. More often than not, depending on the lass, I like to think that I'm teaching a lesson.

If the lass is high on herself, the type that walks around fully confident that she can possess any man that catches her eye, I can bring her down a few notches. I've been known to devastate some egos. Samantha would be the first one to attest to that.

As she grew into the remarkably attractive woman she is today, she may have held onto the hope that I'd become attracted to her, but it never happened. Not in the way she thought.

Over the years, we've reached a level of comfort that's allowed her to change clothes in my presence with less awkwardness than that of a married couple in the same situation. Samantha's told me several times how much of a shot to her ego my passiveness is. According to her, women live, and love, to be looked at; a fact that's guaranteed job security for every cosmetologist and fashion designer for centuries.

In Marney's case, I think she sensed I'm gay because I didn't react to her guiles the way most heterosexual men undoubtedly would. Her open gaze, her fingers playing with the top buttons of her blouse, and the exaggerated swaying of her hips, were fairly useless against me. I appreciated her beauty, but I didn't automatically fantasize about ripping the bloody blouse off and shoving my face into her bosom.

Whatever the cause, she seemed to lose the air of stuffed shirt she had upon our first greeting. In fact, she became quite comfortable around me in a remarkably short time.

A woman like Marney wouldn't occupy my thoughts this much except that, despite my lack of interest, she left a London number scribbled on the back of her employer's business card along with two words: *call me for the sake of friendship.*

A smile creases my lips at the thought of bringing Marney to dinner tonight. What would Mum and Samantha think of the raven-hair beauty with the obsidian eyes, and creamy skin? The idea certainly has merit.

Once I secure all access files and all the electronic signatures in Solutions' digital vaults, I declare my day done.

As I walk past what once was Terence's office, I feel compelled to stop and look into the empty room. It's a much bigger space than my office, and the window faces Old Broad Street. My office window faces Tower 42, a beautiful structure of glass and steel that stretches to the skies.

I step inside and walk all the way to the window. Perhaps it's time I stop being such a sentimental fool and move into this office. I like this fifth floor view of the city. It may very well distract me from my work, but I could definitely find comfort in this little peephole into the pulse of London life.

I just would have to avoid getting caught up staring at the beautiful suits walking in and out of Pinners Hall.

I take the elevator down to the underground level parking garage and text Mum that I'm on my way. It normally takes me a half-hour to get back down to Cadogan Square.

"Last chance to ask Marney to join you," I mutter mockingly at the ghostly reflection on the glass.

Just as I'm about to key in Marney's number, I change my mind. This dinner is all about the ladies showing off their respective lads, after all.

On my way home I stop at the spirits shop, but I realize my mistake before I even park. However, an idea occurs to me. I pull into a tight spot then walk in the store. A few minutes later, I place the paper sack on the passenger seat, and fight my way through traffic the rest of the way.

There are two vehicles that normally wouldn't be parked on Cadogan Square. One is an older model Land Rover, and the other is a sleek Jag. Diametrical opposites, I muse, rugged and utilitarian versus sheer style and performance. I love the lines of the Jag, but I secretly envy the capability of the SUV.

Just like shoes hold a plethora of information about a woman, a man's choice in vehicles gives a fairly accurate tale about the sort of person he is. That's why they call them bloody status symbols, after all. I laugh as the thought crosses my mind that Samantha drives a convertible, easy to undress. What would I be?

I turn to look at the sleek lines of the BMW and find it presumptuous, but I don't know what I would choose instead.

I try to put on my social mask but as I open the door, I start feeling nervous. I don't do so well around most straight men. I never have. At least, I don't do well when the gathering is this small, and therefore more intimate. I feel much more comfortable in a larger group or at least a small group where the women hold the majority.

The discomfort goes back to my days as a thirteen year-old at St. Clement's Prep. Boys were physically cruel, not just with their sexually confused peers like me, but with any lad that showed the slightest sign of weakness.

"Shut the bloody window into the past," I mutter to myself, echoing words I've said to Samantha more times than I could count.

The first thing I see when I walk into the studio is the broad back of Jason McElroy. He's sitting at my computer, checking his work email, perhaps. When I take one step, his head moves, letting me know he's aware of my presence. After logging off, he stands and walks towards me, a friendly smile on his face. He's not that much taller than me, but he somehow fills the room in a way that makes me feel like a little boy.

"Welcome home, Commander," I offer, using his last military rank.

"Lewis, it's a pleasure to see you," McElroy says politely.

I inwardly cringe, expecting the crushing pressure of his solid hand, but perhaps he's finally aware of his own strength, for the bones in my hand aren't crushed.

"I see you redesigned the background on the main site."

McElroy gives off a quiet intensity, like a staring bull about to charge. Around Samantha, he's as pliable as a bloody teddy bear.

"New security measures," I tell him, finding comfort in the topic. "Similar to pigment striations on a currency note."

He looks interested. "What prompted that?"

"Russian hackers hide their worms in picture files, even in the sound of video clips. A month ago, the Yard's computers crashed for two straight days after someone opened up a digital birthday card. No information was stolen, but the breach embarrassed a lot of people."

McElroy smiles. "Scotland Yard," he shakes his head. "Those chaps don't suffer embarrassment lightly."

"No, they don't."

It's strange to feel this level of camaraderie with this bloke. Our friendship started out on loose, rocky terms, but Samantha's been the common, smooth ground where we've built a mutual respect.

"The smarmy thinkers at MI5 developed this countermeasure they call swirl technology. In essence, our server sites are protected by a digital concertina wire of programs designed to ferret out phishing codes, viruses, and other types of invaders. When a threat is detected, this technology attaches itself to the origin, leading our security teams straight to the device where the attack came from."

"Quite impressive."

I nod in agreement. "The advantage of working for Nathan Jeffries is that he gets to sample the latest of the latest."

Jason shakes his head then gazes at me with something like awe. "I have nothing but respect for your intellect."

I realize he's talking about the entire cyber tech divisions working, not only for Lions, but also in law enforcement and the military. Still, the compliment is welcome.

"How was she?" Jason whispers, nodding towards the steps to indicate he's asking about Samantha.

My mouth goes dry when I think of Samantha, brazenly spending the nights curled up next to me. "She was bearable." I try a smile.

"How's she doing with the cravings?"

This question gives me pause. "To tell you the truth, if she had any, she did a fantastic job of hiding them. She never had a low moment, even when she was upset about your extended assignment."

Jason's eyes fall to his feet. "It couldn't be avoided." He grabs the back of his neck forcing my eyes to fix the scars over his ear. He's let his tawny hair grow long enough to cover them, but the shrapnel that burned and tore the flesh also destroyed every hair follicle.

"I hate to bloody leave her. I'm just glad you were here for her, as always."

His voice is so deep, I'm not sure how to read the emotional subtext beneath his words. "Does it bother you?"

He looks up at me, eyes wide with surprise. "Not at all."

I nod, thinking I understand. "Really?"

Jason surprises me by taking my shoulder in a friendly grip. "Because you're her best friend, more like her brother, really. I know how much you mean to her, Lewis."

"She means a great deal to me." I'm trying to figure out where this whole conversation is coming from.

"She told me you've been having a hard time, anticipating some drastic change in your relationship once we get married. I'd like to assure you that I'm not planning on locking her up in some bloody tower, although sometimes she tempts me." He grins mischievously.

I smile back, knowing exactly what he's talking about, and pleasantly surprised at his entire demeanor.

"If I'm not around, I'd feel much better knowing you're there for her."

I frown at him. "Why wouldn't you be around?"

He pats my shoulder and gestures for us to join the others. "In this line of work, you just never know."

There's a cold feeling settling in the pit of my stomach. Some three years ago, Lions lost one of its agents in Syria. To this day, no one's been able to figure out what happened. "Are you saying that because of Donnelly?"

Jason looks thoughtful for a moment then nods. "I thought I'd take a desk job or handle the training, but that's just not me. Sam and I have talked about this at length. I want the field work. I want the tough assignments. It's just who I am."

"That's true, but it's no longer just about you. You'll have a wife to think about."

Jason smiles. "You don't know how good that sounds to me."

"Jason, Sam still has a hard time being by herself. She's still plagued by the nightmares. Do you really want to put her through sleepless nights while you're guarding some diplomat out in Yemen? She's been through enough. You both have."

There's alarm on his face. "She didn't mention the nightmares to me."

"Of course she didn't. It's important to her that you're happy with what you do."

He looks confused. "That changes things."

I nod. "For her sake, limit your risks, chap. She needs you more than you think."

He grabs the back of his neck with one hand and squeezes. "I gather we'll be doing more talking than she prefers. I'm glad you brought this up to me."

I'd like to tell him that I'm not just looking out for Samantha. Once I earned top clearance at Lions, I learned just how much Jason Stephen McElroy has already sacrificed in the field.

We both climb the steps into the living room, where Mum and Samantha are tripping over each other in the small kitchen.

I recognize the man in the living room reading the William Blake poem hanging on the wall. He turns around as we approach. Dr. Richard Bergman wears an affable smile on a Patrician face lined with care. His stare is open, his blue eyes flash intellect.

"It's good to see you again, Lewis."

I shake hands with Mum's boyfriend, wanting to find something to dislike about the chap, but I can't. "Good to see you as well, Sir."

"Please, call me Richard. All my friends do."

I don't have to turn around to know Mum and Samantha are looking at us with big, moist eyes.

"Please, gentlemen," I motion to the couches.

There's a spread of cheese and crackers that suddenly reminds me of the two bottles I left on the credenza downstairs. "Please excuse me."

Richard and Jason nod and engage each other in a talk about their vehicles.

"Where are you off to?" Mum calls, holding a large pot with kitchen mitts.

The mouthwatering aroma of the roast evokes a loud grumbling from my shrinking stomach. "I forgot something. I'll be up in no time."

I feel a pang of sadness as I think of all the small gatherings Terence and I used to host. It was the sole reasoning behind buying this place.

"Hey."

I turn, startled to see Samantha gliding across the floor.

"Oh, you can walk? I thought Jason would drive you right through the mattress."

She twists her face. "If you really want to know, we're eagerly waiting for tonight. Lots of loving to catch up on," she says with a smirk I have no trouble interpreting. "What do you think of Richard?"

"I just got here."

"Come on!"

I pick up the paper sack and there's an audible clanking of glass. Samantha's eyes go to the bag for a quick second.

I smile at her. "It's non-alcoholic," I announce, pulling out one of the clear bottles.

"Eisberg," Samantha looks appreciatively. "Cavernet Sauvignon, nice."

"Love your liver," I quote the Eisberg slogan.

Samantha shakes her head. "You worry too much."

"Consider it my penance for not worrying enough before."

She nods in understanding. "So…" She pauses for a moment. "What'd you boys talk about?"

"You're a curious, little lass."

She gives me a pleading look.

"We were grading your sexual performance, and discussing where you can improve your techniques," I say deadpan.

"Arse!" She gives me an obligatory chuckle, but she looks nervous.

"He just wanted to express his gratitude for allowing you to bask in my superior company while he was away."

She rolls her eyes. "Seriously?"

"He's afraid you'll go astray."

She looks confused. "As in I'm going to run off with someone else?"

I shake my head as I raise one of the bottles. "As in giving in to a different temptation."

"Oh." Her eyes look pained.

"He's just concerned about you, we all are."

"I've stayed dry for over six months now," she says defensively.

"And we're all so very proud of you, luv. We really are. But we know it can be difficult on you, particularly when you're alone."

She takes a deep breath, a clear sign that she's annoyed with all the concern. "I wasn't alone. I was with you."

I sigh. "Come, let's join everyone."

"Not until you tell me what that sighing was about."

She stands in front of me like a Royal Guard, her expression invites no argument.

"Sam, I'm not always going to be there to fill in for Jason, luv."

There's a flash of anger in her eyes. "What does that mean?"

"Lewis, Sammie Kay!" Mum's voice calls from the top of the steps.

"We're coming," Samantha answers then she gives me a pointed look that tells me we're bound to continue our discussion later.

I let her take the first five steps before I start climbing, wondering if I'll have any answers not only to her questions, but to my own, as well.

14

No one makes a pot roast the way Mum does. Every succulent bite is an explosion of flavor, and the non-alcoholic wine proves to be quite an unexpected hit.

The conversation is fluid and entertaining. There's much laughter around the table, and by the time the night comes to a close, I decide I like Dr. Bergman for my mother.

I actually expected Samantha to feed Jason after watching her cling onto his arm, constantly stealing kisses, and giving him plenty of lingering looks that he returned. However, it was Mum who engaged in similar lovey-dovey behavior, surprising the rest of us.

Samantha is clearly eager to have Jason to herself. For his part, Jason deliberately uses every stalling tactic, clearly enjoying Samantha's frustration. For a moment there, I think she's about to knock him unconscious, throw him over her shoulder, and take him away. I take a few shots at her, and everyone laughs in good humor, even Jason, who seemed mortified at first.

Dr. Bergman takes Mum out for a nightcap, jokingly laying the blame on me for bringing home non-alcoholic spirits.

"Richard," I use his first name at his insistence. "Why, you don't need to get this one drunk, she'll give it up for free," I joke.

Samantha's chin nearly hits the floor, before she succumbs to wave after wave of laughter. Jason clears his throat, but he laughs anyway. Richard throws his head back and his deep laughter echoes throughout the house.

For her part, Mum simply offers a wry grin and says, "Don't wait up."

And so, off they go. Two new couples clearly in love. My heart almost aches with joy for them.

As much as I enjoyed the dinner, I don't want to stay home while thoughts of Mum and Richard in bed cross my mind.

I run into my bedroom to change my clothes. The scents of the juicy roast still cling to the fabric of the shirt I pull off and discard in the hamper. In fact, the mouth-watering aroma permeates the entire house.

Heeding to a lifelong discipline for proper grooming, I shower, shave, and change into dark slacks, a rust-colored button-down, black tie, and black loafers. On the way out, I grab a black leather coat and leave the house.

Once in my car, I go through my playlists on the touch screen of the sound system and opt for oldies. REO Speedwagon rolls out "Take It On The Run", and I sing along. According to Samantha, I can't carry a tune in a bloody bucket, but I feel like Elton John without an audience.

I've no destination in mind, as always, whenever I feel compelled to drive while my mind discharges itself. Just the music and the smooth gliding of the BMW, the two things where I find a level of comfort I've never found anywhere else. Inevitably, I think back on when I first found this joy in driving.

Samantha spent the summer after her senior year with Mum and me, in Liverpool. I remember how she bragged about driving a car, while I was forced to motor around on a tiny, midnight blue Vespa 50, until I turned seventeen.

I loved the tiny scooter. Despite breaking down more often than it ran, I loved riding up to the Mersey and cruising around, but it paled in comparison to driving Mum's old Peugeot hatchback. If memory serves, it was an '87 GTI model. As a young, inexperienced driver, the 130 horsepower engine felt like a jet turbine that gave me the feeling of being propelled at the speed of sound.

Samantha usually forgot several essential items when she packed to come to Liverpool. An oddity considering her memory, but she never failed to bring a dozen cassettes full of new music. We would fill up the tank, pop in the newest American tunes and drive.

I remember when she introduced me to Pearl Jam and Nirvana. I tried hard to show nothing but contempt for the sound that ultimately killed Glam Rock, but there was such raw fury in the aggressive guitar playing, and the vocals were full of angst and darkness, making each song quite appealing. Even when you couldn't decipher what Eddie Vedder or Kurt Cobain were saying, you felt the energy of each song in every cell of your body.

I made a feeble attempt to defend Def Leppard and Judas Priest, but Samantha knew I'd go "Grunge" as soon as I heard Pearl Jam's "Jeremy". And I did.

It was infinitely better than some cassette tape of hers that ended up "mysteriously" disappearing that summer. I committed the crime only to save my eardrums. The label read "Gangsta Rap". To this day, I have difficulty finding what was so appealing about it. Samantha loved it. In fact, she still does.

She'd sway to the music and rap along, taking advantage of her perfect memory, though her delivery of each line was lacking, especially after her British tongue set in after a week around me.

I hated rap songs. To me, they were nothing but the perversion of some great older music set as background for the angry rants.

Inevitably, I've changed my mind a bit since then. I am guilty of listening to Eminem, and Flo Rida can really get me going, but I miss the old band days. I miss the cheesy ballads, and the cliché rock anthems. That music reflected softer times, happier even. My generation enjoyed a brief bubble gum period before anger and religious wars dominated the forefront of our lives.

The bloody Berlin Wall became rubble in 1989 after all, taking with it the threat of nuclear holocaust, or so we thought. I often wonder if that's what we celebrated during that brief period. We were all about fun, friends, and the never-ending quest for love.

Samantha had vastly different ideologies, but often lost the argument when I'd ask her how many suicides, or murders my music inspired. My point was further proven with the deaths of figures like Kurt Cobain and Tupac Shakur, just to name a couple.

Music is to me the social reflection of the times. My mother adored the music of the fifties. It made her think of her parents, both deceased before I was born. I learned that soon after the war years, the entire world seemed to exhale a sigh of relief and embraced life. It's no accident places like America experienced the famous Baby

Boom in the years following the fiery end of World War II with the dropping of the bomb in Hiroshima.

The music of the late eighties had a similar undertone, until the nineties brought on another wave of politically driven lyrics that were bound to get worse in this new, ominous era of religious tension between Islam and the West.

But what am I doing theorizing about all this rubbish?

At seventeen I was simply enjoying the company of my best friend, taking in the Mersey Valley countryside, or the Ellesmere Port area. We'd drive for hours, generally engaging in talks about the meaning of life. Our time together was healing for each of us.

For Samantha, it dragged her away from the void she faced when she was overwhelmed by the loss of her parents. For me, it was a welcome stretch of time where I could be no one but myself without the ever present fear I felt each day.

I'm already in Richmond, driving at a good clip on the A316. I can't remember the last time I hopped in the car and drove out to where I'm going. By the time I get into East Sheen, I fight an urge to turn around and race back home.

There was a time when all I did was look for, so called, gay cruises with Terence. He was deep into the lifestyle. I was too for a time. I even started a group in Soho that defended likeminded men, and women, from persecution and prejudice.

I'm having quite a difficult time coming to terms with the fact that I haven't felt strongly about anything for a long time. Perhaps at a subconscious level, I'm here to find some vestige of the base whereupon I once built my persona.

I make the turn on Clifford Avenue, looking for a parking spot. It seems the park is hopping tonight since it takes me some time to finally find a place where a BMW 7 Series doesn't look too out of place.

The weather is mild and the starry sky promises a dry night. I exchange hellos with several blokes walking on the street. I notice a few already holding hands, probably heading to their cars, and possibly some hostel down the road, the kind that cater to the gay lot.

As I get closer to the park, the men and women around are less reserved in their public displays of affection. I turn away from a group of young blokes that giggle way too much for my tastes. It would be bad enough to have an embarrassing loitering fine slapped on me, let alone a drug charge, or some lewd conduct charge.

I pass a couple of young lads, their wandering hands all over each other. I give them their space and continue down a path, following the sound of music.

A tall blonde woman in her twenties is performing an excellent rendition of Joni Mitchell's "Both Sides Now". The guitar carries its music clearly, right into my heart. Her voice is so good that I think Joni would be proud. I begin tapping my foot and mouthing the lyrics when she smoothly takes her small audience through the chorus.

When she strums the last notes of the song, an enthusiastic wave of applause ensues. The woman is actually a man. He pushes back the long blonde hair in a decidedly feminine fashion and basks in the admiration of the audience.

I make my way over to offer a compliment when I feel a tap on my shoulder.

"Is that you, Lewis Bettford?"

I recognize the voice instantly even though the last time I'd heard it, I was in my twenties. "Why, Carmen, what brings you here, old queen?"

Carmen Santopietro is a seventy-something Italian, who was famous for his Burlesque shows in Soho during the seventies and eighties. He loves to entertain younger generations with his stories. Finding him here is slightly disconcerting.

Carmen takes my face in his hands and kisses both my cheeks affectionately. I kiss one cheek for the sake of politeness.

"Where have you been hiding, doll?" Carmen takes my hands and draws back to give me the once over. "You're still a fine morsel, laddie."

I smile, noting for the first time the greyish blotching on his chin and his hollowed cheeks. The baby-smooth skin has given way to the passage of time. The wrinkles are deep, too deep for the layers of foundation to conceal. The artificial lashes that once gave his large, dark eyes, the allure he was so well known for, now look ridiculous on his aged visage. There are only a few wisps of his once lustrous dark mane under the shapeless, curly wig he wears.

I've seen the posters that still hang on the walls of cabarets in Soho. Carmen had the healthy figure of a Betty Page, or a Marilyn

Monroe, but there's a paunch around his middle now that defies the threads attaching the buttons of his trousers.

"You look quite well, luv," I lie.

When Carmen beams at the false compliment, I only feel sadness, and a strange sense of revulsion.

Carmen aggravates that feeling by pinching my lips. "You were always the one with the candy mouth."

It takes a herculean effort for me not to pull away. Carmen Santopietro is the closest thing to royalty that the gay community in Soho has. Recalling his efforts for what he called human equality, more commonly known as gay rights—once he hung his gowns in exchange for business suits—I can't hold anything less than a deep respect for the man.

"And you've always had the gift of flattery," I say, after Carmen releases my mouth.

"I'm no more than a dizzy, old omi with a bad onk, and tired orbs." Carmen laughs at his own joke. "I heard Terry married some polone from Chelsea. Sorry, luv."

"He's finally happy. It's all that matters."

Carmen makes a face and looks over both shoulders. "Depends on who you talk to, pet."

I frown in confusion. "How do you mean?"

"Terry, who's still quite the dish, I say, had some dashing young camp's luppers all over his basket, luv."

A wave of indignation surges through me. "Who was the camp?"

Carmen dismisses my question with a wave of his hand. "Just some chicken cottaging around here."

"How much of a chicken?"

Carmen gives me a wicked smile. "Too young to shave."

Damn him! "When did you see him?"

Carmen shakes his head. "I can't remember well enough, luv, beginning of summer, perhaps. He's been cruising again, not just here, but all over."

"Did you talk to him?"

"I tried, but he pretended to be totally absorbed by some glossy in his lills."

I don't have a lot of trouble following Carmen's Polari. The slang was a product of the 1960's, when homosexuals had a greater need of a private way of communicating. Some people called it closet talk, but most just referred to Polari as gay slang.

In modern day England, there is no longer a need for Polari. Only the gays of old use it, and understand it fluently.

"You seem quite troubled over Terry's antics, luv."

"It's not what you think," I tell him.

His eyes flash disappointment.

"I have no interest in Terence as a partner, but I just wish he made up his bloody mind."

"About what?"

"About who he is."

Carmen looks thoughtful. "All the way out, or all the way in, isn't it, Lewis?"

I nod. "Exactly."

"Where are you?"

"Me?"

Carmen's gaze is piercing. "Are you all the way in, or all the way out?"

I'm suddenly overwhelmed by a wave of nervous hysteria. It bothers me that I'm not sure how to answer. "Carmen, darling," I say in a singsong voice. "Whatever makes you ask me such a thing?"

He doesn't laugh. He doesn't even flinch. His dark eyes continue to pin me in place. "You've been nothing but a teasing naff for as long as I've known you, lad. It's as though you're still pining over Terry and won't bloody move on."

Sweat pebbles on the back of my neck as a column of heat rises up my spine.

"Keep those precious ogles on me when I bloody talk to you, Lewis."

Carmen's voice is so commanding I turn back to him.

"You and Terry were together for a long time. That's why I've questioned him once or, whenever I caught him sampling a different fruit."

I say nothing. I'd walk away, except that Carmen is standing right in front of me, blocking my way.

The Joni Mitchell impersonator picks up his guitar once more and several people shift uncomfortably as they turn away from staring at Carmen and me. They've undoubtedly listened to every word. Not that I care.

"I wanted him to prove that I meant something to him," I say lamely.

"That's bollocks, and you know it. I actually don't blame Terry for chasing other pieces."

I could lie. I could easily come up with some twisted story about worthiness and patience, but I don't feel I need to defend my position on a relationship that no longer is.

"If I didn't know better, I'd say you're as confused as you were the first time I ever saw you walk your scrawny scotches into my theater."

"Aren't you ever confused?"

"Never, darling. I am who I am, no bloody apologies."

I nod, but say nothing.

"It isn't an easy choice, pet, though your lot sure had it much easier than us old queens. We prided ourselves in our discretion, your lot usually airs it out like it's some sort of fad like Terry does, until his mood changes and he suddenly remembers he wants to be straight once more." His eyes narrow and he jabs a finger into my chest. "Then there are those like you, who seem to be hiding from something."

When the guitar begins to play, Carmen and I politely keep quiet, allowing the singer's voice to be the only one in the air.

I don't want to stay here any longer.

For the first time in a long time, I feel alone in a crowd. It's an ironic thought to contemplate, for I escaped loneliness by cruising, finding likeminded people I could relate to. I found friends with whom I enjoyed laughter. I even shared tears and comforting embraces. In all honesty, I've used every one of those friends emotionally.

I join the collective trance as one voice soars through "Chelsea Morning". If I close my eyes, I can see Mum singing along to Joni Mitchell.

Carmen has drifted over to a group clapping a beat, sitting on the grass. Thankful for small favors, I turn to walk away.

I don't stop until I'm at the door of my vehicle, but my mind is in fragments during the walk.

"Pardon me, luv. Care for some company?"

I turn to the sound of the cultured voice to see a young bloke no older than twenty, smiling seductively. He wears a ruffled white shirt, unbuttoned down to his navel. His hair is dark, styled in long cornrows that crisscross over his head. His eyes are dark and glint with street smarts. I quickly look over my shoulders, and down each side of the street, expecting to see his mates. It was a typical technique of gangs in this part of town. They'd send the eye candy to distract the mark before robbing him.

"I'm alone, hoping you could assist me with that," he says with a heavy lisp.

"I'm headed for home," I say, once I'm sure I'm not about to get mugged.

The bloke steps closer, his teeth are so white they gleam in the dim light of the streetlamp.

"No need to spend the night alone. You're quite a dish, what do you say we start at an even hundred."

Few things disgust me more than camps like this young punk. "Get lost, camp. I'm going home."

The lad looks perplexed, his feline smile still in place. "Camp?"

"As in, Known As Male Prostitute," I say dryly.

"I like that. Come now, gorgeous, I'll do anything."

"Great, you can start by getting lost."

"Well, that may cost you at least ten pounds, luv."

His left hand casually reaches behind his back, and although he continues to grin, his eyes have taken on a feral glint.

I take a quick step and unleash a solid blow to the bloke's solar plexus. All the air rushes out of his lungs and his mouth opens and closes like a fish out of water. I hear the metallic bounce of the knife blade hit the ground at about the same instant his knees thud onto the concrete of the sidewalk.

Without waiting another moment, I quickly get in the BMW, hit the starter button and peel away from the curb. I see the would-be-robber reach for something on the ground and I accelerate. Whatever he threw at me falls harmlessly in the wake of my exhaust. My heart beats painfully fast and I can only breathe in quick little gasps.

When the surge of adrenaline finally ebbs, I feel suddenly giddy, practically elated as I cruise back onto the A316. I fight the urge to call Samantha to tell her all about the strange incident. In fact, I pick up my mobile and thumb to her last call when I suddenly remember that she is, more than likely, um... occupied with her fiancé.

Yes, I think things are definitely changing for us.

As suddenly as that wave of elation hits, it leaves me with an unwelcome numbness. Inevitably, I flash back to my conversation with Carmen Santopietro. Besides all the disturbing news about my ex-partner, Terence, and his troublingly accurate observation of me, something else gnaws at me.

While speaking with Carmen I felt I was looking into a future version of myself. I feel I'm holding just a little thread sticking out of the ball of yarn my mind is at this moment. I don't feel brave enough to pull it, afraid of what I may unravel.

I have a passing urge to call Terence. If anyone can lecture the philandering wanker, it's me. What the bloody hell is he doing?

I imagine he'd love nothing more than a phone call from me. The only reason he hasn't tried is because I was adamant about breaking contact after our last row. A row we had when he tried waltzing back into my life after dissolving our partnership. By then, he was already married and I had no intentions of getting in the middle of that, despite his tearful declarations of missing me.

I missed his company more than I would ever admit to anyone else, but thankfully, there were enough things commanding my attention—most notably, a side-trip to America—to prevent me from wallowing in self-pity that might have inevitably worn me down to allow him back in.

This is precisely the kind of thing I need my best friend for, but I have the feeling this one time I'm on my own. I gather it's best if I just begin getting used to it.

15

Mum spent all weekend with Dr. Bergman and other than a text message from Samantha late Sunday, I heard nothing from her.

I slept as late as possible and watched a few football matches. I even indulged in a couple of *Bundesliga* matches.

I love German football.

There is very little individual effort. Each team works the field like a well-oiled machine, their play is fast, their passing crisp, and their shots true. The English game is getting a bit crowded with demanding primadonnas, whose play is lacking and utterly predictable. There is no competition with the Germans, the Italians, even the bloody Spaniards. I take that to heart. Football was born in the Queen's Land after all.

When I was eight, I'd sneak out to the fields and play, hoping Mum never found out. She had nothing against the game. In fact, she is, to this day, a Liverpool Reds fan to the core. The problem was my size in comparison with the other boys.

Kids like Mikey Sullivan and Danny Simmons outweighed me by twenty pounds or more. Those two had been involved when little Kenny Walters ended up with a broken leg. Mum forbade me to play after that incident.

As the song goes, I was as thin as a stick of macaroni, and according to Mum, just as brittle too. What she never understood was that all the dancing I was doing in her studio had given me fleet feet, and quick reflexes, not to mention great stamina. I could run like a gazelle, and just as swiftly.

Ballet gives you such an awareness of where your body is in space, it translates into agility on the football fields. I could leap to avoid slide tackles like no one else. Word was I had to be still for anyone to get me. I was never a good dribbler, but if a midfielder went with the long ball, I could outrun any defender, take the ball and score nine out of ten times.

I was by no means invincible, nor could I run out of trouble forever. When someone found a way to bump me off the ball, the result was frightening.

My secret football playing came to an abrupt end when I was sixteen. Mum taught the class a particular number for months, and I was the male lead, as usual. The culminating move was a *présage*.

With only a week left to perform, I wrenched my knee something terrible when Mikey Sullivan dropped me awkwardly on a slide tackle that I couldn't evade, despite my acrobatics. It wasn't a dirty move at all. It was part of the game. I limped back home and did all I could to hide the injury from Mum, hoping I'd heal overnight in order to hold little Kelsey Berkheimer over my head.

Présage lifts are awe-inspiring, difficult to master, and incredibly demanding on the body. In essence, the male has to lift his mate arm's length over his head, but despite the seemingly obvious, the secret was in the stance of the male. Kelsey was a thin, little lass that I had no trouble lifting. The trouble was that I needed two good legs to hold the position.

The next morning I couldn't even bend my leg, and there was no hiding the discolored swelling of my left knee. It was the one time Mum was angry enough to paddle my arse but thankfully, seeing me in pain spared me from her wrath.

Mum didn't force me to dance. I honestly loved ballet, especially once the moves became more intricate and challenging. Ballet is normally perceived to be boring, but performing is exhilarating.

My love affair with ballet started out as something Mum and I did for fun. I knew what it meant to her that I danced and I threw myself into it from an early age.

I'm well aware of the Freudian implications. I grew up without a father and Mum did the only thing she could, so I danced. Perhaps, the same reason could be applied to explain my infatuation with football. There was something beautiful about scoring a goal, but more appealing than that, was the sense of camaraderie among teammates.

I've watched matches where the winners embrace each other in jubilation, while the losers hold one another, soaking their jerseys with their own tears in collective mourning over their defeat. I've always wanted that sense of belonging.

I didn't follow the league too closely while I was with Terence. He had a most obnoxious habit of commenting on the players' physical attributes while disregarding the match entirely. He probably did that to regain my attention. That was Terence, it was always about him.

I've never been the reflective type, or the introspective type, and yet I find myself having these one-sided dialogues more and more.

In an attempt to clear my head, I select a New Age playlist and within minutes, the haunting and ethereal voice of Enya allows me to quiet my inner voice, dim the mental images, and shut down my mind.

***

When I arrive at the office Monday morning, I realize I have yet to contact Quinn McDermont. I look at my schedule—my once "cleared" schedule, which has been anything but. There are no appointments, and other than the MacAchallies Transports project I have nothing going on. Today is as good as any day to meet the intriguing Quinn. After keying her London mobile number, I lean back on my chair and wait through three rings.

"Good morning, Lewis," says the smoky voice.

"Good morning, Ms. McDermont, how does your day look?"

"It would look a whole lot better if you call me Quinn."

I let the chair straighten up, a wry smile on my face. "My apologies, Quinn. Is that better?"

"Much. My day is clear and I can be up to your office within the hour."

"Can you find your way over here?"

"Yes, I can take the tube to Liverpool Street and walk the rest of the way."

I look around at the Spartan setting of my office and think of the main office, which was Terence's, vacant and empty. I fear it may give Quinn the wrong impression. "May I suggest meeting at Fox's Café?"

"Um… Old Broad Street, right?"

"Righto."

A soft chuckle. "Sounds perfect. One hour?"

"One hour."

"Looking forward to seeing you, Lewis."

"And you as well, luv."

I can hear her chuckling before she ends the call.

To pass the time, I bring up one of the pages of *Famous* to see if I can learn something more about Quinn. To say the tabloid jackals dragged her through the mud would be a serious understatement. After two articles full of quotes from "close friends of the couple", I've had about all I can. I recall the creative headlines that assaulted Samantha when she commanded the New York City spotlight while dating the very rich, powerful, and enigmatic Brooks Waldenberg. I recall reading outright lies about my best friend, made up by "close friends of the couple."

There's a new headline dated a week ago that alludes to the former Mrs. Fischer hooked on dope and having "mysterious men" in her Malibu mansion.

"Un-bloody-believable…" I shake my head and close the browser as I consult the time.

After a quick look in the mirror, I gather my jacket and overcoat and head for the door. The day is grey and the cool air already carries a drizzle that annoys me. I hate the bloody rain. Umbrella in hand, I make my way up the street to Fox's and get there with plenty of time to spare.

I'm never late to an appointment and I expect the same from the people I meet but it seldom happens. Samantha is my biggest offender. She won't think anything of keeping me waiting, and like a bloody fool, I wait for her each and every time.

"Looking for someone?"

I recognize the smoky timbre and turn, surprised that Quinn somehow beat me to Fox's.

My eyes first register the styled, short blonde hair. It surprises me because I expected the long golden locks I saw on the photographs online. Her bangs sweep left over the most vibrant blue eyes I've ever seen. They're resplendent against the California tanned, smooth complexion, which detracts from the Norse goddess image I had upon seeing her photographs. Her bottom lip is luscious and ripe. Her smile grows at the wide-eye look of surprise on my face.

"It's really good to meet you," she says, extending a dainty hand that's dry to the touch, unlike my sweaty palm.

At least I have the presence of mind to subtly wipe off some of the moisture against the fabric of my coat before taking her hand.

"A pleasure to finally meet you," I quip.

The cut of her two piece suit is expensive, simultaneously elegant and provocative in a way that does not show off her body, but clearly states her femininity. The elegant jacket conceals her breasts in a demure manner, though I suspect they are a bit large for her small frame. I notice her eyes giving me a direct once over, her gaze is unapologetic, more appreciative.

"Samantha failed to properly convey how handsome you are."

I curse my muteness. She beats me to the compliment and if I say she looks stunning—which she does—it'll feel forced. "You're too kind."

I haven't let go of her hand. In fact, I'm about to kiss the back of it to give her a proper European hello, when a dark skinned man cuts in between us.

"This place is a bit crowded," the man says as though unaware of rudely interrupting. He stands by Quinn with a possessive disposition.

Quinn seems a bit put off but she manages a smile. "Lewis, this is my friend Firuz Ahmadi." She turns to face the man. "Lewis Bettford, Samantha's best friend."

Firuz Ahamdi extends his right hand. When I offer mine, he squeezes with every ounce of strength. His obsidian eyes glint a warning that's at complete odds with the forced "friendly" smile.

"A pleasure, I'm sure," he says with a slight Middle Eastern accent.

I let him crush my fingers without giving him the satisfaction of a grimace. "Likewise."

He doesn't let go until Quinn looks at him sideways.

Firuz sizes me up the way I've seen men evaluate one another in pubs as they compete over the same lass. His black hair is slicked back. His complexion is brown, adorned by a full beard that reaches to the collar of his shirt, perfectly trimmed. His features are actually delicate, a testament to Caucasian blood, particularly his eyes. They're a startling green. He's attractive in an exotic way and arrogance emanates from the lad in waves. His smile doesn't quite reach his eyes, which are boring into mine.

I've met many blokes like this wanker. I wonder what exactly the extent of his association with Quinn is. Ignoring his stare, I turn to Quinn, charm factor full on, and heed a juvenile urge. "If I may, I'd like to give you a proper English handshake, the kind reserved for a beautiful lady, such as yourself." I bring her dainty hand close to my lips, letting my breath caress her knuckles. Her smile dazzles me.

"I've heard so much about you. Looks like the rumors are true," she says.

"Only the ones I've allowed to be known, luv." I wink at her, drawing perverse satisfaction out of Firuz's rolling of his eyes.

Quinn glances at my hand, which is still holding hers. "Shall we?"

I let go, feeling my cheeks burn, having actually forgotten Firuz's presence. I can't remember reacting this way to anyone before. "Please."

I indicate she should lead the way, and mentally shake my head at the unfamiliar reactions this woman elicits from me in person.

Before I can fall in step behind her, Firuz cuts in front of me and lays a hand on Quinn's shoulder, guiding her to one of the empty tables.

"Oh, I forgot!" Quinn cries, abruptly stopping and turning to Firuz. "Will you be a dear and retrieve my folder from my car?"

Firuz's thick, black eyebrows form a V as he frowns. "Don't you have those in your bag?"

Quinn shakes her head.

The frown disappears. "Very well, darling."

Firuz turns away from Quinn and glares at me before leaving. I give him a blank look resisting the urge to call out "fetch!"

We walk past the square table Firuz chose. We take a seat at a horseshoe-shaped table that doesn't allow us to sit across from each other, but nearly side by side. Quinn places a thick folder and a thin laptop on the table. Apparently, I was too mesmerized by her looks that I failed to notice the supple leather bag slung over her shoulder.

"You keep interesting company, Quinn."

She blushes. "Firuz is a good friend. He's always a bit rough, but he means well. If you knew what I've been through, you'd understand his being protective of me."

I'd like to point out that first impressions are very telling, but I change my mind. I don't know the entire story, but I can't help feeling a bit strange about the man.

A waiter dressed in black from head to toe, introduces himself as Kellen, and takes our drink orders. I opt for a cappuccino while Quinn orders chai tea.

I wonder if she's referring to the tabloids that have apparently hounded her all over the US, but instead of letting curiosity get the best of me, I decide to switch tactics, sensing she doesn't want to talk about it.

"How's Dr. Fitzgerald these days?" I ask, referring to the man from Bionics, citing some common ground to begin our conversation.

Quinn smiles. "Don is doing well. I can't wait for his next seminar."

"How are you tied to Bionics, if you don't mind me asking?"

"Not at all. I headed a research project for them a couple of years ago. It made me spend enough time in London to warrant obtaining my own place."

"I'm surprised you never attempted to ring Samantha."

Quinn frowns slightly. "To tell you the truth, I'm dying to see her. At the time I was here, however, I'm pretty sure she was still in New York."

Now why didn't I think of that? It seems my thought process has been thrown off its tracks. After mentally shaking myself, I decide to go right into the heart of the matter. "Quinn, I haven't felt right about keeping you a secret from Samantha."

She glances at me with interest. "I can understand that, and I'm sorry I placed such a burden upon you, but will it suffice to say that I've got my motives?"

"Only if you are willing to understand that I'm quite protective of our mutual friend, though not as fanatically as your friend is of you," I say with just enough edge in my voice.

She draws back to better look at me. "Well, I'm glad for that. Firuz can be overbearing at times, but—"

"His heart is in the right place." I nod.

"Something along those lines. I guess I was hoping he'd be to me what you've been to Samantha." Her eyes flash as her smile widens. "I can't believe you're real after all."

The expression on her face makes me put my guard down. "Why do you say that? Is Firuz gay?"

"No, he's kind of narrow-minded when it comes to that. You know those government types. I said that because Sam was a tough nut to crack. She didn't say much and didn't talk about herself like the rest of us. We really didn't know much about her for months, but the one thing we knew was that she had a best friend in London that she visited every summer."

"I fail to see what's so difficult to believe."

Quinn nods. "The incredible part was the way she talked about you. At first, we figured you were really her boyfriend, but she went with the friend bit so she could date around. Although despite all the attention guys gave her, she never really dated anyone until Brooks."

I feel the muscles in my face stiffen at the mention of Samantha's ex-fiancé.

"Lewis, I don't mean to be ungracious, but Firuz and I have to meet with an attorney later in the day. Firuz is the only lawyer on the planet I trust, but I know nothing of international business laws." She lays her hand on my arm. "I promise I'll fill you in on the Sam I've known. I'm eager to hear about your version of her. May I?" She gestures toward the laptop.

"Of course."

She lets go of my arms and opens the screen. "I've stored some of my research in here. I want these documents available through a secure net for universities and hospitals. I want complete control over transfers of files and a way to track their visibility. I don't want any of this to fall into the hands of some tabloid jackass."

I think back on all the tabloid headlines I read earlier. I can't even imagine suffering that kind of onslaught on your privacy. "You want an intranet with limited accessibility and controlled data sharing. Will it be open to subscriptions?"

She shakes her head. "No, some of these vultures in the tabloids are very good at fabricating credentials to gain access to information. I don't want to take any chances."

"Very well."

"I also want a safeguard on my own personal information."

"Did the tabloids get access to your personal info?"

She gives me a humorless smile that enhances the sudden frosty expression. "Not exactly. My wonderful ex-husband volunteered much of my information to some bimbo working for *Famous*, who drained not only his balls, but also his head of any pertaining bit of information that concerned me. She obtained tax returns, bank statements, personal photos, and even all of my addresses. I never thought Andrew would do something like that. He claims innocence, of course." She shakes her head. "If things wouldn't turn into a three ring circus, I'd sue his pants off."

So, that's why *Famous* carries the bulk of the Fischers' divorce stories. "I'm sorry you've had to endure so much."

She looks surprised. "Thank you."

When I look into her bright blue eyes, the moment seems to charge itself and renders both of us mute. I haven't felt anything remotely close to this since I was a kid.

"Madame, your tea," the waiter announces, breaking the strange spell. "Sir."

I watch him set the steaming mug of cappuccino before me as Quinn thanks him.

What just happened...?

When she looks back at me, there's a subtle guarded veiling of her gaze, not as direct as before we lost our voices.

"Um... I'm sorry. Usually, Firuz or one of my assistants handles this type of thing but this," she taps the laptop, "is very sensitive."

"Thing?"

She seems to be wrestling with how much to say. "Actually, just about anything I need to do usually gets done by someone else. It's the way it's been for a long time, until the tabloids got interested in me. You see, usually it's an assistant conducting these meetings. This is the first thing I've done on my own in more time than I care to remember."

"I must say, I'm happy about this. I don't usually like to deal indirectly with a potential client. Their participation in the project is quite important to ensure their own satisfaction."

"I couldn't agree more. In my case, I've been having a hell of a time trusting anyone. I do trust Firuz with certain things, but this research is a bit different. It's pretty much the reason I'm here now. I needed to get away from everyone, from everything, and find a way to stand on my own again."

I'm surprised at her candor, but I sense she's surprised herself even more. "Am I to feel you don't trust me as well? I won't be offended, luv. I'm sure I can't blame you."

She smiles. "Quite the contrary." She closes the laptop and slides it over to me. "Do you have a notes app on your cell? I mean, your mobile?"

I nod and put the device on her hand. She taps the screen then composes something in the digital notepad before handing me back my mobile.

"The passcode is there."

"You're indeed playing the mysterious one. Why trust me?"

She looks into my eyes. "Because I feel like I know you, and I'm too tired of feeling alone in all this."

"You're not entirely on your own," I observe.

"Because of Firuz, you mean?" She shrugs.

"He's quite attracted to you."

She seems uncomfortable with my statement. "We've always been friends."

Not exactly what he wants, luv...

"Tell me, what exactly does a biomechanical engineer do?"

Quinn brightens. "Actually the term is a bit deceiving. It should actually be ergonomic engineer. But basically, what I do is study the relationship between the human body and different products. There's a vast range, of course. I normally work with athletes. So I've done shoe designing, pads, even track starting blocks. I work with a lot of injured athletes and help in their recovery. Some of the files I have in here," she taps the laptop, "are implants to replace damaged joints, knees, shoulders, hips, and even toes. The scope is quite broad."

I can tell Quinn is passionate about her work. "How did you get into that field?"

"There are a lot of children who sustain injuries that hinder them later, especially if they want to play sports. I didn't think enough research was being devoted to childhood injuries, therapy protocols, or even implants for children. It's a tricky science, but I felt very strongly that we ought to be taking children into account as well. I also didn't think a child should suffer due to the parent's inability to pay the exorbitant fees, so the foundation picks up the tab. Thankfully, with Firuz's help, we've been able to attract some great sponsors and contributors."

"Thank you, Quinn," Firuz says, taking the opportunity to pat her hand on the table.

So much for pretty women lacking substance, I think as I force myself to ignore the contented smile on Firuz's face. "Quinn, you've got yourself another contributor. Solutions will take care of your intranet at no cost to you."

"Oh, that's not necessary," she says, blushing fiercely now.

"I insist."

Firuz's heavy eyebrows shoot up high, but he recovers quickly, though he's clearly eager to make a more concrete agreement. "Oh, I can prepare the releases and necessary forms right away," he interjects, flashing a wide smile.

I'm willing to wager the bloke is working the figures in his head as to how much money he'll save.

Quinn places a hand on his shoulder, silently commanding him to stop then turns to me. "May I ask why?"

"I don't have children in my life, but I know two little girls that are very special to me and I'd hate to think nothing could be done if they ever wrench a knee."

Firuz drinks as he looks away unimpressed, further irritating me.

Quinn's eyes are riveted on mine. "God forbid! Are these kids your nieces, or nephews?"

"They're the two young ladies who will play the role of flower girls at Sam's wedding. I'm an honorary uncle of sorts."

I catch Firuz's bored, unimpressed expression out of the corner of my eye, but I ignore him just so I can keep my cool out of politeness for Quinn. I don't like the bloody wanker.

"We'd best be on our way, luv," Firuz says, close to her ear as though I'm no longer at the table with them.

Quinn looks at the clock on the screen of her laptop then gives me a look I'm not sure how to interpret, but it makes me feel warm inside.

"I'm afraid I've to go."

I smile as Firuz quickly stands and offers a hand to Quinn. She hands me the bag so I can help her pack the laptop, and I have to strangle the bubbling laughter when he frowns at her. Strange, but for a long moment, his eyes never leave the bag as though he cannot conceive another lad helping Quinn but him.

Not wanting to give him an advantageous position from which to look down on me, I stand too, relishing the fact that I'm a good five inches taller than the lad. I've never before experienced this level of passive animosity towards another man, but this one has more than rubbed me the wrong way.

His eyes remain on the bag, even as he shakes hands with me without uttering a word. With him out of the way, I turn my full attention to Quinn.

"I look forward to working together, Quinn."

Firuz rolls his eyes and mumbles something under his breath.

Quinn dazzles me with her smile. "You just keep getting better and better, the more I get to know you."

So do you, Quinn…

16

The next day, after a long conversation with Dave Reynolds, who runs the Liverpool office, I turn on the answering service and decide today is as good as any to move offices.

I quickly find it's so easy to take things apart, while reconfiguring an entire office is altogether differently. I'd love to give in to temptation and call my interior designer and let him deal with it all, but I need the sense of accomplishment for some reason.

It takes me an hour to figure out how to take the desk apart in a way that will allow me to move the bloody thing. To put it together, I'll need another set of hands.

Since I unplugged my sound system and the computer, I plug my mobile and run an internet radio application, which stops in the middle of Tears for Fears' "Break It Down Again". The shrill ringtone is loud out of the sound dock.

"Yes?"

"Hullo, handsome, what are you doing?"

"Samantha, my beloved, beautiful, best friend. I was hoping you'd call."

"Uh oh..."

"Care to flex your muscles in my office?"

Silence for a few seconds. "What kind of proposition is this?"

"Not those muscles, luv. I'm moving offices."

Samantha chuckles. "Pity. But if muscles you want, muscles you'll get. See you in ten."

Ten minutes later, I hear a bump on the office's outer door. When I step into the reception area, I see Samantha pinned by Jason Stephen against the glass door. His hands are supporting her weight by her buttocks and her arms are tightly wrapped around his thick neck. The lip lock goes on even when I open the door to let them in, startling both.

"Oh, hi luv!"

I shake my head at Samantha as I trade a smile with Jason. "If you need me to come back…"

Jason laughs. "Don't leave me alone with her! She's insatiable."

"For you, I am," Samantha coos in a sultry voice.

Jason kisses her lips once more then gives me a sheepish look and Samantha apologizes.

"No need to apologize. You're in love and in no condition to conduct yourself properly," I allow.

Samantha laughs, gives me a one arm hug and pulls Jason by the hand into the office.

"Wow, you never know what you accumulate until you have to move it," Jason quips when he sees the overwhelming amount of boxes filled to capacity with the contents of my office, taking up different spots on the floor.

"I don't bloody understand how I let it get to this point," I complain. "Imagine if we still kept paper files, like in the stone ages."

"You just have to get organized," Samantha remarks, but it's clear she's overwhelmed by the piles of files and loose papers littering most of the floor.

"She's speaking from experience," Jason adds. "Have you seen her new office at Lions?"

Samantha gives him a dark look.

"I couldn't get past the bloody door last time I was there," I chime in.

"I know exactly what's in each pile. What's in this one, huh?" Samantha points at a random pile.

I look helplessly at her.

"Jason, you put the furniture back together while you," she points at me, "make some sense of this mess. Whatever you haven't used for the last six months, get rid of it."

She goes to Jason and wraps her arms around his neck, pulling him down for a kiss. "I'm thinking Li Chen's, what do you think?"

"I think I'm already anticipating dessert."

"So long as you don't act out her office fantasy," I quip.

Samantha looks stunned. "Hey!"

Jason and I laugh.

"Wait, what will you do?" I ask her, knowing her penchant for weaseling out of doing heavy work.

"I'm on lunch detail. I know what you like, Lewis. I'll surprise you," she points at Jason. "I want all the furniture ready to be moved at my direction by the time I get back."

Jason walks her to the door where they kiss and wistfully look at each other for a second.

I don't blame them one bit, but a sudden pang of jealousy burns through me. I'm not jealous because I want either of them. I'm jealous because I've no one. I flash back to long conversations Terence and I shared in this very office afterhours, disliking how much I miss that.

"I'll be back in a flash," Samantha promises before going out the door.

"Go ahead, say it. I don't know why she makes such a sap out of me. I hate being away from her," Jason mutters still looking at the door.

I blink, trying to clear the images of Terence, not wanting to let nostalgia claim my mood. "Yes, she has a way of doing that. Pretty soon you'll be together every second."

Jason nods as he surveys the desk pieces and the ceramic bowl containing all the hardware.

"Any idea where you want the desk?"

"I'd prefer it against the back wall, but Samantha will make me move it so it faces the door."

Jason smiles. "I thought you were the boss of your own company."

My cheeks burn. "I am, but obviously you consent her far too much not to know her, shall we say, persuasive side."

The smile fades. "The lass knows how to throw a tantrum," he says with a pensive look.

I gather by that look, Samantha has already thrown a few at him.

He helps me move folders and pockets full of printouts out of the way near the back wall. The wooden floors are still scuffed where Terence's massive, ultramodern desk once sat and I decide to use those marks as reference points for the positioning of my more traditional desk. Jason agrees.

We fall into an easy chat about the current state of affairs of the Liverpool Reds and his football club, the Tottenham Hotspur.

"Soderbergh tells me you are quite the striker."

Jason shrugs as he props one of the legs into the frame of the desk. "I can run fast, but my dribbling ability leaves much to be desired. You did a number on Rogers from what I heard. Word is you smoked him like a cheap cigar."

This makes me laugh. The chaps at Lions make it a point to play pickup matches every Saturday. I started playing when Jason Soderbergh, another field agent for Lions, talked me into it while I was using the Lions employee's gym. Playing was far more preferable to the bloody torture devices meant to keep you in shape.

The first time I played, I realized I was in sorrowful condition, but with the help of Jason and Samantha, I can now get through an entire match without the need for bottled Oxygen.

"I wish I would've been there to see the look on Rogers's face when he got megged," Jason says on a laugh.

Megging an opponent is dribbling the ball between their legs, making them look foolish. I liked the move for its psychological value against a defender. There is more to football than chasing and kicking the ball. There is the psychological game within the game. "At the risk of bragging, it was a good move."

"None of those lads could believe how good you are."

"I wouldn't expect them to."

Jason stops fiddling with the screwdriver to look at me. "You know some of them thought gay men couldn't play. I'm glad to see you proved them different. More than I did, at least. Rogers was one of them, of course. He and I had some friction when I first started at Lions."

"Old timers always have a hard time with young fast risers."

Jason chuckles humorlessly. "He's a big homophobe. That was the main problem. I think he still wonders how Samantha and I got together."

"I've heard a few things here and there," I confess.

Like any workplace inhabited by men and women, gossip and speculation reign supreme at the proverbial water cooler, but to hear gossip about Jason was unexpected.

Jason is a war hero, a former commando of Her Majesty's SAS. Upon recovering from the wounds he sustained during an ambush at the end of the first Iraqi war, Jason left the service only to end up with an addiction to pain killers that escalated to a drug problem that eventually left him destitute.

Samantha's alluded to the fact the he even sold his body so he could buy the drugs he so desperately craved. She also mentioned another lad from the service who was always at Jason's side. After Nathan, his former Commander, found him on the streets and got him the right help. Jason emerged as one of the top field operatives for Lions.

Many of the more seasoned agents were jealous of Nathan's pride in Jason and soon dug up his past. Soon words like "queer", and "fag", began floating around in his wake. Jason didn't so much as address the rumors. He embraced them, giving his critics nowhere to go with their speculations. For some time, he even played the part. He was a common sight at gay nightclubs, though he was often playing to the crowd of divorcees and discontented wives who often sought the company of gay men.

Because he never took on a partner once he started in Lions, not even casually, no one believed Jason was gay at first, but the lack of a girlfriend in his life lessened the doubt and they had no choice but to leave him alone in ambiguity.

I know firsthand of several interns and secretaries that fanned themselves whenever Jason walked by. I admit, even I developed an attraction. It was once only physical, of course. Since getting to know him better, I have no doubt he is the type of lad I would have lost my head over if it weren't for Samantha. He's a great conversationalist. Despite his hard exterior, he has a good heart and knows how to make people laugh usually at his own expense.

With far more than a touch of embarrassment, I recall making a subtle pass at him. It was after Terence left me to go find another playmate. I knew how smitten Terence was with Jason and I couldn't think of a better revenge than taking on with him to make Terence green with envy, but the juvenile stunt backfired. The way Jason brushed off my attentions hurt me deeply, humiliating me beyond belief. I knew then that he was using my lifestyle as a bloody cover and I resented him for it. The irony is not lost on me. Is that what I've been doing for so long?

At one point, I'd fantasized of being in a room alone with Jason. Now that I am, I feel nothing but a sense of respect and the brotherly affection reserved for a dear friend. I've discovered there are many things I like about Jason Stephen. The most important is the way he loves Samantha. That's the only thing I need to hold Jason in high regard and out of my fantasies.

"I don't care what's being said about me," he says softly. "As long as they don't involve you or Sam, they can say what they want. Hand me those two bolts there, please."

I retrieve the bolts and place them in his hand. He holds a hex key between his teeth as he starts the bolts into their respective holes then begins to tighten a leg to the desk frame.

"Can I ask you something?"

"Certainly," he replies.

"I'm afraid it's not really something you'd care to answer and I feel the fool for even voicing it."

Jason stops tightening the last bolt and sits up to look me in the eye. "Lewis, I'd like to think that after how we got to this point, we are friends."

I breathe a sigh of relief. "We are. That's probably why I'm vacillating."

Jason gives me a penetrating look and sighs in resignation. "Do you want to know why I claimed to be gay?"

I nod after a moment. "It's just that, I remember seeing you at Soho, or at some of the cruises. You were a hot commodity as far as everyone knew, and everyone heard about you and that other lad from the Royal Navy."

"Taylor?"

"Yes. That's it, I couldn't recall his name."

Jason looks thoughtful for a moment then he stands, forcing me to look up at him.

"Help me move this bookcase."

We each grab an end and lift the bookcase enough to drag it towards the wall opposite the windows. I try not to grunt or beg for a break while Jason looks as comfortable as though he were holding a much lighter object, made of paper perhaps.

"Taylor was a lot like me, lost, addicted, and desperate. I knew him from my days aboard the *HMS August Charles*. He was also part of the convoy we were charged to protect."

"The convoy that was ambushed," I intuit.

He nods and leans his broad back against the bookcase, his eyes losing their focus as the past plays in his mind.

"Out of the four sailors participating in the convoy, he was the sole survivor. Taylor carried a lot of guilt because of that."

"Because he survived?"

"It's not something many would understand. You train with your lads. You sweat and bleed with them. You fight alongside them and when they die, you can't help feeling you ought to be lying next to them as well. It's as though you deserve nothing less." He hesitates for a moment. "I survived the ambush but I never saw that as anything more than the failure that it was. I lost six of my teammates that day. I felt I didn't deserve to live."

I can't even fathom thinking along those lines. Soldiers are made of a different substance than the rest of us. I don't know whether they acquire that over their training, or whether it's something they're born with.

"After our release from the hospital, Taylor and I remained close. We really had no one else to turn to but each other. He turned to me to constantly talk about what he felt about that day, when we lost his friends. I talked to him about my losses which included a girl I loved, who easily forgot about me. He lamented losing his father's respect and I lamented having grown up without a parent."

"I didn't know that."

Jason shrugs. "I had an aunt that raised me until she suffered a stroke that disabled her. I spent two years in foster care and joined the army as soon as I could."

"So you and Taylor had much in common," I say in an attempt to steer the conversation back to safer waters.

"Taylor developed feelings for me and I found such a level of comfort in him. I didn't have the heart to reject him when he openly told me how he felt. There was something about that closeness..." He looks at me. "You'd understand better than most. I didn't want to leave him alone and I didn't want to be alone at that time. Samantha thinks that I needed to feel wanted."

I pray Samantha doesn't barge in. This is a side of Jason I'd never expected to be privy to.

"I can honestly say that I loved that lad," Jason says on a sigh then shakes off a wave of emotion.

"What happened to Taylor?"

Jason's pale blue eyes shut tightly, squeezing a tear that runs down his face. "Taylor lost himself to the drugs. In the beginning, we did what we did so we could eat something other than the scraps we found in restaurants' dumpsters, but then we both were so hooked on drugs…" Jason's voice falters. "You wouldn't believe the things we did for another fix." He shakes his head. "During that winter, he left the shelter to get a fix and never returned. I nearly lost my bloody mind, Lewis. I looked for him everywhere. The anxiety shocked me out of my own fog of despair." His gaze turns cold. "I went to the police only to be physically removed out of the building. Those wankers wouldn't have some queer vagrant demanding something be done about his missing friend. I didn't care about the humiliation, but they wouldn't do anything."

I stand in silence, not knowing what to say or do.

"Tay's body was found at one of the docks in Bernie Spain Gardens a week later. If it weren't for his dog tags, no one would've ever known who he was."

"Bloody hell…"

A bitter smile creases the planes of Jason's face, producing a dimple that slices his left cheek. "When I saw an article on the bloody broadsheet, you'd think Taylor was living behind the picket fence of a quaint home in Kensington. There was no mention of living in the streets after being ignored by his own family after the war."

"I didn't mean to pry, Jason…"

He dismisses my concern with a shrug. "I lost the last person I loved and I didn't want to feel that pain again. It's taken a long time to come to terms with Taylor's death. Between you and me, the nightmares I have about Taylor have much more of a bite than the ones from the ambush in Iraq. It's just something I live with."

I'd like to confirm whether he's admitting to having been gay for that time, but I just can't do it in light of this revelation of nightmares. I can only sit in silence as he slowly composes himself.

He hasn't made an effort to wipe away the tears, which says much about him. I can't think of anyone more perfect for Samantha.

"I haven't talked about this with anyone else other than Sam. And I only talked to her because I knew she'd understand. She's had to calm me down a few times when I'd wake not knowing where I am."

"What's making you open up to me?"

He gives me a look as though it should be obvious. "Your friendship with her. I truly didn't think I'd ever tell anyone else about this." His smile is ephemeral, sad. "Samantha thinks it'd be a good idea for me to see her therapist, but I'd rather talk to a good friend."

It takes a moment for me to find my voice. "I'm inclined to agree with her. I don't know that I can be much help to you, but I'm incredibly grateful for your trust."

"You've been there, Lewis. You're the only other person I can talk to about these things, unless you'd prefer me not to."

"Not at all," I assure him.

"I think you and I have a lot more in common than you think."

I sense a tremendous significance beneath his words. Before either of us can say more, the front door rocks in its frame, prompting us to quickly walk out to the reception area where Samantha is struggling with the heavy glass door. She has both arms wrapped around two large white paper sacks. Steam curls out of one of the sacks. The glare on her pretty face is comical.

"Did you not get my bloody calls?" She demands when Jason opens the door and grabs the sacks.

"No, we never heard any ringing," I offer.

When I look for my mobile, I notice a pile of files has fallen on top of it, effectively muting any ringing.

"Mine's in the Rover, charging," Jason replies to her quizzical glare.

Samantha shakes her head. "Fine, I hope you're hungry, boys."

Back in the office, Jason and I bolt together the legs to the frame of the desk.

"Wow, you've moved two bookcases and put half of the desk together. I'm not very impressed, lads."

"We were talking, Sam. Besides, you appointed yourself furniture coordinator. We weren't going to move anything without your approval," I tell her.

Samantha looks from me to Jason, back to me. "What were you talking about?"

"Men business," Jason says with an irrepressible grin.

Samantha stares at him, mouth agape. "No secrets between husband and wife," she finally chastises, wagging her finger in his direction.

Jason walks up to her to kiss her forehead. "We're not there yet, luv."

"I can get it out of you," she purrs suggestively, turning her face up.

To his credit, Jason puts a finger on her lips and gently pushes her back. "You're incorrigible."

"She's not going to forget, you know," I call to Jason as I gather the hardware for the other side of the desk.

"We'll see…" Jason growls in Samantha's ear, making her swoon.

"Not fair," she moans.

After sharing a little peck, they finally separate to join me at the now assembled desk, where I open all the containers from Li Chen's.

The air in the office becomes redolent with ginger, shallot, garlic, and sesame oil. I look contentedly at the heaping paper platter of shrimp fried rice. Samantha stirs a steaming container of Wonton soup that makes my mouth water. Jason immediately attacks the spring rolls and a container of Dou Ban Yu. I cringe as he adds more of the lethal Chinese version of hot sauce in the already acidic dish.

"You had no idea what to order, did you, lass?"

Samantha sips soup noisily from her plastic spoon, fanning her open mouth. Worst table manners ever, this one.

"Woah! That's steamy!" She takes a drink of ice water. "No, I just anticipated some big appetites from my two hardworking lads."

"She's fattening me up to win the marathon next April," Jason quips.

"I believe it," I agree with him.

"Honey, I can easily engage you in plenty of activity to keep your body nice and hard, just the way I like it. I'm still winning that race though."

When she digs into the Lo Mein, I start laughing, earning a dark look from her.

"Don't you have a gown to fit into?"

"Do you wish to wear this soup?"

Jason laughs around a mouthful of spicy fish. "You two are worse than brother and sister."

"So what were you talking about while I was gone, hunting for food like a good little lioness?"

Jason and I exchange a look that she doesn't miss.

"Was it about me?"

"No, Miss Center of the Universe," Jason says softly. "We were discussing the Reds and the Spurs."

"Oh. Football, of course," Samantha says dejectedly as she stabs a shrimp out of my plate.

I content myself with listening to Samantha go on and on, debating the color scheme of her wedding. She demands we pick between the ice blue chosen by Alicia, and the vivid tangerine tango Lorna Matthews suggested.

Jason makes the mistake of choosing a color without first formulating a reason for his choice, and Samantha makes mincemeat out of him for his lack of consideration.

I gently try to nudge her towards the tangerine, citing all of Lorna's arguments yet again. Samantha listens at length, but I know she isn't really hearing me.

After consuming most of the fare, Samantha volunteers to clean up while Jason and I go back to setting up the modular bookcases. I'm almost too full to move, but this office won't rearrange itself.

"Do you think she's cross?" Jason asks after Samantha leaves to take the trash out to the alley bins.

"Not at all. She's trying to make up her mind."

Jason is holding two bolts between his lips, making me wonder whether he suffers from some form of oral fixation. He pulls one to attach the keyboard tray under the desk, then the other.

"What do you think I should've said about choosing the blue?"

"For starters, you first need to refer to it as Ice Blue, so she knows you've been paying attention. Secondly, if you had mentioned that the color matches her eyes, she would've felt you truly cared enough to take a bigger picture into consideration."

Jason looks dumbfounded. "So, you're saying my, 'because I like it' wasn't good enough."

"For Sam? Not at all."

Jason considers this for a long moment with a grimace. "Next time you should be the one to answer first. I'll follow your lead."

I have to laugh at that. "Sam will see right through the charade."

Jason shakes his head. "Sometimes, I don't know how to talk to her. Not like you do."

"Entirely different relationship, chap."

"Well, I wish you'd teach me just how to communicate well with her."

I listen for any sign of Samantha but with the elevators down, it'll take her a few more minutes to get back up. "There is no trick, Jason. Listen to each word she says, be aware of the way she says those words, and go along with her emotions. Don't point out she's wrong, especially when she is. Give her a chance to come to that realization on her own terms, and when she does, don't take the I-told-you-so stand. Be soothing and encourage her."

"Easier said than done, she can be a bloody test when she puts her mind to it," he gripes.

"I bloody heard that!" Samantha protests from the doorway, arms crossed, tapping her foot. Leave it to her to run up the bloody steps for fear of missing something.

Jason sighs wearily. "I rest my case."

I laugh as Samantha drapes herself over Jason's shoulder and pretends to choke him.

"You'll pay for that, mister."

"Oh yeah?"

Jason reaches back and easily flips Samantha onto his lap. His fingers dig into her ribs and she explodes in a fit of giggles as he mercilessly tickles her.

I watch them awash in a wave of envy. They look so bloody happy. From that point on, as enjoyable as the rest of the afternoon is, something gnaws at my mind.

Just as the sun gives way to twilight, we finish setting up the office furniture. I'm tempted to simply incinerate every bloody file littering the floor since I've no idea what's in them.

The three of us share tea at Fox's in lieu of a stiff drink at the pub before saying our goodnights. We stand at a high table across from the booth I shared with Quinn McDermont. I almost wish she'd be there again, this time without her "friend".

"You know we'd go with you tomorrow if it weren't for the appointment with the florist, right? I messaged Gwen and she replied that it's fine. She said so."

"I know, Sam. I'll bring them to Nathan's straight from the airport," I tell her, referring to Gwen and her little girls, who arrive tomorrow.

"Is it really important for us to be looking at flowers instead of...?" Jason inquires, realizing his mistake as soon as Samantha's expression darkens. "Of course it is."

"I'm not going to be able to sleep tonight." Samantha's expression turns anxious.

"Just remember, keep an eye on her shoulders and block the punch. Hop back a few steps and jab with your right," Jason offers with a sorry attempt at keeping a straight face, making me laugh.

"That's not even funny!"

I shake my head. "She's not going to strike you, Sam."

She looks far from convinced.

"I'll text you as soon as their flight touches down, luv."

She nods. "Alright."

"Thank you both for all your help."

Samantha hugs me and Jason and I face each other aware that we've become closer friends after today.

"Thank you, Jason."

Samantha looks lovingly at each of us.

"Not at all, chap." Jason offers me his right hand. "That's what friends are for."

17

I sit at a booth in Ellie's Café in the concourse of Heathrow Airport, sipping a tolerable cup of black tea when my mobile chimes and lights up the display screen. There's a text telling me the British Airways flight out of New York City has landed. I drink the rest of the tea, throw the cup away, and key in a text.

Sam, Gwen landed, I'll see you at Nathan's

I'm shoving the mobile into my pocket when I feel it buzz. When I look at the screen, I have to roll my eyes at the reply. It's an emoticon, a yellow globe with big shocked eyes and a small, perfect black circle for a mouth. I'm willing to wager she's shaking herself to pieces with anticipation.

My heart is racing a bit. Perhaps Samantha is not the only one feeling pangs of anxiety.

I find a spot near the gate and stare through the glass at the people emerging from the plane until I see a bouncing, light brown bob instead of the usual ponytail Emily favored when I saw her last.

She looks slightly taller than I remember her. She's dressed like a charming little doll in a pink and brown skirt and matching top. Her little arms are wrapped around a plush Hello Kitty. Emily stops, raises her head and turns around. I can't hear Gwen but I know she's called her.

A moment later I see her and her oldest daughter, Brooke, each of them towing a wheeled suitcase. With a matching bob and an elegant pair of eyeglasses, Brooke looks decidedly older than her eight years.

Some of the people emerging from the gate halt and look around for a moment before breaking into a smile and running into welcoming embraces. Others simply keep their eyes on whatever electronic device they hold in their hands and wordlessly walk off, oblivious to everything and everyone around them.

"Lewis?"

I wave at Brooke and smile. I can't believe she's only eight. Her willowy frame has an innate grace and fluidity of movement that's rare in a child.

"Mom! Mom, it's Lewis!" Brooke exclaims before nearly running her little sister over with her suitcase. She shuffles quickly in my direction, drops the handle of her luggage and jumps into my arms.

"Blimey, little lady, you are stronger than the last time I saw you."

"I couldn't wait to see you!" Her arms get tighter around me.

Swallowing a lump of emotion, I kiss the top of her head and straighten up to be dazzled by Gwen's radiant smile that I don't feel worthy of.

The smile falters a bit as her blue eyes fill with tears. Barely stifling a sob, she throws her arms around me after I let go of Brooke.

"I know, luv. I know," I say soothingly as I gently pat her back and stroke her long brown hair. I can only guess at the emotions coursing through Gwen at this moment. My heart is riding its own tempest. "I should've never allowed her to leave without talking to you first. I feel utterly responsible and I can only hope you find it in your heart to forgive us, Gwen."

Gwen nods on my shoulder, her whole body trembling as she cries.

"I'm just happy to see you again," she says in a quivering voice.

Emily looks up at me with honey-brown eyes, wide with alarm. I wink at her and she smiles shyly before hiding behind Gwen's leg.

"Why did you leave without saying goodbye?" Brooke inquires with the forthrightness of childhood we all lose as we grow older, her hazel gaze piercing and direct.

"Because I knew I'd see you again, young lady."

"You did?"

"Yes, I did."

Brooke looks suspicious but nods, satisfied with my answer. If only it were that easy with her mother.

Gwen draws back, dabbing at her eyes. She gives me a nervous smile and looks around with interest.

"I'm sorry, honey. I didn't think I was going to fall to pieces like this. It's not like I haven't talked about everything with Samantha."

"You and I never really did though," I observe.

She hugs me again, tight. "I don't need to talk about anything that happened. I'm here, aren't I?"

I return the embrace, hoping my voice won't break when I speak. "And you won't ever know how glad I am, luv."

I hold her through one last bout of tears while Brooke and Emily patiently wait. I wonder if they somehow anticipated this moment and understand its significance.

Gwen squeezes me one final time and releases me. Her mascara is a bit smudged, but she quickly fixes that.

"Ready?"

She nods as her eyes dart around. "This place is huge. How am I going to find the baggage claim?"

"Fret not, luv. I already sent someone to fetch your luggage. Unless you or the girls need to visit the loo, I'm taking you to Kensington where all your belongings will be waiting for you."

"Mom said you drive on the wrong side of the road," Brooke says with a little incredulous smile.

"We drive the right way, little luv. It's the rest of the world that's wrong."

I feel a tug on my trousers and I look down to see Emily staring up at me. "Yes, littler luv?" In response, she extends her arms in the universal "pick me up" command. "Why, certainly. Shoulder ride?"

She nods, her little lips curving up into a devilish grin.

"That is, as long as your mum and big sis don't need my help with their bags."

"We're fine," Gwen says as she works to smooth her brown hair back down. "Please, take that one. Keep her for as long as you need to."

Emily rides on my shoulders like a sultan's daughter riding on her royal camel along with Hello Kitty. By the time we make it out to the lot, I find a deep well of sympathy for camels all over the world. Emily has definitely grown since I last saw her.

I keep stealing surreptitious glances at Gwen for some indicator of her mood but she gives me precious little. She must be a world class poker player. There's too much background noise to conduct a conversation so I engage Brooke and Emily into telling me about the flight. They chatter incessantly until we are out of the terminal.

When we're near my car, I hit the fob and open the boot. Brooke and Emily run to the BMW and stare in awe.

While Gwen secures the girls in the back seat, I put the two carry on pieces in the boot of the car and climb behind the wheel. Gwen hands the girls their handheld videogames, but they show little interest, their eyes taking in their surroundings.

"We might be lucky enough to have a quiet ride," Gwen offers with a smile.

"How was the flight?"

"Wonderful! I probably should've never accepted the first class treatment. I don't think I can ever go back to less than that."

"Well, now that your husband is on his way to making it big, your days in coach may just be behind you. How's Tony doing?"

Gwen's eyes flash with pride. "He's still in shock with everything."

Tony's first novel is on its way to becoming a television teen drama, and the production team wanted him to oversee the character development. Since the debut of his book *The Composition*, published with Samantha's efforts, the Amaya's lives have been forever changed.

"They're filming the pilot in Wilmington, North Carolina."

"Amazing. Any known actors?"

Gwen thinks for a moment. "Not really, maybe one of the teachers is someone somewhat known, but the director wanted all new faces. I heard there were a few kids from the Disney shows auditioning for parts. It's so surreal."

"Will he come to Sam's wedding?"

"I hope he can. He really doesn't know."

A part of me is just fine with Tony not making it to the wedding. He and Samantha have quite the history, and I fear how things would play out with him around. I know my best friend far too well to believe she's completely come to terms with her role in Tony Amaya's life.

On second thought, after seeing the numerous public displays of affection and the way she stares at Jason, Samantha may have finally put her feelings for Tony to rest. "Let's hope for the best, luv."

Gwen turns in her seat to check on the girls. They're looking out the windows, commenting on the strange-looking cars driving on the wrong side of the road.

I thought about taking on the role of tour guide and point out a few sights to Gwen, but one look at her and it's clear she's not really seeing the scenery. "Is everything alright?"

Gwen shifts in her seat. "One of my best friends back home thinks I'm crazy to be here after everything that happened."

I give her a quick look, trying to judge her mood, but to no avail. "Truthfully, I think you're simply mad to be here after everything that happened."

The day is actually sunny and clear. The grounds of Osterley look quite picturesque from the M4 motorway, but it all seems lost on Gwen, making me uneasy.

"Gwen," I say softly, reaching for her hand. She laces her fingers with mine, just one friend looking for comfort in another. "I don't presume to diminish the turmoil you must have surely gone through in the aftermath of the attack, but I will say that no one, and I mean no one, felt as badly as Sam did."

Her right hand squeezes mine, while her left clears away the tears that have streaked down her lovely face. "How badly?"

Her voice is flat, giving me a tiny glimpse into the depth of her resentment. I don't intend to find Samantha forgiveness by making excuses for her, but I have a feeling I won't have to. Gwen wouldn't be here if she were holding a major grudge. Would she?

No, I decide. Despite her wounded feelings and resentment, I just know she will come to truly forgive Samantha. "Please don't think I'm only going to tell you this because she is my best friend," I warn her. "By the time we landed, I was beyond terrified Samantha would hurt herself. I remember thinking she'd never been so despondent, not even after the death of her parents. You've come to mean the world to her and each day that passed without contact was sheer torment on her."

"I'm sorry. I'm so sorry. I just didn't get a chance to vent at her, you know? It was bad enough that I had to hold it all in while Tony recovered."

"And once he did?" I prompt her, though I can already see the answer to that.

Her expression is so cold, I shiver.

"Oh, I fired both barrels at him."

Hell hath no fury... "I can't imagine you angry," I lie.

"Angry would've been easy, Lewis. I felt nothing. I could actually see the pleading look in his face and I felt absolutely nothing." She sighs with regret. "I didn't share my bed with him until recently."

The cold glint of her normally warm gaze freezes my blood. Time to take this conversation in a different direction. "Are you going for the right, or the left?"

Gwen seems to shake herself back into the moment. "Huh?"

"Which eye are you punching?"

She squints as though trying to figure out whether I've completely lost my bonk, but then understanding softens her face and she laughs. "Oh, I don't think I could pick one. I may just pulverize every bone in her body."

"Do you need me to hold her down?"

We are still laughing when a little voice registers from the back seat. It's Brooke.

"What, baby?"

"I said, who are you punching, Mom?"

"Hey! Punching is not nice," Emily chides.

Gwen smiles at them. "Em is right, punching is not nice. I'm not punching anyone, honey."

Phew!

"Are we there yet?" Emily inquires in such a hopeful little voice that inadvertently makes me floor the accelerator.

"We'll be there in a few minutes, ladies," I reply.

"Woah! Look at that house!" Brooke exclaims.

"Wow!" Emily shares the sentiment.

Gwen is staring out the window at one of the mansions along Queensworth Boulevard.

"Oh, dear God!"

Just past the opulent edifice that caught her eye is another breathtaking estate that elicits more admiring exclamations from my three passengers.

At the end of Queensworth, I turn into the Jeffries' drive. I slow down to a crawl, enjoying the wide-eyed stares as we roll on the crushed stone. The drive veers right then meanders back revealing the large portico of Nathan Jeffries' estate.

I pull around the fountain and notice one of the large double doors opening. Samantha stands at the doorway, her posture radiating trepidation.

The girls are already unbuckling their seat belts, positively shaking from excitement. I can't imagine being that small, so full of energy, and forced to endure an entire day of traveling. These little dynamos needed to do some major energy spending.

Gwen seems not to share in her girls' excitement. "Gwen?"

Her smile wavers a little. "I'm okay. I was just thinking that whatever the case, Samantha did save my husband. I'll try to focus on that."

"If it helps, she also got Tony's novel where it is," I suggest, thinking Samantha needs all the help she can get.

"Boy, you *are* her best friend."

I pull the mobile I purchased earlier at the airport and hand it to her. "This has my number, Sam's, Jason's, Nathan's and Alicia's. Anything you need, don't hesitate to call."

"Thank you, Lewis. You're the best."

"Not at all, luv. So long as this little reunion doesn't turn into a catfight, we can talk more later."

"I'd love that," she says as she absentmindedly cracks her knuckles, leaving me to wonder what she's looking forward to, the talk or the catfight.

"Samantha!" Emily squeals.

Brooke opens the door and both girls are out of the car like a shot. They make a beeline for Samantha, who crouches down and is nearly run over by Emily.

Samantha hides her face over Brooke's shoulder, but she can't hide the racking sobs that shake her whole body.

I want to run around and open the door for Gwen, but she's already out and slowly walking towards Samantha.

"Blimey, both of you are so adorable! I've missed you so much!"

"Why are you crying?" Emily asks with severity.

"Are you crying tears of joy?"

"Today I am, Brookie. I'm crying happy tears because I get to see my two little luvs once more."

Brooke and Samantha lean their foreheads together. It looks as though neither wants to let go.

"Mom says you had an emergency. That's why you didn't come say goodbye."

Samantha strokes Brooke's hair. The gesture reminds me of her mother doing the same thing after Samantha fell and scraped her knee. The memory makes me feel hollow.

"I hope you forgive me one day. But I knew I'd see you again," Samantha soothes.

Brooke smiles. "That's what Lewis said when I asked."

Samantha glances at me with a smile. "So, how was that long, dreadful flight?"

The girls start chattering about every part of the trip until Samantha gently begs them to allow her to say hello to Mommy. Both girls relent, not without hesitation.

"Hey," I call to them. "Who wants to make a wish on the fountain?"

"Me!" The girls call out in unison as they sprint for the fountain.

Gwen and Samantha give me a grateful look then turn to face each other. I quickly dig out some shillings and a few pennies, which Brooke and Emily take before running off, throwing a "thank you!" over their shoulder.

I watch them stop at the edge of the fountain, frozen in thought as they make their wishes. I look back, at Gwen and Samantha, not knowing what to expect.

Samantha has her long chestnut hair in a ponytail. Even in a form-fitting track suit, she has an undeniable elegance, but I can tell she's as nervous as a fox at the sound of barking hounds.

Gwen stands a few inches taller. A slight breeze plays with the layers of her dark brown hair. She sweeps her bangs to one side with her hand and I see her blue eyes are filled with emotion. Her legs are gracefully long, making her faded jeans look far more stylish than their designer probably intended.

I hold my breath wondering what's the first thing they'll say to each other. I knew they had been chatting online, as well as trading letters on a daily basis, but it's easy to omit certain feelings on a letter.

Samantha has a phobia of being judged, and she possesses an affinity for reading facial expressions. With this in mind, I can only stare from one to the other. The tension is as tangible as the ground beneath my feet.

"Welcome to the Queen's land?" Samantha says in a shaky voice as her eyes fill with tears.

By employing the line I suggested for her to say when seeing Gwen again, I realize how frayed her nerves must be.

Gwen seems to have gone rigid. She doesn't reply, but continues to stare at Samantha and because her hair effectively conceals her eyes from my vantage point, I can't even guess at what may be going through her mind.

As though reaching a conclusion after some inner debate, Gwen's shoulders sag and she slowly shakes her head, a tremulous smile turning the corners of her lips.

"Come here, you, stupid bitch," she says, almost sobbing each word.

I don't even blink, wondering what the context of her words is. Samantha smiles warmly through tears and approaches Gwen, her head hanging down.

The two beauties look into each other's eyes once more then embrace, their shoulders bobbing under the assault of their emotions.

The tears are flowing freely now.

Oh, yes. Gwen and Samantha are crying too.

I can't believe how good it feels to breathe again. Samantha is blubbering through a series of tearful apologies, while Gwen just holds her.

"I'll sleep with Jason and we'll call it even," Gwen says and Samantha nods.

I can only roll my eyes.

I approach both women and wrap my arms around their necks. "Since there won't be a bloodbath, I suggest we take this inside, ladies."

They each lean their faces on my shoulders, half laughing, and half crying. My eyes fall on their clasped hands and my mind quickly flashes through time since Samantha wrote that first letter to Gwen.

What a friendship. What an incredible friendship...

18

Who knew that you could cry more from joy than from sadness?

The sight of Gwen and Samantha carrying a conversation as though they're long lost sisters reunited is so heartwarming I can't keep my eyes dry. I even helped Margaret make grilled cheese sandwiches for the girls, and tea for the women, who had yet to let go of each other's hand.

Each time I walk in the library to find them smiling at each other, I feel things are as complete as they have ever been.

The laughter of children has not echoed within Nathan's beautiful home since Samantha and I were kids. It's music to my ears, and apparently to Margaret's as well.

Aware that Samantha and Gwen have quite a few things to iron out, Margaret, Nathan's lovable housekeeper, and I take it upon ourselves to entertain the young guests.

Margaret had asked Samantha for a dinner plan for Gwen and her girls, and in turn, Samantha asked me for help. We suggested an entire shopping list of sweets and cakes, but Margaret, who raised three children, scoffed at our suggestions and offered to take care of everything on her own. I've wondered what she meant and I'm finally getting an answer. Margaret has gone above and beyond by planning a few activities for the girls and preparing a list of nutritious, yet tasty, kids' meals. But for the time being, she caters to their insatiable taste for treats.

The mere mention of cookies sends up a wave of giggling and squealing from the two little beauties, particularly from Emily, now five years old, a small replica of her mother in every aspect, except for the large dark Latin eyes of her father.

"How would you like to be my assistant bakers for the evening?" Margaret asks.

Brooke and Emily look to their mother for approval with wide eyes and hopeful glances. I don't wait for Gwen's answer, I simply usher the kids into the large kitchen, where Margaret presents each with an apron.

"Look! It's just my size!" Emily claps happily as she hangs the apron over her neck. "Can you tie it for me?"

"Why, certainly, little luv," Margaret says in a voice I've never heard her use.

"Do you need help, Brooke?" I ask.

Brooke graces me with a lopsided smile that produces two, impossibly deep dimples. She is tall for an eight-year-old, and unlike the few little girls I've ever come across, who suffer that awkward stage as they go from little kids into big kids, Brooke Amaya is well on her way to becoming quite an attractive, graceful pre-teen. My heart goes out to her father.

I watch her pull a hairband from a little backpack to hold her hair back, transforming her into a kid version of Audrey Hepburn.

"That's okay, I can tie it myself, thank you," she says sweetly.

Emily calls my name and twirls, modeling her apron for me.

"Why, you look ready to bake a fine pastry, luv."

The corners of her dark eyes tilt upward, along with her tiny lips. She's so irresistibly adorable.

"Where's your apron?" Emily asks with severity.

"Yeah, where's your apron? You're going to bake with us too, aren't you?" Brooke adds.

"Where's my apron?" I echo. "Margaret, darling, where is my apron?"

"I don't believe this is such a good idea, but who am I to keep another set of hands from helping?" Margaret muses as she goes to a cabinet.

She pulls a folded apron out of the drawer and hands it to me. Once I cinch it tight, I look expectantly at her. "You're the boss, luv."

For the next hour, I learn the intricacies of the sugar cookie under Margaret's careful instruction. Brooke and Emily mix eggs, flour, and sugar in a bowl. They take turns rolling the dough and we carefully shape our cookies with an assortment of cutters before Margaret slides the trays into the industrial size oven. When the first batch is baked and cool enough to touch, Margaret produces an array of colored sprinkles and tubes of icing, and the girls prove quite artistic at decorating each treat.

I pretend I don't know what I'm doing, and both girls laugh at my feigned inability as they coach me through the process of making smiley faces on a cookie.

I've never seen Margaret smile so much, despite the many times I've spoiled the old bird by treating her like royalty.

We're decorating our fifth batch of cookies, when Samantha and Gwen walk into the kitchen.

"Oh, something smells wonderful!" Gwen says on a breathy voice, basking in the sweet fragrance of freshly baked sugary dough.

Brooke and Emily chatter about their creations, accurately narrating every detail of the last hour. I could listen to those voices forever.

Samantha picks up a cookie and takes a bite. "Mmmmm! These are delicious."

"Don't eat too many, you've a gown to wear," I warn.

Samantha sticks out her tongue, but I don't see her take another cookie after that. I notice that Gwen puts a cookie back on the cooling tray. The pout on her face makes me laugh.

"Flour looks good on you, Lewis," Gwen says pointing at one of her high cheekbones.

When I touch my face, my fingers turn white. "Just a little bit of flour. No harm."

Gwen and Samantha laugh.

"Lewis?"

"Yes, Emily, my luv. What is it?"

"I'm sorry about my hands."

I'm not sure I understand, but it's obviously of some importance, for everyone laughs, even Margaret.

"Your hands?" I ask, taking one of those dainty hands in mine. I can barely believe there are actual bones in those tiny fingers.

"Not my hands," Emily points at my legs. "Those hands."

When I look where she's pointing I see a series of white, powdery hand prints practically running the length of my—no longer black—trousers. "Oh, those hands."

I turn back to Emily, who is regarding me with an impish grin. "Fret not, little luv," I tell her and gently flick her tiny button nose, leaving a white streak.

"Em! Lewis put flour on you!" Brooke tattles.

I'm shocked at the desire for retribution I see clearly etched in Emily's eyes.

"Uh oh," I quip and run around the table with Emily hot on my tail.

Brooke blocks my way and I stop and feel Emily launching herself at my legs and I go down in a giggling heap with both girls amidst a cloud of flour.

***

Margaret makes a healthy looking salad for the women, who reason they can gobble up more cookies as a reward for being so conscientious about their caloric intake.

I catch both little girls yawning frequently, even Gwen looks bushed. "The overnight flight must just be registering in them."

She nods. "I thought it'd be easiest for them. I figured we could sleep during the flight, and we did a little bit, but the girls were too excited so they're probably too tired to even realize." She yawns behind her arm.

"Looks like they're not the only ones done in," I observe.

"I asked Margaret to help me block out the windows in your bedroom. Sleep as long as you can. We can do our all-night girl talk later," Samantha offers.

"Sounds good to me, thanks."

Samantha is quite familiar with the effects of travel, so she and Gwen take the little ones to bed. As exhausted as they seem, it takes another hour for their excitement to tamp down after checking out every part of what will be their bedroom for the next twelve days or so. As promised, their luggage is waiting at the foot of their beds. Gwen is staying in an adjacent bedroom that can be accessed from the girls' room through an adjoining bathroom.

I volunteer to read to the little ones and urge Gwen to rest. She gives me a tight hug and kisses my cheek. Her dazzling smile leaves me with a grin of my own. The scent of her body lotion that tickles my nose is so intoxicating that I take a few deep breaths to steady myself. It reminds me of Quinn McDermont.

Barely four pages into *Green Eggs and Ham*, Brooke and Emily close their eyes and they're off to dreamland. I tuck the covers around them and lay a gentle kiss on their foreheads nearly overcome by a wave of tenderness.

I can't remember ever feeling so alive, so full of purpose. I even allow myself to think of things I never considered.

Gwen left me with a nightlight that I plug into an outlet on the wall. I debate whether to close the drapes. Dusk is just beginning to make its appearance, so it's still pretty bright out.

"Are you that much of a bore, luv?"

I smile at the sound of Samantha's voice. "They went out like a light. When was the last time you fell asleep that deep, that quickly?"

Samantha steps into the room to stand at my shoulder. "I can't remember." There's a soft smile on her face as she looks at the sleeping faces. "Tony says hello. Gwen chatted with him just to let him know everyone arrived safe and sound."

We stand there for a long moment, watching the girls sleep. I don't need psychic abilities to know what's going through Samantha's mind.

Motherhood was taken away from my best friend before she ever got a chance to long for it. She suffered an infection that rendered her ovaries inert when she was only fifteen.

She's never mentioned a desire to have children before, but I know deep down, she'd love nothing more than to have a child of her own. I don't dare voice some hopeful sentiment. The pain of that particular wound is eternal.

"Jason and I talked about adopting," Samantha says softly.

I sense she's working herself up to elaborating, so I say nothing, but I smile so she knows I don't feel the idea is crazy.

"I always want those things I can't have."

I put my arm around her shoulders and she leans into me. My heart breaks when I feel the shudders that tell me she's crying.

"One step at a time, luv," I say in as comforting a tone as I can muster.

Samantha dabs at her eyes and gently pulls out of my embrace. She motions for me to follow her and we reluctantly leave the two sleeping beauties.

"Gwen fell asleep just as quick."

I feel a wave of disappointment, though I completely understand. I couldn't imagine traveling an entire day, alone with two children. "If I'd known Tony wasn't coming with them, I would've gladly gone to help her."

Samantha smiles at me. "You're sweet."

We walk down the hallway towards Samantha's room. "We should go down to the library, luv."

Samantha raises a curious eyebrow at me.

"What? Sound carries pretty well up here."

"Okay…" She acquiesces.

Before she grills me over my sudden concern for sound travel, I head for the spiral staircase leaving her no choice, but to follow.

"Is Jason joining you soon?"

"Not until later. He's conducting a class in Richmond."

"How about Nathan and Alicia?"

"They'll be here by morning. Their conference in Geneva took an extra day."

I sit on an old leather couch and Samantha joins me, her gaze studies me closely.

"What?" I ask, unable to bear her scrutiny any longer.

"You weren't worried about our voices waking up the girls. What is it?"

"I'm just being considerate. You never know when you'll begin cackling like a hyena. To a small child, it could prove quite frightening."

"If you dodge my question again, I will bite you like a bloody hyena," she says, folding her arms and narrowing her eyes. "What is it?"

Sometimes, her intimate knowledge of me can be a disadvantage. "I felt a bit funny about being in your room."

Samantha barks an incredulous laugh. "Since when?"

"I don't want Brooke to get the wrong idea."

She twists her face into a mask of pure frustration. "Be serious."

Her persistence is something I normally admire, but right now, I find it maddening. "How did it go?"

"With Gwen?"

"No, with the bloody Queen of England."

She slaps my shoulder. "You need a new bloody line."

I watch her tuck one leg beneath her, and bring the other folded up so she can rest her chin on her knee. It's beyond me how she's able to contort that way and appear to comfortably settle in for a long talk. "We talked about the wedding. She wanted to know how it all happened."

"Okay, I'm familiar with that story," I quickly interrupt her before I have to hear another syrupy version of Jason's proposal. "What about your sneaking away from the hospital after Tony was shot?"

Samantha purses her lips in thought. "We've gone over that in our letters. Basically, you were right. Gwen wants us to look ahead."

"She was quite nervous about seeing you."

"I was petrified of seeing her."

"When she called you a stupid bitch, I thought her fist was going to smash your eye next."

Samantha's eyes seem to lose their focus. "I wanted her to. That was the first time in all this time that I wanted a drink."

I take a deep breath and place my hand upon hers. "I'm glad you didn't give in, luv."

She looks a bit shaken. It breaks my heart, but I can't allow her to keep thinking of self-recriminations.

Perhaps it's time that I join the "Look Ahead" philosophy. It's clear these two have worked through their feelings. Hopefully Samantha has done enough penance. I don't believe I have to wonder about Gwen. Despite the short time I've known her, she really is a class act. "Enough of the deep stuff. What's the plan for tomorrow?"

"Jason is taking the day off. We'll take Gwen and the girls sightseeing, and hopefully to get their gowns properly fitted."

I was about to invite myself until she mentioned the gown bit.

"Will you join us?"

I was planning on getting started on Quinn's intranet, but I can't tell her that. "How about you bring everyone by my place for dinner, or we can have an after-dinner gathering. I'd like Gwen to meet Mum."

Samantha smiles. "Sounds splendid!"

"Sam, I need to talk to you."

Her posture subtly changes at the severity of my voice. "What is it?"

"It's about Terence."

Her indrawn breath is like water receding from a beach that's about to get hit by a tsunami. She laces her fingers as though bracing herself for some unwanted truth.

"Is he bloody calling you, asking you to meet him because he misses you?"

"No."

The relief in her eyes is only minimal.

"I went cruising in Richmond, ran into an old friend who told me a few things about Terence."

She looks a bit put off, though the reason evades me. I proceed to tell her about Carmen Santopietro and everything the old queen told me. Samantha listens attentively and I sense she is trying to detect whether I want Terence back in my life. She grows slightly more relieved as she realizes that's not the case then nearly panics when I tell her about the punk trying to mug me.

"I really don't want you going to those bloody places."

"Fret not, luv. I probably won't."

"Probably?"

"Definitely."

"So, any action with this friend of yours?"

I feel a wave of revulsion. "Carmen is in his seventies, Sam."

She makes a face.

"You know, the strange thing is that when I was talking to Carmen, I couldn't help noticing how dreadfully ridiculous he looks, or how lonesome he is. I mean, I have no doubt that he can impress some drunken chicken enough to bed him, but overall, his existence is depressingly lonely."

"When you say chicken, what do you mean?"

"Oh, it means young lad."

"Eww."

"I agree."

"What makes you think he's lonesome?"

"When the Joni Mitchell impersonator began playing again, Carmen shuffled over to a group sitting on the grass and sort of invited himself. He kept his eyes straight forward, like he was just staring at the singer, but I got the feeling it was more to keep from seeing the disdainful glares from some of those blokes around him. Think about it, Carmen Santopietro probably has more money than you can imagine, yet he's cruising for trade, or for companionship, I don't know, but the point is, he's got no one."

"When you say trade…"

"It means sex," I tell her. "Carmen must have had a thousand lovers in his lifetime, but he's alone. The false lashes, the lustrous wigs, the elaborate makeup; all of that might have had some allure when he was in his twenties or thirties even, but he's an old man. A very lonely old man."

Samantha is taken aback by my passionate delivery. She stares at me curiously, probably wondering where I'm coming up with this stuff.

"You truly care for this Carmen, don't you?"

"It's not that," I say, frustrated. "I mean, he's one of the most benevolent people you'll ever come across, but he's made his life into what it is, right?"

She draws back. "I don't think I understand, luv."

The sight of that grey stubble on the wrinkled jowls of Carmen's face is something I desperately wish to eradicate from my mind. "I almost felt like I was staring into a mirror, a mirror that was showing me a future version of myself."

Samantha slides closer and takes my hand. "Look at me."

It's a struggle to compose myself, but eventually I do as she says.

"That'll never be you. Okay?"

"Sam, it's not that I'm planning on going drag or anything like that. I just don't want to live a lonesome life when I get old."

"You won't," she says with conviction.

I shake my head. "I'm going to say a few things to you, but I want your promise that you won't turn this around to be about you."

She looks more concerned than upset, and I'm so thankful for that.

"I don't want you to feel guilty, or harbor the erroneous notion that I somehow hold you responsible for whatever this is. Promise me, Sam."

She looks into my eyes for a moment. "Very well. I promise."

My shoulders sag in relief as I fervently hope she keeps this promise. I think I've been feeling like I can't talk to her the way I used to. "I know I have you, okay? I know you'll always be a part of my life and I'll always love you for it."

She nods, silently encouraging me to go on.

"But you're getting married Sam. You and Jason will soon build a life together and I can't, and won't, in good conscience be a constant interloper. I won't presume to burden you with my problems because you'll be having problems of your own. But you'll never face those things alone again. You have Jason now."

"Lewis—"

"I just…" my voice trails off. "I don't know," I whisper as I hang my head under a weight of some unnamed emotion.

Samantha shifts on the couch and drapes her arm around me. "It's almost impossible for me not to make this about me."

"You promised," I remind her.

"I did. I'm keeping that promise."

"You'd better."

We sit in silence and I can't help thinking how much I'm going to miss these moments.

"What do you want out of life?" Samantha asks.

"Out of life?"

"Remember that nice chap that took me to dinner when I first moved back?"

I search my memory until a name comes up. "Joshua something. The professor you met at the old book shop."

"Yes, Joshua. He asked me that question. I didn't have an answer. I don't know that I ever will, but it gave me quite a bit to think about."

"Did he have an answer?"

She nods. "Children."

"Oh."

"I guess we all want someone to grow old with, as cliché as that sounds. But if you don't want to be alone then you have to give someone a chance. Other than Terence, you've never let anyone else in."

Out of the chaos that my mind is at this moment, I see a pattern emerge, like the headlights of an approaching car through a veil of fog. I know it's a car, but the fog prevents me from seeing its make, or model, and of course, there's no way to tell who the driver is. That's what the elusive answer looks like in my mind.

Approaching footsteps intrude just before I get a clearer picture. I tamp down the urge to scream in frustration.

Samantha pats my back and stands to go to Jason's open arms. They kiss and embrace as though they've been apart for weeks rather than hours.

"Lewis, good to see you, chap."

I give him a friendly nod. When I stand, I notice a large bundle on the floor by the doorway. "Did you bring work home?"

Jason smiles at both of us. "I heard someone loves stuffies."

Samantha reaches for the bag from Kenzie's Toys, and pulls a three foot tall, plush teddy bear, brown and cream, with large dark eyes that somehow exude warmth.

"Aw, I want one," Samantha pouts, hugging the bear to her.

"That's for Emily. Brooke gets this." He holds up a tiny case. "Wireless ear-buds."

"Aw, I want some!" Samantha takes the ear-buds case and hands the bear to her fiancé.

Jason McElroy, former Commander in the SAS, and veteran of the Gulf War, grins like a little boy on Christmas morning holding onto his new "Stuffy". He stands there, looking at the little case over Samantha's shoulder with one arm around her middle, both of them the picture of married bliss already.

It's quite something else to see someone through a different lens. The aggressive, tough man made of granite and the once, lost, suffering lass, look destined for parenthood against all odds. Well, so long as the dad manages to remember to bring toys for the mum as well, apparently.

I easily envision Mr. and Mrs. McElroy in the same pose, holding a baby instead of a plush toy. It looks natural. It looks right. I have a sudden sense that nature has somehow reestablished itself. The same way grass and trees grow back after a forest fire; the same way metal rusts and returns to mineralize the earth; the same way we all inevitably return to the dust from which we came. Despite the strange, twisted paths Jason and Samantha each walked in their youth, nature, and love have brought them full circle to something that can be called a normal life.

From somewhere deep within me, a question emerges to the forefront of my thoughts.

Where does that leave someone like me?

19

"Yes, Sir. The layout is a perfect template for any platform," I say into the microphone. "And the encryption will be no less than 1024 bits."

Arthur MacAchallies thanks me profusely in his sonorous voice, his words colorfully tinted with his heavy Scottish Brogue.

"Miss Ballach sends her regards, young Lewis. You know she was fair scunnered with the last lad that set up the old system."

I have no trouble imagining the intriguing Marney Ballach chewing the head off the man responsible for setting up their operations network so poorly.

"I commend you on standing behind the name of your company, lad. Quite apt. Should you need anything, don't hesitate to call."

"Thank you, Sir."

The video conference ends and a silver background with navy blue lettering boldly stating: SOLUTIONS INC. floats on the screen. The sight of the logo normally fills me with an overwhelming sense of pride, but today it fails to lift my spirits.

As pleased as I am with the direction of the work for MacAchallies, I can't help feeling a certain juvenile resentment for having to work today. However, when I look at the flow charts for Quinn McDermont's intranet, I only feel an eagerness to start on her project.

Samantha and Jason are taking Gwen and the girls sightseeing. I regret not being there with them. I would love to see their faces when they get to enjoy the view from the top of the London Eye or while riding on the top deck of an old Routemaster bus. Wherever they are, I hope they're having the time of their life.

The multiline, digital telephone chirps its cold, impersonal trilling. I don't recognize the number on the tiny screen.

"Solutions Incorporated, this is Lewis, how can I help you?"

"Lewis, this is Richard."

"Dr. Bergman, how are you?" I say after feeling a strange pang of disappointment.

I was hoping it was Quinn.

There's a bit of a pause that seems ominous in its nature, and it makes the hair on the back of my neck stand on end.

"Lewis, I'm calling you from Queen's Hospital, the new one in Romford. Do you know it?"

I think for a few seconds. "That site used to be Oldchurch Park."

"Precisely. Your mother was admitted for observation. I thought you'd like to know."

"Observation?" Mum is virtually fanatical about her salt intake and she can still outdance any of her young pupils. She is the unlikeliest person to end up at the hospital for observation. "What exactly for?"

"Don't be alarmed," Dr. Bergman says, hearing the concern in my voice. "She has what's called an atrial fibrillation, or afib for short. It's quite treatable, but there's a strict protocol in place to identify its causes."

"I'll be there in no time. Thank you for calling, Dr. Bergman."

"Not at all, chap. Drive safe."

I drive as safely as a car thief chased by police helicopters. After finding a spot in the lot, I run into the lobby looking for the admissions desk.

"Madeline Bettford," I say to a thin-faced lad in blue scrubs. He taps a few keys on his computer then asks for identification. I'm gritting my teeth as he takes his sweet, old time filling out electronic forms before he finally hands me a large visitor's pass that I must wear around my neck at all times, according to him.

"Room 581. Elevators are that way." He points me down the left wing and I thank him.

When I step out onto the fifth floor, my mind flashes back to a large salt water fish tank, an aquarium actually, like the one I saw at a hospital in Pennsylvania the night Tony was shot. At the time of the incident, I was too busy uncovering the sins of Samantha's tormentor—her ex-fiancé, Brooks Waldenberg—and I didn't properly process the entire affair at the hospital back then.

In retrospect, when I took Gwen to see her wounded husband, the way she held it together left an indelible impression upon me. I'd never seen such strength in someone who would have been easily justified to completely fall apart.

With no small effort, I shut the door on that line of thought and focus my mind on my mother.

The door to room 581 is ajar. I step in and see Dr. Bergman sitting on a chair, delicately holding Mum's hand. The smile on his face does much to inspire a surge of confidence.

"Is that Lewis?" Mum asks.

When she sees me, she frowns at her companion. "Now why'd you go behind my back, Richard?"

Dr. Bergman offers his chair to me after kissing Mum's hand. "I'll fetch some tea for you, luv." He turns to me and looks at his wrist. "Lewis, if I didn't know any better, I'd say you flew like bloody Superman to get here so soon."

Mum gives me a disapproving scowl.

"Yes, it sounded grave over the phone. What's happened, Mum?"

I sit as Dr. Bergman excuses himself to go get the tea.

Mum's hooked up to a heart monitor, and an IV line is running clear liquids into each of her arms.

"It looks worse than it is, son," she says, giving me a beatific smile that frightens me even more. "It's nothing, luv. My ticker was a bit off sync, is all."

The human heart is nothing short of divine design, but as with many anatomical miracles, there's an incredibly delicate balance required to keep these miracles working. One tiny imperfection, one measly fault in the chemistry, and we are faced with the reality of our fragility. And nothing in the human body requires such perfect functioning like the brain and the heart.

I find the very mention of a heart issue petrifying. I can feel the blood draining out of my face. "What does that mean, out of sync?"

Mum extends her hand and I take it, drawing far more comfort than I'm giving.

"Afib, atrial fibrillation."

I recognize the term; atrium is a part of the heart. That's what I get from atrial. If I recall correctly, the atrium and ventricle form the pumps that send blood and nutrients to every part of our bodies.

"Lewis Jonathan, stop shaking your bloody bonk," Mum snaps.

"It's about your heart," I say, my tone heavy.

"Will you snap off, already! I'm not singing with the bloody angels anytime soon, child."

The strength of her voice is reassuring. "You mean devils. And they don't sing, they rap."

Her face is a twisted mask of confusion that makes me lean in and crush her to me.

"Dear Moses and every saint. Lewis, I'm fine," she protests, even as she squeezes me.

I'm not, I'm scared... "You'd best live forever. Heaven won't take you, and word is hell's afraid you'll take over."

My mother's laughter is the most powerful soothing balm, and it keeps my eyes dry when I draw back and sit back in the chair.

"Wherever do you come up with such rubbish?" she asks with a smile.

I pat her foot. "So, what exactly is happening with your ticker?"

"From what they tell me, the heart runs on electric pulses that originate from a point in the top part of the heart. They follow a certain sequence to keep the heart pumping blood. A fibrillation happens when another point tries to take over and be first on that sequence, creating a quiver."

I swallow the lump of fear back down to the pit of my stomach where it seems to turn to ice, freezing me from the inside out. "So, it stops pumping?"

"Not exactly, it just pumps a bit less efficiently. Oh don't look at me like that," she says, waving her hand in an attempt to wipe off the frightened look on my face. "Lewis, this isn't a big deal. Lots of people have this and don't even know it."

"I care little about other people. How do you fix it?"

"Medicines or something like shock therapy; they'll stop my heart and fire it up again, just like that old Peugeot we had when you and Sammie Kay were kids."

I hear nothing after the words "stop my heart".

"Lewis Jonathan, wipe that look off your face," she orders.

"I'm a bit frightened. Is that alright with you?"

"Quite so, but since you're here, you might as well make me feel better, not worse."

She's right.

"I'll be taking medicine every day to keep this old ticker tapping right along. I also have to keep my blood a bit thinner to prevent clots from forming. There's nothing to worry about."

"Clots?" I ask, unable to keep the alarm out of my voice. "Clots lead to strokes, Mum, a clot can—"

"That's quite enough!" Mum snaps. "That's exactly why I'm taking the medicine, every day, like a good little girl. Okay?"

Her smile almost convinces me, but I know what she's like when it comes to taking medicines. I've heard her say more than a few times that she doesn't believe in any bloody pills. I've seen her pick up a prescription only to flush it down the loo, refusing to take it. "Will you, Mum? Will you actually take your medicine the way you're instructed?"

I recognize the pinching of her brows. She's about to bite my head off with some scathing diatribe, but at the last second, her expression softens.

"I will, Lewis. In fact, I will take the utmost care of myself. After all, there's someone I want to live for. Besides you, of course."

"Richard?"

"Why, yes Richard. Prince Charles is an odd-looking wretch now, so I've shut the door on that possibility."

I smile. In Mum's eyes, Prince Charles could do no wrong, despite the years of scandal that have followed the man like a shadow.

"I love Richard," she says softly. "I want to spend whatever time I have left with him."

"Does he know that?" I smile at her.

Mum brings her left hand up. The diamond on her finger gleams with a light of its own.

"Is that…?"

Mum nods and smiles that beautiful, youthful grin of hers. "Yes. We're getting married." Her face suddenly fills with anxiety. "Will you give me away?"

There are certain moments in your life that are so momentous, they'll be etched in your soul forever. This is one of them.

On the one hand, some of my worst fears are coming true. I'm not ready to share my mother, but I'm not self-deluded. My old woman gave me not only life, but a lifetime of love, companionship, guidance, and she deserves this and more. It does take a herculean effort to keep myself composed, though I'll reserve the right to let these emotions flow through me later. I'm technically losing my two best friends, after all.

"Like bloody hell I'll give you away, Mum. But I'll be honored to walk you down that aisle, luv."

A single tear trickles down her cheek.

The door opens and I turn to see Dr. Bergman holding two disposable cups, looking uncertain. The boy has come to ask the family for the girl's hand, I think.

"Here you go, luv." He sets both cups on a bedside table and shifts his weight on his feet. He looks as nervous as a teenage boy suffering the scrutiny of his girlfriend's father.

"Congratulations are in order," I call, standing up and extending my hand.

"Lewis, my boy," he says, giving me a grateful handshake. "I will take good care of our lady."

Our lady... "I don't doubt it, Sir."

Dr. Bergman takes my place in the chair and gazes at Mum with soulful eyes full of love.

"When is the big day?"

"Sometime next year, luv," Mum says, surprising me. "I'm not about to be so tacky as to wed around the same time as Sammie Kay."

I swear she can read minds. "It's a bloody epidemic, Sam and Jason, Nathan and Alicia, and now you two."

"Oh, darling." Mum waves my concern away. "Nathan and Alicia have been married from the second they met, but it is high time they make it official. It would be nice if you were to catch the bug, too."

"You just couldn't resist, could you?" I hold a smile upon my face, but I am a bit peeved she has to bring this up once more.

Dr. Bergman looks around uncomfortably. I'm about to suggest he'd better get used to moments like these if he is to share his life with Mum. "Will they let you out of here by dinnertime?"

"I certainly hope so, luv. The doctors want to run a few tests, but don't fret. I'll be there tonight, I'm not about to miss out on meeting the famous Gwen. And I cannot wait to meet those little girls."

I smile. "Well, then I shall leave you, love birds, to test the suspension of the bed, and be on my way."

"Lewis!" Mum blushes only a shade of red less than Dr. Bergman, who tries to stifle a chuckle under his fist.

"Love you," I tell her, starting for the door. "Good luck, Dr. Bergman."

"Lewis! Can you believe that son of mine…"

Mum's voice fades as I make my way down the hallway.

By hospital orders, I shut down my mobile before going in. I boot it up as I walk to my car and hear three chimes.

Once I sit behind the wheel, I tap open the messages. Samantha sent me a photo of Emily and Brooke from the top of the London Eye, looking down on the old city. There's another photo of Gwen and Samantha posing under the façade of Gucci. The caption beneath reads: *wish you were here, luv.*

"I do too," I think aloud.

The third is a voice mail that comes from a number I don't recognize. For a second I think it could be Quinn, but this is a different number. I press 1 and listen.

"Lewis, I'd really like to talk to you. I'm home all day, please, for the sake of old times, come by today."

Terence's voice brings up a well of resentment and a wave of nostalgia. I can actually hear loneliness in it.

I resist the urge to text Samantha and ask her what I should do. Not only is she out and about having a grand time with Gwen and everyone, but she'd steam if she knew Terence was, yet again, playing the loneliness card.

I have plenty of time before everyone meets at my flat and his house is close by. The prospect of talking to Terence is making my heart race. I'm probably too angry to keep myself composed if he were to say the wrong thing, but we had left the door open for friendship, though I asked him not to contact me for a while. In the time since, we've exchanged few emails, nothing significant, just work-related issues. He was concise and to the point and I gave no more than two-word answers. Awkward didn't even begin to describe it.

***

Terence lives in an affluent neighborhood north of Hyde Park. I've never been inside, though I've driven by during lapses in judgment when I felt I missed him.

Of course, I don't miss him. I miss that sense of having someone in my life, someone there just for me. I miss being needed.

By the time I pull in front of the new contemporary-style home, curiosity is the only force driving me onward.

Like everything else Terence owns, his home is a status symbol. The structure is a multi-tiered split level edifice with flanking galleries overlooking a pond on the west and a manicured lawn on the east. Nearly every vertical surface is tinted glass, especially designed to keep safe from prying eyes. There's some elaborate landscaping that must command a small army and a big fortune to upkeep.

A mutual friend I ran into, told me Sandy, Terence's wife, hired a well-known architect and designed the entire house without Terence's input. I didn't believe it until now. There is no way Terence could've designed this place on his own.

There's a stone path leading to the front doors. I climb the two steps onto the small porch and press the doorbell. A few seconds later a stout, older woman wearing white scrubs opens the door.

"Mr. Bettford?"

"Yes, Madame. I'm here to see Terence at his request."

"Follow me, please."

The presence of a nurse in Terence's house feels like a bad omen. I follow her down a wide hallway into a large, open study where someone is sitting on a recliner.

For a moment I can't speak. Terence looks at least thirty kilograms lighter. The black robe he wears hangs on thin shoulders, severely detracting from the pillar of health I've known him to be.

"I'm glad you came," he says in a hoarse voice.

I can barely meet his bloodshot gaze. "You don't look well."

"Yes... come sit down, Lewis."

I step into the study, unable to restrain the wave of awe that fills me with the first glimpse of his home. "Heavens! Terence, you've certainly moved up in the world."

He shrugs. "It's a house," he says, deliberately diminishing the interior's beauty.

My eyes dart everywhere, from the blonde pine loft overlooking a lovely receded sitting area, to each immaculate setting beyond. No put-together furniture at all in this place, and no antiques. Just tasteful, comfortable pieces in red tones that pop out of the cream-colored wall-to-wall carpeting. Expensive artwork is mounted on matching gilded frames that adorn the walls, each with its own spot-lighting.

Terence gets up off the recliner with considerable effort and ushers me to the sitting area. We both face the glass wall that looks out to an oriental garden, which includes a pond with a babbling fountain.

"Will you need anything at this moment, Terry?

"Not at all, Lisa, thank you."

The nurse nods once firmly and disappears down the hallway.

The beautiful surroundings are lost on Terence, who stares at me with a strange look. Growing uncomfortable with what I perceive to be hopelessness in his gaze, I give him my undivided attention. "What is it, Terence?"

Terence crosses his thin legs and leans back into the couch. "Your little tart is getting married."

"Yes, she is."

"To that young dish," he sighs deeply. "What a waste. How do you feel?"

"Me?"

"About Jason. I know you were growing quite fond of him."

"As were you," I counter.

Terence shakes his head sadly. "Darling, I just wanted to shag him, not love him."

The smile brings the shallowness of his cheeks into stark contrast, making me feel a slight wave of revulsion that I'm unable to suppress.

"What about the little tart? Don't tell me you're not going to miss playing with her tight little fanny."

I bristle. "Her name is Samantha, and we're best friends, practically family. If you take on that tone again, I'm gone."

"My, my…" he says in mock admiration. "You've got strong feelings for the little tart, you always have."

I don't have time for this. "What did you want to see me for, Terence?"

His smile is snide. "I missed you, darling."

"You can't say rubbish like that to me. Not now." I get to my feet.

"A dying man can say whatever the fuck he wants," he says in a flat voice.

I freeze before taking a single step. "What are you talking about?"

"Look at me, darling." Terence spreads his arms out pulling the robe open to reveal a thin layer of grayish pale skin over his skeleton. I notice some bruising and a blistered sore on his chest.

"Jesus…"

Terence covers himself and cinches the sash of his robe. I can't voice the frightening realization, I can't say a word. My blood has turned to ice.

"Fret not, my love, you're quite safe, I assure you."

"When did you find out?"

"That's not important."

"Terence, talk to me."

He rolls his eyes. "Sandy wanted babies so she forced me to test. I tested positive."

"I'm sorry…"

"Don't be an idiot. I didn't ask you here to be sorry," he snaps. "I asked you here because certain things have got to be said."

When AIDS finally made it to the world's collective consciousness, the backlash against homosexuals was the stuff of Orwellian legends. Gay men were vilified, persecuted, and even the church piped in to declare the disease was the work of the hand of God cleansing the world of the worst sinners alive.

So much for love and infinite mercy, I always thought.

When I was an adolescent and my body began experiencing its sexual awakening, the prospect of contracting AIDS kept me up at night. It was the number one deterrent of engaging in a homosexual relationship, or in any relationship at all. I couldn't believe all the people who continually involved themselves in careless sexual behavior throughout that time.

Growing up in the 90's, the initial fear and panic that gripped the entire world during the previous decade, gave way to a quieter level of acceptance, or intended ignorance, as though the disease would cease to exist if no one thought of it. AIDS was ravaging the Far East and Africa at an unprecedented scale while the West turned more tolerant and less fearful, thanks to new successful treatments.

But seeing the disease up close, and quite personal, is devastating. Infinitely more so when it's someone you've known in your life, that has meant something to you. Tears sting my eyes.

Despite our rocky relationship—even unfulfilled in Terence's eyes—it's tragic to face the inevitable loss of someone so intelligent, so talented, with so much left to give, and a whole life to live.

"I didn't ask you here to say goodbye, either," Terence says, his voice suddenly trembling with emotion. "I wanted to tell you that I regret everything I put you through."

I flash back to several times when I was so easily discarded so he could scratch and itch, only to return full of remorse, practically expecting me to simply open my arms and allow him back in my life, which I did.

Terence was familiar, comfortable, and accepting of my limits on the relationship.

"I wanted to tell you that you were right in staying pure." His chuckle is so devoid of humor that I feel a chill run down my spine.

Despite having my fears validated, I can't bring myself to say anything. There's a swirl of emotions that steals my voice, leaving only a quivering of my limbs and a sudden difficulty to draw an even breath. "Terence, I don't know what to say," I finally mutter.

"Don't be daft, luv. I didn't ask you here to come comfort me either, though I won't stop you if you so choose."

"Why did you ask me to come?"

Terence averts his gaze from me and looks out the window before speaking. His once, thick, lustrous hair is now a disarray of dry, brittle strands.

"I just messaged all my clients and announced the closing of the Ancile, citing health reasons. By now, I'm sure they're all aware of what those reasons are, but that's no longer important to me. To allay their fears, I recommended they sign with the capable services of Solutions Incorporated."

I try not to react at the news. We are talking nearly two million pounds in yearly revenues.

When Terence and I split up, he practically stole my clients from underneath me. In all fairness, I was too wrapped up in taking care of Samantha with the help of Jason and the assets of Lions Securities. Her life had been threatened, after all.

At the time, I reasoned my best friend needed me more than my clients, but my absence inspired a loss of confidence. They grew nervous when the Solutions partnership dissolved and Terence gave them enough assurances to lure them away. I hold to this day, that in their shoes, I would've done the same thing. "Can't Sandy run the company? You still have talented techs working for you."

"Sandy is a good lass. I have no doubt she'd do great running the firm, but it's not what she wants, and not what I want either."

"Why not?"

Terence looks as though the answer should be obvious. "I'll be dead soon, Lewis."

Despite this hurtful predicament, I'm glad he reminds me why I didn't give him what he wanted. Selfishness is a real turn off. "What about your techs?"

"They have impeccable recommendations."

"And Sandy?"

He waves my concern away. "Sandy can stand up to her family and finally marry her lover."

"Her lover?" Suddenly I know why Carmen spotted Terence running around on his wife of a few months. "You arranged a marriage to placate her family?"

"Sure, it was quite a convenient arrangement. We presented a hetero image to the world and we discreetly lived our lives as we intended."

"You pulled off a great act, from what I hear."

He nods agreeably. "Sandy is a pretty lass. It was no hardship being with her. Besides, it was easy to do considering all the—shall we call it, training, that I had with you."

I want to know what made them think about having children but his underhanded barb finds its mark. "You told me you respected my stance."

"I was as patient as I could be, luv. We both know that."

A lump of emotion rises into my throat. "There was nothing patient about you running to the cruises to get what you weren't getting from me."

"You mean sex."

I turn my face away as though he slapped me.

"Look at me, Lewis. How does it feel to have your fears realized? I was patient because you knew my history, you had your concerns, but I wasn't going to bloody wait forever. I don't regret living to live."

"No, you made that quite clear," I say bitterly.

"And yet we were still something to one another and I know why. I've been having a deluge of these epiphanies while I lie here, burning in bloody pain from yet, another medicine the butchers try on me."

I turn back to face him, the skeletal visage burning into my memory.

"You aren't gay, Lewis. You never were one of us."

"You don't know what you're talking about," I say hotly.

"You, my darling, are by long and far guilty of living a lie. I was just a convenient screen. It's true and you know it."

My heart flutters in my chest and I'm suddenly lightheaded with hate.

"You're a sham, my luv. A bloody sham."

His accusation is delivered in a strange tone, tinted with something akin to envy, perhaps. Whatever it is, it's disconcerting.

I feel my hands start to shake and there's a large cold lump of ice bouncing in my gut. My eyes sting with tears and my breath is no more than ragged little sighs.

"Listen," Terence says. "I don't care about that. You've been quite the challenge, I must say. It's a strange thing to admit, I know. But there it is." He sighs. "Blimey, look at you. You're still as beautiful as the first day I met you, and I don't mean your delicate looks, luv. You're beautiful all around. Your superior intellect, your drive. Anywhere you go, people are drawn to you. Your loyalty to the little lass is a great example of that."

I feel tears spill over my lashes, though I don't understand why I should cry.

"I respected your choices, and our partnership will always be a fond memory." He smiles sadly. "For as long as this brain continues to fire, that is."

I can only put my head down as the tears fall.

"But still…" Terence reaches for a blanket that's lying next to him. "That's not what I wanted you here for."

"What then?" I ask in a pained voice.

A sudden intensity makes him look more alive than when I first came into his study.

"Break out of your prison, my luv. You have too much to give someone else. Just make certain she is as bright, and as beautiful as you are, and don't settle for anything less. Don't let another Samantha Reddick slip by."

I flash back on nights when we'd sit up in bed, sharing a bottle of wine, and having these deep conversations about every mystery of life. I recall the days leading up to the formation of Solutions. I recall marching together, proudly holding that rainbow flag, along with our brothers and sisters. But I feel the truth of his words in my bones.

"Believe you me, lad," he goes on in a tired voice. "Falling in love is a wonderful thing. Falling in love with your best friend is far more. Now," Terence gets to his feet with some effort. "I'm going to ask you to leave and let me die, knowing I said what I had to say, my luv."

Without another word, he stands and shuffles to the end of the hallway and laboriously climbs the wide steps towards the loft. Only when I hear his door open and shut do I feel I can move.

Like a shell-shocked soldier, I see nothing but the promised salvation outside the door. I get as far as putting my hand on the brass doorknob when something makes me turn around.

I rush back to the hallway and fly up the steps. Without hesitation, I open the door of the master suite and boldly walk in, startling the nurse.

Terence is lying on his back, attaching the wires of a heart monitor to the sensors stuck at different points over his torso. His eyes widen with surprise for only a second. A small array of medical monitoring equipment beeps and whirrs bedside. Finally, he dons a breathing mask and lays his head on the propped pillows.

"You're so glad you're not me, right now." His voice is muffled from behind the mask.

I almost want to demand he tells me whether he put me in danger of contagion by being here, but the presence of Lisa, his nurse, puts me at ease. I glance away from her disapproving glare. On the near side table there must be about fourteen different pill bottles.

"How long did they say?"

"Mr. Bettford…" Lisa throws me a pleading look.

Terence silences her with a raised hand. "Leave me, Lewis. Leave me the way I left you all those times. And don't try to be the better person I already know you are."

His breathing is more labored than it was before. My presence is agitating him.

Lisa takes me by the elbow and guides me towards the door.

"Be the better *man* I know you've always been, luv." Tears appear in his left eye and roll towards his temple. "Leave. I deserve nothing less."

My chest is heaving and my knees barely hold me up. I've admired this lad from the moment I met him. I did for him all I could, just to keep him near me, except for the one thing he always wanted. At the same time I have to wonder if, had I given in, he would be safe as well. The thought is short-lived. Terence was surely addicted to sex. As it turns out, it appears I saved myself, but there's little satisfaction in that.

"Go now."

Lisa grips my elbow a bit tighter and I back out of his room. When I look back, his eyes are closed and his shallow chest rises and falls with irregularity. The pitiful sight will haunt me for the rest of my days. "I won't forget you, Terence," I whisper.

I don't recall walking out to my car and driving back to my flat. A torrent of memories plays in my mind's eye, a collage of a life that until now, I never saw as the lie that it really is. For the first time in my life, I feel I know who I am. And the veracity of that knowledge resonates in every part of me, whittling away everything in me until there's nothing but one single question:

Who am I now?

20

I hear techno music, and the thudding of feet marking a rhythm out of the studio. Samantha, Jason, Brooke and little Emily are dancing in sync, matching the moves of the avatars on the large flat screen. I can easily tell who's winning—and winning big—just by the way she moves.

The music is so loud, and their focus is so complete that they don't even know I'm standing behind them. I almost think I finally got one over Jason, but the clever security man has already spotted me on the reflection of the computer monitor. I can see the smirk that pretty much says, *better luck next time, chap.*

Little Emily copies the moves with surprising accuracy. In a short time, she'll give her big sister a run for her money, but for now, Brooke's score is easily double everyone else's. Samantha gyrates her lithe body and I can guess her expression is tight in concentration, competitive as always, she is. Jason is not a horrible dancer, but his choreography is so pitiful it makes me laugh.

I leave them to their game and go up to find Mum and Gwen speaking animatedly, broad smiles on their faces.

"Hey, handsome," Gwen says by way of greeting.

She walks over to me, her smile faltering as she reads something in my eyes. I shake my head and smile, trying to dissuade her from asking what's wrong. She asks nothing, but she frowns at me before embracing me warmly. It takes a superb effort not to lose it right there.

"Do you want to talk about it?" Gwen asks softly in my ear.

I'm about to reassure her that there's nothing wrong but something in her voice stops me. "Later perhaps. I could really use a talk."

Gwen kisses my cheek and pats my shoulder. In her always positive, melodious voice, she says, "Whenever you're ready."

Mum's at the kitchen again, shoving something in the oven. I suddenly hate the cramped galley kitchen. Whatever is in the oven smells absolutely mouth-watering, but I don't know if I could really eat after what I learned today.

"This wonderful lassie is not going back," she declares, laying a soft hand on Gwen's shoulder. "That husband of yours will just have to move everyone to the Queen's Land, I say."

"How are you feeling, Mum?"

"I feel like dancing, my boy."

I give her a pointed look. "I thought you had a heart condition."

Mum rolls her eyes and shakes her head then exchanges an exasperated look with Gwen. "I have a little flutter, and the medicines are working great. I'll be seeing Dr. Parks regularly every other week."

"Great, so you're staying in London?" I ask.

She nods. "I'm not moving in with you, son, but yes, I'll be staying in London, although I already miss home, no offense to you, luv."

I smile. "None taken, Mum."

Unlike Terence's death mask, Mum's face radiates an aura of energy and livelihood that does more to reassure me than any doctor could, but the question escapes my lips anyway. "Are you sure you're well?"

"Lewis, by George!" She throws her hands up in the air, turns and goes back into the tiny kitchen.

"Where's Richard?"

"He'll be here a bit later," Mum replies. "You're not going to call him, Dad?"

Gwen chuckles, proclaiming the gesture sweet.

"Mum!"

"Don't upset me. I've a heart condition, dear. You ought to do as I say from now on."

"Oh, you're *not* going to pull that, are you?"

Mum grins like the devil. "Oh, but I am."

I shake my head. "We'll see. What's on the menu?"

"Lasagna, American style," Gwen says. "It's all done, Mum, we can all relax for the next forty minutes or so. Why don't you rest for a while?"

"Sounds like a good idea, my sweet girl."

"Oh, of course, but if *I* had told you to nap, you would've bitten my bloody head off," I gripe.

Mum slaps my cheek playfully as she walks towards the steps. "Gwen *asked* me to rest. She's not ordering me to go to sleep. It's all in how you say things, my boy. You ought to change your ways. Spouses tend to walk off when they get ordered around."

Good God...

Gwen laughs and takes Mum up to her bedroom. Mum would readily push my arm away declaring herself healthy as a bloody horse, but she's quite taken by Gwen, and loving her attentions. I follow them up because I need to get into some more comfortable clothes.

I can hear them chattering along before the door is finally pulled shut. Gwen waits until I emerge from my bedroom then we both make our way to the living room. A cheer floats up the steps before another songs begins playing, the rhythm marked by the contestants' dancing feet.

"They've been at it since we got here. Those girls are going to crash hard tonight."

"Yes, I'm surprised Emily's still going," I observe, recalling how the little cutie curled up in a ball when she ran out of energy from how hard she played. "What'd you think of London?"

"Everything is so amazing here. I wish Tony would've seen it all with me. But, we'll talk about my impressions later. What happened today? You look like you've seen a ghost."

"I did, in a way."

Gwen's blue eyes focus on my face and for a moment, I lose myself a bit in her gaze.

It's strange how she makes me feel a little off balance when she looks at me this way.

"Does the name Terence mean anything to you?" I ask after mentally shaking myself.

She nods. "Samantha told me he was your partner for years. She didn't care much for him and she said the feeling was mutual."

"He thought of Sam as competition."

Gwen laughs softly. "Of course, for the attention."

"Not exactly. He thought Sam and I were more than just friends."

"He thought you and Samantha were sleeping together," Gwen intuits.

I nod. "Actually, luv. We have slept together several times. We just never had sex, as everyone else around us seems to believe. Terence was convinced."

"I'll be honest, it's hard to imagine."

I shrug. "She's a little sister of sorts, despite her evident beauty I didn't feel that pull that she seems to exert on everyone else."

"Well, you're both stronger than I am. I don't know what I would've done in that situation," Gwen says, giving me a lustful look.

I feel a wave of heat coloring my cheeks as she giggles.

"So, did anything happen with Terence? Samantha only told me that the break up really upset you."

"It did for a time. He asked to see me today."

Gwen draws back, her eyes flashing concern. I have the distinct feeling that she knows more about me than I've been led to believe.

"Did you go see him?"

The image of Terence's emaciated body, his shallow face, and bloodshot eyes fills my head with a pain I can't begin to describe. I feel my head growing heavier as I nod.

"What did he say?" Gwen asks in a definitely protective tone.

I think back on everything he said to me, not so much what he said, but the way he said it. Every word was filled with regret and a strange acceptance that left me cold. "He's…"

Sensing my plummeting emotions, Gwen lays a comforting hand on my shoulder, her eyes full of concern.

"Gwen, he's dying." My voice is no more than a hoarse whisper.

"What?"

I take a tremulous breath trying in vain to steady myself. The cloak of grief that envelops me constricts my throat and I can only hang my head as a torrent of tears breaks through.

Gwen guides me back into the bedroom and we both sit on the bed then she wraps her arms around me, and places my face on her shoulder.

"It's alright," she says in a soothing voice. "Let go, Lewis. Just let go."

And I do. For the next ten minutes I cry every tear I held back throughout all the deceit, all the betrayals, and all the hurt. I soak the shoulder of a woman I barely know, though I'd bare my soul to her without a second thought.

***

"Did he contract it recently?"

"I don't know. He found out because his wife made him take a test. She wanted a baby."

"Jesus…"

"Terence always needed sex. Every major fight and argument we ever had was about sex."

"But you never…"

"Not once."

"Not even kissing?"

My blood runs cold at the thought of that. "There was kissing, though I wasn't the one to initiate it." I feel a slight wave of nausea rolling through me. "I'm going to have to get tested."

"It's probably a good idea, but I don't think you should worry. Given everything you told me, you would've seen a sign by now."

"I hope you're right."

"I'm so sorry, Lewis. That's awful. But I don't want to even think what would've happened if you ended up catching that and possibly dying too." The possibilities make her shudder. "I'm so glad you're safe. I don't mean to sound insensitive about Terence, but you have to keep in mind that he was aware of the risks, and he still went after it."

I can only nod. I feel tired, emotionally spent.

"Are you going to tell Samantha?"

I shrug. "I don't think I want to bring this up now. You don't know how much she frets over me at times. I'd rather have her happy as a bloody bird out of its cage."

Gwen pats my back affectionately. "Are you going to be okay?"

I nod and try for a reassuring smile. "I have to wrap my mind around it. I just… I think I'm in disbelief right now."

"If you need to talk…"

"Thank you, luv. I will."

"Good." She stands, then gives me her hand and pulls me up off the bed. "I know this may seem cold, but I hope you're starving."

I give her a thin smile.

Images of Terence still float in my head. I make no mention of the revelation Terence forced me to face. Honestly, I wouldn't know how to even get into that with anyone. You grow up giving the world one version of who you are, and more often than not, you do it so well you even convince yourself. I wonder if that's what I've done since I was a boy.

You aren't gay, Lewis. You never were one of us…

Terence's declaration, in that hoarse, ragged tone, continues to bounce around in my head. There's no sense denying any of it, but I'm reluctant to admit it to anyone else other than myself. It's as though I don't know who to be. I don't know how to act.

An hour later, it's not the succulent aroma of Gwen's lasagna that puts a smile on my face. It's the warmth of family, the easy laughter and the undeniable presence of love permeating every confine of my soul.

We are a universe onto ourselves and the two little girls are the very center of it. The rest of us revolve helplessly around them, gravitating towards every gesture, every word, and every grin.

Brooke is in awe of London. Everything is deemed either awesome, or cool. Her exuberance and enthusiasm is so contagious that I decide to take the day off work to spend it with them. And why not?

"I was holding Mommy's leg the whole time!" Emily exclaims.

"It wasn't that scary, until we got to the top, but the view was awesome!" Brooke adds.

I've lived in London long enough to dread the bloody traffic, and give the historic places no more than a disinterested, passing glance. But hearing Brooke and Emily chatter about the old city makes me see it anew.

At the first long yawn, Gwen instructs the girls to gather their sweaters and get ready to leave. Before I point out that it's early, it dawns on me that they're still readjusting. I'm surprised the jetlag wasn't more severe, especially on the girls.

Jason is the first to leave. He gets down on one knee and hugs each of the girls. Samantha walks him out after he bids us all good night. I'm sure he won't leave for another half hour. Samantha dialed down on the affection for fear of setting a bad example for the girls, so I know that she's probably ready to burst if she doesn't get a long kiss good night.

Despite being treated for afib at the hospital earlier in the day, Mum insists on going out for a drive with Richard. I try to give her a hard time but once I get "The Look", I decide it's better for Richard to deal with her.

"You're a sweet girl, Gwen. These two angels of yours are absolutely precious," Mum gushes.

Gwen accepts the praise with evident pride, though later confides to me that she's amazed with how well the girls actually behave.

"You don't get it," Gwen says with severity. "At home, they would've had everything upside down. It's like a bomb goes off every time they play."

"Not those two angels," I muse.

"Yes. Those two angels," Gwen insists.

"Is Sam dragging you to the dressmaker tomorrow?"

"That's the plan." Gwen's eyes flash with excitement, though it's quickly followed by a yawn.

"Gwen, can I keep the girls for you?"

She looks surprised. "Seriously? They can be a handful," she warns.

"I insist. I'd like to take them to Regents Park and the London Zoo. If you allow me, that is. I promise I'll guard them with my life."

Gwen looks incredulous for a moment. "I don't think you know what you're getting yourself into."

"It'll give you and Sam some girlie time."

"Okay, I'm sure they'd love to go. If you run into any trouble, you will text me or Samantha, and we can rescue you, right?"

"It's settled then," I reply confidently. What could be so difficult?

"Hey girls…" Gwen's voice trails off when she sees the two sleeping forms on the couch. "Of course," she says, in a tone reserved only for weary mums the world over.

Before we can move to pick up the girls, Samantha races up the steps, a devilish grin on her face. "Ready to go?" Gwen points at the girls. "Oh."

"Sam, you'd be closer to the dressmaker from here. Just spend the night here."

"Gwen?" Samantha asks.

Gwen yawns again. "Sure. At this point I'll be happy just dropping in place."

"I have a third bedroom with a king size bed, luv. You will all fit there just fine."

"Thank you, Lewis. Except that Brooke snores and Emily grinds her teeth something awful," Gwen laments. "They can sleep on the couch, they'll be fine."

"Are you sure, luv?" Samantha asks dubiously.

"They do that on weekends at home. They'll watch TV late into the night and sleep on the couch."

With the matter settled, I run upstairs and grab two extra blankets that Gwen and Samantha drape over the sleeping beauties. I can already hear Emily grinding her teeth.

"Blimey, that's frightening," I observe.

"It's okay, those are just her baby teeth she's grinding to nubs," Gwen explains, oddly unaffected by the terrible sound of teeth scraping on teeth.

Samantha and I both make a face at the next grinding noise.

Gwen chuckles. "Okay, guys. I'm beat."

"This way, Gwen," Samantha offers.

Gwen thanks me with a warm hug before letting Samantha walk her up to the room. I grab the last plates from the table and load them into the dishwasher. By the time it's filling, Samantha joins me in the kitchen.

"Blimey, I wanted to lie down right next to her and pass out. I'm exhausted."

"I'm sure that's *all* you wanted to do," I say, laughing to myself.

"You ought to be ashamed!"

"Who won the dance-a-thon?"

"Brooke," Samantha says admiringly. "Blimey, can she dance!"

"You weren't doing so bad yourself."

"I was trying. She was doing. Big difference, luv."

I fill two cups with tea and we go down to the studio. I'm surprised to see everything still in order after they shook up the place while playing the video game.

"Are you alright?"

Besides my mother, no one knows me as well as Samantha. There is no point in lying to her, or hiding answers. "I will be."

"Talk to me."

I take a deep breath, not wanting to recall the morbid visit to Terence. "Only under one rule."

Samantha rolls her eyes. "Oh, this ought to be good."

"I talk and you listen until I'm bloody done. I mean it, Sam."

Her eyebrows rise in curious unison but she holds back from asking, and nods in acquiescence.

I go through the visit once more, once again omitting Terence's epiphany. The emotions are easier to control this time around. Apparently I left everything on Gwen's shoulder, so I'm able to keep my voice steady. I probably sound like a recording, but at least I can talk without breaking down. Samantha listens intently. Her only reaction is a slow shake of her head.

When I run out of things to say, she takes a deep breath, holds it for a moment as she holds my hand then exhales a long rush of air.

"I feel so sad for you," she says in a shaky voice. "Why didn't you ever tell me you didn't have sex with Terence?"

"I don't know. You would've never believed it."

"I had no idea you felt so strong about the risks of sex."

"Petrified."

"How long does he have?"

I can only shrug in reply.

"I don't know what to say," Samantha murmurs.

"There's nothing to say, luv. He was bloody reckless. Play and pay, right? I can't help thinking that if I'd given in, he'd be safe."

"Wrong," Samantha says, firmly. "I'd be losing you." Her arms squeeze me tightly. "It's a risky lifestyle."

A sudden anger flows through me. "He's not dying because he's gay, Sam. He's dying because he fucked a diseased wanker. And that happens in the hetero world too."

Samantha is clearly taken aback by my outburst. She flinches at every word I spit at her.

"Lewis, I meant the way he lived *his* life. It had nothing to do with being gay."

I know that but I'm still shaking with a rush of misplaced fury.

She grabs my arm forcefully, her eye brimming with tears. "Listen to me. I've loved you regardless of what you chose. Bloody hell, the day you told Grandmum you are gay, I was never more proud of anyone, and I've admired that strength since. I know what you had to go through. I know what you had to tolerate, and I know how much it bloody hurt to hide who you really are," her voice falters, deteriorating into a high pitched mewl in her efforts to stifle a sob. "I don't bloody care what you choose in life. All I care about is that you're happy, that you have someone to love you the way you deserve to be loved," she cries through each word. "When you meet the partner that takes your heart in their hands, and cherishes it like he should, I will forever love him for that."

My sudden ire evaporates at the sight of the tears in those remarkably beautiful eyes of hers.

She turns away but still holds onto my arm, struggling to compose herself, but she can't.

"I walked with you on that gay march when we were nineteen, remember? I walked with you while those bloody church wankers tossed garbage at us. I heard every hurtful slur and condemnation, and I watched in awe as these men and women marched on. I've never seen anything so courageous in my life."

I silently agree with her.

"When I met them, all I could think about was those times when we were forced to run away from a group of bloody bullies who wanted to beat on you because you danced ballet. I realized all those people marching had a similar story. I remember Mum suffering the disdainful criticism from her neighbors, opining on the wrongful way she was raising you, according to those old cows." Samantha sniffles loudly. "They were not afraid of being who they were, no matter what poison those people spewed at them!"

I reach over for the tissue dispenser from the counter and set it on the table between us.

"I remember Cory Jameson running away from his house because his father told him he'd rather have a dead son than a gay son. There was no one kinder than Cory, as young as he was. He had the courage to stand before that man and announce who he really was. Do you remember him? Grandmum kept him hidden from that drunken wanker of a father, just so he could flee to Dover."

I remembered Cory quite well. He was four years older than us, barely sixteen at the time of that awful incident.

Cory was beaten because he came to see his boyfriend—a former student of Mum's—dance. His father dragged him out in front of us, called him a bloody fag, queer, and all sorts of vile things as he kicked him around back to their house. That night, Cory came out to his parents and paid a terrible price for his confession.

I remember when he appeared at the back door of Grandmum's house. His shirt was torn in places where whatever was used to lash him had struck. Angry, bleeding welts on his back told a horrid tale of what the lad endured. His right eye was swollen shut and his nose was broken. Grandmum immediately called the police but nothing really came of it.

The incident left such an indelible impression on me that made me think I was committing a crime, and I dreaded getting caught liking boys if that was the punishment I'd receive.

Where I was scared, Samantha was outraged. I actually regret all the times she stood up for me, while I cowered behind her.

You aren't gay, Lewis. You never were one of us…

If I weren't, then why did I react the way I did when some little wanker started calling me a fag? Why didn't I ever deny it? Was it just cowardice?

"I was even willing to pretend I was your girlfriend, by George!" Samantha exclaims.

She did.

Kenny Larson and Teddy Chambers were classmates of mine at school. They were known to point out the "faggy" kids to Big Jon Delmar, and then they would watch as the bigger bully beat on somebody far smaller, and frailer.

The boys pedaled their bikes nearly two kilometers to find me coming out of Mum's ballet school, which was my home, and quickly pointed me out to Delmar. I was fortunate to have Samantha there those days, her Easter break, I remember. As soon as she figured out what was about to happen, she draped herself all over me and gave me a scandalous French kiss that actually earned me Delmar's and his cronies' admiration. I was even asked to play football, which eventually led to my injury some time later.

Samantha's rescue methods bring a smile to my face. "We were what, fourteen?"

"Yes."

"You weren't my type," I say, letting my smile grow wider.

"Shut your gob! Jon Delmar would've sat his ample arse on your bony frame if it weren't for me." She flips her hair from one side to the other. "Don't tell me it was such a bloody hardship."

In retrospect, it wasn't, and for the first time, the memory sends a wave of heat through my insides. I force myself to remember it was quite uncomfortable. By definition, that should have put to rest any doubts about my orientation.

Taking advantage of her more composed demeanor, I take her hand and look into her eyes. "Forgive me, Sam. I'm feeling a bit raw inside. I know you're the one person who's never judged me for what I am. I won't ever forget it."

Her gaze is soft and understanding. "I'm sorry too."

I want to tell Samantha exactly what Terence said, but I can't. I need some time to wrap my mind around everything. Perhaps I need to find a way to forget it all.

"Are you alright?"

"It's just a lot to take in right now. You know, he's sending his clients back to Solutions."

Samantha thinks about that for a minute, finally composed once more. "Don't be cross, but that's only fair, luv."

"Perhaps."

She nods and pats my thigh. "I thought you were getting upset about the wedding again."

"Which one?"

Samantha looks confused.

"You are a poor observer, Sam. Didn't you see the gleaming stone on Mum's hand?"

Her eyes widen. "What? Lewis, had she been wearing it, I would've seen it. Us women don't overlook something like that."

"She was doing the cooking so perhaps she removed it."

"Probably. Gwen would've seen it too."

"Okay, let's say I believe you. I'm surprised she didn't tell you."

"I'm not," she says quickly. "She probably felt it inappropriate so close to my wedding. I'm so happy for her!" She scrutinizes my face for a moment. "How do you feel about that one?"

"I think you gave me the answer, lass. I want her to be happy. I want Richard to cherish her heart like it should be cherished. I'm happy for her."

She looks a bit unconvinced. "Okay, you haven't had an easy day, so I'll just pretend you told me everything that's inside that bonk," she says, playfully jabbing a finger at my skull.

"Where will you sleep?"

Her brow furrows. "On your bed with you, duh!"

"I thought you'd spend the night with Jason."

She looks sad. "He's doing Soderbergh a favor and working his nightshift."

"Perhaps he just wanted a break from you," I tease.

"Har, bloody har. What a comedian. If you must know, he can't stay away from this," she says, sliding her hands down her thighs provocatively.

I actually follow her hands with my eyes before a wave of guilt makes me snap my head away though not before Samantha gives me a curious look.

You aren't gay, Lewis. You never were one of us…

"Care for a film?"

Samantha peers into my eyes suspiciously. "What do you have?"

"Hell's Vixens, a Lesbian Odyssey."

She punches my shoulder as I laugh. We were never the type of people to lengthen a sob fest.

"Actually, it's the film based on that book you were reading."

"I read three books a week, which one?"

I motion for her to join me in the studio. After quietly sliding the futon in front of the 32" monitor, I navigate to the film website and start the stream. I hear Samantha gasp when *Bride Wars* starts playing.

"Haven't you seen it?"

"No, but it's not based on a book."

"I thought that's where all films came from."

She shakes her head. "There is such a thing as screenplays, you know."

I sit next to her and soon she arranges me in a position that will allow her to lean against me, the way she's always done. Even as far back as a week ago, I wouldn't have felt so strange feeling Samantha's body against mine this way. I try not to think about it, making an effort to get lost in the hilarious catfights between Kate Hudson and Anne Hathaway, but the feeling persists.

When Samantha goes to bed, I tell her I need to do a bit of work. By then, she's sleepy enough that she doesn't get curious about what I might be working on.

I don't work on anything of course. I stare at the wall, my mind projecting a series of images of a much healthier Terence and the good times we had together.

That's the irony of life's end. No matter what anyone did against you, if that person is dying, you automatically focus only on the positive things. Inevitably, I allow the heartaches to surface as well, but I no longer feel the humiliating pain I once did. I feel numb. So numb that I don't feel the tears that flow down my face as I lean back and let oblivion pull me away from reality, though not before hearing Terence's hoarse voice in my mind one more time.

You aren't gay, Lewis. You never were one of us…

21

Despite the emotional onslaught from the night, I'm feeling better than I expected when I slowly roll on the futon only to feel a soft bundle wedged against me. When I open my eyes, I see little Emily curled up in a ball next to me.

Her eyes are closed, but her smile betrays her feigned slumber.

"Blimey, what a kink in the neck! Perhaps if I rearrange my pillow, let's see," I muse as I carefully pick up Emily and carry her to the top of the futon. The kid is about to burst out laughing but she does all she can to suppress it. I carefully put my head on her little form. "Oh, much better. Perfect. Very well, good night, all." I begin snoring as Emily wiggles under my head, her giggles growing in volume and escalating in pitch.

"I'm not a pillow!" she squeaks in a staccato of giggles.

"Oh, so soft, comfy pillow."

"Lewis! Wake up!"

"What? Who?" I sit up and turn to her. "Emily, little luv, what are you doing there?"

Emily grins. "Mom told me to wake you. Breakfast is ready."

"So it is, pet. I can smell the coffee from here."

"I don't like coffee," she says, wrinkling her button nose.

"That's a good lassie. You want tea, much more refined. It'll make a lady out of you."

Emily considers this with a straight face. "You mean a lady like Samantha?"

I have to laugh. "She's no lady, little luv. Very well, up we go."

Emily jumps out of the futon and her feet are already carrying her up the steps, seemingly before she even hits the floor.

I follow her up to the kitchen where Gwen is busily preparing scrambled eggs on a skillet. I definitely don't remember buying a carton of eggs or half the fare laid out on the counters.

"Good morning, Lewis," Brooke says as she sets the table.

"Miss Brooke, You changed my world with a blink of an eye; that is something that I cannot deny; you put my soul from worst to best; that is why I treasure you my dearest."

Brooke looks at me impressed. Her smile produces a deep dimple on each side of her pretty face. "Wow, I can't believe you don't have a girlfriend," she quips.

I laugh. "What makes you say that?"

"Daddy always recites poems to Mom, especially when he's in the doghouse."

I recall Samantha telling me such a phrase means being in trouble in America. "Does it work?"

She scoffs. "Nope."

We share a laugh that dispels the gloom that saw me to bed.

Gwen sets a platter with a small mountain of steaming scrambled eggs in the center of the table. "Coffee?"

"Thank you." I'm hoping I don't get a case of heartburn, but I'm not going to be selective after she took the time to cook.

Gwen kisses my cheek and motions for me to sit.

Samantha runs down the steps into the kitchen singing a "hullo" as she pours coffee into a mug before sitting by me. She grabs a clump of scrambled eggs in her bare hand and stuffs her mouth, earning a disapproving look from me, and a bemused glance from Brooke.

Emily climbs up on her chair and stares at Samantha with large curious, eyes.

"Samantha, Lewis says you're not a lady because you don't drink tea," Emily says with severity.

Samantha stops chewing and cuts a narrowed glance at me. "Oh, he did, did he?"

Emily nods.

I feel Samantha's foot collide with my shin, making me wince.

"Emily!" Gwen admonishes.

Brooke and Emily look at us with wide eyes until we all start laughing. When most of the egg pile is gone, along with the toast, and the coffee, I offer to clean up and enlist the help of the kids while Gwen and Samantha go do whatever it is women are compelled to do before hitting the shops.

"Where's Mommy going?" Emily asks in a fearful little voice.

"They're shopping, Em," her sister answers for me.

Emily gives me a monumental pout. "I want to go shopping."

"Shopping is boring, little luv," I tell Emily. "Your sister, you and I are going to a far more exciting place."

In an instant, the pout is gone, replaced by a look of pure anticipation.

"Where?"

"The London Zoo."

The girls squeal their approval and proceed to describe to me every zoo they've ever visited as we finish cleaning up the kitchen.

Samantha and Gwen look ready to face the cameras when they finally emerge, but they rush out the door to change their clothes at Samantha's house. I don't even presume to tell them they might as well have gone to Kensington last night.

"Are you sure about this, Lewis?" Gwen asks for the twentieth time.

"Yes, I'm quite sure. We'll have a smashing good time while Sam drags you around the old city."

Gwen looks at Samantha, who simply shrugs. "Alright," Gwen sighs. "Girls, you two listen to Lewis and stay within sight at all times, got me?"

Both girls nod, smiles set on their little faces.

"Okay." Gwen hugs and kisses each girl then gives me another quizzical look.

"I'm positive, Gwen. Ask no more."

Gwen frets about the girls needing to change their clothes.

"Fret not, luv. I've a little something planned.

"What?"

"Go do your girlie stuff," I prod her.

"Okay... They're all yours."

Gwen finally leaves with Samantha, grateful to have some adult time.

I open the double doors to the gallery for the first time in over a year, and the girls run out to the railing to wave farewell at their mum and Samantha as they drive off in the Mini Cooper.

"Are we going to the zoo right now?" Emily inquires.

"Yes, we are."

"Yay!" Both girls cry in unison.

***

I drive the girls through Park Lane so they can get a peek at Hyde Park. Brooke hooked up her iPod to the sound system and they sing along to something called *Kidz Bop*, popular songs rendered in kid style. Could've been worse.

We stop at the St. John's Wood Substation, where I leave my car, and walk to a boutique that caters to younger girls.

"I thought we were going to the zoo," Emily says.

"We are, but your mum was adamant that you look presentable for Mr. Lion."

"Oh."

Brooke laughs. At eight years of age, she can no longer be so easily convinced.

I've known the boutique's owner, a dynamo of a lad named Will Turner, designer extraordinaire. He designed women's fashions for a long time before burning out, according to him. His children designs command a fortune.

"Lewis! Lewis Bettford? Blimey, lad. What brings you to my humble little hole in the wall? Come here, lad."

Will kisses each of my cheeks as he welcomes me to his "humble" shop, which is about as humble as the Taj Mahal.

The girls' eyes dart around, mouths agape in wonder.

"Will, how about you give these two little ladies your unique shopping experience."

Will's grin is impossibly wide. "Ladies, welcome to Lisson Grove. May I have your names?"

"I'm Brooke, and this is my little sister, Emily."

Will is very well in tune with children. He offers his hand to Brooke and compliments her kindly, but leaves plenty of room between himself and Emily, speaking to her through her big sister. I know Emily is more than outgoing, but new faces make her initially shy.

Will then calls two of his assistants and two lovely girls appear. They introduce themselves as Nikki and Susan. They ask if the girls would prefer to shop together, but Brooke and Emily quickly decline. They partner up and go in the direction of the displays labeled by age. Brooke suddenly stops and runs back to where I'm standing with Will.

"Lewis, does Mom know you brought us to this store?"

"We'll keep it a secret." I give her a conspiratorial wink.

"Cool!"

I watch them go after I promise to join them. Soon I hear their chatter and giggles as they tell their respective shopping assistants all about Pennsylvania.

"Nieces of yours?" Will asks.

"In essence. How have you been?"

"I'm well, Lewis. The same can't be said for Terry from what I hear."

I'm a bit surprised by this. "What else are you hearing?"

Will gives me a grin that reveals a severely crooked row of lower teeth. He has thin features and a slight frame. His blonde hair is swept to the side in a style that I associate with old Flock of Seagulls videos, and his pale hazel eyes are deep wells of sympathy.

"Few things here and there. His company is closing down."

"I'm surprised you know that."

"Well, chap, I should. I'm one of his displaced clients. In fact I got an email saying I ought to contact you."

"By all means, Will. But that's not what I meant."

Will's smile vanishes. He looks over his shoulder, as though to make sure we're alone. "There's a lot of resentment in the community. Paddy O'Connor is releasing an announcement on The Flier. Given Terry's penchant for throwing lavish parties, some of those guests may react badly."

The Flier is a web page dedicated to the gay community of the Greater London Area, a social network. The publication often celebrates the lifestyle, and glorifies prominent advocates, as well as vilifies the outspoken opponents who publicly denounce the gay way of life.

"Terence is beyond caring about such rubbish, Will."

He nods. "I imagine you're right, lad. But what about you?"

"What about me?"

"You, Terence, and the talented Audrey Burton are by far some of the most prominent success stories out of Liverpool, lad. You're all well known in this city."

This point gives me pause.

"There are some rumblings about your company already. Hopefully it comes to nothing."

"I'm not concerned with that. Our friend is dying, Will."

"Words fail me," Will says sadly.

"Yes."

He glances over where the girls are sifting through clothes from the displays. "Are you playing nanny today?"

I breathe a sigh of relief, thankful for the change of subject. "Yes, these lovely young ladies are here for my friend Samantha's wedding. They'll be the flower girls."

"Lovely, lovely." Will claps his hands in approval. "We have a charming line of formal gowns for little ones."

"Forgive me, chap. Augusta Flynn already made the gowns."

"Augusta? I wish I could say something bad about that old bird but she knows her stitching," Will says with grudging respect. "You know, it surprises me that you're not the groom in that affair."

"How you do go on," I tell him on a laugh. "Samantha and I, we're best friends."

"Who's the groom?"

"No one you know, I'm sure."

"Try me," Will challenges.

"Jason McElroy."

Will seems a bit stunned. "Of course. I shouldn't be bloody surprised."

"How do you know him?"

Will looks suddenly angry. "That wanker acted as camp as a row of tents, but it was clear he was more of an ambisexterous since he was always deep in the bloody fish. He's nothing but a buggering tootsie."

His use of gay slang takes me by surprise, the last word most of all. Despite its unthreatening sound, the slur might as well be the most venomous curse bestowed upon anyone who pretended to be gay. Playing tootsie is seen as an affront, as a belittlement of a lifestyle that's less of a choice, and more of something ingrained in our makeup.

"When was this?"

Will makes a placating gesture sensing my discomfort. "I admit it was years ago. Many of us wondered just how often he shagged his fag hags."

I have no doubt Jason McElroy caught the eye of women in a nightclub setting, but knowing him as I do now, it's highly unlikely that he made a habit out of sleeping around.

Terence's words come to my mind and I suddenly see just how these people that have held me in such high regard will so quickly turn on me, were they to ever get word that I've been nothing but a pretender for years.

"Lewis, are you alright, luv?"

I blink repeatedly, only now aware of his voice. "Quite, quite. Something I was thinking, is all."

Curiosity makes his eyes shine, but he probably senses I won't get into it. "Let's share some happier news, my friend."

"By all means," I agree.

"Davy finally moved in."

"It's now official."

Will chuckles. "It only took ten bloody years."

"Good for you, chap."

He gestures behind me and I turn to see Brooke in a stylish top and dark jeans. It's hard to believe she's only eight. I give her an approving smile and a thumbs up. She thanks me and runs back with one of the assistants.

"How about you, luv? Anyone in your life now that your own fag hag is tying the bloody knot?"

I indulge Will with a soft chuckle of my own. A fag hag is a woman who loves the company of gay men, though not always innocently.

"No one. And please, refrain from playing match maker."

Will makes an effeminate gesture of feigned indignation. "Keep in mind you're not always going to be this much of a dish, luv."

With a wink, Will leaves me to attend other customers. I walk towards the fitting rooms where the girls are carefully selecting their new clothes. Emily is holding on to a pretty little lavender dress, her eyes downcast, sad.

I get down on one knee in front of her to ask her what's wrong.

"I really like another yellow dress, but Mommy always says I'm only allowed one."

The sadness in those big brown eyes is so staggering I can't trust my voice for a beat. "Well, not today, little luv. Today you can get every dress you can find."

She looks up and her eyes go wide, though guarded, as though waiting for me to say that I'm only teasing.

"But Mommy said only one."

"Well, Mommy is not here, and I say get as many as you can."

Emily throws her little arms around me and squeezes tight before running in search of her assistant who's smiling down at her. I see a pile of garments are already folded and readied for package.

"She has good taste," she says, pointing at the pile.

"I'll take it all, luv. I want a variety of those colorful sacks." I indicate the store shopping sacks.

Somewhere behind a rack of printed tops, I hear Emily's voice. "Best day ever!"

I thought Samantha enjoyed making me wait as she tried on one thing after another, but she falls short in comparison to Brooke, who stares at her reflection with a critical eye as she tries on her new clothes.

Some two hours later, I arrange for Will's assistants to carry the shopping sacks to the boot of my car, only after each girl chooses what to wear for the day. Despite the alarming quantity of bags and shoe boxes, I admire their restraint. I practically insisted they choose more outfits. The grateful smiles on those pretty faces are well worth it.

Our second stop is at the nearest McDonald's. Both girls stare incredulously at my salad while they dip chicken bits in ketchup, and slurp on vanilla milkshakes.

The girls excuse themselves to visit the loo and I hurry up and rush my own bodily function, terrified of not being outside when the girls are done. I quickly wash my hands and rush out. A wave of anxiety courses through me when I don't see them. I've never known how long a minute really is until I count every second, my eyes fixed on the door of the loo. I only breathe when I see the door pulling open to reveal Emily drying her hands on paper towels, followed by Brooke.

Thus improperly nourished, we take a cab back to Regent Park Boating Lake. Earlier, I was worried about the weather turning cold and rainy, which can happen quickly at any given moment, but the day holds its brightness.

My mobile buzzes in my pocket as it has every half hour. I stopped replying to Gwen and Samantha after the fourth text message asking the same question, *How's it going?*

When Brooke and Emily see the paddle boats, their eyes get that spark of excitement that omits the word "No" from my vocabulary.

We rent a boat and carefully board it. Fifteen minutes into it, I'm the only one paddling us around and my legs are beginning to cramp up, despite my improved conditioning. This is where I could use the finely fit leg muscles of my best friend, who runs every bloody morning and has the endurance of a race horse. But I'm on my own, dreading the prospect of walking the endless paths of the London Zoo after this exertion.

I navigate the small torture machine all the way to the bridge of the Outer Circle that leads to the zoo. There aren't many boaters out. A few old timers, some couples, but no other children.

However, every person we pass by waves and smiles openly at the girls, who return the gestures with their unique exuberance. A group of four women on a boat, paddle closer and one even offers to team up with me, noticing my pained expression. I politely decline, but then am subjected to some song the girls make up about me and that nice lass K. I. S. S. I. N. G. in a tree.

Brooke asks me to say different words for her and she repeats them in a pretty good British accent. Emily masters the word water, pronouncing it as *woah-tuh,* and they do what they can to suppress their American dialect.

"Try this," I tell them, recalling a Cockney rhyme. "Got to my mickey, found me way up the apples, put on me whistle and the bloody dog went. It was me trouble telling me to fetch the teapots."

"What?" Emily asks as she laughs.

"What the heck does that mean?" Brooke laughs. "Who's Mickey?"

"That's called a Cockney rhyme. What I said is, Got to my house, found my way up the stairs, put on my suit when the phone rang. It was my wife telling me to get the kids."

"I don't get it," Brooke protests.

"Got to my house, rhymes with Mickey Mouse, so got to my mickey means…"

"I got to my house!" Brooke completes the sentence.

"Apples and pears rhymes with upstairs; whistle is short for whistle and flute, which rhymes with suit, get it?"

Brooke nods but Emily's lost interest and she's looking at other paddle boats.

"Teapots and lids rhyme with kids. That's you, teapots and lids."

Brooke bites her lip in thought. "You said something was bloody."

"Bloody is not a good word for you to say, Brooke."

"Samantha says it all the time," she's quick to say.

"I had a bloody boo-boo once," Emily rejoins the conversation.

"That's actually cool," Brooke chuckles. "It was bloody cool!"

It's impossible not to laugh when a child curses.

"Do you know any more rhymes?"

"A few more," I assure her, though I try to think of one without "bloody" in it.

Sweat is pouring off my brow by the time I guide the paddleboat back to its mooring. The girls easily hop out of the bloody contraption. When I attempt to stand, a cramp sears my thighs. My initial reaction is to tense up and a cramp through my buttocks literally brings tears to my eyes. I've got to run with Samantha more often.

Brooke and Emily's concern and their dependence in me to have a good time, give me enough strength to get out of the blasted boat. I shuffle along the path that is now the longest path in existence as we head for the zoo. By the time we make it through the gates, I'm inwardly begging for mercy.

The girls flutter like butterflies, practically sprinting from exhibit to exhibit. Brooke takes several photographs of each animal on her digital camera and Emily prompts her to show me each and every one. And I look at each and every one, it's the only chance I have to stay still as new pains register in parts of my body I wasn't aware I even had. They leave me on a bench and run to look at an exhibit of Australian water dragons.

A woman walks up and sits next to me. I smile politely at her and she returns the gesture. She's a bit heavy but nonetheless attractive.

"It's a bit hotter than I thought," she says as she pushes her sunglasses up her nose. "Yours?"

I follow her gaze. She's looking at Brooke, who picks Emily up so she can get a better look at the dragons.

"Your daughters are beautiful!" The woman says before I can reply.

I start to formulate a correction but the words die in my throat.

"The little one looks a lot like you. Your wife must be gorgeous."

"Thank you," I manage as I think back on that last rave I went to, when I helped a mum with her infant and ended up in an emotional maelstrom. I can feel something similar to what I felt that day, a strange pressure in my heart.

"How old are they?"

I sigh. "Brooke is eight and Emily is five."

"Bless their hearts," the woman says on a breathy voice. "Well, enjoy your day."

I force a smile. "Thank you, Madame. You as well."

She walks away, smiling at the girls one more time before making her way down the path.

The girls return to the bench to show me the photos of the dragons. I notice Emily's hair is a close match to mine in color. I wonder what if...

"Ice cream!" Emily points, jolting me out of my reverie.

I try to buy a bit of rest by indulging the girls with ice cream, chocolates, cotton candy, and some sugary juice that tastes odd to my adult palate. The girls swear they've never had anything so good, and that gets them another round. Their joy does much to dispel the sudden gloom that threatened to envelop me after hearing the woman comment on "my beautiful daughters".

We spend a long time staring at the sleeping lions, hoping they'd put on a show, but other than an occasional flick of their ears, they don't move. Giraffes, antelopes, and other savanna creatures stare back at us indifferently while birds call out as though demanding our attention.

As we start moving on, Emily turns to me with that pouty, little angel face and stretches her arms up. I don't hesitate for a second, I just grab her and prop her under my arm over a hip. It doesn't take long to realize the design of the female body is nothing short of divine creation. My hips don't flare out enough to provide a bit of a ledge to help support Emily's weight.

Not to be outdone, Brooke takes my left hand. My right forearm burns painfully under Emily, but her little arm around my shoulder, and the smile on her little face make the pain bearable. At least long enough to get through the elephant exhibit.

When we walk up to Gorilla Kingdom, my legs begin to ignore the commands from my brain to keep moving. I set Emily back on the ground and she and her sister run to talk to the apes. Accepting defeat, I text Gwen, asking where she is as subtly as I can.

"Mommy!" The girls exclaim in unison and dash away from me.

My first instinct is to yell for them to stop before they run to some stranger that resembles Gwen, but my muscles vociferously protest and threaten further cramping if I try to stand. I try anyway, but when I see the knowing little grin on Samantha's face, I gratefully sag on the bench though I wonder if I'm only seeing a mirage.

The girls' voices escalate in volume and pitch as they try to outdo each other in their account of their day. Gwen somehow manages to respond equally to each. Once they're done burning off Gwen's ears, they turn to Samantha and repeat their fast chatter with even more vigor. I can only shake my head and smile sheepishly as Gwen sits on the bench beside me.

"I tried to warn you," she says after kissing my cheek.

"Why do I have the feeling you two were following us all day?"

"We weren't. We were about to do an early dinner, but Samantha suggested we check on you after you stopped replying to our texts." She looks sincere.

I exhale a long weary breath. "You and Tony have my utmost respect and admiration. Don't they tire you out?"

"You might have only sustained half the damage if you kept them away from the large amounts of sugar they tell me you gave them." Gwen smiles. "I can't believe how much you spoiled them today. They're never going to want to leave."

"I'd love to watch them grow," I say under a sudden wave of emotion that earns me a curious look from Gwen.

"Did it ever cross your mind?"

I'm helpless to prevent the telling pause.

Gwen looks interested. "How does it work?"

"How does what work?"

She keeps her eyes on me. "How do gay couples raise children?"

"To be honest with you, I really don't know. I don't know any gay couples raising children."

"You know, back home, it's a pretty big deal. Few people defend those couples, saying it's their right. Most people are against it, saying that they'd be keeping the children from making their own decision as to how they'd live their lives."

"In other words, gay couples would raise gay kids," I interpret.

Gwen squirms. "Yeah."

"And what do you think?"

She looks like she anticipated the question. "Me, personally? I think as long as a child receives love, guidance, and care, it's all that should really matter. But the problem is tradition."

I've never heard this argument before. "Tradition?"

"Well, think about it. You and your partner are raising a boy. On Mother's Day at school, the kids make these crafts to present to their mothers. What would your kid do? He'd be inadvertently ousted, not to mention teased by his classmates. How would he feel? And that's just a small example of the many things that would put the kid in that position."

"I've never thought of that," I admit.

"Look, I don't mean any disrespect when I say this, but a child needs a mom and a dad. The basis of his life among society starts at home, and the first, and most important social institution is the family, mom, dad, and children."

"But times are changing," I say, but it feels hollow.

"Yes, they are, but not enough to completely accept something like that, and not just socially, but biologically."

Samantha often told me Gwen thinks herself to be simple, but this frank talk of something so controversial reveals her to possess quite the intellect.

"I think just about everyone will accept two women raising a child," She continues. "Women are nurturing and the image alone is easier to tolerate. Even on a sexual level."

I glance over at Samantha and the girls, who are flagging down an ice cream vendor. Go ahead and sugar them up, I think with perverse glee. "How'd we go from kids to sexual levels?"

"I'm just saying two naked women in bed look hotter than two men in bed."

I grin at her. "Depends on the men, luv."

Gwen laughs and nods in consent. "I don't know, Lewis. I guess. For instance, I can't see you with another man. You know, doing it. I just can't."

I hold a thin smile on my face. I actually can't either. I don't know that I ever could.

"What's it like, anyway?"

I give Gwen a sideways glance. "Two men together?" She nods. "I wish I could tell you."

Understanding flashes in Gwen's eyes, though it fights through a fog of disbelief.

"You never…?"

I shake my head.

"I know you told me you and Terence didn't, but I didn't think to ask you if you ever had another lover."

"I guess you can say I'm a virgin," I tell her with a self-deprecating chuckle.

Gwen laughs her melodious little trill then looks at me with severity. "I'm selfishly glad," she says. "Did you ever want to?"

"Are you offering?"

Her wicked grin unnerves me.

"I'm not sure," I quickly add. "A time or two, I gather. I was always too afraid of risks."

Gwen clearly wants to ask many more questions but Samantha and the girls approach. Emily and Brooke sport a nice chocolate ice cream mustache, and even the tips of their noses are dotted with it.

"Where do you little ladies put all that ice cream?" I ask.

Both girls simultaneously look up at Gwen, anticipating a sound ear boxing.

"How much ice cream have they had?" Gwen asks me, but her eyes are on each of her girls.

They both look to me for help and all three of us put two fingers up. Gwen looks skyward and closes her eyes. I'm guessing she's counting to ten.

"Hello, sugar rush," she says.

Samantha looks at me. "Way to go Uncle Lewie." She winks.

"Come now, both of you. How bad can it be?"

The incredulous looks both women give me are full of foreboding. By the time we go back to Kensington, I know exactly what a sugar rush, and subsequent crash does to a child, and it's something I will remember forevermore. The experience is so traumatizing I simply refuse to share it here.

22

I hear my mobile and groan under the covers. My legs are sore, my back is aching, and the last thing I want to do is make any movement that engages the stiff muscles of my right forearm. I can't believe just how much exercise carrying Emily really is.

Wincing at the stabbing pain in my arm, I grab my mobile and connect the call. If it's Samantha I will scream.

"This had better be bloody good."

"Uh oh, sounds like someone had a rough night."

Quinn's smoky voice makes me jump, bringing a new onslaught of pain that gleefully torments the muscles of my back. "Hullo, Quinn," I manage, covering the device long enough to hiss the pain away.

"You sound rough. Are you okay?"

"No. I got trampled by a couple of flower girls yesterday."

Quinn laughs a soft, melodic, pretty laugh that makes me smile. "Sounds rough, alright."

"You have no idea. What can I do for you?"

"Have you any plans today?"

"You're first in line to demand my superior company."

She laughs again. "Lucky me. I'd like to get together, perhaps go over the last template you emailed me."

Bright sunlight is cutting through the gap between the wall and the blind, forcing me to squint. "You're willing to work on a weekend?"

"Not the whole day. Look, I'll be honest. My friendships in London are purely professional. I don't want you to fall in that category. I don't want to sound pathetic and say I'm lonely and I'd like to spend time with a friend, so I won't say it."

I smile, moved by her sincerity, and resist the urge to ask her about her friend from the other day. "Like I said, first call first served. Would you like to meet at the office?"

"Yes, works for me."

"I shall see you there within the hour."

A giggle. "Bye Lewis."

The hot shower does wonders for the stiffness in my muscles. Perhaps it's high time I join the ranks of the fit on a more permanent basis. I know Samantha could help me in that regard, but I don't want to give her a chance to mercilessly torture me the way she does on the rare occasions we decide to run together.

A part of me feels a tremendous guilt over not telling Samantha that Quinn is in town. Hopefully she at least divulges her reasons to keep Samantha in the dark.

I'm selecting a shirt to go with the slacks I picked out when I realize it's bloody Saturday and I have no intention of dressing formally. I'm almost tempted to call Quinn and ask what she'll wear.

I settle on dark jeans, a light blue shirt and my trusty old Rockports. I grab a black hooded zip up jacket to guard against the chill and leave the flat. The lack of traffic allows me to arrive at the office in record time.

I take the elevator from the underground level where I park and I'm surprised when it stops at the main floor. The custodians normally use a smaller elevator at the back of the building. When the doors open, a now familiar pair of bright blue eyes peers at me over a dazzling smile.

"Are you always this punctual?"

Quinn enters the elevator cab and the doors slide shut behind her. The scent of her perfume gives me the urge to get closer to her.

"My mom is all about punctuality."

Quinn wears designer faded jeans that are tight around her thighs and knees, but flare out around her sandaled feet; a cream colored t-shirt from American Eagle and a light pink fleece zip up complete the pretty picture. The shirt is tight around her chest, which is fairly large for her frame as I suspected. Her short stature makes her curves more pronounced, making me think of the word voluptuous. Her short hair is somehow pulled into a ponytail that bounces atop her head when she moves. She holds her mobile in her hand, no purse.

"Where's my new friend?"

"Firuz?" Quinn frowns. "I could call him for you, if you'd like."

I shake my head. "Not necessary. I think you're quite safe with me." I'm ecstatic about not having to endure the sour disposition of the enigmatic Firuz Ahmidi.

She looks confused, but smiles in understanding.

"No bag today?"

"I left it in my car."

I frown. "Where did you park?

"Under the tower. Arnie lets me use the spot when I need it."

An unexpected surge of jealousy burns in my gut. "Another friend of yours?"

Quinn gives me a sideways glance. "Arnold Braddigan. He's an attorney."

"There are a lot of attorneys working at the tower," I tell her, unable to sound deliberately unimpressed.

"Well, Arnie and his wife are like family. I think of him as my British uncle."

The tightness in my chest vanishes along with the raging jealousy.

What is going on with you, Lewis? Pull it bloody together!

The elevator opens on the fourth floor and after unlocking the door, I allow Quinn to go in first. She looks at the small reception area with interest.

"This way," I tell her, opening the door to my new office.

"Oh, my God! What a place!"

I'm enormously pleased at her reaction. The office is attractive, despite the lack of a more personal touch, as pointed out by Samantha. I may just save money by not calling my interior designer, Milton Stoneworth.

With the extra room, Samantha suggested setting up a sitting area away from the desk. I was finally able to use the tea service I got as a gift from Mum on one of my birthdays, along with other gifts from Samantha and Alicia.

Quinn steps up to the tea service and picks up one of the mugs. "Red got to you too, didn't she?" She says, lifting the red mug. "She has it bad for the Red Wings."

"Do you have a favorite hockey team?"

"I don't watch hockey. I like soccer. I actually played when I was a kid, all the way through high school. Well, until I fell off my horse. I still play on occasion, especially when I'm visiting London. Some of my father's friends play indoor."

"Soccer," I choke the word out as I shake my head. "I've always questioned that term. I often think there ought to be a different name for what you, Americans, call football."

"You won't get an argument from me. I do follow the Premier League though."

I grin. "An enlightened woman! So few of you. Have you a favorite team?"

Quinn nods. "Manchester United."

The grin on my face fades. "You must be joking," I lament.

Quinn raises a fist. "We're Man U and we are loud, Loyal fans and totally proud..." She laughs. "Does this mean you'll unleash a series of viruses into my intranet?"

"For starters," I grumble.

"Could be worse, I could be like Firuz and cheer for Arsenal."

My face goes sour at the mention of her abrasive *friend*. "I wouldn't expect anything less."

She laughs. "Perhaps I should've lied and tell you I'm a Derby County fan. Are they still the worst team in the league?"

I can't believe how a simple taste in English football draws me to her. "They haven't improved much. What position did you play?"

"I was a midfielder in rec league, but once I got on the travel teams I started playing goalkeeper. The net was mine all through high school."

This widens my eyes in shock. Quinn is barely over five feet.

She seems to read my mind. "I know I'm short, but a lot of girls didn't kick rising shots."

"I played striker," I tell her.

"Would you want to play? There's a group playing later. We could use one more."

I notice the hopeful look in her eyes and don't have it in me to say no despite the nagging aches from my excursion to the zoo.

"That could prove quite interesting, given my conditioning, or lack thereof."

Quinn laughs. "Trust me, no one in that group is in the best of shape."

"I'd love to," I agree, ignoring my body's complaints. "When I was a kid, I only played when I was allowed, which wasn't too often."

"Why not?"

"I did ballet and my… instructor heavily depended on me to carry certain sequences at the performances. I was forbidden from sustaining an injury."

"Wow! I've never met a dancer. That's amazing. I bet you're really good."

I expected the usual joke, or the subtle confused look, anything but her assumption that I was good. Modesty aside, I was quite good, but I just never came across someone who would intuit that. Most people often laughed at the fact that I chose ballet over the more glorified sport of football, which was why I never even steered a conversation this way.

"Do you still dance? You look like you do."

I grow a bit self-conscious at the way her blue eyes sweep over me. When I do the same, I notice the definition of her thighs. She looks like she could be playing for the US Women's National Team. "I stopped before college."

"Samantha told me once your mom taught dance."

"She still does. She was my instructor."

She looks more interested. "I hope you don't mind me asking, but how did your father feel about you dancing?"

I smile. "I never met my father. It was just Mum and me."

Quinn's smile vanishes and she bites her lower lip contritely. "I'm sorry, I didn't know."

"Not at all, luv."

"I only asked you because my father didn't really care for me playing soccer. He was a hundred percent behind me on my horse riding though."

"I imagine your father didn't play sports when he was a kid."

"That's the funny thing. He played football. American football. He was a linebacker at UConn, but then he came out here for a study abroad program and when he got back he was all about horses."

"Do you still ride?"

Grief flashes in her lovely eyes. "Only when I visit my parents. It's been quite a while."

"Why?"

"I was living in California with Andrew. My parents live in Connecticut. It was no big deal to hop on a plane and go see them, but I was just really busy with work and Andrew and my father didn't exactly get along. I was always stuck in the middle and sometimes it was easier to just go along with Andrew just so I wouldn't suffer his idiotic mood swings."

Her eyes seem to focus on different times. I wonder if *idiotic mood swings* is a euphemism for an intolerable truth that I don't have the heart to ask about.

"I can't believe I tried to please that idiot, forsaking my own family in the process."

Tears shimmer in her eyes and I step up to her, take the mug from her hand and lead her by the elbow to one of the sofas. She sits in a daze. When I release her arm, she turns and stares at me with a wounded look that pierces my heart.

"I'm sorry." She catches the escaping tears with her forefingers and sniffles loudly. "I'm so sorry."

Regret emanates from her.

I reach for the tissue dispenser Samantha set on the table, grateful for her foresight. Quinn pulls one out and dabs at her eyes.

"I haven't talked about things with anyone. I'm probably starved for a sympathetic ear. I'm so sorry."

"Don't you and Firuz talk this way?" The question escapes my lips before I could think of taking it back.

Quinn thinks for a minute. "He's not exactly the deep type, you know? He's a big believer in never looking back. I'm sorry."

"Don't apologize, Quinn. It's obvious you've gone through quite a lot."

She nods. "The reason I didn't want Sam to see me just yet is because I want to have a better outlook on the idea of marriage. I don't want to say something stupid because my own failed, and I don't want to be reminded of the fairy tale it can be. Does that make any sense?"

I hesitate for only a second. "Absolutely."

She drops her head on her hands. "I'm sorry, I'd better stop. Firuz tells me I wallow in self-pity too much."

This time I take her forearm and give her a pointed look. I can sense how much she needs to unburden to someone. "This isn't Firuz you're talking to."

Quinn' eyes fix on mine. I notice silvery striations in the blue backdrop of her irises. I try not to blink, but she does, breaking the spell. "I think I see now why you didn't want to see Samantha just yet."

She gives me a grateful look. "I wasn't ready to see just how happy two people about to commit themselves to each other can be."

The blush on her face tells me she surprised herself by revealing so much and now she's uncertain how to proceed. I can almost read her mind as she thinks up an excuse to leave, but that's the last thing I want and the last thing she needs. She wants a sympathetic ear? I have two. "I've known Sam my entire life, and it's difficult to be entirely happy for her getting married when I know just how much it will change our friendship."

Quinn looks surprised at my candor.

I shrug. "You're not the only one starved for a sympathetic ear."

Once we both work through our views on marriage, we end up uncovering different things about ourselves. We talk right through the lunch hour, never once mentioning her project.

She tells me all about her parents, her little brother. I tell her all about my mother and Liverpool. We spend a great amount of time talking about Samantha and revisiting some of her most memorable antics. I'm probably learning much more than Samantha ever thought I would, or wanted me to, and Quinn gets to see the Samantha I've known. Not the seductive, drunken overachiever, but the girl that accepted my every fault, the girl who kissed me in front of a bunch of bullies in order to protect me; the girl who somehow survived the horror story her engagement to Brooks Waldenberg really was.

Quinn tells me about the haughty girl who exuded an aura of superiority and sophistication; an elegance envied by everyone who knew her. She tells me about the enigmatic Brit who wrote nearly undecipherable passages of such beauty that depicted a bottomless well of pain no one was aware of.

"I kept some of the things she wrote. It took a long time before I understood that she'd lost someone. And then, there was the dead hole thing…"

"And what's that?" I ask, feeling a knot in my stomach.

"Some stupid stunt we pulled." Quinn brings her hands to her temples as though the recollection is inducing a migraine.

"Are you well?"

Quinn nods slowly. "Lewis, perhaps I just want to feel like Samantha will forgive me for all the things I did, or ever said about her. I'm afraid to see that she's still angry with me."

This confuses me. "You seemed to carry a friendly chat over the telephone the other day."

She nods. "That was great but neither of us said anything of substance. We were sort of feeling each other out."

"Let me guess, you were using your telepathic powers of non-verbal communication to get an accurate read on one another after all these years."

She looks at me with real surprise. "That must be something only gay men understand. You're right."

Gay men…? "Actually, Samantha often refers to that. That's the only reason I know anything about it. It must be true then."

Her reference to gay men produces a chain reaction that locks up my mind behind steel doors. I can feel the locks engaging in my head. Quinn seems unaware of the sudden change in my demeanor.

"What time is it?" She asks.

I glance at the clock on my wall. It's after three in the afternoon. We've been talking for the last five hours.

"Oh, my God!" Quinn exclaims when she takes a look at the clock. "I feel like I totally wasted your time, Lewis."

"Nothing could be further from the truth. It's been a real pleasure to get to know you, Quinn."

Her smile grows uncertain as she looks into my eyes. She's probably sensing the sudden distance that wasn't there before her line about gay men.

"That means a lot." She bites her lip for a moment. "After today, I'm going to envy Samantha even more for having you in her corner all her life. I hope you see me as a friend as well."

"Absolutely."

Just make certain she is as bright, and as beautiful as you are, and don't settle for anything less. Don't let another Samantha Reddick slip by...

Something goes cold inside of me as I let Terence's words play in my mind while looking into Quinn's eyes. Right at this moment, I can't think of any woman more beautiful, or brighter than Quinn McDermont.

Quinn smiles. "So, will you really take the field with me?"

"Only if you agree to dinner if I survive the exertion," I tell her, already feeling the soreness from the zoo trip.

"I'd love to."

***

I agree to meet Quinn at Westbourne Park after retrieving my gear from my flat. The indoor shoes look dusty when I pull them out of the closet. I dig for my old shin guards and a pair of long tube socks. I grin in anticipation of the match.

In less than an hour, I'm pulling into the lot from Tavistock Road. I see a group of eight men and two striking women in warm up suits forming a circle and passing the ball around, trying to keep it off the ground. If this is part of the group I'm about to play with, Quinn was right. All the men, with the exception of two, look overweight. The two ladies however, look in tip top shape.

A wine-colored Jaguar with tinted windows pulls up next to my car. Firuz Ahmadi emerges out of the driver's side. He's wearing gold rimmed sunglasses even though the day is overcast. I wave to him but he stares right through me. He ignores me and walks to the boot of the Jag. I can only shake my head at his rudeness.

Quinn opens her door and hops out. She's wearing a bright green, long sleeve jersey with white piping along the arms. There's a faded crest over the slope of her left breast that I can't make out. White cyclist spandex shorts peek out from beneath her black football shorts.

"Apparently you take these games quite serious," I observe as I register the worn Diadoras on her feet.

Quinn smiles, looks over at the group of blokes kicking the ball and waves as they call her name. "Hi boys!"

"And you have a fan club, I see."

She shrugs. "These men are all good friends of my dad's. They still treat me like a baby."

"And the ladies?"

"The tall one is Katja. She's Henry's wife. Kicks like a mule if you give her the chance. The shorter brunette, that's Meagan O'Rourke. She's a coach, and a very quick defender."

I nod. "Of course."

She gives me a once over. "I thought you'd have a Liverpool jersey with you."

"I have it framed at home, luv. If we were playing outdoors in the mud, I would've worn a U Man, jersey."

Quinn gapes at me. "So that's how it is." She grins.

Firuz slams the lid of the boot and walks up to me, invading my personal space.

"It's a surprise to see you here, Lewis. I've heard these chaps play hard."

I force myself not to step back as I try to read between the lines. "Is there another way to play?"

His smile is enigmatic.

"Got my gloves?" Quinn asks.

Firuz hands her the keeper gloves, never taking his eyes off me. Not that I can see behind the dark lenses of his gold rimmed sunglasses, but I can feel his glare.

"Hey, Lefty!" Calls one of the men standing by the entrance.

"Hi, Timmy." She heads for the doors after giving me a look.

I turn to watch her go when I feel Firuz standing even closer than he already was.

"Ready for a friendly match?"

I nod. "Always."

"I didn't know what to expect when Quinn asked me to come, but I'm certainly looking forward to it."

There's something cold about his smile. We stare at each other for a few long seconds before he nods and walks away.

"Welcome lad, glad to see an infusion of young blood today." One of the men from the group offers.

"Lewis Bettford," I extend my hand.

The man smiles. "I'm Jones."

The man is solid. I judge him to be in his late forties although the lack of hair atop his head makes it difficult to tell. I notice he stayed behind to tie his laces tighter.

"Glad you could make it, lad. I was wondering if we'd have a replacement for Pete. Who's your friend?"

"I wouldn't say friend, Sir. I just met Firuz a few days ago."

Jones seems confused. "Well, this certainly just got interesting," he muses, his eyes on Firuz's broad back noting the green 16 emblazoned on his jersey.

23

The indoor football field is designed for up to eight-a-side matches. Quinn is standing with the two women, chatting away while one of the men, who clearly has the respect of the others introduces himself to Firuz and me as Henry.

"Welcome," he says, shaking hands with each of us.

I notice Firuz doesn't try to crush Henry's bones.

"What kind of experience do you have?"

"I played first liner for Loughborough," Firuz says pointedly.

Henry's eyes go wide for a second. "Impressive. How about you, lad?"

"I'm more of an observant of the game, Henry."

Henry considers this while looking from me to Firuz. "Alright, since you're the newcomers, we'll pair you up for picks, even though Fir.. Firuz?" He gives a questioning glance at Firuz, who nods. "Firuz, here, has infinite experience."

I completely understand Henry's assessment. Loughborough has a strong reputation as a football mecca at the university level.

Henry and Jones toss a coin that awards the first pick to Jones. Without any hesitation he picks Firuz first. Each captain takes a turn making their picks. Jones picks Quinn, and Meagan O'Rourke joins me at the left of Henry.

"Any problem with Lewis playing right mid?" Henry asks the team once we huddle at the south end.

They all shake their heads and break away to go pass the ball around.

"We're going north," Henry points at the far net, where Quinn is bouncing on her feet and wind milling her arms after trotting from one side of the box to the other. I've seen other goalies do the same thing, as though they need to reconnoiter 44 by 18 yard area where they're allowed to grab the ball, just in case they forget.

I glance back at the south net. Our goalie is a thin lad that doesn't seem to move very fast.

A ball rolls to my feet. I tap it with my left foot ahead of me and dribble it up to the top of the box. The flooring has a bit of a grip and it feels somewhat softer than I thought. With a running start, I look up and pick the left upper corner of the net. I plant my left foot just behind and to the left of the ball, and swing my right leg through, making contact with the top of my big right toe. The ball flies towards the center of the goal but the spin forces it into the left. The goalie watches it go in without ever making a move to stop it. Suddenly, every eye is on me.

"Nice bend," Henry says, wide eyed.

"Lucky shot," I comment.

Out of the corner of my eye, I see the lads at the far end of the field looking at me with a new appreciation with the exception of Firuz.

I watch him line up the ball from just inside the box. He is not as wiry as I initially thought. His legs seem as thick as tree trunks. He backs up exactly five steps, looks up and runs into the ball, unleashing a hard shot that Quinn punches to the corner. She shakes her hands, grimacing, before focusing on the next shot. Brave, that one.

I watch her make two other saves, one with her feet, one by leaping to her left. Her eyes never leaving the ball she batted.

"She's incredible," Henry says in appreciation. "Leave it to the Americans to make gorgeous keeps. I dare say Quinn may be a tad better than Hope Solo."

"She's a bit short. I'd go high each time."

Henry chuckles. "You haven't seen her in action, lad."

I frown. "How often does she play here?"

"Not as often as we'd like. Whenever she visits London, she'll ring us up for a match."

A whistle sounds behind me. I turn to find a rotund little man in a striped shirt standing at midfield. He signals with both hands for the captains to join him.

The ball is awarded to Jones's team. Part of the coin toss victory is choosing which team wears the red vests in lieu of uniforms. Henry distributes the vests, subjected to the taunting grin of Jones's team. I look at each member, noticing that they have an advantage in size. I look at our lads, but since I've never played with any of them, I don't know what their smaller frames will bring to the table.

At the whistle, Jones quickly touches the ball up field and charges to the center as Firuz peels around Meagan and encroaches the box. I back pedal to mark their left midfielder until he makes an inside run. The lad playing sweeper for my team is Henry. He confronts the midfielder who gets the ball from across the field and he taps it behind me where Firuz is charging.

I run as fast as I can, but Firuz easily evades Meagan and suddenly he's one on one against our lethargic goalie. The dark skinned man dribbles around the hapless goalie and unnecessarily blasts the ball into the back of our net. He makes a beeline for Quinn at the other end of the field and picks her up in jubilation. I can't help noticing the subtle shove she gives him when he finally puts her down.

"Blimey, chaps! It's looking like a long day for you!" Jones quips as he struts back near midfield.

"We just gave you a gift, laddie. Plenty of time left," Henry counters affably.

I take note of the chap covering me standing as flat footed as a dead duck with a confident little smile after his team's quick scoring.

At the whistle, Henry and a tall lad they call, Max, touch up then turn and pass to the defense. Henry calls out his name, but he's well covered to receive the ball.

"Kenny! Kenny!" I scream until he looks up.

I fake to the inside then quickly run around the outside of the dead duck that's supposed to guard me. Kenny goes for the long ball, his pass bouncing ahead of me. The common move is to take the ball to the corner and center it as the defender comes close but I've got a different idea.

As soon as I feel the defender cheat me to the outside, I twist and hop the ball over his extended foot, easily clearing it with a long leap. The sweeper anticipates a pass to one of my forwards, who's sprinting up the left point, but once again I twist out and gain the box. Quinn tracks the move and slides to protect the near side, which opens up the far corner. I pivot hard, watching the sweeper slide by as I switch to a left shot that I bend around Quinn's outstretched arm. She gets up on her knees, glancing behind at the ball caught in the netting then smiles at me.

"That was a perfect shot!"

I trot over to her. "Fortunate," I correct. "An inch lower, you make the save. How do you leap like that?"

She grins. "I guess the same way you leapt over Cody," she nods at her defender, who looks awestricken.

"You've got quick moves, chap. Quick indeed." Cody shakes his head and smiles at me.

The whistle is blown. The ref, a paunchy middle age man with a no-nonsense demeanor, sternly waves me back to my side of the field.

"Go on, striker, try it again," Quinn says as she slaps my arse hard enough to sting, startling me. "Nice shot, striker!" The brazen move colors her cheeks.

I smile and jog back to the line.

"Pass the bloody ball sometime," Firuz grumbles as I trot by him, ignoring his sour disposition.

When Jones moves the ball, Firuz calls a side switch around our other midfielder. Henry motions for me to stay with Firuz, who makes a power move around me. I'm running with him, staying close to his side, slowly driving him out of bounds when he unleashes an elbow into my lower back. The blinding flash of pain in my kidneys sends me down in a heap of misery. At least the wanker loses the ball out of bounds.

"Chin up, chap. Are you alright?" Henry helps me up with a look of concern.

I grimace when I try to straighten and get back to my feet with some effort.

Kenny nods for me to run up field, cocks the ball in both hands behind his head, and launches it over the midfielder. I can't run as fast because of the pain but I get to the ball first. As I look up to examine my options, Firuz crashes into me, hip to hip, sending me sprawling out of the field. The whistle sounds.

"Red free kick!" The ref calls.

"Are you blind? He didn't even have the bloody ball!" Firuz screams.

I'm still up on one knee, feeling the blossoming of the bruise on my hip. My foot tingles when I stand and my lower back is still in agony.

"Pardon me, lad," Henry calls to Firuz in a taut voice. "Let's take it down a notch. We'd all like to walk off this field as friends."

Firuz merely nods though I detect a faint smirk as he trots back to guard Meagan out of all people.

Kenny runs up to place the ball down.

"Let me take this one, lad," I breathe the words with difficulty.

Kenny looks at me intently. "Are you sure?" I nod. "Hey, I can dish a little payback," he says, fixing his eyes on Firuz.

I put my hand on Kenny's shoulder to turn him back around. Firuz smirks again. Something about the resplendent white jersey, the swishy green shorts and the evenly rolled white tube socks bothers me. Firuz looks like he's ready for a photo shoot, not a pick up match.

"Kenny, drive for the box and peel out," I call in a way that only he can hear.

He nods. After taking a look behind him, he gives me a conspiratorial grin. "I got you, Lewis. I got you."

I look towards the inside where Henry and Max are jockeying for position in the box. Meagan is back as a safeguard with Firuz in front of her. The whistle blows and I take my running start towards the ball. With Kenny encroaching the box, the defense crowds the middle. As I near the ball, Kenny shoots back outside and I send the ball on a crisp roll at his feet. I try to sprint to the top of the box, but the pain in my hip and back is unbearable, so I cover behind Henry as he drives for the front of the net.

Kenny tries to center it for Henry but the defender recovers and gets in the way of the pass. The ball rolls towards me as Firuz screams at his teammates to push the line back to set up an offside trap. He races back from midfield, pretending to cover Henry, but I somehow intuit that he wants to blindside me again.

With everyone covered, I take up the open field. My intention is to race into the box and take the shot, but it's hard to breathe.

"Man on! Man on!" calls Kenny, frantically warning me there's someone coming at me from behind.

I can almost feel Firuz debating whether to charge me shoulder to shoulder into the ground or slide tackle the ball away from me. Either way, he's about to get another hit on me. I try to slant towards the outside, hoping Kenny cuts across, but he backs up to his defensive position leaving me without a wing man.

"Back Lewis, back!" Henry calls from somewhere behind me.

I hold my breath and strain my senses until the pounding of heavy feet registers. The thudding is sharper as I slowly release the air in my lungs.

Quinn starts cheating out to cut down the angle of my shot. Unbeknownst to her, I have no intentions of shooting at the net. When the thud is loud enough to speed things up in my mind again, I wager on Firuz going for a shoulder check. I stop suddenly and execute a quick spin from left to right. As Firuz's eyes grow wide at the absence of the contact he expected, I casually lift my heel and feel the clash of his lead foot on the soles of my shoes.

Despite his athleticism, the move catches him so completely by surprise that he doesn't have the instinct to break his fall with any sort of dignity. By the time he tries to put his hands in front of him, his arms can't extend and the first thing to smack the semi-soft surface is his chin. The rest of his body threatens to bend over his neck, but at the last moment, his momentum stops. I bend the ball over two blokes to the waiting crown of Max's head but Quinn recovers and she springs to the corner, making the save by punching the ball over the cross beam.

I limp up to the goal line and offer her my hand to help her up.

"That was one amazing save, luv."

Quinn is breathing hard. "Saw it at the last second!"

The ref blows the whistle in a long irritating note, drawing everyone's attention to him. Quinn and I watch him rush to the fallen figure of Firuz. He's surrounded by most of his team, still on the ground.

"How'd you know when to spin?" Quinn says with a note of awe in her voice.

"Ballet," I reply.

"I thought so!" Quinn exclaims. "That was too graceful to be a soccer move."

"Football move," I correct her.

"Whatever." She grins and fixes her blue eyes on mine.

The moment is instantly charged and our smiles falter. I refuse to blink. An urge to sweep her blonde bangs tenses the muscles in my arm.

"Hey, asshole!" Firuz screams, breaking into the moment.

I turn, trying to figure out who's the object of his tirade, only to discover it's me.

I can tell the wanker is trying to fight off the pain of humiliation more than the physical pain from such an awkward fall.

"Firuz, take it easy, lad," Henry soothes.

The enraged dark skinned man shoves Henry away then looks at the others, daring them to try to stop him. Satisfied no one is about to get in his way, he clenches his jaw and stomps towards me.

Quinn interposes herself between us and places her hands on his chest.

"Cut it out, Firuz! You went for the hit and he beat you clean and fair. Get over it!" Quinn says tersely.

"Whose team are *you* on? I can't believe you let that sissy shot get past you. Cut the bloody angle next time."

I say nothing. In fact I'm about to walk away from Firuz's glare when he grabs Quinn's arm and spins her out of the way.

Something snaps in place in my brain. The grimace of pain on Quinn's pretty face sends a bolt of cool anger through every muscle in my body.

Firuz invades my personal space, leaving no more than an inch between our noses. His nostrils flare and his eyes look wild, yet there's something uncertain about the way he looks into my eyes.

"Okay, that's enough, Firuz. It's just a game," Quinn says, but this time her voice has a hint of fear.

"Come now, lads, we don't need this type of trouble. We're all friends," Henry takes my shoulder and I let him pull me a few steps away from Firuz.

Jason McElroy teaches a class of basics in self-defense. I filmed the class once and I remember him saying to never take your eyes off an opponent. When Henry turns me all the way around, I know I made a mistake.

Firuz bolts like a race horse at the drop of the gate, but when he readies himself for a high hit, I sink to the floor and roll into his legs. His knee strikes the back of my head, but as he flips on his back and thuds painfully on the floor, I know he's got the worse end of the deal.

I get to my feet quickly just as Firuz seemingly leaps back to his and charges again. This time he grabs the red vest I'm wearing and starts driving me backwards. Meagan and Katja shuffle out of the way, their eyes wide with alarm.

"Stop! Dammit, Firuz!" Quinn screams and manages to wedge herself in between us, almost jogging to keep up.

With her in the middle, I drop my arms from his, thinking he'll do the same, but instead, he grabs her arm and yanks her out of the way. Quinn loses her balance and falls on her side.

Firuz is unfazed, but as Samantha would say, I'm royally pissed off and now I know exactly what that means.

"Let's go, fag…" Firuz growls as he grabs my throat with one hand and cocks his free arm to unleash a punch.

His knuckles crash into my jaw, making everything go black for a moment. He adds pressure to his hold and chokes the breath out of me. Everyone else is tending to Quinn. I'm on my own.

"Are you just going to bleed, asshole?"

I feel something warm running down over my lips. The second or third punch hit my nose. My eyes instantly water and I can only see a distorted shape of my surroundings. When I blink away the sheen, I see Quinn holding her arm.

Another punch whips my head.

I decide that's the last one he gets.

I reach for the waistband of Firuz's fancy shorts and yank them up with everything I have. The inseam cuts into his genitals and he howls soundlessly as his grip finally fails him. I unleash a hard blow into his inner thigh with my knee. The blow threatens to make him lose his balance but he opens his stance and crouches down. The image of Quinn being painfully cast aside closes my hand into a tight fist that I smash down into his upturned face. A splatter of blood flies in every direction when my fist strikes his nose. Firuz goes down and makes no move to stand back up.

I want to spit a glob of blood, but I'm too conscious of the rubbery flooring, so I force it down my throat nearly making me throw up. I feel an ache in my nose when I try to inhale.

"Here, lad!"

I grab the proffered towel from Henry and cover my nose.

Quinn extricates herself from the concern of the others and runs up to me.

"Oh, my God! Are you okay?"

I nod. "Are you?"

Her eyes go cold, her expression fierce. She puts a finger up and runs to Firuz, who's blinking repeatedly, trying to refocus his eyes.

"Firuz," Quinn calls in a cold voice.

The man squints up at her. Bright red blood pours out of his right nostril into his open mouth, coloring his teeth. His hands are still clamped to his genitals.

"We're done. Don't bother calling me again."

I see his eyes go wide in desperation. "Quinn, let me explain…" he says in a strained voice.

He tries to get up but he slips and goes down again, like he doesn't have enough control over his limbs.

Jones stands over Firuz and shakes his head in clear disapproval.

Quinn leaves him to take me by the arm. "Let's get you some ice."

I allow myself to be led to a table at the small cafeteria at the other side of the complex. Quinn leaves me on a chair, but returns quickly with several Ziploc bags full of ice.

"Are you still bleeding?"

I find an unsoiled area on the towel and cover my nose. When I remove it, it's still white. "No, it stopped."

"Good."

"What's with the ice bags, luv?"

She arranges the ice bags on the table and props her elbow on top of them, wincing at the pain. "What a jerk," she says tersely.

"You dumped Firuz over a scuffle in a football match?"

She shakes her head. "Of course not. I dumped him because he's an asshole. That was so embarrassing."

I stifle a laugh. "That's one ugly American curse."

Quinn's hard expression evaporates when she giggles. "Asshole? I suppose it is. Sounds a lot harsher than wanker."

I couldn't argue with that.

Henry appears at the door. Quinn waves him over and soon he's seated at the table with us.

"Well, Quinnie, your friend is no longer welcome. I got that straight from Matt, the owner."

"Good." Quinn agrees.

"Lewis, that was some show, lad. Some show indeed. Do say you'll join the league sometime."

"I don't know. You are a rough lot," I joke.

Henry slaps his knee as he laughs. "That was bloody priceless!"

"I take it this happens often?" I ask.

He shakes his head. "We haven't seen a good scrapping like that in a long time," he chuckles. "We do all we can to play a gentleman's game. How about you, Quinn? Will you still come around?"

Quinn dazzles him with her smile. "Of course, Henry."

"Very well." Henry stands. "We're going to the Chariot to celebrate since the match was called. Perhaps you two will join us?"

"Perhaps," Quinn says with a wink.

He extends his right hand to me. "Glad to have met you, Lewis. That was one sweet move out there, not to mention that beautiful bend."

"I apologize for ruining your match today, Henry."

"Not at all, chap! That was the most fun a lot of us have had in years!"

After Henry leaves, I turn to Quinn. "How often do you really play with these chaps?"

"Why?"

"They treat you like royalty."

She shrugs. "Just about every chance I get when I'm here. Henry is good friends with my father. He and his brother used to run a soccer camp for kids. His brother Lenny is a goalkeeper. He was one of my coaches."

"So, what do you think was Firuz's problem today?"

Quinn shakes her head.

"Where's he from, anyway?"

A roll of the eyes. "He grew up here in London. His mother is British. His father is Iranian. Something to that effect."

"Were you… involved with him?" I'm surprised at the rush of jealousy that boils in my blood.

What's gotten into you…?

Quinn seems taken aback by the tone of my voice. Her eyes search mine. "Would you be jealous if I was?"

It's almost like she can see inside me. "He's just not right for you, luv."

"Oh no? Did you decide that based on today?"

"Not at all, you and him made an awkward couple at Fox's the other night."

"Well, Lewis, do you know what the right man for me would be?" Her smile is mesmerizing.

"I can't say. I don't think I know you well enough just yet."

Something changes in her eyes. "Well, then let's do something about that."

***

I'm waiting for Quinn to retrieve her bag from the boot of Firuz's car, giving them plenty of space to have what appears to be their last conversation. I can't hear what they're saying, but it seems a pretty heated argument. Quinn contributes precious little and there's a lot of looking away on her part. He pulls her bag out and she wrenches it from his hand then quickly makes her way towards me. Firuz looks like he's about to cry until his eyes find me and I can feel his blazing hatred washing over me. Somehow, I resist the urge to smile and wave at him.

"Quinn, just a minute, let me say one more thing," Firuz pleads.

She stops and whirls on him. "How dare you embarrass me that way in front of my father's friends? You have no excuse, Firuz. You're a jackass."

He takes a menacing step towards Quinn, prompting me to push off the BMW and head towards her. When Firuz sees me, he stops and gives me an odd little smirk as his eyes bore into mine.

"Leave your key on my counter and get all your shit out of my flat," Quinn orders.

Firuz props his hands at his waist and turns in circles, clenching and unclenching his jaw. I don't like the fact that he's been staying with Quinn one bit.

"Can we go to your place?" she asks when she joins me.

I'd love nothing more, but since she doesn't want Samantha to know she's here, it's not a good idea. "Have you everything you need in that tote?"

She nods.

"Since you're playing secretive, it may be better to go to my office, luv. Sam's got a penchant for showing up unannounced at my flat.

She looks a bit disappointed. "Okay."

I open the door for her then walk around the back of the Beamer. Firuz glares at me, his hairy hands fisted at his sides. I make sure he finds my face and grin at the way he seems to be shaking with rage.

I watch him get in the car and peel off the spot. In a last effort to let me know he's less than pleased with me, he drives dangerously close to where I stand. Had I opened my door, it would've been taken out by the bonnet of his car.

I have the odd feeling our head butting contest is far from over.

24

"But I look a wreck! People will think you are taking pity on some destitute Yankee if you take me anywhere. Besides, you don't look well enough to be going anywhere. Is there a place that delivers?"

I drape myself over the love seat in the office like an old man. I'm hurting in places I didn't even know I had, and that's not even counting the slight swelling around my jaw and nose where Firuz's knuckles landed more times than I could count. "I can only think of the Chinese restaurant down the block."

She brightens. "Perfect! I love Chinese."

"But for the record, you look stunning and people would actually wonder what a beautiful lass like you is doing with this bloody Scouser," I comment, noting how attractive she looks in her warm up suit, despite the fact that it's emblazoned with a Manchester United crest. The Cristiano Ronaldo jersey beneath the thin jacket complete the ensemble, and the black and red make her hair and eyes stand out.

Quinn drops her eyes, her cheeks turning red. "You're sweet."

"Are you sure you don't want to go anywhere?" I try one more time.

An anxious expression crosses her face. "I'd rather not. Is that okay?"

"Sure."

She looks around at the dual bookcases on the other side of the room then stares at the desk for a moment. I cringe when I spot the loose sheaves of paper lying all over the desktop.

"I really like your office."

"Do you?"

She nods. "It doesn't look like a museum."

"Is it the lack of artwork on the walls?"

"No, silly. My ex-husband kept his office so spotless and organized it was like being in a museum. He hated it if I tried using his computer. He went as far as furnishing one of the rooms for my own office. He got me a decorator and everything. At first I thought it was sweet, but he just didn't want me to find out about his other life."

"His other life?"

She nods slowly, getting up to stand at the window. "Andrew chased anything in a skirt."

"That's the impression I got from some articles on the web," I say softly.

Quinn whips her head around, a cold expression on her face that recedes after a moment. "I don't know why it's so easy to talk to you, but I don't want to abuse that."

I nod in understanding though her apprehension is beginning to grate on me. "It's quite alright, luv. This is what friends do."

She looks hesitant.

"The key to my life-long friendship with Samantha is our brutally honest conversations. Talk to me, luv," I encourage her.

She nods and comes to sit beside me. After taking a deep breath, she starts talking.

"One day something happened to my hard drive and I couldn't access the web. I went into Andy's office and began doing my research. I was researching concussions in the hopes of developing better head gear for different sports. While I was online, someone messaged Andy, some girl with the handle HotCherry..." She shakes her head. "Let's just say I found out a lot about Andy's sexual fantasies through HotCherry."

This seems utterly unimaginable. Andrew Fischer is a computer genius. Why would he not employ one of his own products, such as the Washout software that deletes any and all traces of browsing history. "That seems so strange..."

"It was. I didn't understand how he'd leave something like that so unsecured, but apparently, he had a whole bunch of email addresses he used to subscribe to adult dating sites." Her shoulders sag. "A part of me feels that he wanted me to find out."

"I was thinking that. What did you do?"

Quinn hangs her head. "I did nothing. He would've been very upset that I was at his computer."

I'm trying to figure out what would possibly keep Quinn from unleashing her fury at the betrayal when it suddenly registers in my brain that she hangs her head in shame, and in fear. Anger colors the edges of my vision a vibrant red.

"Andrew would get so angry, I thought one day he'd lose it and start hitting me..." her voice trails off as she begins to cry.

I pull Quinn into me and she lays her head on my shoulder, sobbing quietly.

***

Despite the uncomfortable revelation, the food restores some semblance of levity between us. One thing is clear, after today, we've forged a bond that transcends mere friendship. I can't compare it to what I have in Samantha or Gwen. It's entirely different, mainly because I'm constantly attacked by emotions I don't fully understand. I've never felt so protective of anyone I've just met.

I feel pain every time I move. Adding to my physical misery, a headache settles on the bridge of my nose, blurring my vision. In an attempt to stem the dull, growing ache, I gingerly pinch my nose, close my eyes, and let my head fall back.

"Still hurting?"

I nod as the pain intensifies, making me nauseous.

Quinn shifts on the couch and takes my other hand. She presses her thumb over the top of my hand where the roots of the thumb and forefinger intersect and massages the tiny area. There's a sudden pang of pain then it mercifully fades.

"Better?"

I keep my eyes closed, grateful for the relief. "Whatever you're doing, keep doing it, please."

She chuckles softly. "If I say something, will you get upset with me?"

"That's not exactly fair now, is it?"

"I don't want you to get mad."

I've always laughed at the misuse of the word *mad* by Americans. "Very well. I won't get cross with you, no matter what you say. What is it?"

She hesitates for a moment. "I didn't know a gay man could fight back."

I feel cross.

"I knew you'd get mad," she says contritely. "I'm sorry."

"I wasn't about to let him reduce me to a bloody pulp, luv. It has nothing to do with being gay, it was survival mode."

She keeps massaging the spot, making me dizzy with relief.

"Bloody wanker..."

She sighs. "Firuz and I have been friends for a long time. He helped me set up Play Again. He's always been abrasive, but I guess I underestimated how much of a jerk he really is."

I find it difficult to attribute any nobility to the abrasive bloke.

"I was pretty distraught over the divorce and the ensuing invasion into my privacy, but Firuz helped distract me from all that by engaging me into establishing the foundation. I've been very grateful to him."

"That's part of the reason you're here. The foundation is established in London."

"It is. I couldn't have done it back home. Not when I was constantly under the microscope. There was an article that accused me of having men in my Malibu home while Andrew was away. They even had photographs. Firuz had the idea that if I gave those jackals nowhere to go, they would leave me alone."

Understanding dawns in my mind. "He became your mystery man and his presence put the rumors of wild parties to rest."

Her fingers stop moving on my hand. "Lewis, is there anything you don't know about my troubles with the tabloids?"

Her tone is just a shade shy of being terse. "Forgive me, luv. I couldn't help reading the numerous headlines attached to your name. I didn't believe any of that rubbish. I know better. Samantha also had her bouts with the bloody tabloids."

Quinn resumes massaging my hand. "I remember seeing those, but I never gave in to my curiosity and picked them up. I'm ashamed to say I actually believed it, knowing what I knew about her."

I don't want the conversation to stray from Firuz Ahmadi. I'm suddenly compelled to know exactly what his role in Quinn's life is. "So, Firuz became your pretend boyfriend of sorts."

"Basically, yeah. Except that he took his role playing a little too serious for my taste." She frowns. "I never saw the side of him I saw today, on the field."

"He's a competitive man," I observe.

"He is," she concedes. "But this was jealousy. I've never seen him lose control that way. I mean he's had a way of intimidating other men who take an interest in me, but never so overtly." She chuckles. "You really set him off. Hey, do you have a flashlight?"

"There's a penlight in the top drawer of the desk."

"Perfect."

She lets go of my hand and goes to the desk. I'm expecting the pain to regain its hold on me but it doesn't. I only feel an urge to close my eyes and go to sleep.

"Okay, let's see," she says. "Open your eyes please."

When I open my eyes, she's standing over me. Her left hand holds my face in place.

"Try to keep your eyes open, okay?"

She subjects me to the blazing light of the penlight, moving it back and forth over my eyes. I feel a stabbing pain in the center of my head until she removes the light.

Her right leg is braced on the couch between mine as she bends at the waist to study my eyes. Her face inches closer to mine.

"A bit slow, but I don't think you've a—"

Her foot slips and she lands on my lap. My hands shoot up to hold her and encircle her waist. Her hair tickles my face and our noses touch. When our eyes meet, I'm still seeing spots from the penlight, but in between heartbeats, the beauty of her blue eyes registers in my brain in vivid detail. My heart starts racing, the pulsing rush of blood is almost painful in my head, but I force myself not to wince. Her lashes close slightly. Is it my imagination or is she leaning towards me a little more?

Her bangs lose their hold and cascade over her gaze. She brings a hand to sweep them away from her eyes and we freeze that way. I'm not at all sure what's supposed to happen, but I have the feeling that she's daring me to make the next move, hoping even.

A bolt of lightning strobes in the windows. Seconds later the thunder thrums in our ribcages, it's so bloody close. The spell is broken as she somewhat awkwardly shoves back and stands, looking out the window with an expression filled with disappointment.

When she stares back at me, there's something in her eyes I can't read, but whatever it is, seems to make her a bit sad.

"I bet your head feels great after that," she quips, looking out the window once more.

You have no idea…

***

When night falls, I take her down to the underground level of my building and together we drive into the underground lot of Tower 42, effectively avoiding the downpour. She indicates a white Audi and I pull next to it.

"That's mine."

"Did you just get that?"

"Last year."

"A beautiful car for a more beautiful girl," I think out loud.

"Stop! You're seriously detracting from being gay, you know."

I give her a thin smile. "I meant it."

Quinn narrows her eyes and gazes at me intently. Once again the air around us seems to crackle with electricity as I feel myself pulled into her. With my eyes I follow the pattern of freckles over the bridge of her thin nose and land on her lips.

When I glance back into her eyes, I see she's focused on the same feature on my face. A car's two tone response to its owner unlocking it breaks into the moment. I physically ache when Quinn turns away to find the source of the intrusion.

We watch as a man in a suit opens the door of his Jaguar and climbs in.

"Why is it that when two people meet, it doesn't take long before revealing their sad stories?" Quinn asks, still looking out the window.

"I think that only happens when the friendship is born from trust."

Quinn turns back to me, the sparkling of her eyes making my heart race.

Calm down...

"We've shared a lot since we met. This doesn't happen to me with just anyone. Trust, I mean," she says in a breathy voice.

I resist the urge to clear my throat. "I can relate to that."

She smiles. "Thank you for listening to my sad stories."

I have the nearly overpowering urge to gently caress her cheek with the back of my hand. My arms actually twitch in anticipation of the movement but I force them still. At the last second, as I'm relinquishing control, Quinn looks down and digs her key out of her pocket. I can breathe again.

"Just one of the perks for doing business with Solutions," I say breezily, feeling my stomach flutter.

When she looks up again, she grins. "I hope it's more than that."

Okay, now why does she have to say something like that? It could have so many different meanings. Not to mention the expression on her face that I could be hopelessly misinterpreting.

"I'd like to do this again. Unless you feel like I'm taking you away from Sam."

Sam who...?

I shake my head as I feel a pang of guilt. "Not at all, but I'd like to let her know you're here."

A flash of anxiety in her eyes. "I promise I'll tell her soon, okay? Just give me a couple of days. I needed today. I needed this talk."

Her pleading tone convinces me. "Very well, but it's killing me that she doesn't know."

"Two days. I promise."

"I'll hold you to it."

I quickly climb out and open her door, my eyes scanning our surroundings just in case some undesirable element decides to take a go at us. London, like any other major city in the world, has its share of thieves and danger and it's always best to be watchful.

Working with a firm specializing in security has definitely had an effect on me. Nathan Jeffries holds meetings where we are shown video footage of the aftermath of security mistakes. Not for the faint of heart.

Quinn unlocks her car and turns to me, concern on her face. "Are you okay? You got so alert all of a sudden."

I chuckle. "Wait until you meet Sam's fiancé."

She frowns.

"He's a bodyguard, taught me a few things, such as always being on the lookout for the unexpected."

There's a renewed twinkle of interest in her gaze. "You have a way of making a girl feel safer than you think. I hope to see you soon."

Again with the meaningful little sentences. "Drive safe."

She steps into me and puts her arms around me, clasping her hands over my sore lower back. I pull her into me, inhaling the sweet scent of whatever she uses on her hair.

"Thank you, Lewis," she tilts her head up.

I can't breathe so I nod and try a smile but something has frozen our bodies and we stare into each other's eyes for a long moment.

You can let go now, chap... I ignore the voice in my head.

The lights of the Audi flash twice, indicating the car locked itself again, a safety feature common to German vehicles.

Quinn releases me and climbs behind the wheel after exhaling a deep sigh that I don't know how to interpret.

As she waves and pulls out of the spot, all I can think is that I already can't wait to see her again.

25

When Samantha calls me on Sunday morning to spend the day in Kensington with everyone, I can't get there fast enough.

The weather cooperates by withholding the promised rain in the forecast and the day is balmy overall. Brooke and Emily model every outfit I bought them; it takes quite a while. I don't try to offer another suitcase for Gwen. I simply call my shipper and arrange to send their new clothes to their home in Pennsylvania.

We spend several hours in Nathan's library, which has an untouched section of children's volumes, some of them dating back to when Samantha and I were kids.

The Reddicks visited Nathan Jeffries nearly every weekend. To keep their only daughter out of their hair, they sometimes took me along. Samantha and I always started in the library. When our mischievous natures forced Margaret to chase us out to the grounds, broom in hand, Samantha and I shared wild adventures in the woods. We swam in the fountain when the days were hot, rode a Friesian horse Nathan had for a time, and more often than not, we took a canoe out to the middle of the pond to exchange wondrous secrets.

Brooke and Emily sit and listen as I read excerpts from Frances Hodgson Burnett's *A Little Princess*. They seem to enjoy my over the top, poetic rendition of each passage.

When Emily starts to doze off, I take her to the overstuffed couch and end up napping as well when her little form curls into me, her tiny fist refusing to let go of my shirt.

When I wake, I see Brooke reading Astrid Lindgren's *Pippi Longstocking* by lamplight.

"Brooke, what time is it, luv?"

Brooke peers up at me from behind designer reading glasses that make her look decidedly older.

"It's after dinner, but Mom said not to wake you, guys."

"I missed dinner?"

"Yeah," she cocks her head to the side as though debating something. "And I'm not supposed to tell you, but Sam took a few pictures of you to post them on Facebook."

"She did, did she?"

Brooke nods, chuckling. "Mom also said that if Emily won't go to bed tonight, she's yours to keep."

I can't think of a harsher punishment, but I suppose it's just. Emily becomes pretty wild right before bed, and I'm still smarting from her sugar high and subsequent crash from the night after our trip to the zoo.

"What do you think of Pippi?"

Brooke keeps her eyes on the page long enough to finish what she's reading before answering.

"Oh, she's great! But it's kind of funny."

"What's funny, luv?"

"Well, I'm on page one-oh-three and I have yet to know what town she lives in, they never mention it."

"Really?"

"I'm quite sure."

I'm quite sure spoken in a nearly flawless, clipped British accent.

"You must be a fast reader."

She shrugs. "Daddy and I have reading races. We used to read-race with Dr. Seuss books, but I don't think he realized I know most of them by heart." She grins confidently. "I always win."

"That makes me think of Sam."

"Oh, I want to be just like her when I grow up."

I actually feel my heart stutter at that. "Young lady, I've a feeling you'll be far better."

"You think so?"

I nod. "I know so."

"Lewis, can I tell you something?"

"But of course."

Two pink circles appear high on her delicate cheeks. "You're going to be an awesome daddy one day."

I hold the smile in place, but I feel something breaking inside and I most definitely cannot trust my voice to emit a steady stream of words.

"I mean it, and I'm not talking about all the stuff you got me and Em. It's just the way you are. I'm going to hate going back home and I'm going to miss you like crazy."

Whoever believed grown men don't cry was never subjected to a sentiment delivered with such sincerity and heartfelt emotion, from a young lady such as Brooke Amaya.

Swallowing the lump threatening to bring me to tears, I take a deep, shaky breath and somehow manage to compose myself. I've never been this much of a sentimental wreck. "I'll miss you too, but we'll see each other more than you think."

Her hazel eyes deepen with emotion. "You promise?"

I cross my heart. "I promise."

She smiles contentedly and turns her eyes back to the page. When I get to the door, I hear Brooke padding behind me.

"Lewis?"

I turn back. "Yes, little luv?"

"Thank you for the fun day, and all my new clothes." She leans in, wrapping her arms around me.

"You're very welcome."

"I love you. You know that?"

Tears sting my eyes and I know then I will forever be a part of her life. "I love you too, little luv."

She squeezes once more before going back to her book.

"Don't worry about Em," she says over her shoulder. "She'll probably wake in a bad mood. I'll come get Mom when she does."

"You're a good sister."

She gives me an exaggerated shrug. "I try."

I walk down the hall to the kitchen where the laughter of three women echoes off the high ceiling. I can hear Alicia and Gwen debating the endless arguments of the quirks of men in every marriage. They are giving Samantha a litany of dire warnings of how her life will change, and what to expect after exchanging the "I do's".

Normally I'd saunter in and seamlessly join into the conversation, but I feel strange inside.

I leave a text message in Samantha's mobile, telling her I have a work emergency, and quietly leave to go back to my flat. I kept hearing Terence's voice the entire time I drove.

When I get home, all I can do is get out of my clothes, and stand under the hot spray of the shower just so I can kid myself by pretending that I'm not crying, even as I fall to my knees racked by my sobs.

I'm not prone to such displays of emotion, but something in little Brooke's words have torn something loose in me. It feels as though I'm seeing light through the crack of an obscured window, and learn what a sunrise is for the first time.

***

While Samantha takes Gwen and the girls to another fitting, I spend the entire morning at the office, hoping to finish up early so I can meet with them. Gwen texts me photographs of each girl in their gown, looking positively radiant. Their complexions contrast beautifully with the tangerine fabric.

I'm thankful for Gwen, who ultimately helped Samantha decide on the colors. Even Alicia was pleased once she saw a swatch of the fabric, declaring she'd look ravishing in the new color.

I'm about to leave the office when my telephone rings. I have to consult with a client about a problem with their intra-network for a distribution center in Harrow, which continued to be a headache. I expect the call to be from the same bloke I'd been talking to most of the afternoon, so I'm surprised when a smoky, yet exuberant voice comes on the line.

"Hi, Lewis."

"Hullo, luv. I'm glad you called."

The weariness of the day flees my body, although the soreness from the football match and subsequent fight are still present in every little move I make. The sudden anticipation to see her is reenergizing.

"How are you feeling?"

"It only hurts when I breathe, other than that, I'm right as rain, luv."

She chuckles. "I guess that's good."

"How's your arm?"

"Still attached. I won't need another implant any time soon."

"What are you doing today?"

"That's actually up to you."

I feel warm all over. "Name the place, luv." I can almost hear her smiling.

"I'm in Chelsea Harbour, Townmead Road towards the marina, unit twelve."

I write down the information. "I'm thinking twenty-five minutes until I get there."

"Good, I wanted to call earlier but I didn't know how busy you were. I'll see you soon."

I set the receiver back in its cradle, wondering for the millionth time whether I should tell Samantha. I even key in the text, but for some reason I opt to wait.

Knowing Samantha, she'll most likely want to dress and make herself up in a way to impress her old college friend that will take until tomorrow. I'm not willing to wait at all to see Quinn again.

Traffic on the Victoria Embankment is fluid so I find Chelsea Harbour Drive in only fifteen minutes after leaving the office. According to the GPS, I have less than a minute before arriving to my destination.

Townmead Road is a short, dead end street that curves south towards the river. I follow the numbers on the doors and find twelve at the very end. A familiar white Audi A6 is parked in front of the unit, and I pull next to it. The luxury townhomes surround a small green that provides a lovely view of the Battersea Bridge.

I see movement behind the open door as I get out of the car. Quinn's short hair bounces prettily with every step she takes on her way to the door with such elegance that prompts me to straighten my tie.

"Hi!" She calls from the door.

I get out of the car and as though it's the most natural thing in the world, I give her a tight hug that she returns with gusto.

"I missed you. Isn't that weird?"

"Not that weird." I missed her too.

She was all I could think about at night.

Quinn looks at me appreciatively, head to shoes, and up again. I'm so glad to be wearing my steel grey wool slacks, a wine button down and a graphite-colored tie

"You look so handsome! Please come in."

Although she's most likely one of the wealthiest women alive, her flat is surprisingly humble. The air is redolent of lemon scented furniture polish and something citrusy sweet.

"I'm sorry. This place is such a mess."

She moves to the far end to open the windows, then she excuses herself and runs into what I assume is the bedroom to do the same. I stay in the small living room and sit on one of the comfortable love seats.

"Do you want to come out to the patio?"

I stand and follow her, casually admiring the lovely flare of her hips and her shapely legs that look deceptively long out of the tight little white shorts she wears. Her back is straight, her arms long and trim, there's almost no waistline to speak of. And yet, she's not a thin little wisp of limbs on a tiny torso, she's definitely voluptuous. I often give Samantha grief over the size of her breasts. They aren't huge, like Alicia's, but they're sizable enough to command attention. Quinn's are almost too perfectly shaped, and they sit high and tight on her chest alluringly.

I step out onto a large stone patio where there's a bench swing facing a charming view of the Thames and Battersea's skyline. A stone path leads to a small dock where a gorgeous wooden boat bobs on the slate waters. Its glossy, lacquered finish gleams under the sun, which also makes the chrome prow scintillate.

Quinn notices my attention is riveted on the boat. "Do much boating?" She hands me a cold glass filled to brim with ice cubes and a dark, reddish liquid. "Sangria," she offers.

"Thank you."

She touches her glass with mine and for a moment, I'm dazzled by her clear, blue eyes which don't waver from mine as she takes a sip of her drink.

Her entire demeanor is different from the last time I saw her when she shared so much of herself. I feel like I've known her far longer than a mere few days.

"I grew up in Liverpool, so life in the water was second nature to me, but it's been a long time," I tell her, remembering to answer her question. "Is that yours?"

She nods and looks lovingly at the boat. "I got it in Maryland and had it shipped here."

"I'd hate to even imagine what the cost is to ship a Riva Aquarama across the pond."

Quinn looks impressed. "I can't think of too many men who'd know the maker of that boat."

I shrug and match her smile. "The point of the prow piece gave it away."

"I'm still quite impressed."

"What did you name it?"

"*Shaoirse.*" She pins me with an amused grin, noting the blank expression on my face. "It's Old Irish for Liberty."

It's my turn to be even more impressed. "Sam taught herself that language."

Quinn nods. "That's who I got it from. She always had an Irish book at hand. She used to write quotes in different languages in this notebook she had. I don't remember the exact phrase, but I remembered *Shaoirse* when I got my boat."

The breeze plays with her wispy blonde hair and her white top flutters, revealing a taut abdomen. I've never been happier to know Samantha than I am at this moment.

"She always talked about you, Lewis." The subtle squint makes me wonder just what she's heard about me.

"None of it true, luv," I tell her, feeling a flutter in my chest.

"Oh, God, I hope not." She grins.

Her gaze is so direct I have this irrational feeling that I'm standing naked before her. A chill runs down my spine, emphasizing my sudden attack of nerves. "I'm sure your Moppin sister did quite a bit of bragging, and given her penchant for words, I wouldn't be surprised if she embellished a few things."

Quinn's laughter is almost musical. She throws her head back, exposing a long, delicate neck where a tiny teardrop diamond is nestled in the concavity just above her sternum. I notice a ring of light skin around her ring finger when she brings her hand to her throat. Like a footstep in the sand, the only evidence that someone was once there. Some part of me is wondering if her heart is vacant as well.

Lewis! What's bloody gotten into you?

"Sorry, that just takes me back." She laughs again.

"What's a Moppin, anyway? Sam didn't know when I asked her."

She frowns in confusion. "What? She's the one that came up with it. Well, sort of."

"Sort of?"

"We all had nicknames—I already told you mine, but we all called Sam, Mary Poppins because, well, she's Brit, you know? We also called her Red, short for Reddick, and her dumb obsession with hockey. We tried to include her on everything but she always had a loner streak. I can't tell you how many guys fell head over heels for her, but she didn't really give them the time of day. The times she partied with us are memorable because of how seldom that happened."

She runs a hand through one side of her hair and shakes her head. The gesture makes her look like a child.

"So, this one night, we're all hammered. Sam and I had to practically be carried! Not my proudest moment," she is quick to add. "Well, we were far too noisy and some of our neighbors started complaining. Sam began cursing them in that accent of hers and the rest of us—there were at least a dozen. The rest of us started speaking with a British accent.

"When the girls helped Sam into bed, she blurted, 'I don't need help from a bunch of M... M...Poppins... and she passed out!" She slaps at her thighs as she laughs. "She slurred her words so bad, one of our sisters, Kayla, asked 'did she just call us Moppins?' The name stuck. I'm surprised she doesn't remember that. Hell, Sam remembers everything, but to be fair, she was pretty drunk that night." Quinn rolls her eyes in thought. "Come to think of it, I don't really recall a sober Samantha. Even when I'd see her in New York, she always had a drink in hand." Her face changes in an instant, marking the end of her trip down memory lane. "How is she doing with that?"

I assume the concerned look on her face means she's talking about Samantha's drinking. "She's stronger than she knows." I take one look at Quinn's concerned expression and something in me gives in to an urge to unburden a few things. "Perhaps I've mothered her too much though. I don't know that she's had a tough test with it yet."

"She said rehab was brutal. It's not a good idea to take her out on the town, is it?"

"I'm sure I don't know, luv. It's taken a lot of effort on her part to make it this long."

Quinn looks away, remorse darkening her expression. "None of us thought she was that bad about it. I mean, we all drank, and she always had the best scores. We didn't know. I didn't know."

"It's in the past, luv."

As the silence stretches, I recall Samantha's falling out with her sorority sister. I'm concerned about there being any bad blood on Quinn's end. Despite the gorgeous face, I have to look out for my best friend first, but I don't think the time is right to risk opening an old wound. "When will the rest of your group come in?"

"They'll be here on Thursday, as scheduled." She moves quickly to the bench swing and sits next to me as comfortably as though she's known me longer than a few days. "They can't wait to meet you."

I resist the urge to take her hand in mine, wondering where these sudden impulses are coming from. "Quinn, if Sam mentioned her sorority life, I'm afraid to say I don't remember."

"I'm not surprised."

"No?"

"We were all young and pretty stupid. I did a lot of things I'm not exactly proud of, and so did Sam. It's probably best we all get past all that and start fresh, you know?"

Her words are encouraging. "Sam did mention about your falling out."

Quinn gives me a guarded look. Her lips tighten into a straight line, devoid of humor. "Like you said, it's in the past."

"May I ask what happened?"

She purses her lips in thought and I can't help but stare at their shape, suddenly wondering about their texture. A wave of heat courses through my chest. The lass is more attractive by the second.

What's bloody gotten into you?

"It has something to do with her ex-fiancé. I can't believe he went missing!"

I feel my back stiffen, but I'm able to keep a neutral expression.

"Brooks and Andy were friends for a time. It was inevitable since Sam and I got to be friends." She looks into my eyes. "How much do you know about Sam's ex?"

"Enough to know that his bloody arse ought to rot in the worst prison this wretched world has."

Quinn is silent for a moment as though taken aback by my response. "No argument from me."

"Why'd you ask me that?"

Quinn thinks for a moment as she takes in the Battersea Bridge in the distance. "Samantha and Andrew had a one night stand. He confessed right after it happened, and a day later I got these pictures of the two of them sent to my office by Brooks. It was humiliating."

"Forgive me for prying," I utter with regret as her expression falls.

She shakes her head, her eyes still on the bridge. "I went to Sam, and she gave me this weird story about not having a choice. I was so angry. I never really dug for the whole story. I didn't want to know. It was the beginning of the end."

There's real pain in her voice now.

"I might've forgiven Andy, had he picked up one of his secretaries, or some other bitch I didn't know. But I couldn't forgive him for betraying me with my sorority sister." Quinn pauses to wipe away a tear. "Especially when he knew how inferior I felt when she was near."

I recall Samantha's one sided telephone conversation with Quinn. It sounded like they were getting along just fine, so perhaps I should keep my gob shut about explaining Samantha's forced participation in the brief affair with Andrew Fischer. I'm already regretting asking some questions.

Samantha had not exactly lied about not having a choice. The man that was about to marry her forced her into a scheme, using her as bait to blackmail several prominent men into his business ventures. I was certainly not about to divulge that horrid secret. That was Samantha's choice. "Since you are here, am I to assume that you and Samantha cleared the air?"

Quinn regards me with a serious look. "With Andy out of the equation, it's pretty easy to clear the air. But things got bad in my marriage from that incident with Samantha. I refused to have sex with him. At first he saw it as penance but when he felt enough time had gone by, he decided to find someone else. When I saw the picture of my husband walking out of some whorehouse in Reno in the front page of *Famous*, I knew the marriage was over."

Sensing there's more, I take her empty glass from her hand and set it on the table on the center of the patio.

"I found out later that Samantha and Brooks called the wedding off and I wondered if that resulted from her tryst with Andy, but we moved to California to try to patch things up and I didn't take the time to find out what happened. Long story short, things got much worse between Andy and me." Quinn stares at the water for a moment. "I should've looked for Sam, and hear her side of the story. The night I confronted her she alluded to their affair not being the first Andy engaged in. It took some time to realize, she was right. Andrew started cheating on me even before we got married."

Far worse than I thought.

"I've thought about her all this time."

I see the same wounded look in her eyes she had when she told me about using Andrew's computer and the ugly realization that followed. I need to get her out of this line of conversation. "The important thing is that you're in touch with each other once more, and now you can both move forward."

Quinn nods but she looks dazed, trying to compose herself. After a moment, a ghost of her radiant smile is back and she turns to me.

"So, tell me, Lewis, is Jason Stephen as hot as Sam says he is?"

"He's a good looking lad, sure." The sudden change of topic is enough to give me whiplash, but something tells me she needs it.

Quinn frowns and stares at me as though not sure how to proceed.

"Is something the matter, luv?"

"I'm sorry," she says, regarding me with a curious look. "I don't know why I thought you'd give me a different answer. Don't you find him attractive?"

I've been put in this spot before, and I've infallibly played the role expected of me each time. I can't find it in me to enact the expected gay response this time. I'm deflated as I realize how Quinn looks at me and this reaction is perplexing. "He's pretty to look at," I feign a smile. "He's a good lad."

"What about her maid of honor? Or I should say, matron of honor. What is she like? Is she pretty?"

The image of Gwen standing at the altar in that stunning tangerine gown is sure to raise the collective male heartbeat. "Gwen is a class act, a wonderful woman, and quite striking."

Quinn's thin eyebrow rides up, disappearing under her blonde bangs. "How'd they meet?"

"It's a long story, luv."

"I'm intrigued. I love long stories."

"I think you and Sam ought to get together and talk about it all."

"That sounds great, but I don't want to interfere in her wedding planning. I'm staying for at least another month after the wedding. To decompress, you know? Maybe I'll get to talk to her after her honeymoon. I'd like to take the opportunity to concentrate on myself for a little while."

It sounds to me like my cue to leave. "In that case, I will leave you to do just that, Quinn."

She takes my wrist when I stand. "I could use a friend to help me decompress. Do you have time?"

I can only imagine how many blokes lost their will when subjected to the effectively persuading power of those blue eyes. "Did you and Sam take some special class to use your eyes for evil purposes, such as rendering men helpless to suit your whims?"

Quinn smiles. "Does that mean it's working?"

More than you could possibly imagine…

"Is there a man in your life, Lewis?"

I look away, suddenly filled with unease. "There hasn't been for a while." I say, hoping she won't try to introduce me to someone.

"So, I can have you all to myself for the afternoon?"

"Absolutely."

She grins. "Great!"

She seems to glide towards me, her arms wrap around my middle and her head rests against my chest. As I return the embrace, I'm assaulted by a citrusy scent emanating from her body. For the first time in a long time, I'm perfectly aware of a woman's breasts pressed against me. I try to take a deep breath, trying to relax a certain part of my anatomy but it's got a bloody mind of its own. Before my reaction is discovered, I manage to pull away from her hold, if a bit hesitantly.

"Your heart was racing," she says with another curious look.

"It does, depending on the company." I smile, daring to think myself witty.

"I'm not trying to be forward. It's just that until now, you've had some type of mythical status to me. Like I've told you before, I feel like I know you. Gosh! I always felt a little jealous I didn't have a friend like you." Her brow wrinkles. "For the longest time, a lot of us thought you only existed in her mind, especially me, despite the tons of pictures she's shown me over the years."

"I'm quite sure, Samantha exaggerated. A little."

Quinn laughs. "It looked a little too convenient that you live here while she was going to school in New York. I had trouble believing it because I could never be just friends with a guy. Ever."

I'm not surprised at all. Quinn is a very young looking thirty-five year old. She is destined to be one of those rare humans who only improve with age just like a fine wine. I can't even fathom what this devastating beauty looked like in her teens and twenties.

Spending an afternoon with Quinn McDermont will be no hardship whatsoever. I'm about to suggest dinner when my mobile buzzes. I excuse myself to check the screen, it's Samantha.

Where are you? Dinner, my place? Mum is coming too.

I quickly type a message and look up at Quinn.

"Was that Sam?"

I nod. "The one and only. She wanted to know where I was."

"And where are you going to be?" Quinn says in a playful tone.

I give her a wry smile. "I told her I'm having dinner with a new friend."

26

The inboard Mercruiser Horizon twin engines roar as the propellers bite into the water, raising the gleaming prow. I feel as though we're flying in a smooth glide that barely ripples the river. Quinn grins as she steers the small boat past Battersea Park and under the Chelsea Bridge. A larger boat chugs south and Quinn steers right into its wake, making the Riva jump like a stone skipping on the surface of a pond. She pushes the throttle to the stops and we fly under the Vauxhall Bridge, leaving a frothing wake of our own that forces other boats to slow down as they chop through it. There's no point in trying to talk over the roar of the engines so I sit back and discreetly hold on for dear life.

Quinn only slows to admire the ominous looking MI6 Headquarters building on our right.

"I feel like James Bond!" she yells before pushing the throttle again. My tie flutters in the wind and the choppy waters are slowly putting me in an episode of seasickness but before the queasiness sets in, Quinn mercifully pulls into the Tamesis Dock and expertly guides the boat into a berth. She's obviously spent quite a bit of time in London to know her way around so well.

After we tie the lines and make our way off the floating platform onto terra firma, I resist the urge to get on my knees and kiss the ground. I feel like I'm still on the bloody water and my steps are wobbly at best.

Quinn takes my arm and together we walk down the wide stone sidewalk of the Albert Embankment, admiring the view of the Victoria Tower, the House of Lords, and Big Ben in the distance. I notice men attempting the anatomically impossible to get a good look at her as we walk by. I'm helpless against the sudden pride I feel of the fact that she's holding *my* arm.

Before leaving, she changed into tight, black jeans that leave very little to the imagination. She completed her ensemble with a flannel, plaid shirt in pinks and purples that she tied at the waist, leaving me looking severely overdressed.

We cross the road before we get to the Lambeth Bridge and walk down Black Prince Road. I'm feeling much better, but I already dread the trip back on the bloody boat, especially if she's planning on flying over the water again.

"I have to have Mexican. I'm starved! Is that okay with you?"

"Absolutely." I'd eat off the filthy street just to be near this beautiful creature.

"Good." Quinn licks her lips in a way that makes my heart stutter a bit.

These reactions are beginning to feel a bit more comfortable, leaving behind an unnerving sensation.

A short, dark-skinned, older man welcomes us to *La Casa de Cancún,* and shows us to our table. The place is painted in vibrant oranges and yellows, and the tile flooring is a rich red that somehow blends it all together. It makes me think of Lorna Matthews's talk about the autumn colors of the bouquet signifying change.

There's a curious sequence of Mayan scenes depicted in oil paintings on the walls. The same Mayan is in all the paintings, first talking to a snake, then an old woman, a deer, an eagle, a large beetle, and then finally lying on the ground as though sleeping, while lovingly holding a woman in his arms.

"That's the legend of Sac Muyal," Quinn says as she looks at her menu.

"Who?"

"It's a Mayan tale of faith. Sac Muyal steals that man's lover. To rescue her, the young Mayan is aided by different entities, who give him instructions that he must not question. When he does as he's told, the gods return his lover to him."

"How do you know that?"

Quinn shrugs. "I've an affinity for history. I delved into all the great civilizations, particularly all the eerie similarities between people separated by vast distances, even by an entire ocean."

"And these people are?"

"The Mayans, the Incans, and the Egyptians."

I'll be the first to admit, I've never picked up a history book in my life. "They were similar?"

"Spooky similar." She notices the blank look on my face. "They all built pyramids that required such precise placement and shaping of rocks that we're unable to reproduce today despite our technological advantages. They all had a thing for time and the stars. Their mythologies, all revolve around a sun god. That's just for starters."

Quinn orders for both of us when the server returns, Margaritas, nachos *con carne*, and a chimichanga platter. I've only tried Mexican food a handful of times when I visited Samantha in Rhode Island, although she vehemently swears Taco Bell is no bloody Mexican food.

The aromas wafting from the kitchen are beyond mouthwatering and bespeak of hot spices whose name I can only guess. I make a mental note to visit similar restaurants from now on.

The margaritas are placed before us in gigantic goblets, their rims salted. Quinn stirs hers and takes a delicate sip from her straw then nods in approval at the taste. When I do the same, my face twists as though I just swallowed pure agave tequila. She laughs and indicates I should stir the drink before drinking from it.

By the time we work through half of the heaping platter of the nachos, I'm stuffed. But the chimichangas are so tasty, I continue to shove food in my mouth as Quinn gives me a fascinating overview of the similarities among the aforementioned cultures. Eerie doesn't even begin to describe these similarities.

Somehow, all our dishes are returned empty to our polite server, who replaces our margaritas with barely a sound.

She has engaging theories about a common origin that spawned these dominating cultures, and the way she supports her case is slowly making a believer out of me.

"It's the only thing that makes sense. I think Walt Becker nailed it in his book. I don't suppose you've read it, have you?"

I shake my head. "But I think I will now."

Quinn smiles. "He wrote a novel, titled *Link*. I'm not going to ruin it for you. I suggest you read it and then let me know what you think."

"It's a deal."

She nods contentedly then looks out the window. "Damn! It's dark out there."

I turn in my seat and see she's right. How did the day get away from us?

Quinn waves sweetly to the man and he shuffles over to the table in a remarkably fast pace.

"*Señorita?*"

"Thank you for everything, Carlos. It's all there."

"*Un placer.*"

Quinn puts a bill in the man's hand so fast that she didn't give me a chance to dig my wallet out of my pocket and pay.

I watch Carlos amble past the tables when he suddenly stops, turns around with a dazed look on his face and glances inquiringly at Quinn, who nods and dazzles him with a grin. Carlos mouths several "thank you's" as he retreats to the kitchen.

"He looks like you gave him a fifty pound note."

"Oh, he got an even hundred."

I can only gape at her. Our meal couldn't have been more than twenty pounds. "Carlos will remember you forever."

"That's the idea. It's all about cultivating relationships, you know?" she winks, making me laugh.

Once we're back outside, Quinn wraps her arm around mine and we stroll back across the road, to the boat.

An older van screeches to a stop close to us, making us both turn in surprise. The door slides open and three people jump out, one extending a microphone, one with a video camera and the third blinding us for a second with the powerful flash of his photo camera.

"Quinn! Quinn!" yells the man with the microphone as he runs towards us.

Quinn's eyes are wide with shock. I have to put my hand up over my face so I'm not blinded by the blitzkrieg of the flash. I put my arm around her and pull her down the street as the trio follows us.

"Is this your new lover, Quinn? Why are you hiding in London? Can we get a word with you? Quinn! Quinn! Look this way, Quinn!"

The few people on the street have stopped to look at the spectacle, presenting me with a new obstacle as they encroach to see what the fuss is about. Next to me, Quinn seems to be shaking herself to pieces.

The lad with the microphone appears to be an emaciated teen. He races ahead of us and sticks the microphone in my face, shouting questions I refuse to acknowledge.

"Leave us alone!" I shout but the bloke ignores me.

"Quinn does your ex-husband know where you are? Quinn! Quinn!"

"No comment!" I shout as my temper flares.

"Why don't you let Quinn answer?" the man challenges.

"She has no comment for you, now leave her alone!"

"Look over here, Quinn!" shouts the man behind the photo camera.

Despite the sudden rage shorting my synapses, I have enough presence of mind not to do something stupid in front of the camera.

To my horror, another van squeals to a stop and four more people crowd us on the street.

I pull my mobile and tap the screen. The camera flashes are raining on us from three different directions and are making it difficult to find the right screen. When I do, I tap a three digit number and hit send. I try to tell myself that all I have to do is be patient.

"Quinn, who's your new lover?"

"Quinn, how long are you going to be in London?"

"Quinn, one shot please, honey, just one shot!"

For her part, Quinn has her face buried into my chest. We can no longer move because I sense these jackals are actually hoping for me to shove one of them to the ground.

"What's your name, man?"

"Is Quinn still doing drugs?"

"Are you still paying for escorts, Quinn?"

"How much did you get in the divorce, Quinn?"

My heart is in my throat, not from fear of these idiots, but fear of losing control as hatred makes me tremble with the intention of bashing their skulls with their video equipment.

An old sedan stops behind the second van and a new wave of flashes and shouted questions are about to make me lose my bloody mind.

I feel close to the breaking point when two other vehicles roar into the crowded street. After a few seconds, the camera people are being pulled away from us in not so kind a fashion. They all begin screaming indignantly at the men in black. I recognize Jason Soderberg's thick frame. He's gently, but firmly, pushing the first crew back to their van, calmly citing a series of violations. To my right Jason Stephen takes two men away by the arm. One looks ready to hit him, but one look from Jason and the man wilts under its intensity.

There are six other men escorting the pseudo-reporters to their vehicles. The onlookers on the street turn away and quickly leave the strange scene.

"What's the sitch, Lewis?"

I glance at Jason Soderbergh. "Paparazzi ambush. Tell McElroy to run the mouse."

Soderbergh grins. "Todd's been itching to run the mouse. Hold on." He turns and talks into a microphone. "Coast should be clear unless you want us to take you somewhere."

"Quinn?"

She finally looks up, her face tear stricken. "My boat is in the dock."

Soderbergh nods. "I'll get you there, Madame."

"Thank you," Quinn breathes.

Just as I turn her to go, I hear the clatter of heels behind me. "Lewis!"

I turn to see Jason Stephen. "Thanks for saving us."

He nods, but his eyes are on Quinn.

I sigh. "Jason, this is Samantha's friend, Quinn McDermont. Quinn, this is her fiancé, Jason McElroy."

Jason looks surprised. "Hullo. Sam didn't mention you were here."

"Hi," Quinn says with an awed expression. "I had some delicate business to conduct before I could let her know."

Jason gives her a soft smile. "Am I supposed to keep you a secret?"

She nods quickly. "Just for a day. I'll explain everything later."

Jason shrugs. "Fine by me, but you know Sam and secrets."

Quinn gives him a pleading look.

"Alright. I won't say a word."

"Thank you."

Jason turns to his radio. "Sods ordered a mouse run. Are you sure about that?"

"What's this mouse run?" Quinn asks.

"Anti-paparazzi software," I reply, but the perplexed look on her face does not abate.

Jason nods. "Sods will take you back to the dock. I can keep someone with you, just in case."

"Quinn?"

She looks remarkably composed. "Thank you. I don't know if that'd be necessary right now. I think you guys scared them pretty good."

"Those blokes don't scare easy," Jason remarks, but eventually shrugs in agreement. "Call if you have any more trouble."

A Mercedez SUV pulls up to the curb. Jason opens the back door and Quinn and I climb in.

"What'd you mean anti-paparazzi software back there?"

"As long as those wankers were using digital cameras, our Magnetic Outburst Selector signal will erase anything in those memory cards. It'll only affect devices actively recording so your mobile and mine were safe."

Quinn stares at me openmouthed for several seconds. "Mouse..." she says in awe, a grin spreading on her face.

"Tell her the good part, Lewis!" Jason "Sods" Soderbergh guffaws as he pulls up to a restaurant by the Tamesis Dock.

"The good part?" Quinn looks at me expectantly.

I smile. "When they go to play back the video or upload the photos, they'll only get to see Mickey Mouse."

Soderbergh pounds the steering wheel as he laughs. "That's a thing of beauty. Lewis, you're my hero!"

Quinn scrunches her pretty face in complete bafflement. "What?"

"When they try to play the video, they'll get a cartoon of Mickey," Soderbergh says amidst bouts of laughter.

"When they upload the photos, they'll get a photo of the most famous mouse on the planet."

Quinn smiles. "Who came up with that?"

"I can't tell you who developed the MOUSE—"

"MI6," Soderbergh quips, twisting to grin at Quinn.

I shake my head. "Very well, the blokes at MI6 developed the software. I grafted the Mickey Mouse images."

"I can't tell you how impressed I am. So then that means—"

I nod. "They don't have a single thing with you in it."

***

Quinn starts the engines and hits some switches, illuminating the inside of the boat, the port and starboard lights, and a light bar near the prow. The city glow of London illuminates the Thames well enough to navigate at night, but the lights make me feel much safer. Not to mention she probably won't hightail it back to Chelsea this time.

I'm surprised when she heads upriver again, coasting up to the Waterloo Bridge, from where we can look up at the London Eye, the massive, ultramodern Ferris wheel that takes passengers on a wondrous sightseeing trip.

Since 1999, over three million people a year have taken a ride in one of the ovoidal capsules, enjoying a climate controlled ride up over 135 meters, or 440 feet, that gives them a majestic view of the old city.

Quinn stops the boat away from the traffic lanes. She stands so she can better see the panorama over the Plexiglas windscreen. When I stand she leans into me, taking my arm and draping it around her middle. My hand ends up on her flat abdomen, sending a pulse of heat through my core.

"God, it looks like it's going to fall any second."

"That's why it never stops rotating."

"You're not serious."

I chuckle. "There was a rumor that once they got it going, they realized that if they ever stopped it, it would collapse."

"That's an awful rumor," Quinn observes. "It's so pretty."

"Have you been up there?"

Quinn quickly shakes her head. "Major acrophobia."

I look down to make sure I heard right. "You just flew over the Atlantic at thirty thousand feet."

She shivers. "I sedate myself to fly, otherwise I couldn't do it."

"That's too bad. The view from The Eye is spectacular."

"I'll take your word for it."

It always made me sad to meet anyone who suffered a phobia for the simple fact that such a psychological issue limits the human capability. Fear of heights is stealing a wonderful experience from Quinn.

Samantha asked me not to go on The Eye until she could go with me. Being the accommodating, spoiling, best friend I am, I waited. It was worth the wait. I loved seeing the look of pure wonder on her face as we spotted the different British iconic landmarks from our capsule.

Westminster Palace looks like a golden, jagged jewel, while Big Ben doesn't look so big from up there. You really gain a new appreciation for architecture when looking at the Charing Cross railway station. Only from up there you can appreciate just how vast the Waterloo railway station complex really is. London stretches before you, beautiful, majestic, and timeless.

The boat bobs gently on the river. Quinn disengages from me and we lean our arms over the windscreen. Her hand finds my arm. She seems to always need contact, which is fine by me. It's strange to have this level of comfort, this much contact, with someone I met only days ago.

She gazes around in wonder. "It looks so pretty."

I've been around London enough to forsake the view, easily done when compared to this, most beautiful rendition of female perfection in my eyes. "It is."

"So, do you mind telling me exactly what happened back there? It's beginning to feel totally surreal."

"Jason, well, both Jasons and I work for Lions Securities. The top man of Lions, Sir Nathan Jeffries, is Samantha's father, for all intents and purposes. As the leading security firm in Western Europe, Lions is charged with delicate assignments that often require access to new technologies. Trust me, they've guarded celebrities and their privacy for years. They're good at what they do."

"Jason is absolutely gorgeous…"

There's no arguing that, but I don't care to hear that. "Sods? He's a good lad."

Quinn chuckles. "He was very cute, but Samantha's Jason is dreamy!"

"He's no longer available, I'm afraid."

Quinn notices the odd inflection in my voice, given the mischievous little grin she gives me. "Are you available?"

"Only to the highest bidder, luv."

Quinn laughs. "I guess it's luck that I unknowingly surrounded myself with the right people. I don't understand how anyone would even recognize me out here."

"Is that what prompted you to cut your hair?" I ask, recalling the flowing silk around her shoulders from the photographs online.

"Hardest decision of my life," she sighs with regret. "How did they know where I was?"

I'm about to point out that as striking as she is, someone was bound to identify her, but something about the encounter felt orchestrated. "Does Andrew know where you are?"

She shakes her head. "I thought that too, but other than my family and Firuz, I can't think of anyone who knows I came to London."

"What about your friends from the football match?"

"They are the closest thing I have to family. They'd know better." She gives me a pained look. "I'd hate to think I couldn't trust them. That'd be awful."

"Was it just as bad back in America?"

"These paparazzi attacks? They were much worse. I couldn't leave the house and even then I'd hide in my own home when helicopters started buzzing around." She looks agitated.

"Perhaps it was just dumb luck. Forget about it."

"I'm worried about Sam's wedding. What if these idiots figure it out and storm the wedding? What if it gets ruined because of me?"

I squeeze her hand. "For one, Sam would love the attention," I chuckle. "But I'm sure the boys from Lions won't let that happen. Fret no more about this."

"You're right. I don't even want to think any more about that."

"Good. We can talk about anything you want."

She nods and bites her lip in thought.

The mantle of night has pushed the light of day behind the horizon. The air gusts sporadically, pushing clouds above us, muting the starry sky. Floating on the Thames makes me a bit homesick. I recall Samantha and I sneaking onto bobbing boats, just to float on the water, either talking or sitting in silence. Am I trying to replace Samantha's friendship with Quinn's?

"So, you and Samantha grew up together?"

The typical Yankee stated question. I bite my tongue and decide no one is perfect after all. "In many ways, yes."

"Did she ever email you about me?"

"Like I told you before, I didn't even know she was in a sorority until recently," I tell her honestly. "And when she did, she said you were rotten to her."

She shakes her head. "I know. It took a while before we actually got along. I was pretty intimidated. I've never known anyone like her. She was so driven, so attractive, so damn intelligent."

Samantha was all those things. She was also as fragile as a snowflake in spring. "Wasn't that a requirement to join Sigma Chi Rho?"

Quinn exhales a long breath as she closes her eyes and lets her head fall back. My eyes are drawn once again to her neck.

"That was a bunch of elitist bullshit. We were all so proud for the wrong reasons, and I was horrible to the new girls."

"Sam said the same thing, the part about the elitist bullshit, I mean."

"She did?" I nod. "Well, there you go. She's damn smart. And yes, I was a total bitch to her at first."

"She can be just as bad."

"Oh, don't I know it! But what makes her stand out is how intelligent she is."

"You both are." She cuts her eyes to me, a penetrating stare. "Typical Sigma Chi Rho, right?"

Quinn returns her eyes to the skyline. "Thank you. But as far as the elitist crap? Not all of us grew out of that. Can we sit?"

"Absolutely."

She pulls her legs up on the seat and turns to face me. The air is growing cooler and heavier clouds have moved in from the southern horizon. I actually smell a hint of ozone in the air. I must have missed the lightning.

"I always envied Samantha. I think I envy her now even more."

"Why?" I ask, genuinely curious. "Was it because of her brains?"

"Because of you."

"Me?"

"I told you, I know a lot of people but I don't have real friends. Samantha came close for a long time. So long in fact, that we swore to be each other's maid of honor. And then she and Andy…"

I see tears in her eyes and I silently curse the armrests and the center console that keep me from reaching out to her. All I can do is watch as she struggles to compose herself.

The moment gives me a chance to ponder what is happening to me. I never acted this way around a woman. Hell, I never acted this way no matter how attracted I felt to a man back when I was seemingly living an entirely different life, and most definitely not with anyone I was working for.

"I'm not going to lie, Lewis. I have my own reasons for being here. I'm so angry with myself at times," she says, and I notice her hands trembling as evidence. "I used to blame Samantha for the end of my marriage. I blamed her each time I found out Andy was out fucking some whore again. But now I see that he'd done those things all on his own before I ever found out. In retrospect, the signs were always there, even soon after we were married. And that made me question whether I was ever good enough as a woman…"

Emotion finally overwhelms her and she drops her face in her hands. When I try to move, the small boat rocks as though it's warning me to stay on my side. I reach for her knee and Quinn grabs my hand as soon as she feels the contact.

"The worst thing is," she sniffles, "I didn't just punish him, I ended up punishing myself! I had so many chances to hop in bed with someone else, but I swore I'd never turn away from the promises I made when I got married. I've been so alone for so long, and I feel so stupid for it. Even when I had the chance, I just couldn't go through with it…"

I intuit she's referring to Firuz, but I don't want to even entertain the thought of him putting his hands on my Quinn and—

Your Quinn…?

I dismiss that inner voice, heeding to an impulse that feels new and alien. This time I could care less if the bloody boat rolls us into the cold water. The Riva lists to starboard but it doesn't send us for a swim. Quinn feels my movement and she turns her face into the crook of my shoulder. I hold her close to me, unable to believe that this is the same woman that met me at Fox's in a business suit only a few days ago. Again, I give in to the irrational feeling that I've known her forever.

A bolt of lightning shatters the clouds. Thunder roars from the east like an angry beast whose quarry got away from its claws.

"Quinn, we'd best head back."

She nods into my chest. "I'm sorry."

"Nothing to be sorry about, luv."

She climbs over the center console, perilously rocking the boat, and relinquishes the wheel to me. I start the engines, push the throttles and the propellers dig into the water, easily moving us downriver.

I maneuver around a ferryboat and allow a few faster boats to overtake us before pushing the throttles halfway. The twin motors growl and we're churning the water at a fast clip.

If MI6 Headquarters looked ominous before, it now looks eerily fascinating illuminated at night.

Once we are past the bridges I look over at Quinn. She's holding her knees, retreating into herself. The sophistication and intellect that impressed me so deeply have fled her, leaving behind a wounded little girl. It takes everything in me not to push the throttles to the bloody stops just so I can get to her flat and hold her again.

It takes some maneuvering, but I finally manage to softly bump the boat against her dock. She snaps out of her funk and jumps out of the boat to secure the lines on the moorings. Just as I'm about to step from the boat to the dock, the skies open up and cold rain soaks through my dress shirt, and pastes my hair to my skull.

I expect Quinn to be already under the safety of her covered patio but she's standing a few feet from me, face up to the rain, arms stretched wide, smiling.

"Quinn! We've got to get inside!"

She seems not to hear me. Her clothes are drenched, the white top beneath her shirt is transparent and in the dim light, I can see every vivid detail of her femininity, down to the pulsing of her heart on the side of her neck. For a small eternity, I dare not breathe, afraid of making her move.

Somehow, my feet carry me to within inches of her. When my shadow falls across her face, she opens her eyes to the rain and my arms move out of their own accord around her waist. She squints through the raindrops and gives me a soft smile as she slowly runs her hands up and down my back.

"Damn it, Lewis. Why do you have to be so gorgeous?"

I stare down at her, unable to formulate a reply. My eyes refuse to look away from her lips. They look as beautiful as dew-covered rose petals.

In the distance, lightning sizzles through the clouds, and the ensuing thunder is a booming cannon that jolts us both out of our trance. We let go and run into the flat. She leaves the door open and we are engulfed by the hissing of the rain.

With her hair flat against her scalp, I notice a scar just behind her right ear as she turns for the patio. The sight of that scar makes me ache at the mere idea she ever suffered pain.

We're both heaving after the uphill dash. The water dripping from our clothes is forming a puddle on the floor between us. We are facing each other, our backs against the walls of the narrow hallway just inside the flat. The rain hisses angrily on the shingles and the concrete walk, mercilessly pounding the grass and the flowerbeds into the wet dirt.

I've always refrained from saying "Are you well?" when someone clearly isn't, and this time is no exception. Quinn begins to cry softly, once again drawing me near. I can only see the right side of her face, the left side is hidden in the gloom of the flat, but both her eyes glitter as they peer up at me. Her vulnerability makes me wish I could simply touch her and absorb whatever pain is ravaging her soul at this very moment, which is charged and agonizingly filled with expectation.

She takes my hands in each of hers and drops her head down to my chest. There have been plenty of times when I've held Samantha in the same fashion. I always wanted to absorb her pain when I saw her hurting, but I carried certain limitations in my mind back then that we had both so easily accepted. I always saw her as my best friend and that enabled me to keep from reacting to her contact. It's not that I didn't feel a certain degree of desire. But when it came to Samantha, I would have never done anything to jeopardize our friendship.

Quinn does not inspire such limitations.

Break out of your prison, my luv. You have too much to give someone else. Just make certain she is as bright, and as beautiful as you are, and don't settle for anything less. Don't let another Samantha Reddick slip by...

I've never wanted Terence out of my head as badly as I do at this moment, but only because I'm so afraid of heeding his words.

Quinn lets go of my hands and flattens her palms against my chest. She slides them down the front of my shirt, sending a ticklish flutter through my stomach that makes me flinch then she uses my belt as a handhold and looks up, her eyes brimming with desire. I give in to the impulse to hold her face in both my hands, feeling as though electricity is crackling between us.

My body is at war with my mind, though I have no idea what to do at this moment, so I only stare back, slowly being pulled down into the depths of her mesmerizing gaze.

"I'm sorry," Quinn says as she shakes herself like she's coming out of a dream. "Good God, I'm acting like an idiot. I'm sorry, Lewis." She buries her face in her hands once again.

When she lets me see her eyes, she's remarkably composed, silently asking me to back up a step.

I oblige.

"We've got to do something about these clothes. Take those off and follow me," she says with a quiver in her voice that betrays how nervous she is as she points at my shoes.

She slips out of her boating shoes and I pull the ruined loafers off my feet. It takes some work to slip out of the bloody socks. I hate the way wet cotton feels on my hands.

I finally manage to get my foot out of the sock when a drenched plaid shirt falls at my feet. When I look up, Quinn is turning and walking down the hallway, wrestling out of her top. My breath catches when I get a glimpse of her bare back. Her jeans cling alluringly low on her hips, revealing a tribal tattoo on her lower back. She disappears around the corner before I can make out any details. A light comes on, chasing some of the shadows into the far corners.

My synapses seem to misfire. I've never felt so bewildered.

"Lewis?" She calls.

I follow the light, not knowing what to expect to see when I turn the corner. Quinn's shadow emerges out of the bathroom followed by her, enveloped in a terrycloth robe. She hands me a towel and begins loosening my tie and unbuttoning my shirt.

"I knew it was going to rain, I should've gotten us back sooner. I'm sorry."

It suddenly occurs to me that we're enacting a parody of marriage, but the bubbling laughter evaporates, leaving in place a sense of longing that leaves me cold inside.

"Let's get this off. I'm afraid your tie is ruined," she laments as she squeezes water out of the tie.

The sash around her thin waist loosens its hold and the robe comes apart just enough to reveal a generous view of cleavage. I've never experienced such sweet torture.

"You know I wouldn't be doing this if you weren't gay, right? I remember Sam bragging about fearlessly walking around naked in front of you."

"And you envied that?"

She grins. "God, yeah!"

Bloody great. I'm Caleb in *Eating Out*.

"Give me your pants, oh, wait. Give me your trousers."

I firmly believe the female body is a much better design. Certain reactions to our male bodies are simply far too telling of the state we might be in, and there's nothing that drives the point home like an erection.

I turn away from Quinn, whose fingers have already managed to unbuckle the belt and undo the button.

"I can get those, luv."

She smiles coquettishly. "I'm sorry. I always played sports, so showering with the girls was no big deal."

Showering with the...?

"I'll leave you plenty of hot water, don't worry," she says over her shoulder as she goes back into the bathroom.

"Righto, take your time, luv," I call to her, leaning on the wall, as I whisper to myself, "I could use a cold shower anyway..."

27

The drive back to my flat is one of the longest yet. All I can do is think of the overpowering current of lust that gripped me while I wrestled for the best way to extricate myself from Quinn McDermont's spell. I've never felt so off balance in my entire life. Or perhaps I have.

I was barely thirteen and it was the beginning of summer. Samantha delayed her arrival by one week due to a volleyball tournament. When her squad was ousted, she quickly boarded the earliest flight and came to London. On the ride to Liverpool from Heathrow, I asked her to refrain from being so exuberant around me, which instantly made her dial up her displays of affection more than a few notches, especially when she finally met Tabitha Little, the girl I'd been dating all school year.

Tabitha Little was easily the most beautiful creature in St. Mary of Mercy Prep. She had a reputation for dating an eighteen-year-old named Matthew Krevens, and for calmly accepting the ongoing rumors. She was looked down upon by grown-ups, but revered by every girl under sixteen. She was younger than me by mere months, but she had the figure and demeanor of a much older girl.

The entire universe seemed to revolve around her. I was only one of the many who secretly worshipped her.

I don't know what it was that made her notice me. Perhaps the fact that compared to everyone else, Tabitha and I seemed out of place. We were equally taller than most, fastidious about our appearance, and oddly concerned with older themes. She was sophisticated without coming off as presumptuous and eloquent without sounding pompous.

In our ballet class, we were a great physical match, but her dancing needed some extra work. I was happy to stay after our lessons to help her through some of the more intricate moves. Ten minutes into our first one-on-one conversation, I felt I had found someone very special.

I'd easily get lost in those dark eyes of hers. Tabitha inherited her Italian mother's Mediterranean beauty, and her Welsh father's intellect.

We became steady throughout the year and by the beginning of summer, it was clear our mutual attraction was bound to evolve into a more physical relationship.

There was also a fair-skinned boy, my best friend from school, Charlie Denton, who had given me a note that turned out to be a declaration of his love for me. In one strange, charged moment, we kissed after curiosity got the best of us. I chalked up the kiss to nothing more than experimentation. Charlie was a fragile-looking lad, painfully shy, but we had hit it off ever since he came to Mum's school to dance, and to him, that kiss meant much more.

Tabitha noticed Charlie giving me longing gazes. His animosity towards her only served to make up her mind about me. At one point, she even asked me if I was gay, and I told her I honestly didn't know.

In essence, we were all victims of hormone surges and sexual awakening, our bodies leading far more than our minds.

It's eerie the way we recollect certain events in our lives. They're never in order, but presented to our conscious in a convoluted spiral, severely lacking any type of chronology. It's as though one thing leads to ten more, and we pick a strand to pull at random.

I've never been comfortable with revealing passionate feelings to anyone. I can tell Samantha that I love her, for she's been the closest thing to a sister I have, but despite the many times I've heard someone tell me they love me, I've frozen, unable to return the sentiment.

I stopped talking to Charlie, though not because he had feelings for me. I was hopelessly attracted to him as well. I harbored feelings of my own, but I just didn't know what to do with all that. I knew everyone else thought it was wrong and I was still afraid of what gay kids went through after school hours.

In the end, Tabitha exerted such a powerful pull on me through the beginning of that summer, reducing me to no more than a moth helplessly floating into the flame, blissfully ignorant of the impending destruction.

Samantha couldn't believe I had a girlfriend. In fact, she seemed disappointed, though I never tried to read into the real reason for that. She finally told me that so long as I was happy, it didn't matter who was the reason behind it, though I knew she liked Charlie for me far more.

Tabitha was intimidated by my best friend. They were civil enough to each other on their first meeting, but I got an earful once they got me alone from each of them. Tabitha said that Samantha's attitude of ownership of me bothered her. My best friend merely pointed out Charlie was her favorite.

I've often wondered if Samantha's presence precipitated Tabitha to rush things in order to claim me.

I'd taken Samantha to see *The Princess Bride*. When we were leaving the cinema, I was shocked to find Tabitha waiting for me after the film. She wasn't cross because I'd gone with Samantha, for I had told her my plans earlier in the day. She gave my best friend a sweet smile and kindly asked if she could have me back for a few hours. Samantha only asked that we walk her back home, which we did, only to crush me to her chest before finally going into the house.

"She really cares about you," Tabitha observed.

"Like a sister," I was quick to amend.

"Is that how you see me?"

"No."

I assumed she wanted me to walk her home as well, but she invited me inside. No one was home. She insisted on showing me photographs from some of her other ballet recitals, knowing I'd be interested, and we went into her room where pink and white frills dominated the scene.

We sat on her bed looking at the photographs, at least I was. Tabitha was staring at me with a strange intensity. Her hand landed on mine and slid up my arm, my shoulder, my back. Her touch felt so good it was slowly putting me into a trance. When we started kissing I felt my insides churning. Her hands continued to trace unknown patterns all over me, until they slithered to my groin. I couldn't breathe.

Tabitha deftly unclasped my trousers and let her hand glide over me, sending a current of pleasure through every cell in my body. Suddenly, I felt a pulsing that arched my back, stopped my breathing, and the release came on so quick, I didn't realize what had happened until much later.

Tabitha looked at her hand, my eyes, and then she laughed.

While I hastily stood and pulled up my trousers, she called me a litany of vile things until I told her I wanted to leave. I felt fractured in unimaginable ways as she threw her insults in a barrage of verbal daggers that tore the fabric of my heart. There's no way to describe what I felt that day, but whatever it was, it proved strong enough to keep me from ever putting myself in that position with anyone.

Until now...

The last two decades of my life flash on the screen of my mind and I'm unable to do much more than let the deluge of memories play out.

I've never believed in self-analysis, but some of the insights you gain when you let the past bubble up to the surface are life altering.

I don't know how long I've been sitting in my car after parking. It feels like days, like two decades, perhaps. I'm not sure why that incident of adolescence would be powerful enough to dictate my sexual conduct from that point on. I've prided myself in not allowing sex to dominate my life the way Terence, or Samantha did. Only this time, I'm not sure who's right.

Terence was recklessly sexual, precisely why he was dying of AIDS, alone in his luxurious home; to Samantha, sex was a fun pastime or a divine experience when shared with someone you loved; to me it's been nothing but something to stay the bloody hell away from.

But today, none of my fears, rational or irrational, were enough to keep me from wanting Quinn McDermont so badly.

I could say that I'm thankful she thinks I'm gay and didn't push for more. But there had been something there, something in those eyes, and in the way her touch lingered on me as we stared at each other while dripping from the rain. That something was desire, I realize and it's beyond me what kept us from heeding to it.

I can almost hear Terence telling me I'm not gay in a mocking tone followed by a bemused chuckle devoid of the coughing and the heaving I heard when I was at his home.

"Thankfully, nothing happened, chap." I say to the confused, eyes on the rearview mirror.

No, but you wanted something to happen…

I don't even pretend to argue with that inner voice.

You want her…

***

I don't hear music, but I hear the sound of female voices coming from my living room when I quietly open the door.

"…and I don't mind telling you, Gwen, that I even had a list of baby names for them. I imagined a strapping little lad, who took after Sammie Kay and a lovely little doll with my Lewis's softness."

I hear the unmistakable note of sadness in my mother's voice. It's always put at odds the way she so fiercely defended me while I grew up.

"My parents died young," I hear Mum say. "I'm sure I don't have to tell you that you become acutely aware of your own mortality on the day you first hold your baby to your chest. You realize you only have so much time to turn this baby into a valiant person, whose triumphs will be the only evidence that you lived your life the right way. You breathe easier when they find that special someone, and you accept the inevitable deterioration to come for you because your child won't be alone, because your job is done. It's the only thing that makes a parent see the end of their life as a rightful rest, rather than the imposed tragedy it really is."

"Mum, please don't say that. You're going to live a long time."

Hearing Gwen refer to my mother as "Mum" brings a smile to my face.

"I watched Sammie Kay grow from this pretty little thing into everything I wanted in a daughter despite whatever mistakes she made along the way. None of us escapes fault. I wanted her for my Lewis more than anyone knows, and I've been taking out my frustrations about that on him lately."

"If it's any consolation, I absolutely adore your son. For everything he's done not just for Samantha, but for me as well. He's a real sweetheart, and whoever he lets in his heart is going to be so lucky to have him."

"You're a dear, Gwen. And you're right. But still…"

There's a long pause between them, and it can only mean Mum's crying. Old feelings of guilt awaken somewhere in my chest and bring back even more dreadful memories.

"I should've been holding a baby by now!" Mum sobs. "But it's been quite a blessing to come to know you, and your precious angels, whom I will miss terribly when you go back."

Gwen offers some tremulous, thankful words. It seems they've been talking for quite a while to get to this point. I've always sensed what my mother's been feeling about me, but to hear it out loud in her voice has conveyed to me the depth of her… anguish.

I slide back down the steps, the same way I did when I was little, while sneaking into the kitchen for sweets. When I get to the door, I open it and make a show of shutting it hard enough for the sound to register upstairs.

When I climb the steps and see them, their demeanor is incredibly at odds with the overheard conversation from just a few seconds ago. They're all grins and smiles, their eyes clear and bemused, not a single trace of the mood that I sensed just moments ago. Incredible.

"Out late, were you?" Mum asks suspiciously.

I smile at Gwen, who's scrutinizing my expression, making me nervous.

Sitting on the edge of the couch, I wrap my mother in a bear hug and kiss her cheek. The skin seems so thin and at this closeness, the grey roots contrast starkly with the rest of her hair. Mum pats my arm as I give in to the impulse to rock for a moment.

"Oh, now you only got this loving right before some confession or right before asking me for something expensive," Mum says, gently drawing back so she can better look at me. "Now I know you can afford whatever your heart desires, so what's the confession?"

How could she possibly suspect…? "Mum, you're such a cynic. Can't a son just give his mother an innocent hug?"

Gwen regards us with a pretty smile, but her eyes are fixed on mine and I can almost feel her presence in my thoughts.

"Samantha said you were out with a new friend," Gwen prompts.

"Client, really, but we're quickly becoming friends. Are you the only one here, luv?"

Gwen nods. "I wanted to come by and check on Mum. Sam and Jason Stephen took the girls to a movie. Oh, I'm sorry. I meant a film."

"That's a good lass," Mum says approvingly. "Well now, thank you, dear, for keeping this old bird some company, but I'm expecting a call from my sweetheart."

Both women stand and embrace, drawing back to share a knowing look before bidding each other good night.

"Good night, Mum."

"Good night, luv." She pats my arm and turns for the steps.

When she's gone, I look at Gwen, whose little bemused smile begins to make me nervous. "Tea?"

"Absolutely. Thank you."

"When are Sam and Jason coming back?" I feel even more nervous as she tracks my every move.

Gwen shrugs. "Samantha volunteered you to take me back to Kensington.

"Oh, she did, did she? It'll be a pleasure."

Gwen's stare is deceivingly innocent. Only when we sit at the table sipping at our cups, does she finally drop all pretenses and gives me a pointed look.

"So, what's her name?"

I spit and sputter my first sip of tea. "What?"

Gwen gives me a look that says "give me a little more credit".

"What's her name?"

"Who?"

"Based on that odd look on your face, the flowery smell of your clothes, and the lack of styling gel on your hair, I'd say you were doing a little more than having dinner with a *client,*" she says, that last word enclosed in quotation marks made by her hands. "So, who is she?"

I want to be a wiseass and ask her what makes her think it's a "she", but the flowery smell of Quinn's detergent is a dead giveaway. "First of all, you, my dear friend, are not even supposed to know that look. Second of all, London has a horrid shortage in police detectives, perhaps I can put in a good word for you."

"Nice try, but you're not sidestepping this one," she shoots back, crossing her arms to let me know she's no longer amused by my lame attempts at deflection.

"I heard you and Mum talking."

This time it's me doing the scrutinizing as Gwen's blue eyes briefly dart around, though she keeps a deadpan expression.

"It's quite alright, luv. I'm no stranger to her disappointment."

"She's not disappointed in you."

I look into her eyes and see a deep well of compassion.

"You know, when I was pregnant with Brooke, I asked Tony whether he'd rather raise a gay son, or a gay daughter."

"You did?"

She nods. "I was just raising a possibility. I wanted to know how he felt."

"And?"

"He said he didn't care as long as he raised a happy son or a happy daughter."

"Admirable."

"As a parent we all have these, maybe unfair, expectations of our kids. But in reality, all we want is for our kids not to make the mistakes we made, so that they live a better life than we did."

"Gwen, my mother's been a different person since the arrival of Brooke and Emily. You may have missed it, but she often looks at me with something like pity, when she's around them." I'm feeling more uncomfortable by the second. "She doesn't know how much that hurts me."

"She can't help it," she says quickly. "How was she while you dated Terence?"

I think back for a second. "She loved Terence. At least she said she did."

"I wouldn't doubt it. She told me you guys got along well. She's proud of your company and knows Terence had a lot to do with getting it off the ground. But that's not it. She said it made her glad to see a twinkle in your eye when you talked about him."

I nod, recalling better times.

"Look, in the end this is your life to live. No one can live it for you."

I give her a grateful smile. "That means more than you'll ever know."

"Good. Now, who is she? Does she have anything to do with that fading shiner on your chin?"

Bloody hell...

I see no point in dodging her any longer. "Quinn McDermont."

Gwen could not have looked more surprised if I said Kate Middleton.

"I thought Samantha said she was coming on Thursday."

"She was already in London when I contacted her about the wedding."

"You spent the day with her and didn't tell Samantha about it?"

I nod. "She asked me not to let Sam know she's here for another day."

Gwen narrows her eyes in suspicion. "Did you two end up in bed?"

"Of course not."

She picks up her cup and brings it to her lips, her eyes never leaving mine.

"We ended up in the shower."

Gwen breaks into a coughing fit that makes her eyes watery. I hand her a napkin and quickly fetch a glass of water for her, unable to hide a wry smile.

"What? You're joking!"

"After we got caught in the rain, that is."

"What?"

I can see a new awareness in Gwen's wide stare. "Nothing of consequence happened, luv. I was a perfect gentleman."

Gwen examines my eyes for a long moment then begins nodding like a scientist concluding on her findings. "But you didn't want to be a gentleman," she remarks.

In a flash, that fiery desire is there when I think of that moment, coursing through my body with less intensity than it did around Quinn, but with no less solidity. "I don't know."

"Okay. What happened exactly? And you'd better have a damn good excuse as to why she hasn't let Samantha know she's been here, with you."

I tamp down on an irrational pang of guilt that tells me it's Samantha I should be confiding in before I begin talking.

"Lewis?"

I nod. "I'll tell you everything. Perhaps you can make better sense of it than I can."

She looks worried. "Okay. And for the record, Mum is not the only one acting different. You haven't exactly been yourself lately."

I blow a stream of air in resignation. "Perhaps you can help me with that too."

***

"I still can't believe it," Gwen says for the fourth time since I got done telling her about my evening with Quinn, and the other days we spent together. The only thing I left out was the fight with Firuz. It seems of no consequence now that Quinn sent him on his way.

I can't describe the sense of relief this unburdening gives me. Once I explain enough of the history between Quinn and Samantha, Gwen surprises me by understanding Quinn's reasons for staying hidden.

"She walked in the bathroom, while you were in the shower, only to grab your clothes, and wash them and dry them for you?"

"Yes."

"What'd you do? Sit around naked for an hour until your clothes were dry?" she asks, subjecting me to another pointed look.

"She lent me a terrycloth robe that was probably her ex-husband's. I didn't ask. Then she told me about the many times she's visited London. She went as far as calling the old city the perfect getaway."

Gwen looks at me incredulously. "So, she said 'why do you have to be so gorgeous'?"

"Are you still stuck on that?"

I turn into Kensington Church Street, and only when we drive past The Churchill Arms pub, I become aware of the fact that it's not Samantha riding next to me. It seems incredible that Gwen and I have gotten so close in such a short time.

"I'm sorry. I guess you just don't see the importance of that question."

"Why is that so important?"

"As if you don't know. She likes you! No, that's a little weak. I mean, she wants you!"

I've always heard Samantha claim she can feel herself blushing. I've never believed her until now that my cheeks burn.

"The question is why?"

I give Gwen a questioning, sideways glance.

"No, you *are* gorgeous, but that's not what I mean," she says flustered.

"Are you quite sure?"

This is the least composed I've seen Gwen since her arrival and she reminds me of Samantha quite a bit.

"You are gorgeous, Lewis. Shut up!" She backhands my shoulder. "You've got that cute widow's peak and who wouldn't want to run their hands through that hair? You've got a nice chin, and gorgeous eyes. If I wasn't married, I'd totally do you."

I haven't seen this side of Gwen. Samantha has spoken about it, and I've seen it in her Facebook posts, but I've never been the direct recipient of her legendary humor in the middle of a serious talk, her way of dispelling tension. "Is that the only thing stopping you, luv?" I can't help myself.

"Don't tempt me." Gwen gives me a wicked grin that I fail to interpret, though it makes me laugh a bit nervously. "If I'm so desirable, why are you questioning Quinn's actions?"

"Men," she mutters under her breath with a slight shake of her head. "Lewis, from what you told me, Quinn blames Samantha for the end of her marriage. Now she's here for the wedding, and suddenly very friendly with you. Isn't it obvious?"

I roll my eyes in thought. "Not exactly," I confess.

"Lewis, she wants revenge."

"How?"

"She told you how much Samantha bragged about you over the years, so she knows how much you mean to her. If I was looking to get back at Samantha for something she did, I'd do it through you."

Given recent history, no one has more reason to get back at Samantha than Gwen. However, I just can't see her as the evil, vindictive type. Although I don't doubt the existence of evil within every one of us, Gwen Amaya remains upon a pedestal to me. "But you wouldn't, right?"

"Not now. I love you."

Not now…? "Did you want to get back at her?"

Gwen looks up through the sunroof as though to stare at the empty galleries of the row houses along Leinster Square. I don't feel bad about taking advantage of her unfamiliarity with London by driving in circles just to keep talking to her, but I feel bad that I asked something that she doesn't know how to answer. "Forgive me, luv." I get shivers from the cold expression on her face.

"I've gotten over it, Lewis. Okay?"

I can't say anything for a long moment. "Of course," I say quietly then smile at her. "By the way, I love you too, Gwen."

She smiles and the cold expression vanishes, bringing me a wave of relief. However, the levity is short lived.

"I just don't trust this Quinn," she says thoughtfully.

This is so like Gwen, to become protective of those she considers close to her. "Fret not, luv."

"No. Listen, you don't know her, and you can't possibly trust her. At least not until you figure out just how pissed off this woman is at Samantha."

In my mind, I see Quinn's eyes filled with longing and vulnerability. I'm not willing to believe that I was seeing nothing but an act. "I don't know that I agree with you."

"Fine. Just promise me you'll be careful around her."

"Very well."

"Promise me."

"I promise."

She sighs with relief and looks straight ahead until we pull into Nathan's drive. I stop by the fountain and Gwen pulls on the handle, but she doesn't open the door.

"Aren't you coming in?"

"I've to be at work tomorrow, luv. Some of us have to keep this kingdom running."

"Okay."

She stares at me for a moment before lounging over to hug me tightly. I return her embrace, thinking of something to say, when light spills from the opened front door.

Samantha runs up to the car and bends at the waist to look inside then pulls Gwen's door all the way open.

"A ha! Caught you! Why, Gwen, you double-crossing tart!"

Gwen kisses my cheek and pulls back with a wink before turning to Samantha. "Hi pot, say hello to kettle," she says pointing at herself and they both laugh.

"What kind of dinner were you having, pet?" Samantha asks me.

"Some boring business dinner," Gwen answers for me as she climbs out of the car.

I truly adore this woman.

"Pity," Samantha mutters. "I thought you were having dinner with a potential date for the wedding."

Gwen gives me a pointed look but says nothing. I tell Samantha about work waiting for me in the morning and she commends my sense of responsibility before dragging Gwen into the mansion.

I try to deviate my mind from this whole day by blasting some old synth-pop numbers, and somehow end up playing Alphaville's "Big in Japan" several times.

The song was mistakenly thought of as a gay anthem when it was first heard in the airwaves. The lyrics *I will wait here for my man tonight,* and *Pay! Then I'll sleep by your side* were definitely misleading. Nearly a decade later the lead singer spoke of the song being about two lovers trying to get off heroine, wondering what it'd be like to live without the vice.

Synth-pop became a favored medium of expression for the gay community while I grew up in the 80's. With acts like Dead or Alive, Eurythmics, Falco—who followed in the footsteps of David Bowie and his androgynous depiction of himself—the gay community gained a voice in a time when so many young people were forced to live in the social shadows, ostracizing themselves from the mainstream. The ruling mentality of that time denounced homosexuality as a mental disorder.

With the growing tolerance, born perhaps of social boredom or the inability to censure self-expression, and aided by a more politically correct environment, there seems to be no longer a need for a gay voice. Some television shows like the American sitcoms *Will and Grace,* or the revered *Ellen DeGeneres Show* have brought such unprecedented acceptance that helped me live a life nearly free of the struggles that people like Carmen Santopietro endured.

This attempt at focusing my mind on anything else but Quinn enjoys a short existence.

The memory of her vulnerable eyes, her touch, her very presence, dominate my thoughts, especially when I'm finally in bed hoping for sleep.

28

I get a telephone call early on Tuesday from Kendrimarian Communications, one of Solutions' newest and most lucrative contracts. There's a glitch in the bloody shipping calculator and their subcontractor's servers crashed after a weekly update.

Karl Kendricks, the CEO of the fiber optics firm is willing to pay me anything in order to avoid embarrassment and costly litigation. The subcontracting company is a global firm that operates the programming division, the golden goose of the entire enterprise.

Suspecting cyber-industrial espionage, I start an investigation that leads to file transfers out of the English servers into Eastern China, Indonesia, and Thailand. I leave the investigation side to better equipped personnel and apply my efforts at repairing the damage.

I hold an uncomfortable conference call with Kendricks and several members of their board to deliver the devastating news that there are a dozen accounts forever lost, wiped clean after the hackers sabotaged their own trapdoors by leaving hydras and feed-worms throughout the network.

The six men and two women present look blank, not because they didn't understand the jargon, which most did not, but because Kendrimarian stood to lose half of the year's revenue.

I offer a way to track the traitorous activities of the inside man and they adamantly deny the possibility of a saboteur among them. I'd seen it before, and it isn't long before I find the culprit, who happens to be the scorned ex-wife of the VP of marketing. Of course, it takes me all of Tuesday to find her.

I missed out on dinner with Mum and Richard, and I missed out on spending time with Gwen and Samantha, who kept sending me photographs of their day's activities with Brooke and Emily prominently present in each shot.

I'm adding another layer of protective software to Quinn's intranet before launching the primer. So long as all templates are intact throughout the international network, I can begin uploading content. I'm watching the progress bar advance slowly when the telephone rings.

"Solutions Incorporated," I answer, expecting the same pestering bloke from Kendrimarian.

"Is this Lewis Bettford?"

I glance at the screen only to see the number's identification is blocked. The voice is female, but before I lay down some degree of charm, the events of the previous day flash in my mind.

"I can take a message, Madame. Our president is away on business," I lie. I've always wanted to be president of something.

"How would you like to make a quick thousand dollars?"

"Pardon?" The eagerness in that voice confuses me, making my guards go up.

"I'm offering a thousand dollars for a little information. What do you say, pal?"

The woman is American. "What sort of information are we talking about?"

As the woman launches into her offer, I set up a communication link into the Lions Securities servers and decide to make use of their tracer software. Creepy callers have been easily caught this way. I'm not exactly listening to the woman until Quinn's name comes up.

"So, what can you tell me?"

"What was that name?"

"Quinn, Quinn McDermont."

"What about her?"

"Oh so you do know her!" she exclaims in a disgustingly eager voice.

"Who doesn't? Didn't every tabloid just trash the poor lass?"

"Oh I wouldn't call that little bitch, poor. You know who she married?"

I fight the instinct to simply hang up as the link is finally made. "Some dot com magnate, I know. Why are you calling here about this lady?"

The trace begins bouncing a signal out of my location, searching for the right relay towers in a growing spiral.

"Look, help me out here. I'm trying to get out of the fucking mail room. I'm trying to do this story on my own. I even paid my own ticket to come here." The chugging of a diesel engine comes over the line, followed by the blaring of different horns. "I got a tip that she was running away to London. I swear I've the worst luck. I ended up paying some idiot to get some pictures but he fucking screwed me, swearing he doesn't know what happened. His camera is toast. He won't even give me my money back."

With my instincts confirmed, I desperately will the tracing software to find the lass. I have to keep her talking longer, but she seems unable to shut her gob, so I relax a bit. "Tough bloody break."

"Yeah, no shit. But then my luck turned for the better when I got a call with another tip. The caller said the rich bitch snagged the owner of Solutions. After doing a little digging, I got the number. Now that's where you come in. Is this Lewis Bettford doing Quinn?"

As the map zooms out to show me where the tracer is scanning, I pray this caller is in London. I decide to make a bold and obvious move. "Why don't you give me a number and a name where to contact you in case I find something?"

The caller hangs up.

On the screen a window with the message: TRACE ABORTED flashes three times before opening a dialogue window prompting me to start the trace again.

"Bloody hell…"

Frustrated, I sit in silence replaying the entire conversation in my head. A call to the telephone service proves fruitless in the search for the origin of the blocked call. According to Quinn, no one knew she made her way to London. Still…

I draw a measure of satisfaction at the loss of the photographs. The mouse software worked to perfection. It's safe to assume these so called reporters still want to bleed Quinn's miseries.

As I think back on the conversation, something else jumps out at me. Someone alerted this person about Quinn's activities.

And for that someone to alert them about me…

I make sure the phone doesn't ring again. I don't want any interruptions for what I have in mind.

At the end of the night, I listen to several messages from the alarmed Kendrimarian blokes in the aftermath of my findings. The BBC is about to have a field day with it all. Their loss is my gain. Solutions Inc. will be hailed as the crime solver and the publicity alone will most likely generate more clients.

I make a mental note to alert my Liverpool office staff, and to congratulate them by promising a hefty bonus for a job well done. It's high time I hire someone in London.

There's also a message of dead air. There's no way to identify the caller, though I can hear the familiar horn of a tug boat somewhere on the Thames. The mournful sound brings forth a deluge of images that has me tossing and turning in bed for a consecutive night. The image of Quinn's remarkably beautiful face dominates my thoughts in the dark.

***

I message Samantha to confirm our dinner plans. We are all gathering at Nathan Jeffries' home in Kensington, more of a dinner meeting to discuss the wedding rehearsal. Lorna Matthews and her mousy assistant are to join us as well.

The Kendrimarian debacle threatens to derail my plans, however, and by 2:00 P.M. I'm stressing with solving the bloody problems, cursing the Asian hackers and the treacherous tart that seems to have conspired against me by betraying her employer.

I might have had everything done if I hadn't spent the time working on Quinn's intranet throughout the night since I couldn't sleep. Of course, that resulted in my staying in bed most of the morning. It's one of the rare times I abuse the privilege of being my own boss.

Eradicating hydras was Terence's specialty and more than a few times, I almost dial him up to beg him to help me. I don't call. Not so much out of consideration for his declining health, but more because I'm afraid of being told he is no longer alive.

I make another attempt at neutralizing malware infiltrations by adding packets of code to confuse the bloody programming of the spyware. It's a last ditch effort, but it pays off with dividends.

Kendricks effusively congratulates me on a job well done. He tells me to wait for his call before finalizing the setup of the new server security protocols, but that's been two hours ago. I open an email window and message him to contact me at my mobile then yawn and stretch, feeling a series of pops throughout my neck.

Time to see the bloody chiropractor again.

The afternoon started out bright and warm, but that's not the case now as I look out the window. The rain falls steadily, darkening the concrete and creating fast rivulets that threaten to overwhelm the old city culverts. The people on the street walk up and down, indifferent to the inclement weather under the shelter of their umbrellas. The rain brings with it the memory of Quinn.

The telephone in my office rudely breaks through the soothing hissing of the rain. Rubbing my eyes, I pick up the receiver. "Mr. Kendricks."

"It's Quinn."

"Quinn?"

"Is this an okay time to call?"

"Certainly." I hear a strange static on the line. Also a muffled drumming that I can't place. "Where are you?"

"I'm trying to stay dry, for a change. Look out your window."

I take the cordless receiver with me, rushing to the window. Among the stream of umbrellas meandering up and down the street, there's one person on the sidewalk facing my window, head on a swivel as she scans her surroundings. She's wearing black heels and a dark business suit, the hem of her skirt just above her knees. The umbrella tilts up, revealing Quinn's lovely face, her mobile pressed to the side of her head. The smile she sends my way sets off a fluttering in my chest.

"May I come up?"

I can't help laughing. "I'd say you'd better, luv. A little thing like you may wash off into the catacombs if you aren't careful."

"See you soon," she says after a giggle.

I take a minute to look for anyone giving Quinn more than a passing glance. I even heed the impulse to look in neighboring buildings for the telling silhouette of someone keeping watch on the street. The faint reflection on the window reveals a disheveled version of me that makes me self-conscious, and sends me running into the private bathroom in the corner of the office. I keep a few things in the cabinet for just this type of impromptu meetings, normally with clients. I have a stupid habit of running my hands through my hair when I'm absorbed in my work and by the end of the day, I'm sporting a spike do.

I tame the top strands back into some semblance of order. As I wash my face and brush my teeth, I suddenly feel foolish for acting like Samantha before a date, but I can't help it.

Noting the sweat half-moons under my arms, I quickly discard my shirt and find a fresh one in the thin armoire squatting in the corner. I'm only half way done with the buttons when Quinn pushes the door open, startling me.

"Oh, my God! Did I interrupt something?" She asks with a wry grin as her blue eyes make a sweep of the large space.

"I wouldn't say you interrupted anything. In fact, you have just saved me from sheer boredom."

Quinn smiles, her eyes roving appraisingly over me. "I was in the neighborhood, and thought I'd stop by and say hi."

"Hi, luv. I'm surprised you are out and about by yourself, considering what happened."

She shrugs dismissively. "No one's going to chase me in this weather, hun."

"I didn't think of that."

She laughs and kicks off her shoes, instantly losing three or four inches. "Oh, those things are sheer torture. You guys have it so easy."

"I don't know about that," I say, thinking of the bloody kicks that killed my feet only a few days ago.

She walks up to the window as she sheds her blazer and casually hangs it over the back of a chair. "Nice view."

I thought the same thing, but for entirely different reasons. "You are hopelessly overdressed for a boating excursion up and down the Thames."

Quinn gives me a sideways glance that spills her blonde hair over her face. She straightens up and brushes her hair back into place with her hand, beating me to it. Curse these sudden impulses.

"Well, the rain put a stop to those plans," she grins. "I had some business in the tower, nothing worth writing home about."

I debate whether to tell her about the caller, but I decide against it, recalling how rattled she was after the episode with the paparazzi. "What sort of business?"

"Braddigan and Stoutford, they represent my interests here in London. I'm trying to retain possession of my little flat and my boat from my ex-husband."

I want to ask her where Firuz is, inwardly cursing my curiosity. "Forgive me, luv. You didn't mention your…"

"Firuz?" She shrugs dismissively. "He no longer needs to concern himself with me. Dinner?"

Well, there's something to be said for small favors. I decide to have a little fun at her expense. "Quinn, I'd be honored, luv, but I have an engagement I can't miss."

The corners of her eyes turn down to match the disappointed pout of her lips. "Of course. I should've called much earlier."

"Forgive me, luv."

"Could you use a date?"

"That depends." She looks interested. "Are you ready to see Samantha?"

She looks away for a moment. "Considering I inadvertently met her fiancé, I guess there's no point in keeping Sam in the dark." She glances at me, a smile on her face. "I'd love to surprise her. I'm ready. At least I will be, knowing you're there."

Now what does she mean by "knowing you're there"?

The idea has merit. Not only will my conscience finally clear from keeping secrets from my best friend, but this way, we won't take a chance of another paparazzi unpleasantness.

Recalling Gwen's warnings, I'd like to know what she will think of Quinn once they meet. "Good. It's about time, and I'm sure there's room for one more."

Quinn grins and claps her hands like a little girl, her hands close to her face. "That's not to say I'm not nervous," she points out. "I just have to freshen up and we can be on our way," she says, happily relieved to avoid dinner alone.

I show her to the bathroom and she's in there long enough for me to finalize things with an email for Kendricks, who quickly replies, promising another bonus for my diligence.

Quinn emerges out of the small bathroom, looking impossibly better than she did going in. "Ready," she declares with a shaky smile.

***

"I almost get lost in the tubes, but thankfully there are better signs here than in New York. I once ended up in the heart of Harlem. I was the only white person there, but thankfully people were nice enough to guide me to the right sub stop."

"I can't believe you didn't drive. Didn't you reside in New York? I ask her, recalling bits and pieces from the bio I'd read.

"Reside?" She chuckles. "You're so stinking cute! Who talks like that?" Her right hand comes to rest on my arm, sending a bolt of heat through my insides. "I've lived everywhere over the past few years. Connecticut is the closest thing I have to home."

"Where exactly? I'm a bit familiar with the state."

"North Madison."

I don't recognize the town. "I'm surprised."

"Why? Because I didn't say Greenwich?"

I frown at the sudden defensive tone in her voice, and the fact that she read my mind. "I meant no offense, luv."

Her hand squeezes my forearm. "I'm sorry. I grew up a country girl. I just always hated the assumption that I'm some kind of a snob, you know?"

I smile. "Aren't we all considered snobs, back in the states?"

"Ha! Some worse than others. Take Samantha for instance. She was all high and mighty, a total snob back in school."

I'd love to tell her that I want to hear more about herself, but I sense Samantha is a common theme she uses as a platform from where to launch into more intimate matters. "She was?"

"Well, it was probably the accent more than anything. Back then a lot of us looked at her like she thought herself too good for everyone else. As I got to know her, I realized that it was just the way she was brought up and her sophistication was a natural thing, not an act. It took a while to get past her usual serious demeanor.

"Of course, that went out the window if we were partying. Then she was a lot of fun, but once she started dating Brooks, she became a complete snob, though with more reason this time. She really changed after that."

"There's quite a bit you don't know about Sam's life with the bloody wanker," I remark, unable to suppress the venomous tone in my voice.

Quinn draws back to stare at me. "Will you tell me all about it?"

"I'm not sure. It's not my story to tell."

"You don't trust me," she says dryly, removing her hand from my arm.

"No, it's just not my place to say anything. Ask Sam. She might surprise you."

"She never really trusted me."

I'm beginning to feel female friendships are vastly more complicated than I can imagine. "How do you figure?"

"She never really told me things. Not even when she was smashed."

"Smashed?"

"Okay, not even when she was pissed."

I laugh, understanding the slang for inebriated.

"Why do you use pissed for drunk and mad for angry?"

"Oh no, we're not debating American English versus British English. The tongue was ours first, luv. You, bloody colonists, perverted our poetic idiom."

Quinn throws her head back as she laughs. "I love talking to you. I don't think I've laughed this much in ages."

I pull into Nathan's drive and her eyes grow as wide as saucers.

"Holy shit! Is this where Sam lives?"

It doesn't surprise me that she's in awe of Nathan Jeffries' estate, despite knowing that Quinn has enjoyed the finer things in life— particularly a mansion in Malibu, California that continued to garner architectural awards—Nathan Jeffries's Estate is simply breathtaking.

The mansion sits on a gentle hill on the highest point of the carefully manicured land. It's a wide structure with Doric columns flanking a long marble stairway that leads to its heavy, oak double doors. There's a gallery that joins each wing, adorned with stone arches. Tall wide chimneys crown the multi-tiered roofs and the stone gutters feature maidens holding amphora, as though pouring the rain on the landscaping below. The round fountain acts like a reflection pool and on a sunny day, it enhances the beauty of the structure.

Today the rain makes the roofs glisten, and sharpens every detail of the intricate stonework framing each oriel.

"It's so beautiful!"

I reach back for her umbrella and quickly climb out of the car. Quinn surprises me by getting out and trotting to the shelter of the ample portico, disregarding the rain ruining her expensive navy suit. The rain is so dense that it plasters most of her hair to her head, but she does a good enough job of shaking the water off to style it prettily by the time I join her under the portico.

"You couldn't wait for the umbrella, luv?"

She shrugs. "I love the rain."

I find myself struggling to suppress the urge to pull her to me and the look in her eyes tells me she knows this. Suddenly we edge closer, both of us victims to the building anticipation. Her face turns up to mine and her eyelids gently veil the beauty of her blue gaze. There are giant moths flapping their papery wings in my stomach and my knees begin to shake like the foundations of a skyscraper during an earthquake.

Quinn grabs a handful of my shirt, her wet hands dampening the thin fabric. I feel my eyes close as I give in to the irresistible pull when the snick of a bolt from behind me jolts me out of the trance. For a fraction of a second, I don't even recognize the sound of the rain.

"Quinn?"

Samantha's quizzical look bounces from her to me.

"Hi, Sam."

The two women stare at each other, one with a smile, and one with a perplexed look, allowing each other a long look.

I've seen that same remorseful look on Samantha upon seeing Gwen again just a few days ago. This time however, Quinn looks just as remorseful. They approach each other slowly and then embrace, both overcome by emotion. I wonder how many of these reunions I can take. They hold onto one another long enough to convey unspoken apologies they both accept, leaving a smile on their faces, friends again.

***

Samantha drags Quinn inside and I watch them disappear. Gwen meets me in the foyer when I finally get inside. She gives me a hug and kisses my cheek, a little grin playing on her lips.

"So, that's Quinn."

"She showed up at my office," I say in a confessing tone, as though responding to an inquisitor threatening me with torture.

"She's gorgeous," Gwen says with genuine appreciation. "But I still don't know that I'd trust her."

I offer her my arm. "You fret a bit much, luv."

"Maybe," she muses as she takes my arm.

We join the others gathered around Nathan's gigantic dinner table. Samantha is introducing Quinn to everyone. Nathan and Alicia welcome the young lass to their home and Margaret quickly sets up a place at the table for the new guest. Samantha then beckons Gwen and the three women quickly fall into an incessant chatter pointed by high-pitched questions, and a constant stream of giggling. Curious as always, Alicia joins the younger women and quickly blends in seamlessly.

"I imagine things are still a secret," Jason says from behind me.

I turn, a bit annoyed at the way he moves around like a bloody ghost. "For now."

He winks conspiratorially. "You owe me."

Samantha calls him to his side and she makes an overly proud introduction of her fiancé. Jason nods in greeting as he is introduced to Quinn, who shamelessly remarks on his physical attributes, sharing some telepathic commentary with the other women. Jason can only blush in response to the blatant scrutiny, eliciting a knowing grin from the normally reserved Nathan.

After dinner, the women continue to carry on, ignoring the rest of us. Richard, Mum, and Nathan take Brooke and Emily into the studio to play board games, and probably to escape the squeals and giggles, while Jason and I aren't so lucky. I only escape to spoil my Margaret with my special spot of tea, while Jason takes care of some work stuff on the phone. I casually ask him to find me in the kitchen when he's done with his call.

Once I'm satisfied that Margaret's been properly spoiled, I start for the living room when Jason comes in.

"Everything okay, chap?"

"When you check the security logs, you'll see I traced a call. The caller ended the call before I got anything."

Jason looks thoughtful. "What was the call about?"

I quickly summarize Quinn's struggles with the paparazzi and lay out my concerns. I offer to hire Lions to provide Quinn with a measure of protection and mention her fears of the paparazzi invading the wedding, ruining the day for Samantha.

"I'll start a celeb detail right away. Any specific threats that you can think of?"

"She hired me to build an intranet for her biomechanics research. I got the impression she's mostly afraid of someone stealing those documents."

"You'd know better than me how to protect from industrial espionage," Jason points out.

"I'm ahead of you, the intranet is secure."

Jason thinks for a moment. "Whoever called that reporter knows who you are. Can you think of anyone?"

"I don't have many acquaintances in London, and those of you I call friends, I trust implicitly. Besides, no one knows about Quinn other than Samantha and she's not privy to this paparazzi mess."

Jason nods. "What about someone who knows Quinn, here in London?"

"Similar situation. The people she knows here are friends of the family. I met a few of them. I can't speak for all of them, but they treated Quinn like family."

Jason looks curious. "How much time have you been spending with her?"

"A few days. She invited me to play a football match." I grin in recollection. "You ought to see the lass make a save."

Jason cocks his head, looking at me with renewed interest.

"You think it's someone she knows," I state, hoping to distract him from whatever he's thinking.

He nods slowly. "It's obviously someone who knows both of you. Does she have any enemies she might've talked about?"

"I can't say."

"Alright, fret not, chap. As of right now, your lady is under our protection." He pats my shoulder.

"She's a friend," I say lamely.

"Of course, she is," he grins knowingly.

"Lewis!"

"You're being summoned," Jason quips. "I'll get everything under way."

"Thanks."

I follow the sound of Alicia's voice, rejoining everyone in the living room.

"There you are, luv," Alicia cries when she catches sight of me. "We were just discussing the new Dandy look. What do you think?"

Four sets of eyes pierce me in place as though I'm some kind of fashion authority. The Dandy look is a female fashion with a generous touch of masculinity. It normally involves tight trousers, or stretchy leggings, complimented by straight cut, double breasted jackets over stylish blouses and short dress combinations. It was the latest fad in European fashion, a more elegant improvement from the tuxedo trend and the military fashion that severely detracted from a woman's femininity. "I think you ought to be a skinny little trollop like Samantha to pull it off."

The women turn to Samantha, who feigns indignation, and good-naturedly joke about her thin hips and nearly non-existent waistline.

"Not for me, I'm a mom of two, I'm lucky I don't need baggy coveralls to cover this body," Gwen laments.

The women take turns complimenting each other's figure. Samantha makes a funny reference to her breasts, and Alicia jumps at the chance to point out her own ample cleavage. Suddenly the conversation deteriorates into a multitude of jokes about breasts, and the ceaseless debate of natural versus surgically altered.

An image of Quinn's breasts, easily exposed through her damp clothes fills my mind, forcing me to shake myself.

Eventually the conversation turns to the upcoming wedding. I notice Samantha becoming uncomfortable about not having Quinn as a bridesmaid, despite Quinn assurances that she's okay with that.

However, Alicia suggests it'd be a great idea to make Quinn a bridesmaid, and soon it's unanimously agreed. The dressmaker will most likely curse Samantha to the ends of hell, but I will gladly compensate the old bird generously.

I can only imagine what Quinn will look like in the stylish gown. Imagining Gwen and Alicia, I can't help thinking that so much beauty in one place should be outlawed.

For her part, Quinn insists that she couldn't possibly add herself to the wedding only three days away. She is the only one who thinks of the overworked dressmaker, but Alicia and Samantha double their efforts to convince her until she relents. With Quinn's acceptance settled, the women turn to the quest for another escort.

As it stands, I'm paired up with Gwen and Alicia with Nathan. Quinn is solo and Alicia and Samantha are making a list of possible escorts out of Jason's colleagues at Lions.

All those lads seem to have come out of the same mold, very masculine, tall and thick with muscle, their voices deep and commanding, every woman's ideal of what a man ought to be.

I'm helpless against the sudden resentment I feel. I'm so bothered by the prospect of another lad standing next to Quinn that I have to walk away from fear of Samantha or Gwen noticing the change in my mood.

Perhaps I can make Margaret another cup of tea.

Not so long ago, I would've put in my opinion and even suggest a grading scale as we discussed men. Back in our late teens Samantha and I engaged in some sort of competition for the attention of some lad that had caught our eye. It was one of the things that slowly helped her break out of her depression after the loss of her parents. Of course, she always won that challenge though once the lad was hooked on her she easily dismissed any romantic possibilities, frustrating not only them but me as well.

Once Terence and I were together, she was on her own. Even as I think of nights filled with profound conversations with him, I realize that despite being attracted to him, I never once felt any shred of desire, and certainly nothing remotely close to the sensations that had literally rocked my core with Quinn.

It's oddly liberating to feel the emergence of this truth in myself, but at the same time, there's a devastating quality about it that confounds me. How did I get so far when I didn't know who I was?

What's more, who am I now?

"...he'll know, trust me. Jason? Jason!" Samantha calls.

She calls out his name two more times before he finally emerges, his mobile in hand.

"What's the matter, luv?"

"Quinn needs an escort."

"For the wedding!" I quickly add drawing several curious glances.

Jason smiles wryly. "Certainly. Are you calling off the wedding?"

Gwen and Alicia laugh so hard while Quinn is a bit more reserved. Samantha's eyes glimmer with fury for an instant.

"You wish," she says.

I know that tone and apparently, her fiancé knows it too, but his smile only widens.

"Who do you have in mind?" He asks.

"We're not sure. Lewis, you need to help us too. Come here."

I join them at the table, exchanging an uncomfortable look with Jason. I feel like he's reading me like a bloody book.

"Okay, there's William Leighton, he's pretty hot—"

Jason clears his throat and everyone laughs at the scowl he gives his bride.

"I mean, he's okay," Samantha rectifies before leaning over and planting a soft kiss on Jason's lips.

All the girls exhale an *Aww* that turns his face crimson.

"There's also Keith Olson, Jason Soderbergh, and Travis Kent," Samantha continues.

"How about Mark Connolly?" Alicia asks.

Samantha scoffs. "Trisha will kill him. That crazy tart changed the locks in his flat because she saw him drive me to work one day."

"Sure," Gwen quips. "Did he drive you to work or did he just drive you?"

The question elicits another wave of raucous laughter from the group. This time even I join in. Samantha playfully slaps Gwen's shoulder as she calls her a tart, but she's also grinning. For some reason, I sense Gwen's little barb isn't so playful.

"How about you first ask Quinn what her type of lad is?" Alicia suggests.

Everyone turns to Quinn, who looks a bit startled to be put on the spot.

"Come now, Quinn, what's your type of lad?" Alicia asks.

"Tall, strong, rich, and in possession of a third leg," Samantha quips and Gwen nearly chokes on her tea.

Quinn shakes her head at Samantha as she doubles over, laughing.

Alicia is a bit slow in figuring it out but when she does, she gasps. "Blimey, perhaps it's time to update *my* type."

More girlish laughter.

"I've seen those lads in the locker room. No luck there, Quinn," Jason quips, sending another bolt of euphoria through the girls.

"I guess I got lucky with my pick," Samantha adds and the women instantly turn to Jason as though expecting a confirmation.

"On that note, I believe I will go take a swim in the Thames now." Jason stands, kisses Samantha on the top of her head and keys in something in his mobile on his way to the studio.

"So," Gwen drawls. "How big is it?"

"Big," Samantha replies with a shameless grin.

"It would have to be," Gwen quips.

The women throw their heads back in laughter.

"Okay, okay," Gwen says, trying to catch her breath. "Quinn, what's your type of guy?"

Quinn looks from Samantha to Gwen, trying to figure out what their last exchange was about, most likely suspecting something, but she is too polite to air it out.

"My type of guy?" Her head slowly turns towards me until her blue eyes pierce me in place for the briefest of moments.

I ignore the pointed look Gwen sends my way, and the little smile of understanding that curls Samantha's lips. I focus instead on Alicia, hoping she's blissfully unaware of the subtle current of tension, but one look at those eyes tells me there's no solace there.

"My type has to be strong when it counts, confident; unafraid of being himself; a good listener and well groomed. Of course, physically attractive, but I want a good brain attached to the pretty face. He has to love the rain, and music." Her eyes focus on me once again. "And he has to love Mexican food."

Gwen's smile is gone and she looks from me to Quinn with a pensive look.

"Bloody hell, lass! If we find someone like that, I'm calling the bloody wedding off and taking him from you," Samantha quips.

"You, my love, must be wanting a week's worth of nights alone on the bloody couch," Jason says, suddenly standing right behind his bride.

Her eyes go wide and everyone laughs, everyone with the exception of Quinn, whose gaze seems to etch itself into the depths of my soul.

29

I'm forced to answer a call from Kendricks so I retire to the ball room. It seems a safe distance from the lewd comments and the girlish laughter.

The man has apparently forgotten that the reboot of his new servers can't be done until all the diagnostics return with a green light. I allay his fears, but the man goes on and on about the lost accounts. I'm tempted to inform the chap that I'm a software security specialist, not a shrink. I'm even willing to direct him to the nearest pub.

When I end the call, I'm surprised at the reigning quiet, but I welcome it.

"Out with it, Lewis," Samantha startles me. "Did you and Quinn shag?"

"Quinn?"

"Don't play dumb with me!"

Obviously, this is no time for jokes. "Sam, on Grandmum's grave, I swear I did nothing of the sort."

The mention of Grandmum gives her pause, but the scowl on her face lessens only minimally.

"Well, then why is she so chummy with you?"

"Chummy?"

"Friendly, flirty, forward, tartish. Don't play bloody games with me!"

"That's just Quinn, friendly, flirty, forward, you know, luv, like you."

"That's different."

"What makes you think she and I did anything?"

Samantha crosses her arms. "You two have been running around all week, behind my bloody back."

"Forgive me, luv. She asked me."

Samantha waves her hand. "I'm not upset. I understand why she felt she needed to do that. That's not important anymore."

I sigh in relief.

"She's obviously fond of you."

"Isn't everyone?"

"Wipe off that bloody grin, you lout. What did you do?"

"Nothing you would've done."

She looks stunned. "So below the belt."

I want to make another impromptu joke but the tense look in her eyes keeps my gob shut.

"She seems quite taken with you. The funny thing is she knows you as being gay from everything I've told her about you. So, either you are some kind of a challenge to her or you're playing her. Which is it?"

"I'm sure I don't know, but I'm not playing her."

"She described you to bloody perfection. You are her type," she thinks aloud, as though forgetting I'm in the room with her. "The way she looked at you..." She whirls on me. "Are you attracted to her?"

"I just met her."

"Please," she says, rolling her eyes. "You looked at a photo of Gwen, and you were ready to convert right then and there. I was actually jealous that you found her so bloody enthralling."

"Well, in Gwen's case, she's no longer attainable, right?"

"Exactly, but Quinn is. What's going on with you?"

"Sam, she just finalized her divorce," I say, hoping to deflect her question.

"Yes, she did, so she's ready to heat up the sheets again."

It's my turn to roll my eyes. "Are you wanting me to shag your friend?"

"Do you want to?"

"You frighten me."

"Do you?"

Her prying is actually making me cross. "Why is it so important to you?"

"Because you are, and always will be, my dearest and bestest friend and I bloody love you more than you know, and ever since you went to Pennsylvania with me, you've been acting very different. Are you still gay?"

My heart races. "I really don't know how to answer you."

Samantha takes my hand. "Quinn is a beautiful girl, sure, but I've never seen you act this way around beautiful girls. What's changed?"

"I don't know how to put it into words, Sam. I'm so confused. Whatever attraction there is between Quinn and me is unfamiliar, but enchanting. I don't know if I'm feeling this way because of certain things Terence said. I just don't know how to feel."

"What certain things?"

I say nothing.

"Lewis," she says softly. "I don't care who wins your heart, so long as he or she deserves it, okay?"

I feel warm inside. "You don't know how good it feels to hear you say that."

Her eyes fill with concern. "It's the wedding thing again, isn't it?"

The pool reflects the accent lights into the ball room, projecting the water's movement onto the walls and ceiling. My thoughts match their indiscernible pattern perfectly.

"Perhaps," I finally concede. I get off the chair, towering over Samantha as I make my way to the windows.

She follows, stands behind me, and wraps her arms around my torso, leaning her chin on my back. "What is it, Lewis?"

"Do you remember how many times I harped on you about your inability to let go of the bloody past?" I feel her nodding. "I think I do that worse than you ever did."

"How so?"

I feel walls going up in my mind and my tongue feels large and heavy in my mouth as though to prevent me from speaking further. I push back the odd sensation by recalling all the times Samantha bravely confessed her every sin to me, and finally muster enough courage to utter my declaration. "I'm still a virgin, Sam."

Samantha lets go and walks around to face me. "Bollocks! If you didn't shag Tabitha Little, you must have done it with someone else. What about your days in Soho, what about Dean? Or Perry, or Paul, or Terence?"

"I told you Terence and I never did. And how do you bloody remember so much. I can't even see the faces of Perry or Paul."

Samantha has never looked more shocked. "You and Tabitha were hot for each other. Is that why it ended?"

"She's the reason I developed an aversion to the idea of sex, Sam. I think I understand that now, anyway."

"She must have been lying when she told Tamara that you and her shagged."

"Who's Tamara?"

"Tamara Laurent, the baker's kid in Liverpool. They lived two blocks from us."

"You and that bloody memory."

"So that was a lie? What a bitch!"

"It wasn't a total lie," I confess. "We did some touching, but it didn't end well."

Samantha frowns. "Go on."

My throat feels constricted. "It just didn't end well."

"Why? How?"

My cheeks have never burned this bad. "It ended too soon, alright?" I snap.

Samantha's eyes are wider than I've ever seen them.

"If you so much as snicker, by George, I will give you the black eye Gwen did not."

Samantha backs up a few steps. "You never told me this. Am I not allowed to react?"

The old feelings of humiliation bubble up to the surface. "Tabitha said some unspeakable things and I never forgot. Sam," I call her name in a pleading voice. "I truly don't wish to speak of this, luv. Please."

Samantha relents, something uncharacteristic for her. "Blimey, forgive me, Lewis. I just... Bloody hell, I don't know what to say. How did you do it?"

"Do what?"

"How'd you stay away from sex? I mean, have you never had an urge?"

"Of course, I'm just as human as the next lad."

"So how'd you...?

I've confessed many sins to her, but this one is a struggle because I never thought I'd be telling her something I knew was so pathetically humiliating. "Let's just say I loved myself quite a bit."

I give her a dark look to deter any laughter, but I don't need it. Samantha is looking at me with something like awe mixed with sadness.

"I'm so sorry, Lewis."

"Don't be daft."

"So you're a virgin."

I nod.

"You're getting sexier by the second!" she exclaims with a grin.

"Sam!"

"Okay, okay, I'm so sorry. It's just that... Fuck, this is the second time I don't know what to bloody say."

"Good. Silence is golden, you know."

"Suddenly, everything makes sense."

Noting the unfocused stare as she looks into the past, I slap her arm. "Oh, Sam, don't do this now, okay?"

"Ow!" She moves a couple of steps away then she turns, her eyes seething. "You're an idiot, you know that?"

"I did not strike you that hard."

"I know that, but you're still an idiot."

"That's no big surprise," I shoot back although I have no clue what she's talking about.

"I would've totally slept with you."

My throat goes painfully dry. "Oh, bloody hell, Samantha!"

"What? I totally would have. Didn't you ever want to know what it's like?"

"Not nearly as much as you did."

"You say that like it's a bad thing. Lewis, when you pull off the layers of bullshit of every one of us, we are by default sexual creatures at the core. And we humans are the only beings in all of nature who do it for the pure joy of it, rather than for the genetic directive of procreating and ensuring the survival of our species." She looks at me with something like pity that I resent. "Blimey, all you had to do was ask."

"Will you please shut your bloody gob?"

Her smile is feline. "You're sexy when you're cross."

"I'm leaving."

"Lewis," she pleads. "I'm sorry, okay?"

I say nothing.

"So, is this what's going on, is Quinn your sexual awakening?"

I stand and glare at her.

Her palms go up. "Lewis, it's an honest question."

There's no amusement in her eyes, just a deep well of concern.

"I feel very attracted to Quinn, but I'm still gay to her. I think that's the only reason she feels so comfortably flirty around me."

"Like me."

"Like you?"

"Lewis, I've walked naked right before your eyes like I was daring you to attack me, knowing you wouldn't, but at the same time, sort of hoping you would. You didn't, and I figured if I can bare my body without you ravaging me, I can bare my very soul to you. You have an undeniable magnetism, and you're a bloody doll. Even Gwen gets lightheaded around you. I bet if she didn't have Tony, she'd be putting the moves on you."

"Gwen aside, didn't you just freak out on me when I teased you about you wanting to shag me not too long ago?"

"Of course. At this point in our friendship that would be terribly incestuous. Gwen would be different and well within the range of possibility. If she wasn't an exemplary faithful wife to Tony, that is."

"She said as much."

Samantha looks put off. "Did she? Okay, I'm beginning to feel jealous of how much you talk to Gwen lately. She can't go back to the States fast enough for me."

That makes me laugh. "You're full of it, always the competitor."

"You're a prize." She smiles.

"Why yes. Yes, I am."

She rolls her eyes. "Arse!"

I try for a laugh, but it doesn't happen.

"Come now, what are you so conflicted about?" She playfully backhands my stomach.

"So many things."

"It's not that complicated, luv. Boy likes girl, girl likes boy, simple. All you need is a bed."

Her light take on sex is beginning to grate on me. "To you, perhaps."

Samantha nods and shows surprising restraint by not snapping back at me. I can see the roiling fury in the depths of her eyes.

"Very well. I won't pry anymore. It'd just be a shame though."

"What would be a shame?"

"I've known Quinn and I know you. She's definitely sweet on you, and you're definitely attracted to her. It'd be a shame if you couldn't see that."

I avert my eyes from hers and stare at the pool.

"D. H. Lawrence had it right. Love is the flower of life, Lewis. It blossoms unexpectedly, without law, and must be plucked where it is found, and enjoyed for the brief hour of its duration."

"Who is Lawrence?"

"David Herbert Lawrence? You're bloody joking, right?"

"I'm not the literature major with the perfect memory, remember?"

Samantha returns to face me and I know I'm in for it when she demands I meet her gaze.

"You don't need to be a bloody novelist to decipher the bloody quote. Take a fucking chance for once. Look how much you've missed out on already."

I have the distinct feeling she means I've missed out on her.

...Don't let another Samantha Reddick slip by...

I shudder at the memory of Terence's words. "Sex isn't everything, Sam."

"Who the fuck is talking about sex?" she says in a taut voice. "I'm talking about much more than that. I know Quinn well enough to know when she's smitten by some chap, and that chap happens to be my conflicted, insufferable, pain in the bloody arse, best friend. Stop hiding from the possibility of suffering. You're never more alive than when you're in love."

"Says the woman who made a monumental mess of herself because of love," I retort in a scathing tone, instantly regretting my words.

Samantha is unfazed. "That's right, Lewis. I've been a mess because of love. Sometimes it's fleeting and it leads to more pain than you can imagine, and sometimes it's the source of a joy so profound it begets a new life. Don't deprive yourself of what makes life worth living."

The quiver in her voice makes my eyes sting.

"Once you come of age, love is what life's about. Without it, you haven't lived and the book of your existence will be forever incomplete."

30

"Are you okay?"

"Right as rain, luv," I reply, accelerating on the open roadway.

"You're too quiet."

I glance at Quinn and smile, hoping to elicit a similar response, but she continues to regard me with a concerned look. "It's well past my bedtime, that's all."

"Okay," she says, clearly unconvinced. "So, this isn't a good time to talk?"

"I have a most willing ear, luv. What's on your mind?" I glance quickly at her, trying to gauge her mood.

She has her lush lower lip trapped between her teeth like she's nervous. I wonder whether I'm projecting that state onto her. I can't keep my hands from shaking.

"I like this new Sam so much more."

"You mean, this sober Sam."

She nods. "I feel guilty somehow."

"No more than I do. I was her biggest enabler."

Quinn leans to curl her hand around my bicep. "She told me what you said to her about her drinking. At least you tried to help her. All we did was egg her on and pour alcohol down her throat then we sat back and watched the show."

"I think we're all guilty of youthful stupidity."

The rain hasn't let up, if anything it's falling in thicker sheets, driven in different directions by the erratic wind, and heavily taxing the windshield wipers, forcing me to slow down to a virtual crawl.

"I really like Gwen. She's so fun, although at first I felt like a child next to her."

"Because she's tall?"

"Watch it with the short jokes, *lad,*" she warns. "Because she's such a lady in every sense. Samantha is right to make her the maid of honor."

"You shan't get an argument from me."

"At first, I thought she had a thing for you, she's so protective. She turned my blood to ice when I first met her."

This makes me laugh. "Gwen is kind to a fault."

"I don't know. There's an evil streak there. Well, we all have that, I guess."

I had thought something similar not too long ago, and I could easily recall that cold expression on Gwen's lovely visage.

"I hope she liked me well enough."

The note of anxiety in her voice is not lost on me. I would never have thought Quinn McDermont, formerly Fischer, to have any sort of insecurities. Particularly when taking into account her profession and what her life must have been in the arm of a millionaire. However, a voice in my head reminds me that fairy tale lives can indeed turn into hellish nightmares as it paints a picture of Samantha's New York life in my mind.

"I'm sure she does. She just doesn't trust you," I utter without thinking.

Quinn uncoils her arm from mine and looks away. "She's right not to," she says softly.

"What do you mean?"

She whips her head around, her hair catching the glow of the streetlights. "I mean, I'm no longer part of the in-crowd. I'm an interloper, so I don't expect someone like Gwen to trust me. Or you."

"What makes you think I don't trust you?"

She gives me a look that says I ought to know better but doesn't reply. Instead, she expertly navigates through the onscreen menu of the sound system.

"Great songs," she comments.

"I take it you drive a BMW back home."

"Andrew had Beamers. I drive a Chevy truck."

I frown at this. "You drive a Chevy truck?"

She nods. "Surprised?"

"You drive an Audi."

She shrugs. "Chevy trucks are hard to come by here."

"I must say, I am surprised. It seems there's much more to you than I was led to believe."

"I told you, I grew up a country girl. Oh! Here we go!"

Quinn turns the volume dangerously high and sits back in the seat, staring at the screen. Colbie Caillat's flawlessly smooth voice softly moves to the forefront of the music. Quinn taps the beat on her thigh with her hand and begins to sing along. Taking advantage of the sound controls on the wheel, I lower the volume, catching the sound of her voice, which is remarkably beautiful.

She keeps singing, even as she slaps my hand in warning before turning up the sound again. Her arm coils around mine and she leans her head on my shoulder.

For each time Colbie sings the word *you*, Quinn gives my arm a subtle squeeze. Suddenly I love the fact that there seems to be a million *you*'s in "Falling For You."

Unable to ignore such a clear signal, I allow the grin to spread on my face, and I dare think that this is exactly what I want my life to be. Despite the torrent that blurs everything outside my windscreen, the sun is shining in the confines of my soul.

My elation climbs with every passing second. Quinn sings "Everything" along with Michel Bublé with an infectious glee, never once letting go of my arm. I let up on the accelerator, not wanting this ride to ever come to an end.

Inside I feel out of control, I feel I could laugh out loud and simultaneously cry. I don't see the ugliness of the rusting industrial site near the marina gas station, or the noxious smoke wafting out of the stacks of a factory in the distance. When the Thames comes within sight, I can't remember having seen anything more breathtaking than the rain sizzling over its silvery waters. I feel alive, far more alive than at any point in my life.

Every song playing causes Quinn to tighten up her grip on my arm, yet I feel like I'm the castaway who finally found a mooring.

When I pull next to her Audi, she reluctantly draws back. Lightning flashes over Battersea and a moment later the thunderous ovation rolls over the Thames.

I shut the engine off, but leave the system on, not wanting the spell to end. Quinn turns in her seat and is about to say something when Marie Digby's angelic voice sings the first lines of *Say It Again.* I never saw this moment coming.

Blue eyes glitter in the semi-darkness and I'm once again trapped by their allure. I can't look away. I expect some wave of awkwardness to wash over us, but it never comes. Being this close to Quinn feels familiar somehow. It feels right.

As though we're following Marie Digby's cues, we drift closer and her hand comes up to my face. There's trepidation in her eyes that makes me hesitate for only a moment before my hand reaches for her face out of its own accord. Her skin is soft, warm. For a brief second I half expect to wake up and realize I'm touching the petals of a rose. Her face turns slightly up, her eyelids close ever so slowly, and her lips part invitingly.

This time my eyes close and I lean in until her lips touch mine. Her hand tilts my head slightly at an angle and then she's kissing me, softly at first, but quickly conveying a sense of urgency. She reaches for the back of my head and pulls me into her, making me curse the bloody center console and the steering wheel that's painfully digging into my side. I gladly endure the pain, however. The taste of her is well worth it.

The tortured sky roars again, the angry rumbling finally breaks into the moment and Quinn pulls away, startled.

"That was close," she says in a breathy voice.

I'm not sure whether she's referring to the thunder, or the direction our kiss was taking. The latter, I imagine.

She turns the volume down and keeps her eyes fixed somewhere ahead of her. "Would it cross the line if I asked you in?"

"I'd like to come in," I reply in a thick voice.

She holds her breath for a beat, and then climbs out of the car. I reach back for her umbrella and gingerly open the door. As I wrestle with it, my jacket gets caught in the door after I climb out, nearly tugging me down to the wet ground. I open the door again to free the fabric when a gust turns the umbrella inside out making me curse the bloody thing.

I hear Quinn laughing over the hissing of the rain that has gained strength since we parked. Rain trickles into my eyes, making them sting. I shuffle blindly in the general direction of the door of her flat, when she stops me, pulls my head down, and kisses me, making me forget all about the cold rain.

Angry drops lash at my back and shoulders, but I don't feel anything other than the warmth emanating from Quinn's whole body. She pulls back for a breath, her hands grabbing fistfuls of my shirt as she pulls me to the door.

Once inside, we find the power is out. Quinn doesn't bother to fumble for a flashlight or even a matchbox. She just leads me by the hand into her bedroom.

"Quinn—"

She silences me with a forefinger on my lips and begins pulling my jacket off, her eyes never leaving mine. I let my hands encircle her waist, allowing the weight of my arms to rest on the alluring flare of her hips. She stands on her tip toes and silently commands me to kiss her. I oblige, a tiny part of me wondering at the ease with which my entire body responds to her.

It's bloody impossible, we've just met, says a fading voice in my head.

Whatever pretense of hesitancy has fled both of us and our kisses turn more demanding, hungrier. Her fingers make quick work of unbuttoning my shirt while I fumble with the buttons of her blouse. Quinn grabs at the collar and rips the garment off her, sending buttons bouncing against my chest that clatter to the wooden floor.

I gasp involuntarily as my hands feel the heat of her smooth skin, exploring the contours of every muscle along her back. I hook my thumbs on the straps of her bra, not knowing what to do next, but Quinn saves me from awkwardness by unclasping her bra from the front. She presses her chest against me and a needful moan registers in my ears through the rush of my blood within.

My trousers slide down my legs and her hands pull at my boxers, her hand accidentally brushing against the pulsing, most sensitive part of my body.

Old fears resurface like a rogue tide and suddenly my mind is transported back to that day when Tabitha touched me.

Quinn senses my hesitation, but she only pulls harder on the back of my head and her kiss melts away the memories. I let my hands glide to the elastic of her knickers wondering if I've ever felt anything as wondrous as the texture of her body. I play with the thin fabric, sliding it down over her hips and bringing it back up again, tugging just enough to make her quiver.

With a gasp, she forces me to pull down her knickers and they pool on the floor over her wet skirt. My hands become explorers happily lost in the geography of her body. I trace every hill and valley with trembling fingers, eliciting a moan of pure pleasure out of her lips, still fused to mine.

She pushes me back and pins my arms over my head, her hair tickles my face as she looks down, her hand closing around me, making me stiffen.

Quinn delivers a soft, lingering kiss as she guides me into her, effectively shorting out my brain impulses. I can only hold on to her exquisite body as she moves in an easy rhythm. Each sensation threatens to make me black out.

She holds my gaze in a way I've never experienced, every nerve ending in my body ablaze. Afraid of letting go far too soon, I clamp down on her thighs and keep her still. She bends down to kiss me deeply, careful not to move. When she somehow senses I relax, she rocks her hips gently in a slow, languid rhythm that she keeps with little sounds of pure contentment.

Her breathing grows ragged and she pulls on my hair, almost painfully as the first wave of ecstasy crushes over her. She holds her breath interminably for a while before biting her lip so hard I'm expecting to see a droplet of blood any second, but then she lets out her breath in a long rush as she throws her head back. When the wave recedes, she fixes me with an unreadable gaze that conveys such a sense of safety that I allow the tide to take me wherever it will as every muscle in my body tenses and screams its release through every cell.

As we lie in her bed, still joined as one, I realize I've never felt more alive, more lost, yet never before so complete.

***

There's a cold draft chilling the sweat on my skin that wakes me. For a moment, I don't know where I am until Quinn's fingers wiggle in her sleep, tickling my chest. I turn my head but I can only see the top of her head. Her face is nestled on my chest and I can feel my arm around her shoulder riding the movement of her breathing.

The rain is light now, but the wind drives it into the windows, uttering a soft drumming. I hear the wailing of a tugboat's horn from somewhere along the swollen currents of the Thames. The sound is no longer mournful to my ears.

"You're thinking so loud," Quinn says softly as she lifts her head to look at me.

Her eyelids are heavy with sleep and her lips look a bit tender from the ravaging of our kissing.

"If you aren't tired enough, maybe I should redouble my efforts," she says lustfully as she straddles me.

"Are you truly this insatiable?"

If we engage in what's quickly becoming my new most favorite activity once again, this former virgin will achieve expert status in no time.

She leans down to kiss me softly. "I have to make up for lost time, and you probably do too," she purrs.

In between bouts of passion, Quinn and I decide to forego the normal tentative revelations among new lovers and dive straight into the heart of the matter. I hold her as she relates to me how devastating it had been to watch her ex-husband change so drastically, and she holds me as I talk about Terence. The contact easily morphs from comfort to passion and I make love to her again, under her loving tutelage.

The aurora of the day is slowly pushing back the shadows behind a soft purple line, and the morning chill prompts us to cover our naked bodies for the first time since shedding our clothes.

Quinn nips at my throat, her breasts pressed against my chest.

"I knew you were ready," she quips in a throaty voice.

"You're a great teacher."

"You're a quick learner."

I try to kiss her but she draws back, a smile on her face. I try to reach for her but she forces my arms up over my head once more, looking at me like a lioness looming over her prey.

"Now, be a good lad, and don't move."

"Why?"

"Just close your eyes and don't move."

I feel a current of exhilaration amidst the sudden fear that makes my hands go cold. "What are you trying to—"

She shushes me by putting her forefinger on my lips. I open my mouth and playfully bite her finger. Her indrawn breath is loud in the near perfect silence.

"Now, close your eyes and don't move."

I do as she says, and soon I feel her lips on my cheeks, my lips, my neck, my chest. I can feel her sliding down on the bed and before I can say a word, she puts me in a trance out of which I never want to return.

31

The long single note of a tugboat intrudes into the most blissful sleep I've ever known. Quinn is no longer curled into me, but lies on her stomach, her head turned to the side, arms under the pillow. I take a long moment to admire the muscle tone of her back when I notice the long scar on the back of her left shoulder.

I shift on the bed as gently as I can before getting up for the loo. I've never been one to walk around in the nude like my best friend is so fond of doing but to keep from waking Quinn, I pad out of the bedroom naked as the day I came into this world.

I stifle a chuckle as my wobbly legs nearly fail me, threatening to send me sprawling on the cold wooden floor.

"What's so funny?"

I whip around, my hands instantly covering my groin, arse to the wall in an attempt to hide.

Quinn smiles confidently from the security of her robe. "Um... there's nothing I haven't seen," she says in a throaty tone.

"This seems hardly fair, luv," I protest.

Quinn raises a curious eyebrow, unties the sash of her robe and lets it slip to the floor. "Better?"

"No. You don't have a part of your body that betrays your state of mind," I complain, pushing my hands harder over my groin.

She laughs. "I've never been this brazen with anyone before."

I can't say I believe her and she can see that in the expression of my face.

"I mean it. It's almost like you bring something else out of me."

"I was going to the loo," I offer lamely, awash in embarrassment.

"Good. I'll be right behind you."

I start backing towards the bathroom door, but Quinn follows just a step behind.

"You're coming in too?"

"Is that a problem?"

I can feel my cheeks burning. "Quinn…"

"Oh! Okay, I'm sorry. I'll wait."

"Thank you."

I walk into the loo, close the door and lock it.

After washing my hands and my face, I unlock the door. Quinn must have been standing at the door the entire time I was inside.

"Here." She hands me a green towel that matches the one wrapped around her body.

"Thanks."

"Lewis, I really don't mean to make you uncomfortable, but after last night, it seems silly for you to feel so awkward around me."

I agree with her, but this is far too new for me. "I'm comfortable."

Quinn lets out a sarcastic chuckle. "About as comfortable as a cat in a dog pound."

She begins filling the tub then pulls a bottle out of the cabinet below the sink, opens it, and pours its contents into the tub. The scent of lavender fills the steamy air inside the small room.

"I'll wait until you're done."

Quinn frowns. "This is for both of us, silly."

"Oh. I was hoping."

"You first."

I climb into the tub. The hot water is biting, but I clench my teeth and lower myself into it.

"Too hot?"

"A bloody tad," I reply, hissing.

Quinn laughs and opens the cold water tap. After a few minutes, she checks the temperature by putting her bare leg into the water, nodding in satisfaction. She removes her towel, allowing me to bask in the beauty of her body before gingerly climbing into the tub. I expect her to lean her back to me, but she surprises me by sitting in front of me to face me.

"I was hoping to hold you," I murmur.

"Well, I wanted to look at you. My place, my rules." She winks.

Despite the cold water taking some of the bite out of the heat, I'm breaking a sweat. My hair is pasted on my scalp and salty droplets course down my temples.

"You'll get used to it in a little while. I promise," she says, flicking away a sweat drop.

I notice her face is flushed, sweat pebbling over her lips. "Is there a reason you are so determined to boil us alive?"

She laughs, leans closer and gives me a salty kiss. "Don't be so dramatic. It's good for you after what we just did."

I smile back but a part of me, a part that has finally regained some measure of control tamps down the initial wave of desire I began to feel. "How did this happen?"

Quinn looks down. "I don't know." She raises her head and looks into my eyes. "I didn't think anything like this would ever happen with you. There's so much I want to say, so many things I want to ask."

"In that case, let's do some soul bearing, luv," I quip, recovering some of my wittier self.

"Not just yet. I don't want to overanalyze things the way I usually do. I just want to enjoy these moments with you."

She turns around and ensconces into me. She leans her head on my shoulder and her arms rest on mine, which are wrapped around her middle.

"Let's just relax for a little while, okay?"

Her fingers trace patterns over the skin of my arms. My eyes follow every line of her body. The sight of her breasts half-submerged in the water, stir a wave of desire in me. She smiles as though enjoying what she's doing to me. She's able to turn her head enough so that I can kiss her and I take full advantage.

When the water cools and our fingertips are as wrinkled as prunes, we silently agree to get out of the water. The scent of lavender clings to our skin.

"That was so nice," Quinn says in a breathy voice.

The grin on my face fades when her eyes flash remorse, making me think of something Samantha said to me after one of her numerous one night stands. She told me she hated that awkward conversation that ensued in the morning, when the dark of night no longer fueled the forbidden passion. I'd hate to think that's what's about to happen here.

Without a word, I quickly wrap a towel around my waist. I step out of the loo briefly, only to retrieve Quinn's robe. When I join her, she is already drying off and takes the robe, shrugging into it.

We each find our clothes and don't look at one another until we're dressed.

"I'm sorry," are Quinn's first words.

I resist the urge to take her hand and instead sit in the most non-threatening position on the other side of her couch. Her eyes focus on the empty space between us for a second then she covers her face with her hands.

"Can I ask you something?"

It kills me that she has her pretty eyes hidden from me. "You can ask me anything."

She lays her hands on her lap, still not meeting my eyes. "What did it mean to you?"

This is where I'd give anything to have Samantha's affinity for putting words together, especially when it comes to expressing what I'm feeling at this moment.

I realize there's no point skirting any issues, no point in playing games. It seems unnecessary after what we just shared. A cautious voice in my mind tells me not to admit anything, but I just don't see the point. "It meant more than you know, Quinn..." My voice trails off. "Considering it was my first time."

Her head whips towards me, beseeching me with her eyes. "Your first time?"

I nod. "You may not believe me, but I've never been with anyone before."

I expect an array of different reactions, but crying is not one of them.

Quinn drops her head in her hands and hard sobs rack her body. I want to draw her into my arms, but I sense it's not what she wants at the moment. It takes a while before her emotional storm abates enough for her to talk.

"I didn't know..."

I say nothing.

"You don't mean your first time with a woman…" she intuits. "But Samantha told me you had a boyfriend for years!"

"I had a partner for ten years, but I never…"

"Not once?"

I shake my head.

"It's hard to believe."

I shrug. "I was afraid of it, luv. Judging by your reaction, I have a feeling I should've never lost that fear."

Quinn recoils as though from a physical blow. I didn't intend to hurt her, although I'm battling a bubbling anger of unknown origin. "Why did you ask me what it meant to me, Quinn?"

"I don't deserve you."

Her words make me feel cold inside.

"Did I just confuse you about who you are?"

I resist the urge to laugh. "I think I've been confused all my life, up until recently."

"Recently?"

I take a deep breath in the hopes of dispelling some of the emotional turmoil that's slowly claiming my senses. "Up until a few months ago, I was gay."

Quinn looks at me with alarm.

"I'm not confused because of you, and what's happened between us. It's been coming for a long time. Ever since I saw what I really wanted in my life."

"Which is?"

Moments of clarity are rare. We seldom realize we have them, and when we do, we don't know how to voice them in order to make them concrete in our minds.

"Lewis?"

"Tell me what about you? What are you confused about?" I ask her in a frigid tone that surprises even me.

Quinn looks at me for a moment. "I don't know who I am around you. When I came here, all I wanted to do was to find myself again. For the longest time I've felt I was nothing more than Andrew Fischer's trophy wife, a trophy he no longer wanted."

I can't ignore the wistful note in her voice. "Do you still want to be that trophy wife?"

She tugs at the sash of her robe, her eyes focused on the past. "I met Andrew during my internship at Lincoln Medical Center. It really felt like love at first sight."

I resist the urge to shift and will myself to listen, although the last thing I want to visualize is Quinn falling in love with someone else.

Why Lewis...?

"I don't know that I want to tell you my whole sad story. Why are we always compelled to do that?" she says, blowing a stream of air in frustration.

It doesn't make sense for either of us to put up our walls after what we just shared. They don't call it intimacy for no reason. Perhaps we got to this point too fast, I think. Perhaps we need to bare our souls, now that we've bared everything else. "I think it's something we do when we feel that the person before us matters."

"You think this is a one night stand," she states.

I decide to take my own advice and let her know that at this moment, she matters. I'm very big on the give and take of things, but right now, I want to give her everything of me and I actually don't care whether she returns the favor or not.

"I didn't want to get involved with a man for a while," Quinn says softly. "I felt that I was going to be afraid of getting hurt for the rest of my life, but I wasn't counting on you."

I can't help smiling. "I understand more than you know."

Quinn smiles back. "I had a plan. I always have a plan, but getting to know you and feeling like I do, was not part of it. I didn't know I was going to feel so damn attracted to you."

"If you keep blowing my head up, we won't have any oxygen left in this place, luv."

She slides over to me and leans her head on my shoulder. "I want to know everything about you."

I've never made a habit of talking about myself, but I start talking and without realizing it, I open rooms in my mind that I didn't even know I had.

My mother becomes a central topic and I even get choked up when I confide in Quinn about the ever-present guilt I've carried at the knowledge of dashing her hopes with my choices in life.

The thought gives me pause. Am I done with being gay? According to Terence, there's nothing to be done with, if I never was to begin with.

"What about your father?"

"I never knew him."

"But surely your mother at least gave you his name."

I shake my head. "Mum played a double parental role so well, I never really thought about asking. At school, there were other boys without fathers, so it didn't seem unusual. It's only lately that I've wondered who I'd be had I known a father."

Quinn looks up and takes my face in her hand. "I don't want you to think I'm not glad you grew up without a father, but selfishly, I wouldn't want you to be any different."

I love the feel of her soft hand on my cheek. "What about you?"

"My parents?"

I nod.

"They're a treasure. My brother and I are lucky to have them."

"You have a brother?"

She nods. "Little brother actually. The accident in the family," she chuckles. "I kind of always wanted to be an only child. Billy was born fourteen years after me. I still remember my parents sitting me down to tell me their news. Dad said to me 'your life is about to change' and he wasn't joking."

"You became nanny by default, then?"

Quinn tilts her head away from me, static standing her hair on end a bit.

"In a way. I was in high school and heavily involved in equestrian competitions, so I wasn't expected to babysit Billy. My first two years in college were a different story. I swear he made me never want to have kids!"

A pang of sadness touches my heart. I can't imagine feeling that way though I quickly realize that's not entirely accurate. Back in the day when I felt my partnership with Terence was permanent, the thought of children was as distant as the furthest galaxy in the cosmos.

I think of the time I stayed with Gwen and Tony, and fell completely in love with their daughters. Is that the turning point of my existence?

"Are you okay?"

I blink out of my reverie and glance at Quinn's worried blue eyes. "Yes, quite."

"You had that deep-in-thought look."

"I feel like so much has happened."

She smiles. "Me too. I can't shake this feeling that I've known you all my life."

My heart flutters in my chest.

"Does that scare you?"

"A bit," I confess.

"Me too."

"So, your little brother is the reason you and Andrew didn't have children."

"No. Andrew wanted a child as soon as we got married, but I wasn't ready. Truthfully, I don't want children. This world is a little too screwed up to raise a child anymore."

"I didn't peg you for a pessimist."

She shrugs. "I'm a realist. What would I be doing now if I did have kids with Andrew? They'd be enduring their parents' divorce."

"You don't know that," I counter. "He may have been a different person. Wouldn't fatherhood change a man?"

"Not *that* man. I remember something not feeling right between us. Intuition, I guess. He definitely realized those fears by running around on me each chance he got."

I frown trying to construct a time line in my head.

"I know what you're thinking," Quinn says, without even looking at me. "Samantha was the first time I got to confirm my suspicions. It wasn't long before I realized that he wasn't sleeping alone during the many business trips he'd take."

"Why did you make me think that Samantha was the catalyst of your divorce?"

She looks up, stunned at the defensive tone in my voice. "I'm sorry," she says genuinely contrite. "I've been an emotional wreck since signing my divorce papers. I have a horrible habit of venting out the wrong things. I'm so sorry."

I immediately soften at the pained look in her eyes. "Perhaps it's not me you should apologize to, luv. Samantha's carried a heavy burden of guilt all these years too."

Quinn is lost in thought for a moment. "I'd like to win my friend back."

"You make me think that you two were quite close, but Samantha always led me to believe that she was a loner."

"Oh, she was," Quinn confirms. "At first she came off as being too good to hang around us. When Gina and I recruited her, the only thing we had in mind were her perfect scores. The girls thought she'd come around, but it always took drinking to get her to spend any time with us." Quinn shakes her head. "I was horrible to her. I wanted to knock her off her high horse and bring her down to earth. She was such a closed book."

I recall Samantha mentioning as much. "What exactly did you do to her?"

Another shake of her head. "Just stupid shit, you know?"

"What falls under that category?" I pry.

"There was some silly stuff, like going without makeup for an entire day, which didn't hurt her in the least or parading them in bathing suits and calling out their flaws, but nothing beat The Dead Hole."

"The Dead Hole?"

"It wasn't my idea. The triplets were behind the whole thing."

I jot my memory for a few seconds. "The Mason girls."

Quinn nods. "Kayla hated Sam."

"Let me guess, Sam slept with Kayla's boyfriend."

"No. Sam stayed out of the dating circle until she met Brooks, but Kayla's guy was infatuated with Sam."

"So, this dead hole was supposed to be revenge?"

"Yeah. It was a big joke. We talked a few Theta Gammas into scaring our pledges. The dare was to spend the night in this abandoned chapel while the boys sneaked around making ghoulish noises and stuff. It was next to a cemetery in the middle of nowhere, a few miles from the campus. We were visiting the Alpha Chi Rho's at UConn, right before spring break, and their sisters told us about the dead hole. It was supposed to symbolize that no matter how dark things got, the sisters always had their back, but we sort of missed the point and drew perverse joy out of scaring those poor girls."

I can't see Samantha scared of boogiemen.

"One of our girls got so spooked she peed her pants and left the sorority. She even transferred out of Columbia the following semester."

"What about Samantha?"

"We went to spy on the girls sometime before dawn. They never slept of course, scared to death all of them, except for Sam."

"I believe it."

"We couldn't find her. In the morning, we spread out and walked the grounds of the cemetery. I found her lying down on a grave. I'll never forget it…"

"She slept on the cemetery?"

"Lewis, it was freezing. I don't know how she didn't get hypothermia. I felt horrible."

"What happened?"

"I asked what she thought she was doing and her answer was calm and eerie. She said, 'this woman is the same age as Mum'."

The hair on the back of my neck stands on end.

"I tried to hurry her away and out of the cold, but she started talking. I thought she was delirious from exposure, but then I spotted two bottles of vodka placed at the foot of the gravestone. She told me how she lost her parents." Quinn's gaze is troubled. "I never looked at her the same way again. We became guarded friends and grew closer as we lost our appetite for juvenile elitist games the Alpha Chi's were so famous for, and dedicated ourselves to our studies. I met Andrew and she met Brooks right before graduation and we agreed to be each other's maids of honor. Our lives looked perfect."

I catch the tear running down her cheek in my thumb and brush it off, cradling her to my chest, allowing her to give in to her tears.

"The ironic thing is that so many people thought we had it all. They didn't see Sam's vulnerability and they didn't see my insecurities. A lot of them simply thought we had it all handed to us. I guess that's why it hurt so much."

"What did?"

"Andrew and Samantha. Sam and I knew the truth about ourselves and I saw what happened as the ultimate betrayal."

Despite knowing what was behind Samantha's actions during that time, I actually feel a wave of resentment towards my best friend.

But Quinn is not crying about that one time her husband took her best friend to bed, she's crying about all the times Andrew left her at home to be with someone else as soon as the honeymoon ended.

I squeeze tighter, drawing her in, wanting nothing more than to absorb whatever pain she feels and make it mine so she can be rid of it.

"Lewis?"

"Yes, luv?"

"Will you do something for me?"

"Anything."

She cries quietly for a moment. "Make love to me again."

32

I once heard a line in a movie in which the lad tells his lover, "You know how to drain the will and strength out of a man", and the pretty lass smiles wickedly at him. I never thought I'd know exactly what he meant, but I do now.

After training me in the exquisite art of pleasing her, we fell asleep. This time, we were perfectly content to just breathe the same air, our exhausted bodies finally overriding our desire.

So when there's a knock on the door, it barely registers in my drowsy brain. I hear it, I know what it is, but my eyes close of their own accord easily dismissing the rapping. However, when I hear the knob turn, my eyes fly open and I quickly sit up to listen. Next to me, Quinn shifts a bit, but continues to sleep.

I hear footsteps in the living room then the hallway. I quickly scan the room, finding only the alarm clock as a suitable weapon. I can see a pair of legs cutting off the light coming in through the gap under the door.

"Who's there?" I whisper loudly.

"Lewis?"

For a moment, I entertain the crazy notion that it's my mother behind the door, but it's not. It's Samantha.

"Sam?" I needlessly ask.

"No," she whispers loud enough for me to hear. "It's the bloody Queen of England."

I look around the bedroom in the hopes of finding my trousers. It takes me a full minute to remember they're piled up at the foot of the bed. I get up off the bed and Quinn reaches for me. Not finding me next to her, she wakes and stares at me with untroubled eyes.

"Sam's here."

She tenses briefly but then she smiles. "Good one."

"Quinn?"

Samantha's voice wipes off the smile.

"Holy shit! It's Sam!"

With that, Quinn becomes a flurry of motion and she somehow manages to slip into a pair of cutoff sweat pants and an old, black, faded Nickelback t-shirt while I'm still naked and bewildered.

I stand frozen in place but Quinn picks up my trousers and throws them at me. I'm almost tempted to jump into them but I'd only succeed in attaining a concussion if I miss.

Apparently, I'm dressed enough for Quinn because she opens the door wide, giving Samantha a broad, sleepy smile. "Hi Sam."

Samantha looks at her up and down, shaking her head, a knowing smile turning up the corners of her saucy mouth. "You bloody tart," she says with a strange grin.

Quinn fidgets with her hair. "Yeah, well. Um… I always wanted to be like you when I grew up?"

They share some secret communication via that female telepathy Samantha always brags about then they turn and pierce me with their gaze. Never have I seen such diametrically opposed expressions on two striking faces.

"Sam," Quinn calls softly to her friend, but Samantha's shocked expression mutes her.

"You didn't answer your bloody mobile. Neither did you," she says to me then turns back to Quinn. "You said you'd go with me to get the Moppins at Heathrow."

Quinn nods quickly. "Okay, just let me grab a quick shower."

"No time, luv. Gwen is in the bloody car, waiting."

Quinn puts her head down and cuts a fearful glance at me. I'm not faring much better.

"Just three minutes, it's all I need. I won't even put makeup on, I promise."

"Fine, I don't think you need any lipstick to make those lips of yours look any bigger." Quinn bites her lip. "So, how'd my best friend taste?"

"Sam!" I call, loud enough to startle her.

"I'll get ready, quick." Quinn scampers out of the room.

Samantha turns to me, her brows raised. "I guess I should ask you the same thing. How did she taste?"

"Must you be so vulgar?"

She shakes her head again, a knowing smile on her face. "You crazy kids…"

I can't help smiling. "You know, this could possibly be the result of your encouragement from the other day."

"You're welcome!" She grins. "I'm going to wait in the car with Gwen." She turns on her heel and starts for the door.

"Sam," I call out to her.

She turns around and steps right up to me. "I think I made her nervous."

I nod. "Quinn is probably crying in there," I point in the general direction of the bathroom. "Bloody hell, I almost started crying."

Samantha stifles a current of laughter with her hand. "Serves you right for that stunt you pulled in Washington with me, remember?"

I only give her a blank look.

"Samantha, dear, your shirt is inside out and if you're looking for your knickers, they're peeking from under the bed," Samantha says, deepening her voice in an attempt to sound like me to quote me verbatim, crossing her arms for effect.

I said those very words to her, hoping to properly shame her after she seduced Tony Amaya in Washington D.C.

"Revenge looks bloody ugly on you."

She laughs again. "How was it?"

She knocks me off balance with her cheerfully curious demeanor. "Like I'm going to bloody tell you."

She rolls her eyes. "Come now. She's only going to be in there for another minute. How was it?"

I try to gather my wits about me. "A gentleman doesn't kiss and tell."

"I'm not asking a bloody gentleman, I'm asking you. How was it?"

No one enjoys a sordid story more than Samantha Reddick, but I'm not about to cheapen this glorious experience with an inadequate account from last night. I don't know that I'd ever be able to describe the things Quinn made me feel.

"That good, I see," Samantha says, nodding.

"You could say that."

She shakes her head, feigning sadness. "First timers, so easily impressed."

"Says the expert," I shoot back.

"I'm joking. Don't get your knickers in a twist. Oh wait, are you wearing any?" She hooks her fingers on the waist of my trousers and I jump away from her, sending her into a fit of giggles.

"Are you bloody done?" I glare at her as she struggles to compose herself.

"You and I are going to have a few words about this, promise?"

"Not on your life. I'm not divulging every detail like you are so fond of doing."

"Fine. So, this really meant something to you, didn't it?"

I meet her eyes firmly and nod. "More than you'll ever know."

Her eyes turn skyward. "First timers…"

"You must really want that wedding portrait with you sporting a blackened eyeball."

She puts her hands up in surrender then her expression turns serious. "What did it mean to her?"

That's a good question. "I've the feeling you intend on interrogating her about it."

"Better bloody believe it, pet." She turns to look at the door. "I'm going to apologize to her. Go talk to Gwen, keep her company for a few minutes, okay?"

I nod.

Samantha stands and walks to the bedroom door. I find my shirt and throw it on, completely mismatching the few remaining buttons. I curse and re-button the bloody thing, suddenly realizing how much sense t-shirts make.

"Lewis?"

I look up at my best friend, who regards me with an unfamiliar look. "What is it?"

"I'm really happy for you."

"But…?

Her smile reminds me of a cloud darkening the sun on a summer day. "Be a bit selfish with your heart."

***

"So, I guess I'm playing second fiddle after all," Gwen says when I climb behind the wheel of Samantha's Mini Cooper.

"You'll always be tops with me, Gwen, my luv."

She bows her head, grateful for the compliment. "Are you okay?"

"I am."

"Was that really your first time?"

"Why do I get the feeling you and Samantha knew exactly what was going to happen last night?"

"No, I'm just going on an assumption. Quinn made it clear she likes you. Anyone can see you're both attracted to each other, and finding you here confirms the assumption. So, what happens now?"

I blink a couple of times, awed by her logic. "It's up to her."

"No, no it isn't," Gwen says in an eerily calm voice. "What do *you* want?"

In that moment, the answer that flashes in my mind carries with it such finality, and I know I've crossed all the way over a line I never thought I'd even approach.

Gwen nods in understanding. "You two make a cute couple. Listen, if you want to stand beside her at the wedding, I'll be okay with that."

There's a note of sadness in her voice that says she'll be anything but okay. "Never, luv. Lorna Matthews would hang me by the thumbs."

"Good. I would've hung you by different appendages."

Samantha and Quinn finally come out of the flat, declaring they're ready to go. Gwen winks at me as I get out of the car. There's such an air of anticipation created by the curious glances while Quinn and I shuffle on our feet, casting nervous looks at each other. Neither one of us knows how to act now.

"I've a suggestion," Gwen says. "Why don't you and Quinn go get your sisters? I'll stay with Lewis and we'll meet up later with you."

"Are you sure, luv?"

"Positive. I won't know any of them, and you'll all probably start reminiscing. As much as I can't wait to hear those stories, I'd feel like a third wheel, and you won't be able to just relax with your friends."

"Gwen," Samantha says in an anxious voice.

"It's alright, hun. Really. You two go ahead." Gwen gets out of the car leaving no room for further argument.

Samantha climbs behind the wheel and asks Quinn if she's ready. The blonde beauty looks nervously around before grabbing the open door that Gwen held for her then turns to me. "I'll see you later?"

"Count on it," I reply.

"Lewis, kiss your girl, for Pete's sakes," Gwen chides.

"Quinn, kiss your lad, by George." Samantha adds.

I step up to Quinn and lean in, but I only succeed in laying a gentle kiss on the cheek she offers. As I pull away, she takes my hand and kisses my knuckles, her eyes full of promise. When I look into her eyes I know without a doubt I've fallen for her.

"Bye."

It takes a monumental effort to keep my tongue in check. What I want to say needs no witnesses.

Samantha leans down so she can see me. "Love you!" She says in a sing-song voice. "Try it, it's not so hard, luv," she says to Quinn, whose face turns a bright crimson. I watch the Mini Cooper drive away, feeling like it's taking my heart in it.

"You knew they wanted to talk about this, didn't you?"

Gwen nods. "I also know you could use a talk."

I smile gratefully at Gwen, my eyes still down the street until the Mini Cooper turns at the corner and disappears from view.

My mobile buzzes in my pocket.

Q is on the clear, no special interest. Following. Sods.

I sigh in relief, glad Jason Soderbergh is keeping an eye on Quinn. He's only second to Jason McElroy in skill and instincts. I reply a quick acknowledgement.

"Important message?"

I shove the mobile in my pocket. "Work stuff." My eyes are still fixed on the last spot where Samantha's car turned.

"No doubt about it, honey," Gwen says as she puts an arm around me.

"What?"

"This is exactly what falling in love feels like."

***

I treat Gwen to a drive into Battersea, pointing out the different London landmarks. Although she's properly awed by the sights, her heart is not really into it.

"Who's got the girls today?"

"Nathan and Alicia. They're taking them to the ballet. I've the feeling they're going to end up with a bunch of dancing stuff. They were already burning Alicia's ear off about slippers when Samantha and I were leaving."

Everyone's lined up to spoil the girls. "It's so easy to spoil them."

"Of course, it'll take years to undo the damage all of you have done to my discipline strategies."

I laugh. "Are you hungry, by any chance?"

"Always. But I imagine you are the one who needs the nourishment after burning off, God knows how many calories."

I can feel my cheeks burning. "I'll take that as a yes. How do you feel about Mexican?"

"Here in London?"

I laugh. "The world of today has a piece of home wherever you go, luv. Well, except for the bloody Middle East. But here, where civilization reigns supreme, you can find a very good Mexican restaurant."

I bring up the navigation system on the screen and request the nearest Mexican restaurant. Seconds later a course is set.

"Great! I've a platter of nachos with my name on it!"

"What is it with Yankee women and nachos?"

"Are you kidding? It's the food of the gods!"

"Weren't you doing the diet deal along with Samantha and Alicia?"

She makes a sound of derision with her lips. "You weren't there for the feast Margaret made. Our diets went to hell after that."

"Should I text the dressmaker and warn her about the impending alterations?"

"Be nice!" she warns.

I hear Five for Fighting's "Chances" playing and I turn up the system as we cruise down Queensworth Road into Queen's Circle, a large rotary that branches off into Battersea Park and Prince of Wales Drive.

"I love the British names," Gwen says. "Everything is Queen something or Prince, or Royal, it's like being in a fairy tale. Tony would love this."

"How are things with the chap?"

Gwen makes a face of discontent. "He says it's a constant argument with some of the screen writers. He's always defending his characters to keep them from being modified. Hell, they wanted to do away with Aunt 'Rish and have a male actor play some wise uncle, or something. Can you believe it?"

"Utter bollocks!"

"He doesn't get it. The executive producer told him the Aunt 'Rish character was going to be the anchor of the entire show. They even had Annette Benning in line to play the role. Tony was so excited about that."

"Who's playing the lead role?"

"Gordon Lennon plays Marcus and Danica LeRoux plays Sofia Malone."

"I know the lad, but I don't believe I've ever heard about the girl."

"She was part of the cast of a teen show that was recently cancelled, she's perfect. Apparently, she read the book and told her agent to be on the lookout for it to go on the screen. Tony said she's not only beautiful in every sense of the word, but she's also down to earth."

"Rubbing elbows with the famous," I remark.

"The beautiful, and famous," she corrects, crossing her arms.

I pull into a spot on the side of the road and soon we're strolling on the wide stone sidewalk on Kessalee Boulevard.

"*Bienvenida al Mariscal,*" I utter in passable Spanish.

"*Gracias,*" Gwen replies.

"Do you speak Spanish now?"

"Are you kidding?"

"Doesn't Tony teach you?"

"I can't learn from him. We both get impatient with each other. That's the funny thing about couples, you know? If anyone else wanted to teach me, I'd pay attention and take their correcting me as guidance. When Tony tries, I end up getting all pissy because I think he's just picking on me, and he gets so impatient quickly."

My mind wanders to the hours of instruction I received from Quinn in the art of love making. There was absolutely no getting "pissy" with her instructions.

"What's that grin on your face about?"

This lass misses nothing. "Just thought it was funny."

"Sure you did. You were thinking of Quinn."

"Is it that obvious?"

"Absolutely."

"Come now, lass."

Gwen laughs. "You are so stinking cute! Just get a good look at you. I've never seen you this disheveled. You're *that* distracted over Quinn. You've got a haggard face, bloodshot eyes, and a brown rat's nest over your head to go with the stubble on your chin and cheeks, and yet, you're positively glowing!"

I'm mute with embarrassment.

"I should mess up my hair and wrinkle my clothes and we'd look like lovers who just got done doing it."

"I should change first," I mutter, feeling more self-conscious by the second.

"You look fine."

El Mariscal is a brick structure with a tile roof, the only one of its kind in all of Battersea. The food is severely overpriced, but the atmosphere is second to none. It never fails to inspire in me the need for a vacation in the white sands of the Yucatan. I'd most likely blister to a crisp, but I'd love to be in such an alien setting.

Our waiter looks utterly out of place. With his carefully trimmed red beard, freckled face, and stout frame, he'd look more at home in the highlands of Scotland, wearing a kilt and playing the bagpipes.

He takes to Gwen, blatantly ignoring me. I don't blame him. For her part, Gwen is immensely enjoying the lavish attention bestowed upon her.

We settle on Margaritas and salsa and chips until our entrees are done. After the heaping platter of nachos, I don't know where we'll fit the chicken fajita platter Gwen orders or the *bandeja del sol* for me. And yet, I manage to clean off my plate. I vow to never scoff at the notion that sex leads you to the excessive consumption of food. I'm living proof that's exactly where it leads.

"So good," Gwen declares as she chomps on another salsa laden corn chip. "Tell me, are you and Quinn a couple now or was that just a one night stand?"

I sip at the citrusy mix before answering. "Things just happened. I'm not sure where we stand."

"Things just happened," she echoes thoughtfully. "Interesting. What exactly happened?"

To my surprise, I describe every detail of my night with Quinn. Unlike Samantha, who'd bury me under an avalanche of lewd comments, Gwen listens intently, her eyes glistening with tears as I make a poor attempt at describing the emotional rush that affected me far more than the physical overload of stimulation, and that's saying something. I only stop talking when our very Scottish server gently places another round of drinks before us, his eyes roaming over Gwen's neck and cleavage. He leaves us with a reminder to call him should we need anything, and moves on to another table. I notice the new diners having the same expression on their face Gwen and I did when the lad came to our table.

Gwen sighs and wipes at the corners of her eyes. "Oh, Lewis," she says on a breathy voice. "I miss those first moments. I wish I could go back in time just to have that first kiss with Tony all over again. I wish I could relive each of those first moments. Oh, my God, you're going to make me cry!"

"Isn't it better when you're married for a long time?"

Gwen considers the question for a moment. "It's a little different. Tony is different than a lot of my girlfriends' husbands. He's always telling me I'm pretty or that he loves me. He writes me little notes all the time. His favorite line is 'I've yet to stop falling in love with you'. It's so sweet and all, but nothing can beat those things I felt that first time he held me, feeling everything you felt with Quinn."

I smile, remembering only too well the tempest of emotion that enlivened me like nothing ever has.

"Of course it's infinitely better when you know that person you feel these things for, feels the same way for you."

Her words give me pause.

"Lewis, love is a risk. Sometimes you win, most times you lose."

"I can't help thinking you are somehow warning me about something."

Gwen looks away. "I'm afraid for you, that's all."

Something goes cold in my chest. "What are you afraid of?"

She shakes her head as she pushes her plate away. "I don't know. You live here, she lives back in… well, she lives across the ocean."

"North Madison, Connecticut."

Gwen's eyes widen is surprise. "You're kidding! My in-laws live in Connecticut."

"Quinn's going back to live with her parents for a time, luv. I think she needs to do some healing, surrounded by family. Her divorce was a very public and hurtful affair."

Gwen smiles approvingly. "Glad to see you actually did some talking."

And we had. I could no longer see Quinn as the overachieving ex-wife of one Andrew Fischer. Her photograph on the article in *Architectural Wonders*, as she showed off her Malibu home had nothing to do with the woman she revealed to me last night; the woman I held close to me as she bravely recounted her heartbreak in stark detail. I cradled her beautiful face as she told me about her dreams, her fears, and all the things that make her far more than just a pretty face.

"You're in love with her," Gwen ventures.

"I'm sure I don't know, luv. I do know I've never, ever felt this way about anyone, but I don't know that I can call it love."

"Why not?"

"For starters, I don't know how she feels, and as you pointed out, her life is in America and mine is here."

"So, what are you saying? That this all happened because you two got caught in the moment?"

I've been entertaining a particular thought that up until now, I didn't want to allow to the forefront, but without Quinn around, a little perspective has been restored. "I know very little about relationships, or being in love for that matter, but I do know that after a major break up, most people look for some pseudo-relationship that enables them to cope with the grief of heartbreak."

"A rebound."

"Precisely."

"If you were a rebound, you would've never shared as much of yourselves as you obviously have. And I'm not talking about the physical part."

I didn't realize how much I wanted to keep this sudden hope from rising any higher. "What if Quinn is like Samantha? Whenever she got lonesome, she'd find some chap and involve herself with him, if only for a night."

"Is that really what you think?"

I look down at my hands. "No."

Gwen reaches across the table, silently commanding me to let her hold my hand. When our fingers are entwined, the way I held Quinn's only hours before, she squeezes gently. "Why are you so afraid of these feelings you obviously have for Quinn?"

"I don't know what feelings you are referring to, but if you mean love, I can't believe it's something that happens so quickly."

"You'd be surprised. What's scaring you?"

"Did anyone ever break your heart?"

"Yes," she confirms in a cautious tone. "Tony broke my heart."

I wince inwardly, not wanting to steer the conversation to the events of last winter. "I didn't mean to bring up Samantha and—"

"That's not what I'm talking about. I mean, back in the beginning, when we first got together. He and I had something so incredible that left me craving for so much more, but he left me for a year."

I know that during that year, Tony met Samantha, inadvertently entwining the destiny of all of us. Life is much stranger than fiction alright.

"I was head over heels in love with him, so when he left, I was crushed."

I'm taken aback by the pain I see in her eyes.

She blinks several times then gives me a tentative smile. "It all worked out though."

"But what if it didn't? What if you had lost him?"

Gwen shrugs. "The way I felt that spring was worth it. I knew I'd get over it sooner or later. It would've hurt for the rest of my days, but eventually you move on, and that's what I was doing when he showed up in my life again. Now, here we are, happily surviving and raising two terrific little girls."

I'm happy that life worked out kindly for her, but I still recoil at the infinite possibilities of my situation with Quinn.

"Lewis, if love was so easy to attain, if it didn't hurt so much when you lose it, it wouldn't be the force it is and none of us would struggle to find it the way we do. You haven't lived until you've loved."

"Sam told me the same thing last night."

Our server comes by to offer us a refill but we decline and I hand him my credit card, that's the only time the man bothers to glance my way and grudgingly at that.

"See? She's right at times." Gwen shakes her brown hair.

It's several inches longer than when I last saw her, enhancing her already sultry image. She's apparently opted to allow Samantha to have a say so on her makeup, for I recognize the green eye-shadow that brings out the unique shade of blue in her eyes, ever so resplendently. She's wearing a white camisole under a bright, yellow top that matches the wedges on her feet. Her dark blue jeans are form fitting, making no secret of the graceful curve of her hips and accentuating the length of her legs. Small golden hoops hang from her delicate earlobes and a small diamond teardrop is nestled at the top of her cleavage.

Having had the night I had, I'm shocked, and ashamed, to feel the stirring of desire within me, making me miss Quinn even more.

Welcome to the sex-driven male mindset, Lewis…

"I'm off to the loo," she says and giggles. "Then you and I can go meet these Moppins I've heard so much about."

33

Just as I feared back when Quinn contacted me, the Moppins have one thing in mind: to celebrate their reunion by visiting the nearest pub. And jetlag? What jetlag?

I drop Gwen at the Royal Academy of Dance, leaving her with Samantha. Somehow they've made plans to go to the Blue Lioness, a posh pub on Vicarage Crescent in a converted shipping building that overlooks the Thames, almost perfectly across the water from Quinn's flat in Chelsea Harbour.

I beg off on account of needing a fresh change of clothes and a shower, and then I'm forced to endure Samantha's references to why I need a shower. I'm secretly hoping Quinn goes with me, but she stays behind and I drive like the devil is chasing me to clean up. On the way home I text Gwen a simple instruction, *Don't let Sam drink.*

By the time I make a futile search for a parking spot closer than a few blocks to my bloody flat, my mood is sour and I curse my impulsive decision of buying the old house on Cadogan Square instead of a simpler flat with an attached garage. Some changes are definitely about to take place.

I run the two blocks from my car to the front door of the flat, wondering what concerns me the most, being around Quinn or keeping Samantha from having a drink. I'm impatient for both.

I kick my shoes off and I'm tearing at the buttons of my shirt even as I take the steps two at a time. I'm so focused on getting into and out of the shower as fast as possible that I don't see Mum until she calls my name from the kitchen, causing me to slip and skip down the steps, driving my toes into the backboards and twisting my knee, adding to my already foul mood.

"Good heavens, son, where's the bloody fire?"

I bite my tongue in order to keep from spewing every curse in the English language and stop to wince at the throbbing in my big toe.

"Hullo, Mum," I manage through a grimace.

"Well, I must say, that was graceful."

I give her a pained look and hobble back up the steps. "I need to clean up, Mum, I'll be back in a few minutes."

"Very well, perhaps we can talk about last night over tea, luv."

I freeze at the top of the steps.

"Don't forget to wash behind your ears."

Great... Instead of arguing with her, I quickly shower, shave, spend more time than I want on the rat's nest crowning my head, and finally feel human once again after donning black slacks, a cobalt blue shirt, and black Rockports. I leave the tie in the closet and heeding a rebellious impulse, roll the sleeves up over my elbows.

When I shuffle into the living room, intending to drink the tea Mum made in one gulp, I'm crestfallen to find a small meal waiting at the table. I can't in good conscience refuse her efforts, knowing how deeply that would hurt her feelings and given the little smile on her lips, she knows this. She has effectively entrapped me.

"Mum, this is great, but Sam and Gwen are expecting me back."

"And Quinn?" She smiles.

I nod. "And Quinn."

"Son, I already texted Sammie Kay, they'll wait for you. Now sit."

"You texted Sam? When did you learn how to text?"

"Don't be daft. I keep up with the new culture as good as the next bird. Of course I know how to bloody text."

To emphasize the point, she picks up her mobile and shakes it at me.

"I'm convinced. You've just never texted me, that's all."

"Why would I not actually just talk to my own son?"

"Good point."

Mum suddenly grows quiet as an array of emotions plays over her face. She attempts to speak twice, but both times she falls silent, slightly frustrated with herself.

"What is it, Mum? Did Richard knock you up?"

"LEWIS!"

I laugh so hard I nearly tip my teacup over.

"You're incorrigible," she chides, shaking her head. "Always been. In that regard, you're far too much like me."

Her silence and deadpan demeanor sobers me up quickly. "Mum, what is it?"

She steeples her hands and lets her eyes go out of focus, making me nervous.

"I've been rehearsing what I wanted to say to you, but now that the moment is at hand, I don't know where to start, luv."

"Does this have anything to do with your heart malady?" I ask, filled with fear.

Her eyes bore into mine. "I'm not bloody going anywhere. Not for a long time to come."

My fear diminishes only slightly. "Well, what then?"

Mum offers me her hand. I look down at the diamond ring Richard placed upon her dainty finger and place my hand in hers.

"Would you believe me if I tell you that I was never ashamed of you?"

I feel my back stiffen. "What exactly are we talking about?"

Mum's eyes well with tears. "You were only nine years old when I began feeling I was doing you more harm than good by getting you into ballet. I put it off only because you were a child and you danced like you loved doing it, despite what the other kids were saying behind your back."

"Mum—"

"Let me speak, please," she says with a smile, squeezing my hand for emphasis. "When you were sixteen, I went into church once to beg for advice. That bloody sanctimonious windbag of a priest had the bloody nerve to condemn you to hell without knowing a single thing about you."

Her eyes are focused in the past. Sensing this may be the only time she purges these thoughts, I say nothing.

"Lewis, I once asked God how to accept the way you were. I hoped your lifestyle was more of a passing fad, and not part of your identity." Her smile falters slightly. "When you brought Terry home, it broke my heart to face the possibility that you'd go the rest of your life a gay man."

I'm stunned by her frankness. "I knew you were disappointed."

She shakes her head emphatically. "I was disappointed in myself, my boy, for I'd forgotten the one teaching from the Savior that tops them all, even the bloody commandments upon the sacred tablets. Only then, I found enough peace in my heart to love my gay son."

"What teaching, Mum?"

Tears spill over her lashes. "Love thy neighbor."

The words are delivered with such reverence that I bow my head, as though in prayer for the first time since I was a child.

"You see, the Lord didn't say love thy straight neighbor or love thy chaste neighbor. There was never any labeling, no categorizing. It's simple, elegant. Love thy neighbor." Her eyes are intense. "You are more than that, by George. You are my son, and I fell to my knees asking God for forgiveness for my disappointment in my own flesh and bone. I should've asked for your forgiveness all along, my boy."

I can't remember having ever seen this level of passion in my mother. At this moment, I love her more than I ever thought possible.

"I did allow myself to grieve however. Your choice meant a drastically different future than the one I envisioned for you. It meant I wouldn't get the chance to see a woman grow old with you. It meant you were the last baby I ever held."

Overcome by emotion, she cries. I get off the chair and throw my arms around her, holding her tight to me. I don't realize I'm crying until everything blurs before me.

"I want you to know," she says haltingly. "I want you to know that I love you, my baby boy, no matter what. What I want for you is no different than what any other mother wants for her children. You can ask Gwen, she'll tell you. I want to leave this world knowing you are loved, knowing that you are happy."

"I love you, Mum. I love you so much," I say, pressing my cheek to the side of her head.

Her hand reaches for my face and I press it against my wet cheek after kissing her palm.

"Mum," I say softly, once I recover enough of my voice. "Why are you telling me all this now?"

"Because I've never seen you look at anyone the way you look at Quinn, and suddenly you've altered my visions of your future. You've once again shaken the fabric of my being. And I want to believe, Lewis Jonathan. I want to believe that you will not go on alone."

I think this is the point where I ought to warn Mum that Quinn and I are not exactly a couple, that envisioning a future between us is far too premature, but I can't do that because suddenly hopes of my own are soaring.

"How do you feel about Quinn?"

"Why?"

"Because it's obvious how she feels about you, luv. I just want to know whether it's mutual or not."

I smile. "I can't think when she's with me, and when she's not, she's the only thing I can think about."

Mum dabs at the corners of her eyes with the sleeve of her top and smiles knowingly. "You be sure to let her know that, my boy, and don't drag those big feet of yours. She's quite lovely."

The image of Quinn brings with it a reminder that Samantha is at the mercy of a bunch of women intending on having a celebration involving alcohol. My feelings for Quinn may be undefined, quickly evolving into something that can be named, but my feelings for Samantha are crystal clear and right now I just want to make sure I'm there to keep her from making a fatal mistake. At the same time, I can't think of leaving my mother alone in this flat after such an emotional tempest.

"You go on, my boy. I shan't keep you any further, luv," she offers as though reading my thoughts. "Richard will be along any second now."

Relief floods through me in waves. Knowing she won't be alone, a sense of urgency over Samantha grips me tighter than before.

"I can wait until Richard comes by," I offer, though I pray if she agrees, Richard doesn't take long.

"No need, luv." Mum suddenly chuckles. "Who knew one day you'd have so many women waiting for you?"

This attempt at levity does so much to restore my composure. I kiss her forehead and tell her I love her then I run out of the flat when I hear a voice behind me.

"Lewis, is everything alright?"

I turn to the deep basso voice, at once relieved and envious that Richard got a spot right in front of the bloody flat.

"Quite so, Mum's waiting for you. The place is yours until sunup."

Richard gives me a broad grin. "At my age, son, it's far more than enough to enjoy the very presence of a fine woman, such as your mother."

He pats my back affectionately and goes into the flat. I trot down the street in search of my car, suddenly able to understand why it's so important to leave behind those we love with someone who loves them just as much.

34

The sound system announces a call coming in. I tap the screen and connect the call.

"I made some progress on your caller." Jason Stephen's no-nonsense tone is not as positive as I'd like it to be. "It's an American mobile, originally from Los Angeles. It's been quite active with calls to the States and one single London number, another mobile with blocking privileges."

I grin. "You have her name?"

"Mandy Martinez. She's employed at *Famous*. She was sort of a rising star until a sensationalized article on a movie star landed her in trouble to the tune of a two million dollar lawsuit. She's been demoted since."

"She's not working alone."

"No, but it seems she hired some camera people. They're abundant in London, what with all these people chasing after Prince William and Kate..." Jason's voice trails off.

"Makes sense. Jason, we've got to get that blocked number."

"I was coming to that. You know we can uncover any blocked number except for one type."

"Government types..." I think aloud.

"Right you are, chap. Call me when you get a name."

"Thanks."

I end the call. Now all I have to do is ask Quinn which of her friends has any ties to the British government.

With the matter of the mystery caller settled in my mind, I focus back on Samantha. I try to think of a time that she was near alcohol and how she handled it, but it's soon clear I managed to keep her away from it, perhaps a bit too well.

As long as the setting is calm, I think she'll be alright. In a rave type setting, she'd cave in, no doubt about it. When I slow down to make the turn into the lot, I spot a sign that sends a bolt of unease through me.

"You have got to be bloody joking!" I nearly scream as I read the sign standing outside of the Blue Lioness: *Tonight Male Review*.

After I park, I resist the urge to kick the sign and pull out my wallet to pay for the exorbitant fee to get past the mountain of a man holding the door. When I walk inside, I hear him call me a fag under his breath. My step falters, but I'm not suicidal enough to whirl on the cheeky bugger and give him a reason to reduce me to a bloody pulp.

The music is loud and the DJ has such a deep voice that it comes out of the speakers like a T-Rex clearing its throat. A stage is set up on the dance floor. Perilously narrow catwalks spread out like a child's portrayal of a sun from the stage. The iconic Union Jack, Rolling Stones logo is emblazoned on the black curtains that serve as background. Someone on speed must be controlling the laser lights; their bright, chaotic pulsing is already giving me a headache. When the DJ mumbles something over the speakers, the women in the club lose their minds as they erupt in a screaming frenzy.

A striking lad with roguishly long dark hair steps out through the curtains. He openly leers at the women and begins dancing to a techno number. The bloke wears the tightest jeans I've ever seen, making me wonder how he's breathing. A ripped white tank top is spray painted over the bulging muscles of his chest. His powerful arms are a flurry of motion as he glides from one side of the stage to the other, eliciting louder screaming from the women he approaches.

I scan the crowd for a familiar face, alarmed at the quantity of fancy glasses, and clear bottles that litter the small tables. I look around for Samantha with renewed urgency.

A scantily dressed lass who disturbingly looks no older than twelve, approaches me with a crooked smile, a small tray propped on the palm of her hand.

"For the right price, I can get you backstage with the boys," she says with a grin.

"Not at all, luv. I'm looking for my friends."

The girl nods her head to her right. "They're all there. Keep them under control, would you?" She leaves me with a wink.

I look to where she gestured and see a small crowd of young men in their twenties making a spectacle of themselves with their catcalls and lewd commentaries on the dancers. I can't fault the waitress for pinning me as one of them. Not so long ago, I might've engaged in such behavior.

Suddenly, a sharp long whistle rips through the electronic music, making everyone turn to see the source of such earsplitting sound. I'm actually not that surprised to see it's Quinn.

I grew up a country girl...

I can't help smiling and shaking my head at the way she said those words.

Samantha and Gwen each grab an arm and pull her down to her seat. Three women I've never met are carrying on, slapping high fives and hollering at the stage. These must be the Moppins.

Once I catch sight of Quinn, I become so focused on her that I apparently miss the dancer stripping down. I see the lad in a G-string that makes no secret of the bulge between his legs. His naked arse wiggles around, causing some women to fan themselves while others reach for the stage.

I recall my ballet dancing, sophisticated and dignified. I didn't always have a problem with stage fright. If anything, dancing was the only time I felt I garnered some sort of respect from my fellow man. This lad twisting his body every which way is one courageous soul. I can't imagine dancing that way for this crowd.

Out of the corner of my eye, I notice other dancers on the floor, shaking their bodies for clusters of women who are blatantly reaching out, and cupping a feel of the entertainment. I check a different corner and I'm shocked to see a young woman kneeling before a dancer who's holding her by the hair, rubbing her face all over his groin.

I've heard of these hen parties before. They were usually secret affairs carried out by invitation only. The women that attended these parties conveniently forgot their beaus and spouses for a few hours, and they acted accordingly, which meant there were no bounds to what they did in the name of fun.

I feel a rush of anger at Samantha. This is just like her, a sex fiend if there ever was one. Why would she bring Gwen and Quinn to such a bloody place?

Quinn's earsplitting whistle breaks through the noise once more. She's dancing with one of the muscular dancers, straddling his thigh and doing an even better job of moving her body lasciviously. The women around her—Samantha included—are cheering her like she's winning a bloody contest.

Jealousy floods my heart like oil. I take two steps towards the group when Quinn plops back in her seat, laughing hysterically to give her friend a chance to ride the wiggling wanker's thigh. The woman taking her place is fairly large. Her thick arms are raised and waving in the air while her sizable rear end bounces over the dancer's thick thigh. Her breasts are bouncing out of the confines of her bra and I gape in shock when the dancer grabs a handful, grinning like a butcher's bloody dog.

The sight fills me with indignation.

Even Gwen, my Gwen, the woman I hold in such high regard that I feel no ladder is tall enough to reach the top of the pedestal upon which I've placed her, is acting like a randy little tart. She brackets the dancer from behind, both her hands on the smooth curves of the dancer's arse.

Suddenly I want no part of any of this. Not even when it's clear this wanker's got his eyes on Quinn. With Gwen behind him, holding onto his narrow hips, and the large woman rocking herself on one thigh, he pulls Quinn up on his other leg and blatantly wraps a large hand around her middle, using the bouncing of his body as an excuse to caress her perfect little arse.

I've never wanted to hit a man so much, not even when I conjured all my anger from years of belittlement for being gay to drive my fist into Firuz Ahmidi's face.

"Lewis? Lewis Bettford?"

The voice is male, pleasant and bemused, and it has thankfully pulled me away from some unexpectedly dark part of my mind I wasn't even aware I had until recently when Firuz made the mistake of hurting Quinn in my presence.

When I turn, I can't help staring at the face before me as recognition dawns. "Paul?"

He grins, displaying a perfect row of white teeth that seem to glow in the dark. "It's been a long time," he nearly shouts in my ear so I can hear him above the din.

"It has," I agree in a similar tone.

Paul Simms and I attended University of Liverpool. He was a close classmate of mine through our basic courses before we each departed to our specializations. Paul went into journalism and I went into Computer Science. No matter what your sexuality, gay or straight, it was undeniable that Paul was one of the most beautiful human beings in existence. I haven't seen Paul for over ten years, but he looks as though he hasn't aged a day past twenty.

"I don't think you're hanging out with that lot, are you?"

He gestures to the far corner where the male audience continues to be ignored by the majority of the dancers. I see two of them have pulled their shirts off, revealing skinny torsos in an attempt to catch the dancer's eyes and failing miserably.

"No, my friends are here."

"Is Terry one of them?"

An old wound bleeds anew, surprising me. "Terence is not doing well."

Paul's green eyes scrutinize me for a silent moment. "I've been hearing some things."

"Like?"

"His name was on *The Flier*, under the black column. I thought it was a sick joke at first." He cocks his head to one side, thinking. "I saw him at a cruise in Lambeth. He looked a bit frail, but I thought he was just doing one of those bloody diets."

That's as close as Paul will admit to hearing rumors about Terence's illness. I don't want to get into Terence dying of AIDS. "I haven't seen him since we parted ways," I shout as the music thumps louder.

"I understand. You made a good pair, but life goes on, right? So, where are your friends?"

There's quite a bit of history among all three of us, but I'm glad Paul decides to remain in the here and now.

"Did you hear that whistle above this noise?" I can feel the strain of my vocal chords, shouting like this.

Paul motions for me to follow him and we walk to the far side of the stage through a door marked: KEEP OUT. The noise is reduced to a distant roar once the door shuts. We're standing in a service hallway that leads all the way out of the building. There are some doors on each side marked with large signs. I follow Paul to the furthest door marked, REST-ROOM, the label giving me pause. Some dance clubs are notorious for what goes on in their restrooms.

"It's just a resting room, lad," Paul says, chuckling at my hesitation.

When he opens the door, I'm pleasantly surprised to see a sitting area in the middle of a large, open floor. The entire far wall is a mirror. Two men sitting on comfortable stools are applying the final touches to their costumes, and fixing their hair with an array of hair products littering a long countertop. They glance at us on the mirror without a word and simply continue to primp themselves.

"Have a seat. Care for a drink?"

I shake my head. "That's quite alright, thank you."

"So," Paul sits on a love seat. "The whistler is your friend."

I nod. "She's also here with another friend and Samantha. I don't know if you remember her."

Paul smiles broadly and nods. "Who could forget someone like Sam Reddick? Certainly not me, chap. I didn't recognize her out there, but then again, I'm not up for another hour and I haven't gotten a good look at the crowd."

"How do you remember Sam?" I ask, dreading some sordid revelation to come.

"She used to call me 'Deaner' after the guy in that old hockey movie, *Youngblood*, remember? She used to say I looked just like Rob Lowe." He laughs.

Personally I think Rob Lowe's legendary good looks are merely ordinary next to Paul Simms. He's the best a German and Irish mix can produce. His hair is dark and thick, and the slim, yet well-defined, build of a midfielder covers his remarkable bone structure. Few people have ever gotten past his striking eyes.

Back in our school years, every girl crushed out badly on Paul, but he never made a secret of his homosexuality. I'd see him holding hands with his partner, both their heads held proudly high as they walked to class. Even Samantha and I fell prey to his appeal and disarming personality. As my best friend had been so fond of pointing out, Paul was too pretty to look at.

At one point, things had lined up for a chance at a relationship between him and me, but by then, Terence was in the picture and nothing ever came to be.

Samantha campaigned hard to get us together, but she wasn't around long enough to influence our lives that way.

"You bear a striking resemblance," I say admiringly.

"You're too kind," Paul says with that irrepressible grin I remember. "Did you come to check out the action?"

"No. I'm trying to save six grown women from their own mischievous inner child."

"You always had a way with words," Paul says with a note of affection. "Don't read anything into it, no matter what they do. They're just having fun."

"I was under the impression that there's to be no contact between the audience and dancers."

Paul scoffs. "That seems to apply only when the dancers are real females. With us, just about everything goes."

"How far does it go?" I ask, unable to keep the dread out of my voice.

Paul frowns. "All the way sometimes. Well, it depends on the dancer. I might let some lass get a feel, but I won't kiss or anything. Other blokes are much more lenient."

"I can't believe you're doing this. Whatever happened to journalism?"

Paul grins. "Dancing pays much better than writing obituaries for the *Times*, and it gives me the chance to write."

"Different articles?"

"I'll contribute to The Flier with articles that won't portray us as the godless heathens the church says we are. Every now and then, the Associated Press will pick up the articles I write, pay me, and exploit them through their secretly unrelated channels."

"It's good to hear you're still chasing your dream."

Paul laughs softly. "My dearest, that's not exactly my dream. I've been working on a novel, my very first."

"That's terrific! What's it about."

"Life as a gay youth."

"A memoir?"

"I bloody hope not," he says, his eyes taking on an animated gleam. "I'm just hoping to put a few readers through what it's like to be one of us, the good and the bad. I'm not making us into heroes, or undeservingly glorifying our lifestyle like others have. It's just an honest account of things I've seen, or have gone through in my life."

"You've got yourself a reader."

"Thank you."

"When are you publishing it?"

"Soon. I was going to send a copy to Solutions, for you and Terry."

This surprises me. "You were?"

"But of course. You and Terry gave me some basis for my characters. I hope you're alright with that."

I feel suddenly quite flattered. "Who am I in your story?"

Paul stares at me for a beat. "One of the good ones."

When the blinding tide of flattery recedes, I realize I need to clarify something. "Paul, I'm not sure you should keep a character based on me in this story."

Paul looks deflated. "I understand, but may I ask why?"

Out of the whirlwind of phrases that fills my mind, like a screaming mass fighting to get out of a burning theater, one simple truth emerges. "I'm in love with a woman."

35

Paul stares at me in stunned silence. I avert my eyes so I don't see judgment in his eyes. I'm expecting him to curse me for a bloody tootsie, and even spit in my face. He does neither. He just stares, unable to form a single word.

"I will still read and promote your book, Paul." When I muster enough courage to look at him, I'm taken aback by his grin.

"You'd bloody better, Lewis. So which one is it, Whistler or Sam Reddick?"

"The Whistler," I reply as a strange elation builds within me.

Paul nods in appreciation. "She stands out. But I always thought you and Sam would end up together."

"You are not the only one."

"I bet. So, is this your 'coming in' party?"

I laugh. "Did you just make that up?"

"I always thought there should be an opposite for coming out parties. You're not the first lad to revert to the mainstream, nor the last."

I blink several times, not knowing what to say.

Paul consults the large clock over the mirror. "When I started writing this book, I was fortunate to truly talk to different people about being gay. Some of the most compelling stories belong to blokes who practically grew up gay until one day, they decided to change. It's more common than you think, particularly with women."

"Why women?"

"Isn't it obvious? Children," he answers his own question.

"But nowadays, a woman can buy some sperm and have a baby without the need for a man."

"True enough, but it's not about the manjuice. It's about our natural instinct to form a family with the proper roles. Many gay couples have tried to raise a family, but the stressful social burden they face is too much most of the time."

"You researched all this?"

"Of course." He takes a deep breath and continues. "Truth is, it seems one needs to be rather selfish to maintain some given lifestyle. I'm not just talking about a gay lifestyle either. It all revolves around family. Say you want to serve the church, or lead a military lifestyle. You want to serve God, Queen and country for life, that type of commitment doesn't usually afford you the luxury of having a family that will detract from your devotion. A homosexual faces a similar issue."

My head is spinning, mainly because I can't conceive that this beautiful, and superbly intelligent, lad is dancing on a stage in nothing more than a G-string. "What are you really doing here?"

Paul laughs. "You wouldn't believe how good the money is, Lewis. Once you get past the piss-inducing fright out there, it can even be fun."

"When you're ready to publish, call me. Sam knows the ins and outs of the publishing industry. At the very least, she's a smash of an editor."

"Do you mean that?"

"I know she'll be glad to do it."

"How much do you think her time is worth?" He asks nervously. "Editors and proofreaders command a pretty penny these days."

"Don't give it another thought. Allow me to contribute to your future success."

Paul bounces out of the love seat and wraps his arms around me, laying a kiss on my cheek, taking me completely by surprise.

"Forgive me, I couldn't help myself. You'd be shocked to hear what some wankers are charging just to read through the manuscript. I always thought you were one of the kindest individuals I ever met."

My mind goes back in time to tender moments I shared with Terence. It seems like another life altogether. "Not at all, my friend."

"If I may, you've earned my admiration today."

"You're too much. I'm not even going to be the one editing the book."

Paul laughs. "I'm not talking about the bloody book. I'm glad to see you've found yourself. I just hope you never speak ill of us, perhaps enough people like you can convince others that we aren't monsters."

"In that case, Paul, I'm an admirer of yours. Nothing takes more courage than to stand proudly and being who you really are, regardless of opinion." I laugh as a thought crosses my mind. "And to pay a compliment back, I actually recall Samantha lamenting the fact that she didn't stand a chance with you. She called it a waste."

Paul looks amused. "I really think it's all about being happy, you know? I can actually say that. Me and Michael have been together for nine years now."

I've never met Michael but I hope he's just as good a lad as Paul. "I wish you many years of happiness, Paul."

"Same to you, Lewis." He grins. "And if you are doing the family thing with that beautiful lass of yours, your children will be absolutely striking."

He blushes at his own words, but I don't have the heart to tell him that Quinn doesn't want children.

"I'd best get out there. Happy coming in, Lewis!"

We stand and embrace like two brothers at Christmas. I give him the only business card I have in my wallet and he deposits it in his locker, thanking me profusely for my future involvement in his book.

***

The DJ is going off on another unintelligible diatribe that is somehow deciphered by the crowd of screaming women who cheer and raise their drinks in salute. More techno music blares out of the speakers as Paul takes the floor. I watch him dance away from the outstretched arms reaching for him, a playful smile on his face. Some women are inexplicably crying and one has fainted and fallen face first on her table. I can't imagine men succumbing that way to a woman's beauty, but I might very well be wrong.

When I look for Quinn and Samantha, I see other faces in their place. I make a full circuit through the place unable to find them, so I quickly key in a text message to them. As I make my way back towards the front door, my mobile finally buzzes in my hand. There's a text from Samantha.

Where the bloody hell are you? We're at Quinn's. I assume you know your way, lol

I run out to my car and wrestle it out of the parking lot, somehow avoiding smashing into another parked vehicle. Within minutes I'm flying across the Thames on the Battersea Bridge on my way to Chelsea Harbour.

The music in my system is interrupted by a trilling that announces an incoming call. I hit the connect button on the steering wheel with my thumb and answer the call.

"Hello, Lewis, this is Lorna Matthews, my apologies for the late call. How are you this fine evening?"

"Miss Matthews, very well thank you. What can I do for you?"

"I just wanted to confirm the time for the rehearsal. I have it down for ten sharp."

"Consider it confirmed, luv."

"Excellent! Augusta will be at hand for last minute alterations for the gowns. I trust we can get all the participants in, correct?"

"I don't foresee a problem Miss Matthews."

"Good night, Lewis."

There's a loud click over the speakers before Norah Jones graces me with her soft, hypnotic voice, doing much to calm me down as I find the narrow road to Quinn's flat.

I pull behind Sam's Mini Cooper and wonder how they fit all those girls in that little car. The door is open but I don't see movement inside. I wonder if they decided to take a boat ride.

"Quinn? Sam? Gwen?"

"Out here, luv. On the patio!"

I walk through the flat, my eyes going to the bedroom as I walk to the open back door. I can't believe how quickly my body responds at the thought of what happened in that bedroom.

American country music is playing from an mp3 dock speaker. The guitars and melodious vocals are a stark contrast to the techno rubbish to which I subjected my eardrums while at the Blue Lioness.

Gwen gives me a lazy wave, her eyes half-closed and a little grin that says, she's had one too many. Quinn gives me a shy smile, looking unsure of herself, quite the contrast from the way she acted last night. I don't fault her. I'm gripped by a similar feeling with Gwen and Samantha around.

"Had to get them out of there before they drank another gin and tonic," Samantha offers with one of her nervous smiles.

My heart almost breaks when I notice the slight trembling of her right hand. Aware of my scrutiny, she traps her hands between her knees, leaning forward on the bench she's sitting on.

"Hi, sweetie," Gwen sings out the words.

"How many did you have, luv?"

Gwen puts one forefinger up and looks at it as though she can't remember it's hers. "One." She exchanges a look with Quinn and they both giggle.

"One of each," Quinn adds.

"I hate being the bloody grownup," Samantha gripes, shaking her head.

I breathe a sigh of relief and turn to Samantha. "Everything alright?"

"It wasn't easy. But it wasn't impossible either. I'm fine, luv. Stop worrying so damn much. Gwen would drink anything Gina and the others tried to give me."

I breathe a second sigh of relief. "Where's the rest of your group?"

"Either naked or drunk somewhere, probably both!" Quinn exclaims and Gwen joins in, laughing drunkenly.

"These two can't hold their alcohol," Samantha observes.

"I see that."

"We're just a little tired, that's all," Gwen protests.

Samantha smiles. "She really protected me, Lewis."

"That's usually my job," I think aloud.

"It's quite alright. You missed the Moppin reunion."

"I didn't see you, ladies, hurting for male companionship," I say a bit too bitterly.

Samantha laughs but Quinn has gone utterly still.

"We were just having fun, it was innocent," Gwen says quickly, giving me a glimpse of what a father must feel upon seeing his daughter drunk for the first time.

"Oh, I can't wait to tell Brooke and Emily about this," I joke.

"Hey! They'll ground me!" She taps Quinn on the arm. "No, wait! They'll box my bloody ears!"

I'm beginning to feel like Samantha and I are the wiser, older siblings of these two.

"They didn't have that much. I think they're just happy," Samantha says softly. "They're funny, aren't they?"

"Slap my bloody knee funny."

Samantha glances curiously at me. "You're sexy when you're cross. You ought to show that side of you to Quinn."

"You're mad. All of you."

"Hey, it's my bachelorette party, you know!" Samantha cries.

"You look like you are having less than a good time."

"Let's go inside for a minute."

"Alone?" I don't want to leave Quinn's side.

"I promise to behave myself. Not easy after watching hot men dance naked, but I'll do what I can." She makes a face and goes inside.

I take a look at the other two, wondering why I haven't heard them laugh again. Apparently, the music has lulled them to sleep. I smile to myself. Quinn must be exhausted after the night we had, and Gwen, usually responsible mother of two, never goes to bed past ten. I think I recall her mentioning that the last time she really drank was in her twenties.

Both their eyes are fully closed, their breath deep and even.

When I step inside, I find Samantha composing a text on her mobile. She hits send and puts the device away. "Hey."

"Hey." I can tell she's got a lot on her mind. "So, how many Moppins were there?"

"Gina, Lynn, and Keri came today. Leah will be at the wedding but she couldn't take an earlier flight because of work."

"Is this a good thing?"

She nods. "They were put off that I didn't join them on a crawl."

"A crawl?"

"A bar crawl, what we used to do when we were in school. I felt kind of disappointed that they haven't grown up. They all have children now. It's bloody crazy."

"Life happens," I muse, carefully gauging her reaction.

"Gina's gotten so big, I couldn't believe it. She was a size zero at one point. Keri is still the same old Keri, her sisters still hate me," she says on a laugh. "And Lynn is so different now…"

"I'm not sure what you were expecting, luv."

She looks at me. "Oh, it's not what you think. It's just that I only now really feel how much time has gone by since those days."

"Were you afraid of going with them?"

She nods. "I started feeling nervous, watching everybody down their drinks, moaning in pleasure from the flavor. I contented myself with a virgin daiquiri, and like I said. Gwen watched me like a bloody hawk. Gina wanted to do shots and Gwen drank in my place. Well, she and Quinn, both."

"I'm glad they helped, but I'm also proud of you." I step forward and crush her to me. "I'm sure it wasn't easy."

"At least they couldn't pull rank and make me drink like they used to." She chuckles then draws back. "What took you so bloody long?"

I relate most of the unexpected conversation with Mum. At one point, Samantha gets teary eyed and tells me virtually the same thing Mum did. After that, I bring up my running into Paul and tell her about his book. She listens with the interest of a trained professional in manuscript evaluation.

"I'd love to work with Deaner, that'll be a smash! Is he still as hot as he was?"

"In your eyes, probably hotter."

"I can't believe we left without seeing him."

"You'll see him soon enough."

She nods. "It might be good for me to get into the field again."

"I don't know, Sam. Nathan is counting on you."

"He is, but at the same time he doesn't really want me to be away."

"That reminds me, are you moving in with Jason?"

"We are scouting some properties."

"You can buy my place. I'll even give you the best friend discount."

"Throw in a bloody private drive and it's a deal."

"Can't blame a lad for trying," I lament. "What about you? Lorna called me to confirm the ten o'clock rehearsal."

"I'm excited. A bit nervous. I'm terrified of getting up there. I'll be shocked if the bloody church doesn't crumble around me."

"You get to be queen for a day, luv. Enjoy it."

We share a comfortable silence that takes me back to a collage of memories with my favorite lass.

"I talked to Quinn about you."

"Best friend report?"

"You know it."

"What's the verdict?"

She grins wickedly. "I never knew about your cute little birth mark on your right arse cheek. Can I see it?"

"Oh, bloody hell…"

Samantha laughs openly at my chagrin.

"But seriously, she told me you practically rocked her world."

I can feel my face burning.

"Your first time shagging, and you pull an all-nighter. I'm so proud!"

"I don't know that I want to listen to this." I shake my head at her.

"I asked her where this is going."

"And?"

Samantha bites her lip in thought. "How do you feel about her?"

"I wouldn't know where to start, Sam. She's incredible."

"Remember what I told you. Be a little selfish with your heart."

Each time I get these warnings, something goes hollow in my chest. "Whatever it is, I can handle it, so just bloody tell me already."

"I can't tell you what I don't know, okay?

Frustration makes me exhale long and loud. "Okay."

"I'm taking Gwen home. I'm sure you'd like to visit with Quinn," she smiles and bounces her eyebrows. "Just give yourself plenty of time to properly groom yourself afterwards. Promise?"

"Cross my heart," I say sarcastically.

"Good."

It takes some time to help wake an exhausted Gwen, but eventually she leaves with Samantha.

I go back to the patio and crouch down next to Quinn's sleeping form.

"Quinn?" I rock her gently.

She shifts and stretches her arms over her head, her chest rising alluringly.

"Hi."

"I'll help get you in bed. Come now."

I get my arms under her and help her sit up. I don't have to carry her all the way to her bed, but I refuse to let go of her until I have her stretched out on the mattress. I'm hoping she tells me to stay, but her eyes close and other than the rise and fall of her chest, she doesn't move.

Only when my feet begin aching do I realize I've been standing at the side of her bed for an infinite time. I try to keep the tide of desire that engulfs me when I stare at the contours of her body, opting to kiss her forehead and quietly leaving the bedroom.

The need for her touch becomes an ache that keeps me from taking a deep breath, but a pile of luggage in a corner of the living room reminds me Quinn has guests. It may explain why she didn't ask me to stay, though I wish she'd at least have made mention of it.

I have no way of knowing whether Gina, Lynn and whoever else have keys to get in, so I don't lock the door when I go out, but I don't leave either. I decide to wait on the Moppins to show up. I can't bear the thought of leaving Quinn defenseless.

It's almost three in the bloody morning when a cab pulls up to the flat, its headlights stabbing the dark, hurting my eyes.

I step out of the car and the three women regard me with suspicion.

"Good evening ladies, I presume you are the Moppins?"

Their cautious expressions melt behind a trio of smiles.

"You must be Sam's guardian angel," says the larger woman. "I'm Gina. This is Lynn and that skinny little thing is Keri." She turns to the women. "Girls, this is *The* Lewis."

"Oh, so you are real!" Lynn exclaims, extending her hand, which I gently shake.

Lynn is a pretty brunette with dusky skin and black hair that falls around her shoulders. She peers at me out of a set of dark eyes through the lenses of her stylish glasses. She has a mole to the right side of her lips that makes her face memorable.

"I'm real enough, but no guardian angel, I fear."

Keri smiles tentatively. Her hair might be red, or light brown and short and spiky. Her clothes hang on a thin frame, making her look like a child, though her gaze speaks of a much older soul.

"We've heard stories about you for years. Always thought you were too good to be true."

"Thank you, Gina."

"Is Sam still here?"

"No, she took her friend Gwen back to Kensington."

"Gwen seems nice," Lynn offers. "Is she the good influence on Sam? She sure has changed for the better."

Gina and Keri mutter their agreement.

"Will you ladies join us at the rehearsal?" I ask them with a smile.

"We'd love to," Gina replies. "But the rehearsal is normally reserved for the participants of the wedding. It's sweet of you to ask. We thought of spending the day with Quinn until we found out that she'll be a bridesmaid, so it's shopping for us for the whole day."

"I see."

"Quinn's better off anyway," Lynn says, her eyes suddenly downcast.

The other two nod in agreement, a note of sadness in their expressions.

"Am I missing something?" I'm suddenly accosted by dread.

The women share a look and seem to come to a mental consensus about something. Perhaps Samantha's theory on female telepathy is no rubbish after all.

"She needs to stay away from her asshole, ex-husband."

The venom Gina infuses in her words has piqued my curiosity. "I thought the divorce was finalized."

Keri scoffs. "He's never going to let her go, even if it's the best thing for both of them."

"Yeah, I can't believe she's even thinking about a reconciliation with the jerk."

I feel like a battering ram just slammed into my chest.

"At least she got away for a little while." Keri comments.

"This was good for her, to clear her head," Gina adds. "I just told her, find someone to wrinkle the sheets with, get those juices flowing again."

"You did not!" Lynn cries.

"Worked in college," Keri quips and the three share a laugh.

I don't share in their laughter.

"Did Samantha leave just now?" Gina asks, noting my serious expression.

"Um, no, they left right before midnight."

Three pairs of eyes pin me in place and I can see judgments and speculations whirling in their minds.

Gina stands a little straighter and raises a curious eyebrow. "Oh?"

"I didn't know whether you had keys to come in and Quinn was done in," I explain, resisting the urge to lecture them about drinking.

The trio relaxes a bit, but whatever their opinions, they're irrelevant. I feel an oncoming flood of desperation and pain that I won't be able to hold back much longer.

"Since you're here, I shall take my leave. I gather I will see you all at the wedding."

Gina smiles tentatively. "We wouldn't miss it."

"Lewis, are there more of you?" Lynn asks.

"More of me? I'm afraid I don't understand."

"Sorry. I was just hoping there were more of you out there. Well, more nice guys like you that aren't gay, no offense."

I give her a thin smile. "None taken, luv."

"Alright, forget the shopping, I'm planning on sleeping all day," Keri says, the last words spoken in the middle of a jaw-cracking yawn.

"Good night, ladies. It's a pleasure to meet you."

They bid me good night in unison and I get in the car. Once I'm sure I'm out of their sight, I pull off the street and brace my arms on the steering wheel as I begin to shatter with things Gwen said during our conversations about Quinn.

I don't trust this Quinn…
…I'm afraid for you, that's all…

Samantha's words are right behind,

Remember what I told you. Be a little selfish with your heart…

She said that right after screaming at me about taking a chance at love. Did she find out about Quinn's intention to reconcile with Andrew Fischer after she put it in my head to go for it?

Did that explain Quinn not kissing me before Samantha whisked her away? Was her expression one of apology and not one of promise as I had originally thought?

Lines float in my head from Mum's tearful conversation from just hours ago, doubling the gut-wrenching pain that folds me over the wheel. I'm hurting so much I don't dare even move. I try to set aside her words only to have Samantha's surface.

I've been a mess because of love. Sometimes it's fleeting and it leads to more pain than you can imagine...

The words reverberate through the deepest confines of my soul as a cold, merciless fire envelops my heart. I feel a fool for leaving the safety of the identity I held for so many years. This is exactly what I've never wanted to feel. I've never been witness to the coexistence of anger and grief in a single heart, until now.

A sedan goes by fast enough to rock my car in its wake. I look out the windscreen at the industrial park that looks like an abandoned relic from a lost civilization. When I start the car, music comes on, but I shut the system off, terrified of hearing some lyric that will exacerbate this tangled mass of feelings burning through me. I drive back home listening to the muffled roar of the engine.

Sleep eludes me as a continuous loop of images of Quinn tortures me until the sun comes up. By then, I don't feel pain or anger. I feel nothing, not even the beating of my heart.

When the sun blazes through the window, I curse its brightness as I get up and shower, wondering how I'll ever face Quinn without hurting this bloody much.

36

I can't do it.

It's barely six when I quickly dress and leave the flat before Mum wakes. I don't want to see anyone right now. I don't want to be the recipient of a sympathetic look. More than anything, I want to stop feeling whatever this is.

I stop at the office to pick up one of my encrypted laptops in order to keep up with work should a situation arise that needs my attention. I quickly compose several emails, delegating ongoing work with my techs in Liverpool then quickly leave. I'm tempted to destroy my mobile, but I have to be available to my clients. I've never wanted some dreadful emergency more in my life, something that could consume my every thought just to drive the image of Quinn McDermont's face out of my conscious.

I've been driving aimlessly more than ever as of late. I no longer care about the rising cost of petrol that normally limits my preferred longer excursions. All I want to do is get away. A fool's errand if there ever was one. I can go to the moon and my mind will still be there constantly reconstructing the memory of Quinn's passionate touch, her words, her kiss…

I race north on the A10 towards Enfield, wanting nothing more than to break out of the M25 ring that circles London. When I do, nearly an hour and a half later, I feel only a mild sense of relief.

The stretch of road before me is beautifully desolate. Farming fields stretch east and west as far as the eye can see until

Broxbourne appears like a concrete oasis in the middle of a green desert. I drive into the small town and make my way to Hoddensdonpark Wood, not interested in sharing any space with another human being.

I force the BMW into a dirt lane with ruts so deep, the undercarriage drags on the muddy bumps that make me bounce my head against the liner. A tiny voice of reason pleads for me to turn back but I can't even if I want to. The only way out is by driving in reverse back to the mouth of the dirt lane, but if my memory of this place is intact, I will eventually emerge at the southern tip of the lush woods near a main road that can take me back to town.

Tall grassy reeds narrow the lane until my side mirrors push their blades with the passage of the car.

My mobile buzzes in my pocket. I can't believe I have any sort of signal out here in the middle of nowhere. I try to ignore it but the bloody thing reminds me I have a message every thirty seconds with a mocking buzzing.

There's a covered bridge spanning over a thin ribbon of water. It looks like it has seen better days two centuries ago, when horses were the only means of travel. The old wooden boards squeak in protest but I make it to the other side.

The woods clear enough for me to spot the lake in the distance. The smell of baking mud wafts through the vents of the BMW and it's redolent in the air when I climb out.

I had not given any thought to this day beyond getting to this point. Now that I'm here without any distractions, I let the images out of their box in my head and let the bloody pain consume me like a flame.

I don't even realize it's my scream cutting through the silent fabric of the landscape until I get lightheaded from a lack of oxygen.

I fall to my knees under the weight of a thousand irrational recriminations.

I want my old life back.

I want to reverse the hands of time to a day when I knew nothing about Quinn McDermont. I want to stop feeling this altogether.

Suddenly I have a clear understanding of why Samantha depended on alcohol to numb her mind. Right now the idea holds tremendous appeal.

Exhausted from the sleepless night, the zoned out drive north to this spot, and the crushing pain of disillusion, I sink into the weeds and stare at the copses of the trees until an encroaching darkness veils my vision.

***

There's a vice painfully tightening its hold on every joint in my body. I can almost feel my freezing skin cracking when I try to move. For a second or two, I don't know where I am. I fish my mobile out of my pocket to check the time, but the screen is dead. Only then, I remember the buzzing alert that has eventually taxed the battery.

I feel tattered as I get back on my feet, but at least this pain can be treated, unlike the other, more torturous gnashing in my heart.

A pang of guilt twists my insides when I think of missing Samantha's wedding rehearsal, but I know I would've been less than good company in the presence of Quinn.

When I'm back within the overwhelming comfort of my car, I start the engine and turn the air temperature to its stop. Every bone in my fingers aches from the cold.

"What the bloody hell are you doing?" I say angrily at my own reflection on the tinted glass of the rear windscreen of my car.

It occurs to me at this moment that I've momentarily lost my mind on pure hearsay. I've never given in to such an irrational urge, and never to such unadulterated suffering. And yet, I didn't need for Quinn to confirm what Gina said, I could feel it.

After a tense half hour during which I fought the gripping power of the bloody mud, I make it out to a strip of pavement. Mud splatters off the wheels into the wells in a barrage that doesn't cease for almost two miles.

I remember to plug the mobile to charge and when it boots up, there's a seventeen next to the message icon. I take a major chance of wrapping my car around a tree as I scroll through the message headings. None of them are from Quinn.

I cross the same thin river from the park, this time on a solid concrete and steel bridge. I vow to never again take for granted such engineering marvels.

Safely heading south back to London, I dare relax, though I wonder if I'm losing my bloody mind. The ache that drove me on this insane side trip has receded to a dull stabbing, so at least it was somewhat productive.

The display on the screen of the sound system flashes an incoming call alert, when I connect the call, Samantha's voice comes through the speakers like a plea.

"Where are you? We've been worried sick!"

I can't help hoping Quinn is part of that group. "I had to do an emergency house call in Enfield," I lie.

"So, you couldn't find a fucking phone?" Now that she thinks I'm safe, her voice gives me a taste of the wrath to come. "You're full of shit. I called your office until I realized you either forgot how to use the bloody phone or you weren't there. I even called Burns in Liverpool, but he asked me if I knew where you were. What the fuck, Lewis?"

"I fucking had something to do, alright?" I snap, finally sick of her Yankee cursing. "Some of us have to work, you know."

"What the fuck is that supposed to mean?"

"It's not about you. Curse again and I'm hanging up."

"Fuck you!"

I hit the disconnect button and I enjoy a long measure of perfect silence.

I ignore five more calls before I give in and connect the call.

"Lewis, it's Gwen."

The soothing tone of her voice instantly shames me for letting everyone down by dodging the rehearsal on account of my broken heart. How did I allow myself to be this pathetic so easily? "Is Sam still cross?"

"I'm holding the guts of her phone together so I can talk to you."

"Where's the mobile I gave you?"

"I gave it to Brooke to play a game and needs charged."

"Sam has a habit of busting up mobiles."

"Can you talk to me?"

"Are you by yourself?"

"I claimed a headache. Samantha and Jason took the girls to some toy palace."

I smile. "Little Prince's Palace of Toys?"

"Yup."

"And Quinn?" I ask, unable to keep a wistful note from tainting my voice.

There's a long silence on the other end of the line. "She was worried sick about you, and she hasn't been herself all day. What happened, hun?"

"If you'll pardon my American, I think I fucked up."

Gwen doesn't laugh. "What happened?"

I summarize the conversation with the trio of women, trying desperately to detach my feelings from the account. I can't.

"You didn't ask Quinn, did you?"

"No. Am I an imbecile or what?"

Gwen takes a deep breath and exhales slowly. "Actually, Samantha and I were afraid of that."

Whatever hope I harbored, flees at the seriousness of her voice. "Oh."

"I'm so sorry, Lewis."

"You win some, you lose some," I reply dejectedly.

"Are you close to home?"

"No."

"When you get there, I'll be there, okay?"

"Okay," I reply, numb.

"Get home in one piece, promise me you will."

Her adamant tone of voice makes me reply. "I promise."

"Be careful."

I disconnect the call and swallow up the miles unable to dispel the notion that Gwen and Samantha set me up. Before I know it, I'm parking on Cadogan Square behind a Land Rover as twilight softens the sharp edges and pushes the light into the western horizon.

***

I climb the steps with leaden feet, my joints still aching from the cold. Gwen, Jason, and Samantha are standing in the middle of the living room. When I step towards them, Samantha runs and throws herself into my arms, squeezing the breath out of me, a series of muffled apologies fill my ears. All I can do is squeeze back.

"You do this all the time, lass," I tell her. "I'm the wounded one and here I am trying to comfort you."

"I'm sorry," she insists as she chokes up.

Gwen walks up to us and puts her arms around us both. I almost blurt out "One for all and all for one", giving in to a nervous impulse.

When they finally untangle from me, Jason hands me a mug filled with dark tea.

"Thanks."

He nods, clearly uncomfortable with the entire situation.

"How's Quinn?" I ask Samantha.

"Never mind how's Quinn."

Gwen shoots her a disapproving glance before turning to me. "I talked to her. She'd really like to talk to you."

"Perhaps you should, luv. Her mind was clearly a thousand miles away." Samantha says softly.

The three of us sit on the long couch with them clinging onto me.

"I don't know that there's anything to talk about. Where are your girls, Gwen?"

"They're in Kensington with your mom and everyone else."

"Forgive me. I missed them in their gowns."

Gwen pats my arm. "You'll see them tomorrow."

I turn to my best friend. "Forgive me for missing the rehearsal."

"I don't bloody care right now. Forget it. I just want you to be alright."

Samantha is seething. I can tell by the tightening of her jaw that I feel on my arm each time she clenches her teeth.

"I should've never invited that bitch."

I want to agree with her, remembering that's exactly what I wished alone in the woods. But if I'd never met Quinn, I would've never found the real me. The epiphany does nothing to lessen the ache in my soul, but it's a good starting point for healing.

At least I hope it is.

"Samantha, Quinn is not exactly unscathed from this," Gwen, always the voice of reason, risks Samantha's legendary temper.

"You don't understand. She's done this shit before," Samantha counters.

I pat Samantha's arm. "It doesn't matter, Sam. We have a wedding to prepare for. I'm fine. I just needed to clear my head a bit."

Samantha grinds her teeth. "I'm going to—"

"You," I interrupt her, "are going to get ready for the first day of your married life, and be the bloody Queen of England for one day."

"I'm sorry."

I cradle her head over the crook of my arm, twisting my hand to reach for the top of her head. "It's nothing you did, luv."

"I can stay with you," Gwen offers.

"Oh no, despite your loveliness, I just couldn't have you fall hopelessly in love with me after subjecting yourself to my sexual prowess. I consider Tony a friend therefore we shall only add our names to the list of victims of bad timing."

Gwen smiles in appreciation of the untimely levity, but it's easy for me to draw strength from her friendship.

"You are something else, Lewis Jonathan Bettford," Samantha says with a smile. "There's not a lass alive who deserves you."

"Hey!" Gwen protests.

Samantha takes a long look at her matron of honor. "Nope, not a one."

"Tart!" Gwen snaps.

"Ah!"

"We can set up a mudwrestling match after the wedding to settle this," Jason offers unexpectedly, earning a wide-eyed look from them before we laugh.

Jason looks like he wants to offer some piece of advice, but he is clearly reluctant to delve into these matters in front of Gwen and Samantha. I hope he sees the understanding in my eyes.

"I'll be fine," I reinstate to respond to their unspoken question when their laughter abates.

"I was ready to deploy a search team for you," Jason says with a lopsided smile.

Gwen looks at Jason for a second then to me before standing. "Hey, Sam. Give me a hand with something."

"What?"

Gwen's eyes flash.

"Oh, right, something."

When they leave, Jason surprises me by coming to sit next to me. "When you and Sam left for Pennsylvania, I was in a pretty dark place."

I turn but his eyes are focused somewhere else.

"I didn't care whether I lived or died. I've been shot, stabbed, beaten… but there's no pain akin to heartbreak."

I nod in agreement. "How'd you make it stop?"

A humorless smile twitches on his lips. "I went into The Vipers' Nest, started a brawl and let a trio of bulls trample me until the bobbies broke it up. I was pissing blood for a few days after that."

"Did it work?"

His eyes roll towards me. "Not for a second. That's the reason I didn't follow you. I was too battered to do much good to you or her."

"Jason that sounds mad."

He shrugs. "It was. The point is you've got to keep yourself together, Lewis. Perhaps you feel alone and insignificant, typical when we feel sorry for ourselves. But don't forget for one second that you matter to many of us."

I feel utterly foolish now.

"Keep that in mind. And as far as Quinn goes…"

I feel a tightness in my chest.

"I don't presume to know women, but she really was not herself today. If you have questions, she has the answers. You've just got to be brave enough to live with those answers, and move on if that's what it means."

I look at him in earnest. "Would you have moved on without Samantha?"

I can see that he wouldn't have.

Without replying to my question, he wraps his thick arm around my shoulders and gives me a brotherly embrace. "Chin up, old chap. I wish there was something useful I could tell you."

Before I get a chance to thank him, footfalls on the steps mark the progress of Gwen and Samantha returning to the living room. Jason grips my shoulder before letting go.

"Okay," Samantha narrows her eyes at us. "What were you talking about?"

"Men business," Jason quips.

"This had best not become a habit of you two."

"Do you want me to stay?" Gwen asks.

I smile wryly at her. "You must be really randy. I'd better not spoil you for Tony."

The line has the intended effect, everyone laughs, dispelling the last of the tension.

"Fine. I promised to tuck the girls in anyway, although Alicia is some story teller and she does this little song number before they sleep. They love her," Gwen says on a sigh.

"You shan't be replaced any time soon, luv," Samantha assures her.

"I'll go get the car," Jason offers. "If you need to talk…"

"Thanks, Jason."

He nods. He stops to gently kiss Samantha on the lips. I notice a wistful look on Gwen's face. She must be missing Tony.

I walk them to the door where Gwen hugs me and kisses my cheek. "If you need to talk, call me."

"You'd best get some beauty rest, lass."

"Love you, good night."

"Love you," I reply.

Gwen turns to Samantha. "Make it a quickie before you tie the knot, *lass*."

Samantha manages to spank Gwen's bottom with a well-placed backhand that makes her yelp before she can get away.

"You're a bad influence on her, Sam."

"Oh, I pale in comparison to her deviousness."

I laugh. "Are you ready for your big day?"

Samantha looks nervously at me. "I think. I'm worried about you."

I spread my arms and she leans into me. "You don't need to worry about me. Forgive me for missing the rehearsal. I feel utterly foolish."

She shakes her head. "I want this for you. I want you to be this happy. I can't feel complete until I see that."

"That means everything, Sam, but I'm happy. Believe me. Now go. I'll be there bright and early tomorrow."

"You're lying, but okay."

"Did Mum say she was coming home?"

"She and Richard have become quite close with Nathan and Alicia, but I imagine she'll be by soon, luv."

"Tomorrow, then."

Samantha smiles. "Love you," she mimics Gwen.

"Oh, the love," I say on a breath. "It's just raining upon me."

She makes a face. "No, I just refuse to be outdone by Gwen."

"Always the competitive one."

"But you still love me, right?"

I look into her pretty eyes. "Forever."

I watch her saunter away from the door, illuminated by the headlights of Jason's Land Rover. She opens the door then turns to me. "You missed one little thing at the rehearsal, but you'd best not screw it up tomorrow."

"What did I miss?"

"You get to walk me down the aisle and give me away."

"It'll be an honor, Sam."

She grins.

I'll walk you down the aisle, but I'm sure as bloody hell never going to give you away, Samantha Kay.

***

The odd nap I took in the woods effectively prevents me from getting any sleep, despite my body screaming for it. My mind won't stop racing. I open up a bottle of wine and sit in the studio, giving in to an urge to listen to music.

I have an external hard drive nearly filled to capacity with music, almost twenty gigabytes of an array of playlists, songs, and even entire albums. I stare at the screen for a long time deciding what to play. I read somewhere that if you find yourself unable to stop feeling down, your best bet is to channel it through a healthy outlet. These included writing, reading, watching a film, and listening to music. I settle on a playlist that contains all the songs with the least play count and sit back to listen.

I feel it's my duty to toast the bride and groom tomorrow and I have yet to prepare what to say. This seems to be the perfect time to do it.

While the lovely Aussie, Angie Hart from Frente softly sings their cover of "Bizarre Love Triangle", I hum the words along and look through hundreds of famous quotes about new beginnings.

After the last ringing note of the guitar, an unfamiliar riff begins to play. I don't recognize the song, but that's precisely why I opted for unfamiliar tunes. I click on another quote website while the song plays. I try not to follow the lyrics, ignoring the reference to love being no more than a game where someone wins and someone loses.

I sigh and let the notes resonate within me. I'd be okay if I just got to kiss Quinn one last time. Some fraction of my conscious mind is fascinated at the irrationality that takes a hold of me.

In an attempt to further clear my mind, I bring up a secure server from the office and decide I'd best finish with Quinn's intranet so I can cut all ties with her.

When I access the mock up, I see four access flags that almost make my heart stop. Several research files have been transferred out of the main server. When I look up the permissions, the screen comes up blank. Someone hacked into the server. I sift through the code until a horrifying pattern emerges.

"Buggering hydras..."

After an hour of careful studying, I realize no hacker broke through the outer firewall. The databases were accessed with the password. The only person in possession of that password is Quinn. The hydra was infused after the breach and the file transfer. Someone is trying to sabotage the entire intranet.

I grab the phone with the intention of calling her, but I can't. The last thing I need is to worry her with my incompetence. I set the receiver back in the cradle and rub my eyes before examining the code. My eyes begin to burn. When I look away, I catch sight of the very first hundred pound note Terence and I framed upon signing our first client. I stare at the intricacy of the striation patterns on the note that are said to be impossible to duplicate. The Queen's broad visage stares back at me, her dark eyes penetrating.

"Shit, of course!"

Cursing my mental lapses on account of my disillusionment with Quinn, I activate the concertina wire protocol I installed earlier on. I run the scan and wait a full ten minutes. The screen suddenly fills with the flagged code as the software throws a net that begins snaring the infected code from the hacker.

The elation is such, I have to resist the urge to jump up and down. The software begins the disinfestation process. I picture in my mind a series of pulses frying every worm from the elaborate hydra. I don't dare even yawn or allow my body to persuade me to bed.

The screen flashes again, telling me the software has initiated the retrieval of the stolen files. To my surprise, they all have the same heading: Play Again Foundation. I recognize the format as money tracking spreadsheets. I had only opened one to import the main layout and was shocked to see the foundation had over a billion dollars at its disposal.

I open one of the documents and see a requisition of funds that makes me frown. On a whim, I access the Lions severs and run a check on the accounts listed in the requisition document. I'm not at all surprised when the accounts prove to be off shore relay transfer accounts.

"You're going to be one sad wanker when you try to withdraw a single bloody penny," I muse, comfortably confident now.

A smaller window flashes on my secondary screen. The tracking program is surfing the web at unimaginable speeds tracking the point of origin of the recipient of the stolen files. I expect a red line to extend out of the UK into China or Russia or even the US. But to my surprise, it flashes a local London address in the embassy district. A reverse directory finds a match and provides me with the name of the hydra initiator.

I quickly compose an elaborate confession and attach the necessary evidence of cyber-espionage and industrial theft, along with other ethical grave charges then prepare a neat, innocent looking requisition package power point presentation and set up a file transfer into the main drive of the server's owner.

On a hunch, I access the tracer software and easily find the file on Mandy Martinez. I crosscheck her mobile calls to the file at hand before me, and I'm not surprised when I find an email.

Quinn McDermont is now dating the owner of Solutions Incorporated, one Lewis Bettford. They're at La Casa de Cancun right now, get some cameras there. I'll throw in an extra $10,000 if you get the article running tomorrow. I'll call you soon.

The email heading belongs to PersianKing16. I easily decode his profile. The name puts a grin on my face.

I compose another email and after consulting the web, I assigned eighteen recipients, eight are American and ten are British. Mandy Martinez will get all the credit. I imagine she'll ascend from the mailroom back to the investigative reporter, at least until the next time she inevitably crosses a line. Everyone deserves a fleeting triumph. She only gets one because she suits my purposes.

I set up the message to be viewed one time and only visible for exactly sixty seconds. Any attempts at printing, copying, forwarding, will simply delete the message forever.

A smile creases my lips when I recall Terence's jubilation at creating the software for these burn bag messages. The attachments will automatically take a spot on her desktop. If she's smart enough, she won't call too much attention to them and use them as background information only. I read it once more before sending it.

Ms. Martinez,

Attached to this message you'll find irrefutable evidence of tampering, espionage, and an attempt to sabotage the Play Again Foundation. Once you understand the mission of this foundation, you'll see why this can easily become the scandal of the year, and I am perfectly aware of how much your profession thrives in scandal.

The man responsible for this attempt will be on his way to the French embassy at 9am on Monday. I suggest you get your camera people ready.

In exchange, I trust there will be no more invading the privacy of Ms. Quinn McDermont.

I shall warn you that there are dire consequences, should you ever decide to test this condition, but I imagine you'll have your hands full with the articles you will be writing on a lawyer and statesman named Firuz Mohammed Ahmidi for a long time to come.

Yours truly,

A man capable of burying your career.

37

I wake on my computer chair. A painful kink on my neck prevents me from looking around, forcing me to swivel the chair. An army of ants runs over my arms, calves and feet as normal circulation is slowly restored to my limbs. I don't know when or how I fell asleep, but apparently, Mum couldn't wake me so she draped a throw blanket over me. The blanket with the white winged-wheel logo popping out of the crimson wool was a gift from Samantha a few Christmases ago. I smile at the memory of her trying to explain to me the rules of hockey while watching her Detroit Red Wings battle it out with a team from Colorado.

In a few hours, she'll be married to Jason. Today is their day, and I won't allow my ongoing drama to spoil it for them.

I pad through the living room and shower. The hot water feels like heaven on my sore neck.

By the time I emerge from the tiny bathroom amidst a cloud of steam and make it to the second floor, Mum's standing by the stove brewing tea.

"Good morning, luv."

"You look ravishing, Mum," I tell her, affectionately smiling at the crinkling of her nose at the sarcastic compliment.

"Wait until you hit my age and see how ravishing you look in the morning," she grumbles.

Every ten minutes for the next two hours, Mum asks me whether her digital camera is charged, every ten minutes without fail! I patiently reassure her that not only do I have my own camera, my mobile, but there was also a professional photographer who was hired to take a minimum of five hundred shots for the bride to choose from.

"I want my own bloody photos. There's much to be said for personal touch, son. Now, is the bloody thing charged? I can't have it quit on me today. What about spare batteries?"

She is relentless.

When Richard arrives to take Mum, she's still not ready.

Dr. Bergman looks quite debonair in his charcoal suit and ox blood red tie. His spine is straight and his shoulders are still wider than his middle, not a common occurrence in many men his age.

We engage in football talk, discussing the latest imminent trade of one of the better players in our favorite squad when Mum finally declares she's ready.

She wears a red blouse, that matches Richard's tie, under an elegantly cut taupe pant suit. A slight shade of pink draws her smiling lips and pearls adorn her earlobes and neck. She looks so striking that neither of us remembers to offer a compliment until she demands one from us, clearly not content with our stunned silence to be enough.

I leave the lovebirds and drive to St. Mary Magdalene Abbots Church. Since I'm part of the wedding party, I'm allowed to park in a small lot at the back of the impressive stone structure.

Father Thomas Scheller, a florid, handsomely bald, rotund man in his sixties, greets me warmly, despite the fact that I've only met him one other time when Samantha and Jason were taking a marriage course. He proclaims this to be a great day before guiding me to where the men are changing.

Nathan is already looking like the lead man in a James Bond film, while Jason Soderbergh looks the part of an Italian mob hit man, his barrel chest testing the seams on the jacket of his tux. He greets me amiably but I can't help being a bit cold, knowing he'll be the one escorting Quinn for the day.

Reminding myself that he is not at fault, I ease into a quick exchange of security measures, and of course, football. I change into the tuxedo, noting with a bit of vanity that the jacket hangs well on my tall, slight build.

Out of all the men there, I spend the most time getting my hair just right while Soderbergh and Nathan rib me good-naturedly.

Jason paces by the window, his eyes never leaving the looped drive of the church grounds.

"She's late," he says, giving the clock on the wall an anxious look.

"Get used to it chap," Nathan jokes.

"I sent her six texts so far, she hasn't responded yet," Jason grumbles.

"She'll make your wait worthwhile," I say soothingly, knowing there's nowhere in that dress where Sam could keep a bloody mobile.

Jason gives me a grateful look. "Thanks, I needed that."

"Not at all."

"Hey, she's here!" Soderbergh points out the window. "What is that?" Soderbergh asks in awe of the long vehicle gliding on the drive.

Nathan squints for a second. "That, gentlemen, is a 1960 Rolls Royce Silver Cloud. One of the finest British luxury sedans ever built."

The limousine's long bonnet is adorned by a gleaming chrome grill, and a bumper that protects the exaggerated curve of its fenders. Its rear swoops down from the roof, giving it an aura of perpetual motion. A chrome triple-pronged hubcap pops out of the center of each whitewall tire, and the paint seems to glisten like wet pearls under the sunlight.

The Silver Cloud rolls to a stop at the bottom of the main stone stairway leading to the large front doors. A driver, smartly dressed in a long jacket and white gloves, affixes a cap on his head and walks to the rear where he holds the door open.

Alicia is a vision of resplendence as she emerges from the limo.

Lorna's exorbitant fee is justified just on the suggestion of adopting the tangerine tango color for the gowns. The former model glides elegantly over the stone walkway and up the steps, a small bouquet of deep reds and tiger lilies in her gloved hands.

The next beauty to climb out is Gwen Amaya. With her hair held up in a French twist, with delicate, wavy tendrils of brown silk framing her lovely face, she is by far the most ravishing mother of two I've ever seen.

"That Tony is quite a lucky man," Nathan comments.

I look at Jason for a reaction, but he holds a pleasant smile on his chiseled face.

Soderbergh looks awestricken. "I love American women." He gives us a sheepish look when we all turn to look at him in surprise. "I mean, right you are, lad. Lucky indeed."

We laugh.

The next two figures out of the limo are Gwen's daughters, Brooke and Emily. My heart bursts with pride and a deep affection as my breath is taken away by the sight of them. Brooke, raven-haired, and willowy, as elegant as her mother, puts one dainty foot in front of the other and reaches out to hold her little sister's hand.

With her light brown hair bobbing as she walks, her merry dark eyes, and the knowing little grin I've come to adore, Emily's tiny features look even more elvin than usual.

"Will you look at that," Nathan says in awe of the tiny doll.

"Adorable," Jason adds.

There's something quite heartwarming about seeing combat veterans turn to marshmallows at the sight of a little girl in a dress. Jason has a terribly soft spot for Brooke and Emily, who lovingly regard him like a brand new toy. I can't help thinking I should've spent more time with them, instead of...

"Never have I seen a car full of so much beauty," Soderbergh quips, earning a pat on the back from Nathan.

"Be nothing less than a gentleman, lad."

"Yes, Sir," responds Soderbergh, his mouth hanging open.

Quinn McDermont's height puts her between Brooke and Samantha, but there's no denying this heavenly creature is a fully grown depiction of devastating feminine beauty.

I almost give in to the impulse to utter that I know every inch of that beautiful body, just to wipe the awed smirk from Soderbergh's face.

I try to peel my eyes off Quinn's figure and I'm able to do so only when I hear someone gasp. When my eyes find the limo, I notice the driver offering both hands to the last figure to climb out, Samantha.

Everything blurs into the background sharpening the focus on the breathtaking loveliness of the bride.

"Don't look, chap. It's bad luck," Soderbergh warns. When I look at Jason, I'm surprised to find him facing the wall, heeding his friend's advice. His eyes are shut tight, as though in fervent prayer. I'd be praying too if I was in his shoes, I think with a smile.

Nathan reaches into the inside pocket of his tux and pulls out a handkerchief to wipe at his eyes. "May Kath and Jack look down on their daughter from above," he says reverently.

"And Grandmum," I add silently.

With a sense of family, forged by common loss, I put my hand on Nathan's shoulder and Jason does the same.

"Lewis, no woman has ever had a finer friend," Nathan says to me, causing a large lump of emotion to form in my throat.

"Jason, I'm proud to see you as the man you've become, and I'm thankful, knowing Samantha Kay will be in good hands when I'm gone. May you live forever in love, son."

I clench my fists hoping against hope not to break down right here. Given the quivering of his chin, Jason is struggling to contain his own emotions.

Behind us, Soderbergh blows his nose into a handful of tissues then shrugs sheepishly when we turn, unable to believe that Jason, "Granite Man" Soderbergh, cries like a child at weddings.

"It's all so… beautiful," he manages in a shaky, gravelly voice, before honking his nose once more.

A knock on the door pulls our focus away from the window. "Lewis?"

"Mum?" I quickly go to the door and open it.

"I need you at the anteroom for a minute, luv."

"What is it?"

"Our lovely flower girls are a bit nervous. I think seeing you will help them settle down. They won't have it from the girls."

"Let's go."

***

Jason is pale, so pale I'm wondering how I could possibly keep his muscular frame from hitting the ground should he faint.

Weddings do funny things to men, especially those of us so heavily invested in the affair.

"Are you well?" I finally ask.

He nods slowly a few times, eyes wide. "Not at all."

"Guess that's why they have the girl walk down," Soderbergh muses.

I have to agree. Easier to stand in place, by the looks of it.

"Just breathe a few times, clear your head," Nathan coaches.

"Yes, Sir," Jason responds in a robotic voice that prompts Nathan to exchange a concerned look with me.

"Come now, Jason. Relax, old chap," Nathan soothes.

"I think I'd be more relaxed facing enemy fire, Sir."

This time Nathan takes Jason by the shoulders and pierces him with a hard gaze that stops the trembling of his hands.

Nathan nods once. "Alright?"

"I think so, yes. Thank you."

We are standing to the side of the altar with Father Thomas, watching anxiously as the groom becomes unresponsive. As groomsmen, we collectively offer our moral support until the last second, which has finally arrived.

Father Thomas motions for Jason to follow and we straighten our backs and follow them. The groom cuts a strapping figure, his face a mask of determination as he joins the smiling priest at the altar.

"Relax, son," Father Thomas whispers. "I pray you only do this once."

"Yes, Sir." Jason smiles, finally looking more relaxed since we were told it was time to start.

The three of us stand in our assigned places, uncomfortable with the scrutiny of over two hundred and fifty people. We know the majority of them since they work at Lions Securities.

The pianist begins to play Pachelbel's "Cannon in D Major", the music effectively settles my own nerves which short circuit when the doors open and I see Quinn.

She holds her bouquet in a demure two hand grip in front of her, her blue eyes soft, a subtle smile on her lips. Her blonde hair falls across her face and I feel my legs tense up as I quell the urge to run up and sweep the silken gold but with a shake of her head, the strands are back in place.

I'm fully aware of where I'm standing, and who's watching over me from the cross. With the memories that assault me at this moment, I expect a bolt of lightning to reduce me to a pile of ashes any second now.

Quinn's eyes focus on Father Thomas, who smiles at the lovely sight in a much more benign way than some of the men in the pews.

Nathan pats my shoulder, a proud smile on his patrician face.

As much as I want to look away, my eyes mutiny against my brain, tracking Quinn's every movement as though my very existence depends on keeping the lovely image in sharp focus.

I try not to notice the dopey smile on Soderbergh's face, though several male visages sport the very same expression.

Quinn smiles brightly at Jason then casts a sad glance at me that is bound to haunt me for the rest of my existence. When she takes her place at the far end, her eyes remain downcast and her lips move in silent prayer.

I'd give anything to stop this horrid needful ache to touch her.

There's a current of murmurs when Alicia glides down the aisle. She's easily the most distinguished woman in the entire kingdom. As she makes her way to her place, Alicia blows a kiss to Jason producing the first hint of color on his face since Father Thomas came to fetch us from the changing room.

"Way to go, boss," Soderbergh quips to Nathan, who smiles proudly.

There seems to be more unfamiliar faces than I expected. But just when I start trying to put names to the faces, every pair of eyes turns back to the top of the aisle and fixates upon the beautiful woman walking down the aisle.

Gwen gives the groom a decidedly sexy wink and a grin that seems to do much to put him at ease. He's at least breathing normally, though his face is still a bit chalky.

"You're doing fine, chap," I encourage him.

"Thanks, Lewis."

At first, I was stunned when I was asked to stand at the right of the groom, as the best man soon after the engagement was announced. Jason Stephen McElroy enjoys celebrity status at Lions, and I could think of a dozen blokes who are better friends to the groom than I've ever been. I mentioned this, but he only smiled and said, "Sam and I would've never happened without you, and that makes you the best man there is."

In typical Lewis Bettford fashion, I shed some tears. I couldn't help it. The memory makes me stand a bit straighter. When I recall some of the conversations Jason and I have shared lately, it does much to put me at ease, as though justifying my position as best man.

The crowd makes a unanimous *Aww* as the flower girls stand at the top of the aisle, looking uncertain until their eyes find mine. I take a moment to bask in the sight, which grows blurry before a curtain of tears that I blink back.

I'm praying this part goes without a hitch.

Earlier, after Mum came to get me, I approached the girls, who regarded me with a grateful look, making me feel like a hero.

"I don't want people laughing at me," Emily said with severity, her pouting lip emphasizing her plight.

"I'm so afraid of messing up," Brooke said in a small voice.

I gave them my best smile and huddled them closer. "Remember our little game of silent talk?"

The girls exchanged a look then nodded.

"I'm good at that game," Emily stated proudly while Brooke rolled her eyes.

The smiles on their faces told me they just may be receptive enough for the second part of my plan. The game consisted of mouthing words and seeing who can guess what the word was, a lip reading exercise.

"Very well, we're going to play while you make your way down the aisle. I'll mouth the word, but you may have to step closer to guess it. You'll have to keep your eyes on me the best you can, and each time I give you a signal, you throw a handful of petals on the floor."

"On the floor?" Emily said with wide eyes.

I nod. "On the floor, get it nice and dirty with petals."

Emily's eyes narrowed in suspicion. "Is Mommy going to make us clean it up?"

Mum and I couldn't escape the sudden laughter that echoed off the walls of the anteroom.

"Not at all, little luv. We'll make Mommy clean it up later."

"And if she doesn't, we'll beat her butt," Emily said eagerly.

"Brooke, are you in?"

"Keep our eyes on you, throw petals when you give the signal, and guess the word. Got it."

"And beat Mommy's butt if she doesn't clean it up," Emily reminds her.

More laughter echoed in the anteroom.

"Great."

"Wait, what's the signal?" Brooke asked anxiously.

I rubbed at my nose with my thumb. "That's the signal."

"Okay," they agreed in unison.

After that, I could only hope they'd do well on their flowery assignment.

Their moment to shine is upon them and I hope they didn't forget our little game.

They look around nervously until they see me wave at them from the altar. When I have their attention, I mouth the word *chocolate* and rub my nose with my thumb. Brooke nudges Emily and together they reach into their decorated baskets and pull a fistful of red petals that they gently scatter as they walk. I see Brooke squinting and I mouth *chocolate* once again.

Emily smiles wickedly as a blitzkrieg of flashes opens up before them. The lightshow catches their attention for a brief moment before their eyes are fixed on me once again. I rub my nose and they scatter more petals. When Brooke mouths the given word, I rub my nose twice and they scatter the petals in a celebratory fashion, no longer intimidated by the adoring gazes bestowed upon them.

I then mouth the word *butterfly,* and the girls approach the altar with dazzling smiles. When they reach us, Gwen leaves her place to usher the girls to their seat on the first pew alongside the bridesmaids. Before sitting, Emily runs to me and looks up.

"Butterfly!" She exclaims and I nod as a current of laughter mingles with another *Aww*. "See? I told you I was good at this game," she says primly.

Gwen reaches for her little hand and walks her back to the pew, instructing her to be quiet after kissing her little forehead. When I look for Brooke, she winks and mouths a thank you, gracing me with her dimpled smile. I wink back.

"It's time, young Lewis," Father Thomas instructs.

I smile, pat Jason's back one more time, and quietly walk off to the side door we used to come in. I quickly turn the corner back up to the anteroom where my heart stops at the sight of my Samantha Kay standing alone, her pretty face lightly covered behind her veil.

I remember holding her hair at the bridal shop to simulate an updo, the image on the mirror leaving me speechless. With the professional touch of a stylist, Samantha's chestnut hair is neatly arranged in a perfect twist that shows off her lovely visage. The light, earth-toned makeup brings out the opaline quality of her gorgeous eyes and her lips are shaded in a peach hue that I can't look away from.

I stare at her, wanting to etch this image in my head forevermore.

"I was going to ask you what you thought," she says in a less than even tone, tremulous with emotion.

My only response is a pair of tears that run for the corners of my lips as I manage a smile.

Samantha steps up to me and takes my arm. "I was hoping you'd say that."

After Pachelbel's timeless composition rings to an end, I hear the shuffling of everyone standing, turning to the doors. The pianist plays a soft melody that reminds me of a music box I heard when I was a kid. The music springs a deluge of memories of one of the kindest women I ever knew, Kathleen Reddick, my best friend's mum.

"Is this…?" My voice fades as a choked sob escapes my throat.

Lewis, get it bloody together, by George!

But I ignore the voice because with the simple notes of this particular song, the true extent of our bond fills my heart with feelings I can't name. God, I love this woman like the little sister she truly is to me.

Samantha nods and her eyes glitter with unshed tears that tell me she shares my sentiments. "First Love," she says with a lovely smile that helps center me. "I still have the music box."

After our last ballet recital together, when we were ten, Kathleen and Jack Reddick presented me with a box of expensive chocolates, flowers for both of us, and Samantha got a tiny music box.

"Whenever you listen to it," Kathleen told us in her soft voice. "Remember how proud I am of you both."

On each of her visits from America, Samantha brought the music box and sometimes allowed me to keep it until she returned. Today it's the center piece of a glass cabinet where I display some of my academic and business achievements. It's been there since Samantha asked me to keep it while she was in rehab.

The memory of Samantha's parents makes me choke back another sob. "They're looking at you right now, luv."

She squeezes my arm. "Lewis, don't do this to me right now. I'm barely holding it together."

With a herculean effort, I manage a wry grin. "You're right. I can't keep everyone waiting from basking in my good looks."

She sniffles once and shakes her head with a smile. "You're such a diva, sometimes."

I take her hand in a delicate grip, both of us facing straight forward. "For the record, I'm not ever giving you away."

She smiles. "I was hoping you'd say that."

Two ushers open the doors and I hear a collective gasp of adoration. I doubt that anyone will blink while Samantha glides over the scattered petals on her way to the altar.

Have you ever lived a moment in your life where absolute perfection reigned supreme? I'm happy to say that as I walk with my best friend, my little sister, my confidant, my enabler, my lovable pain in the bloody arse, my Samantha Kay, I am living a moment of pure perfection.

A Dante Alighieri's quote resonates in every confine of my being, and I finally understand where such timeless inspiration can be found.

The moment feels like a final passage from turmoil to peace. The union of these two, once broken, souls has the power of healing not just themselves and their past wounds—like those of losing your parents, like Samantha or losing yourself, like Jason Stephen. It can also heal those of us who may be away from the one we love, like Gwen or to those of us who struggle with the disillusion of flawed love, like Quinn, and to those of us nursing a broken heart, like me.

I manage to give Quinn an understanding smile, finding such needed relief in her reciprocation of the gesture, that the worst of the pain fades enough to allow me to bear witness to the forging of the two souls at the altar.

If life decides I don't get to write my own love story, then I'll be quite happy having a small part in today, for I realize I'm not a witness to the end of something as I previously thought. I will be a part of my best friend's life forever.

As the vows and rings are exchanged, I realize we are all here to celebrate an important part in the book of our lives. I know now I'm not losing my best friend at all. We are here together to begin writing the next chapter.

***

After a heartfelt sermon, pointed with just the right amount of humor, Father Thomas prompts the couple to hold hands and look at each other. The entire congregation stands and goes still to allow two voices to be heard in the exchange of vows.

Father Thomas nods to Jason.

"Today, Samantha Kay, I join my life to yours," Jason says in his strong voice. "Not merely as your husband, but as your friend, your lover, and your confidant. Let me be the shoulder you lean on, the rock on which you rest, the companion of your life." There's a hitch in his voice and given the gleam in his eyes, I can tell he's struggling with the emotion of the moment. "With you I will walk my path from this day forward."

Samantha's visibly shaking. She tries to smile but it looks more like a grimace as she fights to compose herself.

"Samantha," Father Thomas nods in her direction.

She nods at him then turns her tear-filled gaze to her groom. "Jason, I was lost and alone. No sense of purpose or being. No comprehension of family, love, friendship or honor, and then I met you." She stifles a sob as best she can and continues. "Where there has been cold, you have brought warmth; where my life was dark, you have brought light. You invited me into your world and asked for nothing in return."

A wave of emotion makes her look down for a beat.

"So what can I say to you that I haven't already said, what can I give you that I haven't already given, is there anything of me that isn't yours already, my body, my mind, my heart, even my soul. Everything that is me belonged to you long before this, and it shall be yours long after this. I will go wherever you will go. Hand in hand and heart in heart."

I'm so choked up I can't even breathe. A quick glance around reveals tearful smiles everywhere I look.

Father Thomas blesses the rings, prompting me to hand them to him.

Jason takes the dainty golden ring and slides it on Samantha's ring finger. It joins her diamond ring perfectly.

"With this ring I thee wed. Wear it as a symbol of our love and commitment."

Samantha's smile has never sparkled more. She takes the proffered thicker band and shakily slides it onto Jason's ring finger.

"With this ring I thee wed. Wear it as a symbol of our love and commitment."

Father Thomas stretches his arms wide and speaks in a voice full of merriment. "May this couple be prepared to continue to give, be able to forgive and experience more and more joy with each passing day, with each passing year. Jason Stephen and Samantha Kay, are now beginning their married life together, we hope that they may have loving assistance from their family, the constant support of friends, and a long life with good health and everlasting love. In so much as Jason Stephen and Samantha Kay have consented to live forever together in wedlock, and have witnessed the same before this company, having given and pledged their troth, each to the other, and having declared same by the giving and receiving of a ring, I pronounce that they are husband and wife."

With a twinkle in his eye, Father Thomas says, "Jason, you may now kiss your bride."

Samantha seems to leap into Jason as he lowers his face and kisses her softly, long enough for a resounding cheer to echo off the walls as the pianist and a vocalist join efforts in a poignant rendition of Innuendo's "Until The End Of Time."

38

The Rolls Royce Silver Cloud whisks the bride and groom away. The rest of the wedding party boards a minibus and we follow the limo out to Rosenthal Gardens.

"That was so beautiful!" Gwen gushes to Alicia and Quinn.

It's taking a great effort for me to keep from staring at the blonde beauty. At times, she tries to find my eyes, which I quickly avert. It's torture enough to be enclosed in the same vehicle with her. So close, yet so far away.

I'm sitting at the back of the bus, flanked by Brooke and Emily. They lean against me as though they've run a marathon.

"Are we going home?" Emily asks in a hopeful little voice.

"Not just yet, little luv. We are going to get our photographs taken."

"Em, they're going to take pictures of us. It'll be fun!" Brooke promises.

Emily pouts, not happy with having to follow directions.

"Yes, and after the photographs, we're going to have the biggest cake you've ever seen!"

Emily's eyes go wide as a smile spreads across her face. "For real?"

"Absolutely. That's why you have to listen to what we tell you and smile pretty for the camera. Do we have a deal?"

Emily mulls this over. "Okay, but I want two pieces of cake." She shows me two little fingers so there's no mistake.

"If you can manage, I'll spring for three pieces," I offer.

Emily sits back, an eager little grin on her face.

"Did you not learn enough about sugar rushes, from the other night?" Gwen says in her mommy voice.

"How many pieces of cake will you have?"

"Knowing I probably won't have to wear this gorgeous gown again? Probably ten!"

Everyone laughs at this, but I only hear Quinn's pretty laughter, cutting into my heart. I glance at her and she quickly looks down at her hands, pretending to listen to whatever Soderbergh is saying.

When the minibus stops, we step out into the sun. I'm grateful for their decision to set up the wedding for this time of year. The cool breeze keeps our skin dry and comfortable. Gwen told me about the torture she endured during her friend's wedding in August. American summers are notorious for the blasted humidity and I break into a sweat just thinking about facing that climate in a full tuxedo.

Rosenthal Gardens boasts one of the most extensive collection of roses in the entire United Kingdom. Their perfume elicits a gasp from every visitor.

Lorna Matthews and her assistant are busily propping Samantha's train under the direction of the photographer. They strike a series of poses from every angle. After running through what sounded to me like a hundred shots, the man turns to the wedding party and we subject ourselves to his whims.

Carson proves to be a creative photographer. At one point he has all the men wear sunglasses and tells us to look fierce, which reduces the women to a fit of giggles. Carson also has Samantha lay across our arms. Nathan takes her feet and Soderbergh takes her thighs, his face reddening at the contact. I'm the lucky chap to support her fanny and Jason easily holds the rest of her.

I stand proudly, holding Gwen in my arms as Carson blinds us with the powerful flash that seems unnecessary, considering the brightness of the day. I can feel Quinn staring at us as she waits in line to pose with Soderbergh.

Nathan and Alicia strike a series of classical poses. The camera loves Alicia, according to Carson.

When Soderbergh stands behind Quinn and wraps his arms around her, I feel a pang of jealousy that leaves an acidic taste in my mouth. Heeding his creative nature, Carson instructs Soderbergh to lift Quinn into his arms. I have to bite my lip and turn away as his arms move under her body, making me fume. When they're done, Quinn gives me a look that seems to say "doesn't feel too good, does it?"

"Hey." Gwen takes my arm. "Why don't you try talking to her a bit more and glaring a bit less."

I curse myself for being so obvious.

Brooke and Emily steal the show as their beautiful smiles captivate not only Carson, but the entire wedding party. Emily asks Carson whether he's done after every shot, frowning when he begs her for one more, but smiling wide before the shot.

When Carson pronounces his job is done, Emily is so happy she hugs the surprised photographer.

"Where's the bloody cake?"

Everyone laughs with the exception of Gwen, who gives her little girl a stern look to which Emily replies with an exaggerated shrug.

We follow a graceful stone walk up to the back of the building where Lorna's assistant double checks hair, gowns, and bowties, before sending us into the reception area.

I can hear a DJ talking out of the speakers make an announcement then calling out Soderbergh and Quinn's names. Holding hands, they enter the hall to a wave of cheer.

Nathan and Alicia are next and when they get to the door, Nathan grins mischievously and shocks everyone by picking up a squealing Alicia off the ground and carrying her into the hall to a chorus of hoots and laughter.

I glance at Gwen with an impish grin.

"Don't you dare!" She warns.

Samantha and Jason laugh behind us.

"Please welcome the best man, Lewis Bettford and our matron of honor, Gwen Amaya!"

Gwen takes a deep breath, fixes her dazzling smile upon her face and steps forward. As we cross the threshold, I take her hand and raise it high in the air like I'm announcing the winner of a boxing match. We join the other two couples and turn as the DJ announces our little flower girls.

Brooke wears a nervous smile, quickly shuffling over to us, but Emily stops halfway, turns in a circle waving like Queen Elizabeth and then bows in every direction.

"Oh, she's such a ham!" Gwen exclaims, pride oozing from every word.

"And now, ladies and gentlemen, please help me welcome the couple of the hour, our bride and groom, Jason and Samantha McElroy!"

As soon as the fairy tale couple enters the hall, the entire assembly begins chanting a demand for a kiss. Samantha stops and stands in front of Jason. She yanks his head down and kisses him so hard, every woman over forty blushes fiercely while the younger lot hoots, hollers, and whistles in approval, the loudest and most piercing one coming from Quinn, who is regarded by Soderbergh with complete and utter admiration.

While Jason's complexion rivals the hue of the bridal roses, Samantha looks very much at ease, queen of the unashamed public display of affection.

Never before have I ever witnessed so many tears of joy. I've picked up three empty tissue dispensers in my efforts to help Margaret and the caterers with the cleanup, after they agree to extend their service another two hours. When Lorna Matthews frets over the costs of keeping her help on the clock, I hand her a blank check and kiss her cheek before propping a tall flute of champagne in her pudgy hand.

The caterers do a fantastic job of synchronized service and have everyone fed and happy in time for the real festivities. The videographer ends up sending his assistant out for a dozen more blank digital tapes since nearly everyone in the place has something to say to the bride and groom. The photographer moves around with several expensive looking cameras hanging from his neck. I don't believe I ever get a good look at the bloke's face since half of it is always covered by a camera.

Nearly everyone working at Lions asks me to introduce them to Gwen and her girls. I'm glad for the chore. It gives me something to focus on, other than Soderbergh swooning over Quinn, who politely laughs at his terrible jokes.

The cutting of the cake brings everyone to their feet and they let out a disappointed groan as neither bride, nor groom, smash a handful of icing on each other's faces. Something about the way Samantha looks around tells me it's a ruse. She rubs a handful of red velvet and vanilla moose icing all over her husband's handsome face.

Jason Stephen picks her up over his shoulder and threatens to dip her, face first into the cake to the clamor of the crowd. When she threatens to call off the wedding night, Jason relents and takes another handful of cake to the face.

The cover band Lorna hired sets up after the string quartet departs once the dinner is concluded. After tuning their instruments, the lead singer, a pretty little redhead announces the first dance and launches into a beautiful, poignant rendition of Norah Jones's "Come Away With Me", making me smile in approval.

Samantha looks adoringly into Jason's eyes as they glide gracefully, cutting a striking depiction of idealistic romance. They seem to have eyes for no one else, and that's exactly the way it should be.

In order for the rest of us to join the bride and groom on the dance floor, Jessie, the vocalist asks the bride and groom to make a request to one another.

Jason surprises everyone by quickly whispering something in Jessie's ear, as though he's been anticipating the question.

After passing along a few instructions to her band, the keyboardist plays the familiar intro to Franki Valli's "Can't Take My Eyes Off Of You," and invites the rest of the wedding party onto the floor.

Gwen laughs with delight as I send her into different spins and lead her through maneuvers I haven't practiced in a couple decades, but which I never forgot. Soderbergh and Quinn are severely outdanced and I draw perverse satisfaction out of her less than pleased expression on her face.

Jessie calls Samantha to get her request.

"She's going with a Beatles number."

"She's going hip-hop," Gwen says.

"At a bloody wedding?" I ask in disbelief.

"I've twenty pounds that say I'm right."

"It's a wager."

No one is more astonished than I when Jessie bops and raps to Salt and Peppa's "What A Man" with infectious glee.

"That'll be twenty pounds Sterling, *luv*. I take cash, check, credit, or we can come to a business agreement," Gwen teases.

"Sheer bloody extortion!"

Gwen laughs prettily.

Samantha grinds her shapely form against a blushing groom, eliciting a barrage of camera flashes and raucous laughter. Not to be outdone, Gwen moves in a way that defies the anatomical limits of the human body. She gets down so low, her face is only inches from my belt buckle. Around us, several men have stopped to stare, their mouths a perfect O of lustful bewilderment.

Out of the corner of my eye, I see Quinn shooting daggers at Gwen. When she looks into my eyes, I blink away from their intensity and I actually feel a pang of guilt.

The number concludes with an ovation.

When the applause dies down, Jessie calls my name. I raise my hand and heed her call to the microphone.

"Hullo everyone, is this a smash or what?"

A loud cheer floats up into the cupola of the spacious hall.

"For those of you, who don't know, my name is Lewis Bettford and I've known our lovely bride, Samantha, my entire life."

A wave of applause crests over my words then quickly ebbs into a silence filled with anticipation.

"When they say opposites attract, they surely had Sam and I in mind. She's into books, I'm into doing. She's smart, I'm not; she's quite attractive, but I'm downright beautiful, and—"

My voice is drowned out in another deluge of applause, laugher, and cheering that doesn't abate until I politely motion for quiet.

"She is the writer and reader, so naturally the gift of gab was bestowed upon me perhaps for just this occasion, for I've been charged with making The Toast." I scan the smiling faces, careful not to let my focus stay on any one person for very long, and continue. "Samantha and I have shared everything in our lives, cribs, tutus, mothers, fathers, grandmothers…" The image of the beloved Lady Reddick of Birkenhead rises in my heart, choking my voice for a moment.

At the head of the table of honor, Samantha is sitting on Jason's lap, holding on for dear life as the tears threaten. I quickly look away from her to keep us both from crying and address my captivated audience. "For thirty-four years we've seen the best of each other, as well as the worst. Our friendship has survived intact despite the passage of time, or the entire Atlantic between us for a good part of our lives. Samantha, luv, I haven't told you how good it is to have you home."

Samantha mouths a thank you as another wave of applause echoes in the large hall.

"We've also survived circumstance, and in Samantha's case, perhaps more tragedy than any one person ought to endure. You're a survivor, Samantha, the strongest person I know."

I pause to collect myself before continuing. "I've also known Jason for a number of years. First by name, and now as a dear friend, who's going to need all the help in the world when Samantha has one of her infamous moments."

"HEY!" Samantha yells, wagging a finger at me, as laughter bubbles up from every corner in the hall.

"My best friend has grown into a magnificent woman, a true feat considering some earlier history that shall remain in the dark where it belongs, for as a great friend once told me, it's better to look ahead. The past is past." I nod as Gwen blows me a kiss.

No one moves, waiting for more, but my words give many a reason to reassess Samantha.

"Jason Stephen McElroy may have been cut out of the same tough cloth, for his own story has instilled in me a profound admiration and respect. Few people have an idea of what it's like to don the uniform, and fight for Queen and country, and I trust you are all grateful to them."

Several of the men, clearly combat veterans, stand to give me a quick ovation.

"Thank you, lads. As if that's not enough, Jason's protected my best friend more than she even knew, and I know for certain he'll protect her heart with his own life. Perhaps it's their past that brought them together. Perhaps it was the recognition of a kindred spirit; seeing in one another that part of themselves they once thought lost, and it's a privilege to be a part of their lives. I believe it was a moment such as this that inspired one Dante Alighieri to ink these words upon a piece of parchment, and the best way I can express to you to look ahead." I pause, hoping to hold back the lump of emotion stealing my voice. "Remember tonight... for it's the beginning of always." You could hear a pin drop in that second.

"Here's to you Jason and Samantha McElroy. I wish for you success, love, and health, today, and every day. I love you both."

Hundreds of glasses are raised and as I look around, it's difficult to find a dry eye in the house.

Mission accomplished...

It's a struggle to find my way back to my seat as people shake my hand, pat my back, and even kiss my cheeks, congratulating me on a great toast. It dawns on me that I never wrote a single word of that.

"My name is Gwen Amaya."

Gwen's classic good looks easily command the attention of every guest. Her voice is clear and infused with a pleasant dialect that cancels out the expectation of a New York accent, and quickly rivets everyone's attention.

"Lewis, you did such an amazing job that I'm not sure how to follow. Didn't he?"

A deafening wave of applause ensues, forcing me to stand and acknowledge the ovation. I blow Gwen a kiss and she smiles brightly as some people plead for her to continue.

"Back home, in Pennsylvania, we usually reserve this opportunity to poke fun at the bride and groom, and Samantha knows I could deliver some pretty fatal blows."

A current of laughter moves through the crowd and it grows in volume as everyone registers the fearful expression on Samantha, along with the subtle shake of her head.

"I will say that Samantha and I have indeed shared *everything*, once or twice, right Sam?"

Samantha's face has never looked more crimson that I can recall. Her nervous giggle carries with it a pleading note for her matron of honor to shut her gob.

A cold rock drops in the pit of my stomach as I recall Gwen's demeanor when I made the mistake of bringing up the events of last winter, when Samantha seduced Tony.

"So, I guess we're now sisters under the skin, and I couldn't be happier to see my sister in the arms of a man who would gladly lay down his life for her. Jason, I'll never forget our conversation, Samantha is a very lucky woman to have you, but as the matron of honor, it is my duty to add this. Jason Stephen, take care of my sister, take care of each other, and remember the way today feels.

It's so much better later. And no, Sam, I'm not talking about the bloody wedding night."

As the guests applaud and laugh heartily, Samantha leaves Jason and runs barefoot up to Gwen who spreads her arms and they embrace as the sisters under the skin they really are.

Pity, I think. I really wanted to see Gwen punch the bride in the eye.

Jessie takes the microphone from Gwen and in a shaky voice, calls out for the bride and groom. Once they stand in the middle of the dance floor, Jessie hands the microphone to the nearly unrecognizable Audrey Burton.

With every step she takes, the jingling of the chains around her heavy combat boots rings out of the speakers. Audrey is wearing a dress however, and her face is actually passably human.

All she offers is a heartfelt "congratulations" before unveiling the portrait I saw the last day I talked with her. The reaction to the painting is somewhere between awe and rapture. Audrey took a still frame from Disney's *Beauty and the Beast*, and morphed the characters into accurate likenesses of Samantha and Jason, rendered in amazing detail. To make the painting her own, she made a few changes, like putting Samantha in a jade Versace gown, and Jason in full armor. To anyone else, it was a remarkable painting. To those closest to the couple, it had quite a bit of meaning.

In the typical style of an Audrey Burton painting, there were elements in the painting that the average eye wouldn't normally catch, such as the clear tall bottle standing on a small table on the far side of Lancelot. The checkered floor also contained a little clue about the couple depicted in the foreground. One of the tiles was shaded in the shape of the Conspicuous Gallantry ribbon that Jason earned during his time in the SAS. A seemingly innocent looking column over Samantha's shoulder is decorated after the First Gulf War Medal ribbon that had once been emblazoned on his uniform over his heart. I only know this from having read Jason's profile at Lions Securities.

The open book on Samantha's hand is no accident either. On the spine, you could make the back half of the Spades Publishing logo and a stenciled word on the cover that is almost unreadable but I know it says, *The Composition*.

After what I said in the toast, it feels like Audrey is conveying the same message. Audrey's painting easily makes my eyes see it as a three-dimensional depiction where Samantha and Jason are at the very front of the scene while everything else is behind them. The book in her hands may be symbolic of marking the point at which they fell in love.

I watch Audrey embrace the couple before a line of people rush to get a better look at the portrait, and to congratulate the artist, who's become far more gracious with praise than I could ever remember.

Once she finally extricates herself, Audrey comes to stand by me, a proud smile on her face.

"Blimey, this makes me want to tie the bloody knot. What do you say, Lewis? If we can't trap someone in the next two years, we should just get it done, and pull ourselves off the bloody market."

I smile at her. "Sounds tempting, but you snore too loud."

Audrey laughs.

"Beautiful work, as usual, Audrey."

"Thanks, luv. I can't wait to paint yours one day."

I can only sigh as I catch sight of Quinn stepping up to look at the painting.

39

The band returns and launches into a musical celebration themed after recent decades, doing much to allow me to put Quinn out of my mind for the time being.

Jessie sings everything from Annie Heart to Pat Benatar then gives the crowd a chance to rest by doing a set of ballads from Celine Dion to Matchbox 20. Before accepting requests, she once again calls my name and Samantha's. We stand on the dance floor and Jessie again instructs her band. When the first notes of Carole King's "You've Got a Friend" start playing, her eyes instantly liquefy.

I lead her into an easy waltz that allows me to hold her close enough for me to sing the words in her ear, meaning every single one, despite the worsening of her crying. I need her to know that I'm happy for her. I need her to know that I understand that I'm not being cast aside. I need her to know that I love her, more than words can say.

"And now," Jessie calls. "We've entered all your names into a computer and we're going to scramble everyone's dates. For one song, you will have a different partner than the one you came in with. Allow me to warn you, a lot of extra weddings have spawned off these scrambles. Now, be nice and polite and ask your matched partner 'may I please have this dance?'"

The crowd laughs as they surreptitiously find a desirable mate to dance with.

Two of the band members bring in two large flat monitors and after a minute, two columns of names appear on them.

"Let the scramble begin!" shouts Jessie and the names on the screens begin spinning like markers on a slot machine.

When the screens are still once again, there's a mad scramble as people hurriedly try to find their mates. Total strangers grin shyly at each other as they take up a position on the dance floor. The matching produces some comical pairings, like my mother dancing with a puppy-eyed lad who works in the mail room. He's barely out of secondary. Gwen somehow gets Nathan, but Alicia gets a nervous lad I know from accounting, clearly intimidating at having to put his pudgy hands on the boss's fiancée. I feel for the lad.

Soderbergh gets Margaret, and I'm happy to see how politely he regards her. Jason and Samantha are exonerated from the matching. They stand at the center of the dance floor looking around with interest.

Jessie warns her audience about her next request before the band plays a familiar melody. It's an older ballad from Bad Company.

The picking of the guitar prompts every couple to hold on a bit closer, I recall the name of the song, "If You Needed Somebody."

"May I please have this dance?"

I recognize Quinn's voice and I turn to look for the fortunate lad who'll get to dance with her. That lad happens to be me.

Her eyes don't waver from mine. I can tell there's so much she wishes to say and I'm helpless against the outer shell of ice I project as I stand before her. Inside, my mental landscape is far different.

You can have anything you want... at least whatever is left...

I nod, unable to form a single word as the lyrics seem to do the talking for me.

Her eyes sparkle with intensity and I can't look away from them. I'm helpless against the tide of emotion that constricts my heart. Is this really goodbye?

How many times can a heart crumble? How much can you hurt before you ache for the need to cease to exist just to stop the bloody agony?

A part of me resents this angel before me, for placing me back in that sea as though in an attempt to drown the last of my breath. Another part of me tells me this is all I wanted, a way of saying good-bye perhaps...

I succeed in avoiding her gaze for only a few seconds. When I look into her eyes, I instantly feel the pull she so easily exerts upon me. There's apprehension in them, and an aura of remorse that I don't know how to interpret.

She places one hand on my chest and lays her head gently against me. I'm almost thankful I don't have to look into her eyes, but my entire body becomes aware of how perfectly she fits against me and a series of images from our night together awakens a terrible ache.

Though my mind formulates a plan to appear indifferent, her fingers tracing patterns on my chest easily vanquish any semblance of distance. Her eyes hold mine as I glance from them to her lips at the same time she whispers the lyrics, *like the way that I need you...*

As the song reaches its crescendo and the lead singer breaks up the song in soulful high melodies of longing, I lean my head down and Quinn raises hers. Her smoldering blue eyes are veiled under her delicate eyelids and her lips part in invitation. I know there's no retreating from this moment.

I kiss her and drink in the taste of her, not wanting to ever let go, not wanting to accept this is the last time ever.

When the song ends, so does the kiss. Quinn puts her head down and shuts her eyes tight in an attempt to keep from crying. Her hand closes around the fabric of my shirt and she doesn't move.

"I'm sorry," she whispers.

I try to ignore the ache I feel at the remorse I hear in her voice. It's not fair for her to break my heart anew. "No apologies, luv. I was glad to be your rebound."

Quinn releases my shirt, looks up with a fiery glint of anger in her eyes.

"Is that what you—?"

"I hope you enjoy the rest of your stay in London, Quinn," I cut in, surprised at the coldness in my voice.

The wounded look in her eyes doesn't match the angry expression. "Well, if you ask me, I can't wait to get home soon enough," she snaps.

"In that case, have a good flight and thank you for coming." I step back and reach into the pocket of my trousers for a tiny flash drive. "By the way, your intranet is up and running. Expect a few phone calls that will require some tough decisions. You shall obtain all the material you need via electronic correspondence."

I've never seen her look so off balance.

"I don't understand. What decisions?"

"You'll find out when you open this," I hand her the flash drive.

Quinn is visibly trembling. She takes the flash drive and looks into my eyes.

"Lewis, I—"

I can see tears in her eyes and I do all I can to harden against their effect.

"Goodbye, Quinn." I take one last look into her eyes and force my body to turn away from the love of my life.

***

The rest of the night is filled with great conversation and enough dancing to exhaust even my little dynamo, Emily. She leaves little footprints on my shoes after using my feet as stilts so she can dance like a grownup.

It's a joy to teach Brooke how to waltz. I make it a point to suggest ballet to Gwen. Brooke's long frame and graceful limbs are easily the envy of a lot of prima ballerinas. Gwen agrees and Brooke gives me a grateful hug.

I even treat each of the Moppins, Gina, Lynn, and Keri, and even a late comer named Leah, to a dance despite the resentment I irrationally harbor at them for stomping all over my sandcastle.

Jason and Samantha McElroy are subjected to a seemingly interminable round of hugs from virtually every person present before finally climbing into the limo. Gwen and I are left to argue on who got the longest hug, just another proof of Samantha's influence on Gwen, making her competitive. Best friends forever, all of us.

When the last of the caterers takes one final box out to their vans, I grab my jacket and head for the door when I hear my name called.

"I don't expect you to believe me, but I must say this was the most amazing wedding I've ever taken part of."

I smile tiredly at this energetic wedding planner. "Lorna, you did a magnificent job."

"Thank you, kind Sir. Thank you. But I'm not here to fish for a compliment, though I will reject none."

I return her broad smile. "I could go on all night."

I'm not sure why she blushes, but blush she does. "A young lady left this for you earlier." She hands me a folded note. "I don't mean to presume, but should you ever need my services, I'll gladly accommodate my schedule and allow you a handsome discount."

"I will keep your card near my heart, luv."

"Thank you, ever so much. Good night."

"Good night to you as well."

I recognize the scent of Quinn's perfume instantly.

Sometime later, when I sit in my car, I hold the folded note for a long time debating whether to even read it or not. I think of simply burning it several times, but I know the curiosity would rob whatever peace of mind I may have left.

I guess I can look forward to some time alone. It may make some departures easy to bear; though I have a feeling tomorrow will be one of the most difficult days of my life. Mum will go back to Liverpool with Richard. I couldn't be happier for her, and knowing she's but three hours away, I can stay in London, knowing she's being taken care of, knowing she is being loved.

Gwen and her adorable girls will go back to their life in the US, back to a man I envy terribly at this moment. I make a mental note to remind him the dream life he leads, that work is not all there is in life, that he needs to love Gwen and their little girls with everything he is.

I've made a great friend in Gwen, and I'm going to miss Brooke and Emily more than I can say. I'll never be able to look at a park the same way. I don't want to think of how changed they'll be the next time I see them. I don't doubt there'll be a next time, but life rolls on and its demands set limits on what we really want to do despite our defiance.

I drive back home, my eyes going to the unopened note lying on the passenger seat every few seconds. When I park the BMW, I stare at the folded paper and opt for revenge, or at least a measure of it. I give it the same sad look Quinn gave me before wordlessly walking away then I climb out of the car, abandoning the note.

***

Morning comes unmercifully fast. I quickly shower and get dressed, fretting over the impassable traffic I'll have to fight through to get out to Kensington this time of day.

Gwen sends me a text to inform me all their bags are packed, except for the four boxes full of toys and clothes that Brooke and Emily accumulated during their stay. Even Margaret, Nathan's lovely housekeeper, put in her token of affection in the form of large teddy bear shaped cookie jars, and a handmade apron for each of the girls. I vow to treat that lovable, old bird to the finest spot of tea London has ever tasted.

Mum stayed the night in the company of Gwen and the girls. I was surprised to hear the entire Kensington household enjoyed their first official slumber party, with everyone sleeping on the plush carpet of Nathan's formal living room.

I only stop to top the tank of my car then drive quickly to Kensington.

While Gwen insists on helping Margaret clean the mess the girls make out of their breakfast, I take them into the library. A pang of nostalgia fills me as I see Emily climb the spiral staircase that leads to Samantha's room.

Margaret told me all my best friend's belongings are packed and ready to go to their new home in Highgate, whenever the paperwork is finalized. They're in no rush, of course. Their honeymoon is scheduled to take the better part of a month, traveling to different destinations through the European Union.

Brooke comes to stand next to me, looking at her sister climb up and down the steps.

"Did you have fun in the Queen's Land, luv?"

"I did. I don't really want to go home yet, but I can't wait to tell my friends about my trip."

"Well, your daddy is eagerly awaiting your arrival."

"I know what *eagerly* means," she says with guarded pride. "It means impatiently, or fervently, or excitedly."

"A bookworm, are you? Where did you learn that?"

She giggles. "In a book."

Say hello to a future American novelist…

"Daddy says books are best friends."

"He's right. They can be."

She bites her lip, a gesture she does whenever she's composing a reply, and it reminds me of Quinn.

"I like a different kind of best friend," Brooke says in a sad voice.

"And what's that, luv?"

"Someone like you."

My eyes sting. "I'm honored to be your friend."

Each time she smiles, her dimples become as deep as pits on her lovely little face.

"Can I ask you something?"

"Anything, little luv."

"Do people usually cry when they're in love?"

She's got my full attention with these words. "Well, that's a pretty grownup question. I'll say that when someone's in love, they don't always cry because they're sad. They may be crying happy tears."

Brooke seems to mull this over. "So, the more they cry, the more they love someone?"

I can think of at least a hundred people I saw shedding tears at the wedding. I know because I'm one of them. What would that do to a child, other than frighten them with the realization that grownups also cry, sometimes far more than kids? "May I ask why you are so interested in this?"

Brooke looks away as she composes the answer in her head. "Last night at the reception, I went to the bathroom and found Quinn crying."

My mind flashes to the note Lorna Matthews handed me last night. I've yet to read it. "Did you ask her why she was crying?"

Brooke nods.

"And what did she say?"

"She said she was crying because she was in love. I didn't think it made sense and I told her so."

"What did she say to that?"

"She said that she really needed to start listening to her heart."

My eyes go out of focus for a moment. What would that mean? "Do you remember when this happened?"

"It was late, way after you and Mommy made everybody cry with your stories about Sam."

I tamp down the rising hope, no way am I going to allow myself to walk up to that ledge again.

"I saw you dancing together. You looked like boyfriend and girlfriend. Do you love her like a girlfriend?"

Some rational part of my mind warns me that Quinn may have been thinking about her reconciliation with her ex-husband, or husband while she cried in front of Brooke. I have no way to know of course but it's more than likely, especially after the way I pushed her away.

Brooke calls my name, expecting her question to be answered. "No more than I love you, little luv."

"I didn't mean it like that. Are you like…" two pink discs appear high on her cheeks. "Are you in love with Quinn?"

The earnest tone of her voice surprises me. "Are you sure you're only eight?"

"Eight and four months," she corrects.

"Well, why do you ask me something like that?"

"Because I asked her if she was in love with you."

My heart is suddenly gallops. "What did she say?"

"She smiled at me then she cried a little." Brooke frowns. "She said she needed one kiss to find out."

There's a buzzing in my head as my mouth goes dry. A thousand voices in my head denounce me for a fool, a proud fool, too blinded by his own self-pity.

"She's really pretty, and she'd make an awesome mum."

I smile in an attempt to hide the emotional turmoil within me. "Mum, is it?"

She grins shyly. "You guys talk so cool. I'm going to miss that."

"I've a feeling you'll be back. Hey, if it's okay with your mum and your dad, I'll fly you in for a couple of weeks each summer. That's how Samantha and me got to be such good friends."

"I'd love that! But Mommy says it's expensive to fly."

"Only when you have to pay for it."

"I couldn't pay for it. I don't have a job yet. Not old enough," she says apologetically.

I laugh. "It'll be my treat. Deal?"

"It's a deal!" She slaps my palm with her hand. "Bloody hell! This is awesome!"

"Brooke Elizabeth Amaya, I will not have you use such language," I say, trying to stifle my laughter.

"Sorry, it just sounds so cool," she says sheepishly.

I grin at her. "It does, doesn't it?"

She nods.

"Okay, just don't say it around your mum or she'll box my ears."

Brooke laughs. "I'm sure I don't know what that is, luv."

I put my arm around her thin shoulders. "I'm going to miss you like crazy, little luv."

"Me too." She turns her face into my side and quietly dampens my t-shirt.

"Hey, don't cry, little lady. We'll see each other more than you think."

She sniffles. "Maybe you're wrong. Maybe we all end up crying so much more when we love someone."

I can only confirm her theory by allowing one single tear to trickle down my face.

***

When I glance at Gwen's coach plane tickets, I quickly march up to the British Airways counter and slap my business credit card in front of a startled woman, demanding the upgrade to first class immediately.

The bespectacled brunette behind the counter can't type fast enough to make the changes. I also ask to make a call to the crew members on first class and quickly negotiate for preferred treatment for Gwen and the girls.

While waiting for the call to board, I sit on a molded plastic seat with Brooke and Emily sitting on each of my legs, their little faces long, nestled between my neck and shoulders, quietly grieving over the impending departure.

Gwen is on her mobile with Tony. They exchange a series of "I love you's" before she finally ends the call and brings the device to her chest, making me smile. Love, when successful, is an oasis amidst a burning desert.

Their flight number is announced over the speaker and I mentally curse the unstoppable march of time.

Neither one of the girls has let go, even when I stand.

I'd love to encourage them and tell them we'll see each other again quite soon, but I can't trust my voice.

Gwen intercedes by using her soothing voice to calm the girls enough for them to give me one last hug and kiss before pulling their carry-on luggage behind them.

"Love you, girls!"

"Love you too!" They call back in unison.

"Go on, Miss Evelyn will take you to the nice seats we talked about," Gwen says, referring to the attractive stewardess whose bright smile calms the girls all the way.

Gwen sighs and gives me a sad little look that matches her girls' to a T.

"I had the best time, but I can't wait to be in my house. Why don't you just come with me?" She grins even as a tear rolls out of the corner of her right eye.

I take a deep breath and let it out slowly. "Gwen, I thank you for being there for me. You are an amazing person. Tony is a very lucky man."

"He sure is," she says with another tearful grin. "Anything from Quinn?"

I shake my head, deciding to keep the last note a secret.

"I'm sorry."

"Love's a game we all must play, right?" I say, quoting one of the songs I heard.

"Maybe, but guys like you should always win." She throws her arms around me, squeezing me tight. "I'd damn well better see you soon. You hear me, mister?"

"Aye, my lady." I hold her tight, not wanting to let go.

"That was the best toast I've ever heard. I'll never forget it."

"I shan't forget yours, luv."

"Thank you for being so amazing to my daughters. They'll love you forever."

"I feel the same, Gwen."

"I'll love you forever." She says as she lays a tender kiss on my cheek, then the other, then surprises me by kissing my lips, not a lover's kiss, more of an affectionate peck to a close friend. "If Quinn doesn't come to her senses, call me. We'll just run away together." She winks.

Levity during an emotional crisis, Gwen's gift. "Don't tempt me, luv."

A last call to board is heard over the speakers. Gwen takes her bag, the last passenger to board, and hands her ticket to the young man who's been staring at her the entire time.

"Don't say good-bye or something final like that. We say, 'see you soon', and we bloody mean it."

The British curse out of her pretty mouth makes me chuckle. "See you soon, Gwen."

"Love you."

"Love you too."

With one last wave, she disappears into the boarding sleeve.

40

"Solutions Incorporated, Lewis speaking."

"Good day, Lewis, this is Marc Ascasubi."

The name surprises me. I've known Marc for years. He was one of the first techs Solutions hired when our operation enjoyed its first growth spurt. He left with Terence when we dissolved our partnership to work with him, where Marc essentially became Terence's right hand. "What can I do for you, Marc?"

"I gather you did not hear about Terry."

My pulse begins to race. He doesn't need to tell me what I already know. "When...?"

"Yesterday," Marc says in a numb voice. "I didn't see you at the funeral, but I know how close you and Terry were and I just thought you should know."

I'm only half hearing his words as a barrage of memories floods my shattering mind with grief.

"Lewis?"

"Yes, I'm here."

"I'm terribly sorry, chap."

"I can't believe I missed the funeral..."

"That's why I figured I'd call you. The burial is today, in London."

This takes me aback. "In London? Terence wanted to be buried in Liverpool."

"Apparently too time consuming for the bereaved widow," Marc says in a tight voice.

"Where in London, Marc?"

"Bunhill Fields."

Bunhill Fields is the resting place of William Blake, Terence's favorite poet. Suddenly Sandy does not seem the cold fish I've taken her to be.

Terence and I loved great quotes and poetry. One of our games was trying to stomp the other with a quote or a poem, and we'd sit up half the night exchanging beautiful pieces of literature.

"Five o'clock. Will you be there?" Marc asks.

"Yes, of course."

"Good day, Lewis."

"Good day."

"I'm very sorry, chap," he adds before disconnecting.

I recline my chair and stare at the ceiling for a long moment. Terence's death is the final page of a chapter I may never read again.

Sitting up straight once more, I reach into a deep bottom drawer where I keep a stack of photographs. There are a lot of photos of the inauguration of Solutions. Terence looks like the picture definition of health, and his eyes are vibrant with intellect. There's a photo of us at Anfield, both of us wearing our Reds football jerseys, our faces painted red and white. The grins are a testament of much happier times.

Before I succumb to the growing grief, I open the drawer intending to put the photos back in when I see a folded sheet of paper. It's *Songs of Innocence* by William Blake.

"Piping down the valleys wild,
Piping songs of peasant glee,
On a cloud I saw a child,
And he, laughing, said to me:"

"Pipe a song about a lamb! So I piped with merry cheer. 'Piper, pipe that song again;' so I piped: he wept to hear," I recite from memory.

The verse overwhelms me and I crush the paper in my hands as the tears come, and come with a vengeance.

***

I take the tube to Old Street and walk all the way out to Bunhill Fields once I emerge into the grey light of day. Soon I'm navigating my way past the mausoleums, noting their patina of the London soot blackening the edges of the stone, and the cracks the rains have carved on their faces.

Behind the green metal fences, the flat stones stand like the rows of a legion, forever awaiting orders. Some of them are leaning as though tired from looking over their namesakes' eternal slumber.

With *Songs of Innocence* still playing in my mind, I walk over to the lone stone and stop to reverently pay my respects.

NEAR BY LIE THE REMAINS OF
THE POET – PAINTER
WILLIAM BLAKE
1757 – 1827
AND OF HIS WIFE
CATHERINE SOPHIA
1762- 1831

I give the Blakes a respectful moment of silence before making my way to a group of people in dark clothes surrounding an ornate casket that sits on a bed of flowers of rich hues. I didn't bring flowers. I don't want to leave something with Terence that will ultimately disintegrate. My final gift is meant to last forever.

Sandy sits next to an intense looking older man with a stooped back. She wears a black veil that covers her face, but I can tell she's crying from the way her thin shoulders tremble. A woman with delicate features sits to her left, a stoic, blank look on her face.

When I approach the group, I see faces I haven't seen in several months. There's a flicker of recognition but given the occasion, no one so much as smiles, let alone gives me a few words normally reserved for anyone you haven't seen in a while. Instead, they part like the Red Sea and allow me a clear path to the casket.

The priest is delivering his conclusion to the service, a distinguished man of solemn expression. He wears a green decorative scarf with Celtic designs rendered in gold thread over his black cassock.

"May the road rise up to meet you," he begins, right hand raised. "May the wind be always at your back. May the sun shine warm upon your face; the rains fall soft upon your fields and until we meet again, may God hold you in the palm of His hand."

No one moves, the perfect silence broken only by the melody of a flute. A young man I've never seen before steps up and begins singing *On Eagles' Wings*. The touching lyrics simultaneously soothing and heart wrenching.

The soft pitch of a woman's voice behind me makes me think of Quinn's voice. Suddenly I'm fighting an urge to turn around, wanting nothing more than to see her standing somewhere behind me, as irrational as that desire is.

I feel someone take my arm and I turn to find a weeping Carmen Santopietro. He nods and tearfully continues to sing. As the song draws to an end, Sandy stands, takes a handful of the dark earth and pours it over the top of the casket. She casts a sad look in my direction before she's led away by her partner. I follow her retreating form until she gets into a dark sedan.

"I was hoping to see you here, lad."

"You too," I say, patting the old queen's hand.

Carmen wipes off the tears and squares his shoulders. "We talked, Terry and me. He was glad you went to see him."

I turn away from the casket to meet Carmen's mournful gaze.

"Carmen, I never meant to—"

"Hush, now child. You and Terry will forever have a soft spot in my old heart. Whatever your choices, whatever you're running from, I only hope you find yourself, lad."

I swallow hard, trying to keep a degree of composure. "I can't believe all these people here."

Carmen reaches for something in the pocket of his coat. "This is how they knew."

I take the two sheets of paper and unfold them. It's a print out of *The Flier*. The article is written by Paul Simms and each new line widens my eyes more than the last.

"Paul did a smashing job," Carmen quips.

"He did. Is this for real?"

"Aye, lad. Terence liquidated his estate and called me to oversee the project."

"The Daugherty Scholarship Fund," I utter in awe.

"I've already been on the phone with donors. We hope to establish three more scholarships."

I skim over the impressive list of academic accomplishments and read over the last lines of the article. "How much exactly went into AIDS research? It doesn't say here."

"Enough to build a new facility and recruit some top talent."

Terence Daugherty's net worth had to be in the neighborhood of a few hundred million pounds in property and global market stocks. "I'd like to contribute as well, Carmen. Call me."

"It means quite a bit, my dear Lewis. Thank you."

Carmen takes my shoulder and pats my cheek with his other hand. "For what it's worth, I couldn't be prouder of Terry, and you."

"Thank you, Carmen."

Carmen's eyes grow moist as he takes one last glance at the casket. A younger man meets him at the head of the path and helps him walk all the way to his vehicle.

Although the dying sun still shines bright into the landscape, a few clouds unleash a soft rain in a strange display of climatic opposites.

"Thank you, Terence, for helping me find who I am," I say with the last of my voice.

Sun and rain, I think. Apt for Terence, the most selfish and self-centered prick I've ever met, my partner of ten years, who handed over the considerable fruits of his labors to the benefit of others.

I loved him, plain and simple, though I did in my own way. I did not understand him at the time he unmasked me at his home, the last time I saw him alive. But I do now, and that's what I'm thankful for.

I retrieve the flash drive out of my pocket and stare at it as rain drops bounce over its glossy plastic cap.

Every photograph of our time together is in this tiny technological wonder, along with every poem William Blake ever wrote and my own personal good bye letter. I step up to the casket and tuck the flash drive into the little mound of dirt Sandy left.

The rain grows colder and heavier as I make my way back to the station as Terence's last words echo in my mind.

Break out of your prison, my luv. You have too much to give someone else. Just make certain she is as bright, and as beautiful as you are, and don't settle for anything less. Don't let another Samantha Reddick slip by...

A small sedan skids to a stop in front of me when I'm about to cross the street.

"Lewis! Get in the car, chap!"

It's Marc Ascasubi. "No need to repeat yourself, lad," I reply as I open the door and fold myself into the compact Renault.

"Bloody rain," mutters Marc. "Where can I take you, my friend?"

"I was headed back to the office."

Marc nods.

He looks vastly different from our early days together at Solutions. His head is completely shaved, a ploy to cover his badly receding hair line. Marc is in his late twenties, thin and wiry. His brown eyes flash with kindness.

"I imagine," I tell him. "You are now the hot name passed around in the industry."

Marc barks a sarcastic laugh. "Not at all. No one wants to give me so much as an interview. Some wankers spread the rumor that I got to where I did by spending quite a bit of time under the boss's desk."

"Who would do that?"

"Buggering bigots, that's who," he exclaims angrily. "I'm looking to move back to Dover, although I'd hate to leave London. I like the schools for my kids far better here."

The decision I make at that moment is effortless. "What do you say you stay in London and work for me at double the salary."

Marc gives me an incredulous look. "Lewis, I wouldn't know what to say. I didn't exactly leave Solutions in great terms."

"Water under the bridge."

"Lewis—"

"Marc, listen to me. I'm getting an avalanche of Terence's former clients and no one knows the inner workings of their systems like you. I'd be mad not to hire you."

Marc looks stunned. "Lewis, I'd be forever grateful, and you don't have to double my salary. I'd feel better if you give me some time to prove myself."

"Nonsense, lad. I know the caliber of person you are. Your networking prowess is just an added bonus."

He is thoughtful as he navigates through traffic. "May I make a suggestion?"

"Sure."

"Ben Cooper is unemployed now that the firm closed. He'd be an excellent addition to your company as well, and I could use his help."

"Ben Cooper is hired."

Marc finally smiles. "I don't know what to say."

"Nothing to say, Marc. Take the rest of the week and come by next Monday. You may have to organize an office by yourself."

"How about I come in tomorrow and start right away. I've been idle long enough, ever since Terry…"

I nod in agreement. "It's settled then. Tomorrow it is."

Tower 42 rises in the distance, growing as we near the offices of Solutions. Marc pulls alongside the street and reaches back for an umbrella. I have the feeling he'll brave the maddening traffic just to come around and open my door.

"Don't trouble yourself, Marc. I don't mind the rain."

"Thank you, Mr. Bettford."

I raise my eyebrow at him. "Marc, I'd like to think we're friends."

He looks chagrined. "Force of habit."

I smile. "Until tomorrow. Welcome back to Solutions."

Marc waves as I casually stroll to the glass double doors. I stare at the parade of umbrellas streaming up and down the street. I used to be one of them, huddling under the widest possible umbrella just to keep my head dry. That was until Quinn McDermont showed me the pure, unadulterated joy of standing in the rain. At this moment I miss her so much I suddenly envy Terence's never having to feel heartbreak again.

41

Three weeks later

When I check my local news feed, I'm pleased to see another scathing article on the fall of Firuz Ahmidi. He will have his day in court soon, looking into a small eternity in prison. I followed every article, thankful that besides naming Quinn McDermont as one of the benefactors of the Play Again Foundation, her name is notably absent from the papers and the bloody tabloids, which harassed Firuz since the day I anonymously sent that condemning email to Ms. Martinez. She's done a terrific job of keeping Quinn out of the limelight.

I'm relieved to see her name less and less. I don't need the painful reminder.

"Greetings from Madrid," I read the post card out loud.

I get up off the chair and walk to the large cork board hanging on the wall. I pull a tack off an old business card and look at the board, wondering where I can fit another post card. Spain, Italy, Lake Como, Zurich, Geneva, all the destinations the McElroys have visited since leaving London three weeks ago.

I've felt the passage of each second of each night of every day for the last three weeks. The hurt and anger in Quinn's eyes visits me unfailingly during the most vulnerable hours.

I tap the space bar of my keyboard to bring the screen to life. Brooke and Emily's pretty faces peer at me from the screen. I click on one of my folder icons, grudgingly placing the bloody frames upon my face not wanting to acknowledge how much better I can see, and begin working code for a server setup.

After two hours of writing code, my eyes are stinging and my heart is no longer into it. Actually my heart is not into much these days.

I've yet to read Quinn's last note, but I irrationally hold onto it as proof that our time together was real, if fleeting. I stuck it between the pages of my copy of Tony's book, *The Composition*.

My last conversation with Brooke replays nearly every night, teasing me with some revelation that eludes me as soon as I feel I can grasp it.

The telephone rings. "Hullo."

"Hullo, my boy. I need a favor."

"Anything for you, luv. Are you taking your medicine?"

"Child, I'm the adult. Of course I am taking the bloody pills. Richard will box my ears if I skip."

I laugh. "What can I do for you, Mum?"

"I need a couple of photos enlarged."

"Sure. Let me have them."

"Richard prepared the email attachments. I'm sending them right now."

Within seconds, I see the new message pop up on my screen.

There are three photos in the file, I download them and open them in the viewer. They're photos from the wedding.

"You and Richard look great on these."

"Thank you, luv. Can you enlarge the shot so it's just us in the photo?"

"Easily. What size frame do you have in mind?"

She thinks for a moment. "Letter size, I'm sure."

"Do you want me to print them for you?"

"I'd love to have you deliver them personally on your visit."

I hesitate. "Of course, Mum."

"Ta ta, luv."

I end the call and take a deep, frustrated breath. I don't like feeling obligated to see Mum, but I like hurting her feelings even less. I hope for once she can't read my expression like a book and fret endlessly about me.

After rolling my head on my shoulders to work off a kink in my neck, I set about cropping the photos. It's a fairly easy task and I waste no time in correcting the light settings, fix a couple of blemishes, and produce a striking portrait of the couple. They look so happy, I find myself envious and longing to know if I will grow old with someone by my side.

I pull up the second photo and quickly set about to crop it, trying to preserve Mum and Richard while cutting off faces on the edges.

The tangerine tango of the bridesmaids' gowns catches my eye. I see Alicia being dipped by Nathan in the background on the right side. There are two other smiling faces near them. On the left side of the picture, I see Gwen smiling at someone off the shot. Right behind her, I see Quinn's face, and my heart stops.

Like a slow-moving montage, I recreate that exact moment. I took this photograph. It was shortly after Quinn walked away from me. Mum came up and handed me her camera, asking me to take the photograph. Unlike all the other faces, Quinn's expression is so wounded, I'm instantly transported back to the moment when I lashed out at her.

I cancel the cropping of Mum and Richard and set the square around Quinn. I thank God Mum's camera is so good that the resolution is fairly intact when I enlarge the face that's haunted my thoughts since that day.

Quinn's eyes are fixed into the lens of the camera. She was looking right at me. Her beautiful eyes gleam with the tears that are trickling over her lashes, forever suspended on the delicate planes of her face.

Her stare is so direct that I stop breathing as the full meaning of her expression registers in my heart, branding it hotly, making me grab at my chest as though to stop a bleeding wound from spilling the life out of me.

"She said she was crying because she was in love. I didn't think it made sense and I told her so."
"What did she say to that?"
"She said that she really needed to start listening to her heart."

"You bloody imbecile!" I curse myself as Brooke's words flash in my mind.

Forcing myself to tear my eyes from Quinn's longing gaze, I grab for the bookshelf, pulling volumes carelessly off the shelves until I find Tony's book.

I pull the note out of its pages and stare at it. I've done this several times before. The brittle paper no longer smells like the intoxicating perfume Quinn wears.

Unable to face the possibility of forgetting her, I carefully open the note and begin to read her elegant, loopy print.

Lewis,
This is not a note of farewell...

"I need wine," I declare, getting up and pouring a glass of merlot with shaky hands.

I go back to the desk and set the goblet down. There's something in my eye and I pull at the eyelid one way then the other, but whatever's lodged inside now begins to burn painfully. In an attempt to swivel to get off the chair to use a mirror to find the bloody intruder, I bang my knee against the desk causing it to shift. With one good eye, I watch in horror as the goblet topples over spilling the dark liquid all over Quinn's note.

"Bloody hell! Shit!"

I jump out of the chair just as wine spills off the edge of the desk. I don't know what kind of paper this is but it quickly soaks up the wine and the carefully printed letters become illegible blotches. I quickly try to pick it up but the wine-laden note rips like gossamer.

"NO!"

I leave the paper in place committing to memory the only lines I read. As though mocking me, the only word that survives the wine bath is her name, *Quinn.*

I let out a litany of curses, venting my rage at my stupidity. I grab the innocent goblet and throw it with all the strength I can muster, but I only draw minimal comfort from the bloody thing pulverizing when it hits the wall.

After leaving the house, I feel a need to be close to Quinn that makes me look to the southwest. I recall that she planned on staying in London for a month and I curse myself for a bloody fool for wasting so much time.

I get in the car and clench my teeth in frustration as I crawl through heavy traffic all the way into Chelsea Harbour before driving down the familiar street passing by the industrial park.

In the distance, the Battersea Bridge's lights come to life, greeting the coming night.

I don't wish to entertain the possibility that Quinn is not at her flat.

"Please...please..." I implore, willing the Audi to be parked in front of the flat, but there's only an old VW Beetle that looks beat and tired when I pull into the spot next to it. The front door is ajar.

With my heart in my throat, I climb out of my car and get as far as the door. I rap softly at first, then a bit harder, but no one answers.

I push the door in and the hinges squeak in protest. Two of the loveseats are covered with opaque plastic and all the side tables are gone. I venture into the hallway, leading to the bedrooms, and peer into the empty spaces, feeling the walls closing in on me.

When I find myself in the master bedroom, I see a large, bulging, clear trash bag on the same spot where our clothes pooled on the night she changed me forever.

My eyes return to the trash bag, but other than some old fashion magazines and several editions of the London Times, I see nothing that tells me anything. I stare out the uncovered window at the Thames, snaking its way through the old city. The memory of our first dinner in London plays vividly in my mind, and I shut my eyes as new blinding pains scour my soul.

Something compels me to look at the trash bag again and I nearly give into an impulse to dump it and go through the refuse when there's a clatter out in the kitchenette.

"Quinn?" I call frantically as I race back out to the living room.

An older woman wearing an apron is stacking utensils in a box on the short counter.

"Madame?" I call but she appears not to hear me. I don't want to frighten the old bird. You never know who has a bad heart nowadays.

"Excuse me, Madame?" I raise my voice and the woman goes still.

She slowly turns around and as quick as a cat, grabs a sauce pan that she holds up in defense. I try to smile and raise my palms in the least threatening pose I can manage. With one hand she turns the volume up on a flesh-colored hearing aid and stares at me, wide eyed.

"Forgive me, Madame, the door was open. I'm a friend of the owner."

The woman narrows her distrusting, pale eyes and seems to inspect every inch of me. Satisfied I'm not the next Jack the Ripper, or a close imitator, she lowers the sauce pan and brings a hand up to her ample bosom.

"Boy, ye gave me a fright, ye did."

"My apologies, Madame."

A little smile plays on her thin lips. She looks to be in her seventies, her left hand has a bit of a palsy and is as wrinkled as a prune. Her silver hair is braided behind her and she stands on thick legs that support her short, but stout frame.

"Ye know Mr. Harry, do ye?"

"No, Madame, I know Quinn. Quinn McDermont."

The woman sighs and smiles sadly. "Aye, ye'r looking for the good little lassie, Ms. Quinnie."

"Yes, Madame. I was under the impression she was still here in London."

She regards me with a confused expression. "Ye's part right on that, laddie. Ms. Quinnie right gone back, but she left two days ago."

This time it's my turn to look confused. "She left two days ago?"

"Aye laddie. Ms. Quinnie sent me for her doctor right last week. Little lassie was hurting, she was."

My heart begins to race to the point that I begin to wonder if I'm bound to have that same flutter in the heart that started plaguing Mum, afib, I recall. "Was she sick?"

The woman shrugs her round shoulders. "Aye, though a day later, Ms. Quinnie was right as rain, at least of the body," her pale eyes are watery, but they've taken on a new gleam. "Ms. Quinnie is hurting in here, she is," she says with severity, tapping her palm over her heart.

What was Quinn doing this whole time? Decompressing?

"I've been cleaning this flat. Mr. Harry up to sell, he is."

"Pardon me, who's Mr. Harry?"

"Ms. Quinnie's Poppa," she says like the answer should be quite obvious.

"Did she leave an address?"

The woman regards me with suspicion again. "Ye'r a friend. Don't ye have a way to call Ms. Quinnie, laddie?"

"Please, it's important," I plead, pulling a fifty Euro note and offering it to her.

The woman scoffs at the money and shoves her hands in the pockets of her apron. She pulls out a crumpled bank check and shows it to me.

Harrison McDermont
1042 Green Hill Road
N. Madison, CT 06443
USA

My heart soars at the mere thought of seeing her again, but where's all this urgency coming from?

I thank the old woman and go back to my car, intending on boarding the first flight out to New York City. I figure this is as good a place as any to make this call so I fish my mobile and begin tapping the screen when a young couple walks by, pushing a baby stroller.

The mobile drops from my hand, eliciting a sickening crack as the plastic base splinters. The couple gives me a curious look before speeding up their pace. I never get a look at the infant.

My mouth is as dry as a bed of cotton.

I storm into the flat, ignoring the old woman's scream, and run into the bedroom where I go down on my knees to inspect the contents of the trash bag through its clear membrane.

"What's the matter, laddie, bloody frightened me clear off me knickers, by George!"

The woman gasps when I tear at the knot holding the bag shut and spill the trash all over the floor. I push the larger newspapers and magazines aside, knowing my brain registered something my eyes were too slow to catch. There's an abundance of crumpled tissues and my heart aches with the knowledge they hold Quinn's tears.

I find a discarded notepad. I recognize it as the kind Lorna Matthews favored to take notes for her planning. The pages match the folded note I held unread like a bloody imbecile.

"Vellum..." No wonder the note disintegrated. After drying out to a brittle wafer, the spilled wine destroyed the fibers.

I even find the pen she most likely used. After staring at it like a native calling forth the power of a talisman, I shove the pen in my shirt pocket. Sweat begins to trickle down my temples as I push the refuse aside, making a monumental mess.

When I finally find it, I let my hand hover over it like it's toxic. It's a small cardboard box, with an inch square base, and about ten inches long. The back wall of the box extends into a label with a hole punched for the item to be displayed from a wire rack. I picked up a similar box discarded at Audrey's studio. The label is predominantly white with some pink stripes and blue letters, *Welford Pregnancy Test.*

I can't breathe.

A heavy hand clasps my shoulder and the greasy smell of the woman's apron nauseates me further.

"Aye, I knew, it was no bloody flu," she observes.

I pull the pen out of my pocket and jot down the McDermont's address on the inside panel of the pregnancy test package, then I stand and bolt out the door, nearly trampling the old woman. She's about to scream at me some more, but I trap her wrinkled hand and deposit a fifty Euros note in her hand, kiss her dirty knuckles and fly out the door.

I call on the way to the airport and demand the first available flight to New York City, wishing we were still enjoying the days of the bloody Concorde. While waiting for the boarding call after getting financially raped for one first class ticket to New York, I navigate into an American rental car service and quickly make a reservation. The wait is agonizing.

42

I watch helplessly as the mobile's battery dies after my repeated attempts to get a hold of Samantha and Jason. I scan the displays at the concourse kiosks, but no one has a charger compatible with my mobile. I quickly sign for a new one and spring an extra twenty Euros for an instant charger and a headset.

The first call I make goes to Audrey.

"This had better be bloody good," Audrey snaps in way of greeting.

"Audrey, luv. I need your help."

"Lewis? Where are you bloody calling me from?"

"The road. I need you to do something for me."

"Blimey, lad... shoot."

"Get to my flat, there's a key under the third planter in the backyard. There's a safe behind the flat TV. Do you have a pen?"

"I'm bloody painting, just shoot the blasted number."

I give her the four number combination twice and make her repeat it back to me. "Grab my passport and two bundles. Meet me at Heathrow at the British Airways counter."

"Passport, two bundles. Off I go."

The call ends.

Audrey is not one to mess around when an obvious emergency is at hand.

There's just enough power in my mobile to text a telephone number into the new one before it finally blinks off. I pull up the text and insert an international code. After four rings, a male voice answers.

"Hello?"

"Tony! This is Lewis,"

"Oh, hey! How are you, Lewis?"

"I wish I could tell you that I'm well, but I don't know right now."

"What happened?."

"I'd love to tell you, but I may not have much time. I need to talk to Gwen," I reply, trying to keep the urgency out of my voice.

"She should be here in a minute. She had to pick up a prescription for me. Hey, I wanted to thank you for everything you did for my girls. They can't stop talking about you."

"Not at all, it was a true pleasure. How are they?"

Tony chuckles. "They can't wait to go back. We're working on some type of a vacation plan. Brooke said all I need to do is call you."

"Yes, I told her I'd happily fly her over the pond. Anytime, I mean it. You just need to tell me and I'll happily get the entire family across the pond at no expense of yours."

"Lewis, that is very kind, but—"

"Please, Tony, it's the least I can do after everything you went through."

"Thank you, Lewis. You're one of a kind."

"Not at all, chap. I consider you family."

"Thank you." We endure a bit of an awkward pause before either of us speaks again. "I hear the wedding was a good time."

"We were sad you missed it."

"I was too, but I had no choice. At least production is wrapped up and they're now filming the pilot. It'll air in the spring."

"Congratulations on all your success."

"Thanks, Lewis. None of this would've happened without you and Sam."

"Perhaps, but you had the talent all alone."

"Thank you, that means a lot." There's a clutter in the background. "Hey, here she is. Hope to see you sometime soon, my friend."

"Likewise."

There's a shuffling noise amidst the static then the melodious voice of Gwen fills my eyes with tears.

"Hi, honey!"

"Gwen…" My voice falters.

"Lewis? Are you there?"

I swallow hard, trying to clear my voice. "I'm at Heathrow waiting for my flight to New York."

"What?" She asks in shock.

"I need to find Quinn."

"Oh, my God! Did you finally hear from her?"

"In a manner of speaking, yes."

"Oh, my God. This is great!"

"There's more."

"Are you coming here?"

The hope in her voice sears through me.

"It's likely," *especially if Quinn doesn't want me…*

"Well, what is it?"

"Quinn's pregnant."

"What?" Her voice escalates in pitch and volume.

I quickly summarize my accidental discovery for her. She doesn't interrupt until I'm done and feeling suddenly empty.

"Honey, why don't you call her?"

"I don't have her number anymore, and the address I have doesn't list one, so it must be private."

"Would Samantha know it?"

"I think she is somewhere in Spain right now. I tried to get a hold of her, but my mobile died and I can't remember the last time I actually keyed in her bloody number."

"What will you say to Quinn?"

"I'm sure I don't know. But she left a note."

"What's it say?"

I feel like an idiot as I recall the wine spilling and destroying the note. A quick look at the clock on the wall tells me I don't have a lot of time before they call me to board the plane. "I can't remember off the top of my head, but even if I did, I'm not sure I could tell you what it means."

"Don't you have it with you?"

I can feel my cheeks burning. "It was destroyed. Long story."

"Jesus! Do you remember any of it?"

"Just a few lines. Um..." I try to jot my brain, wishing, not for the first time, that I had Samantha's perfect memory. "It's not a farewell note... It's not a breakup note... I was supposed to be safe...Her husband was once all she wanted..." I blow a frustrated breath. "I can't even remember if that's the right order. Gwen, she's pregnant. I don't know what to do!"

"Okay," Gwen says.

I can almost see her thinking furiously.

"Okay, I want you to keep something in mind. Are you listening?"

"Yes."

"Did Samantha ever mention my pregnancy when I was sixteen?"

"She's big on confidence, luv. I didn't know until just now..." I'm stunned by her revelation.

"Well, it happened. I'm only telling you because I don't think age matters when a woman gets pregnant by accident, and right now, Quinn is probably very afraid, and very troubled with the decisions she might have to make. Do you understand?"

I nod as though she can see me. "I think so."

"Lewis, now that you know, all you can do is support whatever decision she makes, okay?"

"You're saying that if she wants to..." I can't voice the hateful word. Suddenly part of our conversations leaps to the front of my thoughts. Quinn didn't want children with her husband. "...terminate the pregnancy... I've to be alright with her decision? Dear God, is that what you had to do?"

"No! I couldn't even think of that. My baby was given up for adoption. It was the only choice I had."

"Oh, Gwen..."

"It's okay, it's in the past. It'll be something I live with."

God, I love this woman. "Do you think that's what Quinn would choose?" I try to drive away the memory of Quinn telling me she never wanted kids.

"Honey, I wish I could tell you no, but I don't know where she is with all this, other than that she's probably very scared right now."

"Bloody hell..."

"Lewis, you have a heart of gold. I know you'll let it guide you through this. Give me the address."

"Gwen..."

"Lewis, every second counts. Tony can drive me to the airport. I'll fly into Hartford and see her."

"Gwen, I couldn't possibly—"

"Lewis!"

"Gwen, I can't."

I hear a frustrated, but resigned exhalation on the line. "It's going to be alright, Lewis."

I actually believe it in my very core when she says it. "I'll call you, soon."

"I wish you'd let me help."

"Gwen, if I see in Quinn's eyes that I'm too late. I will need you more than you could possibly imagine."

There's a burst of static. "Okay, I think I understand. Whatever you need, I'm here. Call me."

"Thank you."

"Love you, hun."

"Love you too."

***

I'm pacing, boring a hole on the floor in front of the row of metal detectors. Two men of the security personnel are tracking my movements with a sharp eye.

The jingling of chains snaps my head up and I see Audrey shuffling as fast as she can. I dash closer to her.

"Do you have time to bloody tell me what this is about?" She huffs.

I grab the passport and one of the bundles of cash. When Audrey tries to hand me the second one, I push it towards her, offering her to keep it.

"Don't be bloody daft! You're going to need this more than I do."

"I'm not thinking straight," I tell her, taking the second bundle and shoving it into the front pocket of my trousers.

"Where's your luggage?"

"No time. I can get anything I need when I get there."

She regards me as someone who's lost his mind. "Tell me."

"It's Quinn. I've to see her."

Audrey's sharp inhale is not lost on me. "Sam said she was your girlfriend…"

I can see her thinking furiously.

"Audrey, I was a bloody fool. I need to see her."

A garbled voice calls all passengers to flight 2485, destined for New York City.

I give her a pleading look.

"On your bike, luv. Whatever it is, do things right."

Smiling, I grab her face and plant a kiss on her lips before running to the nearest metal detector. The lad by the conveyor belt looks from me to Audrey as he meticulously runs a wand over my body, despite the fact that I didn't set off any bloody alarms. I retrieve my mobile and keys, submit myself to the shoe inspection then I'm running for the gate as the second call goes out to the passengers of British Airways flight 2485.

***

No flight has ever taken so long. I feel as though I've counted every bloody second of it, too strung out to sleep, too conflicted to eat, and even the wine I asked for, remains in its holder untouched and no longer chilled.

In an attempt to escape the torturous chambers of my mind, I call forth my earliest memories and entertain myself with the mental documentary of my own life.

I've never been so conscious of what growing without a father has meant for me until now. In my heart, I elevate my old woman to Saint status as I recall the many times she defended her only son from the prejudice of others.

Now, facing the possibility of being a father to a child, I feel as though it's the chance I've been waiting to atone whatever fallacies my family has suffered.

I wonder if that's what inspired me to give my all to my two little honorary nieces, Brooke and Emily. I can easily, and truthfully, say that I've never felt such unadulterated joy of life as I did when Emily giggled at some funny thing I said. I've never felt such a powerful current of emotion as I did when Brooke spoke to me in her older-than-her-years voice.

You're going to be an awesome daddy one day...

The day she said those words to me, I ached with the acceptance that I'd never experience parenthood. Now I have the hope that I will one day hold a child and pour all of me into that new life.

It's strange in a way. I've just learned of the possibility of a baby, who came out my own flesh and blood, and I love the very thought of this baby more than I've loved anything in my life.

I can't help thinking that whatever love I have that Quinn doesn't want, can be devoted to this baby. But I don't even know if that's the case. Were those tears Brooke saw Quinn shed meant for me?

At the very least, I want her to know that I want to be someone in the life of this child. And if she's inclined to terminate the pregnancy, I want to at least have the opportunity to stop her.

Our child...

On some level, I've tried to rationalize that without actual confirmation, there's no sense jumping to conclusions and allowing such a fragile hope to soar so uncontrollably. As I just learned, in an emphatically painful fashion, there was no greater pain than an unrealized hope, but something deep inside tells me I'm right.

***

When I land in New York at 3A.M. local time, a customs official, along with a dour Homeland Security officer, are very interested to know why I carry no luggage. The first thing they do is take my mobile from me, just as I'm dialing Gwen.

They even accuse me of presenting falsified documents, ignoring my business travel permits stamped all over my passport that allow me entrance into virtually any country in the world for a seven day period. A slight variance of the typical diplomatic travel passes, attained exclusively by Lions Securities.

My bloodshot eyes and disheveled clothing severely work against me. They interview me at length for another hour, making fun of my accent and referring to me in terms I've already heard more than enough times in my life.

When the thick wanker leaves me in an office for further interviewing, I spin the phone on the desk and dial in the codes into Nathan Jeffries' private line at his home.

"Lewis, what the bloody hell are you doing in New York?"

"Nathan, I need your help."

I quickly outline my situation. When I mention the possibility of Quinn carrying my child, there's a long silence on the line after which he promises to handle it.

I thank him and set the receiver back in its cradle as the self-important arse sits his ample rear on the ratty chair and begins screaming at me, demanding to know who I called.

When I don't answer, he stands and braces his thick hands on the desk as he leans into me, showering me in a spray of spit while screaming in my face.

He's stabbing a sausage-like forefinger at the picture on my passport, suggesting the photograph is a fabrication. He seems proud of himself for coming up with such an intricate word on his own.

The phone on his desk rings and the man angrily snatches the receiver, barking into the line that he's in the middle of something.

Within a few seconds, the transformation is astonishing and I go from "British fag" to "Mr. Bettford" in record time. It's good to know Nathan Jeffries.

The man trips over himself with apologies as he leads me out of the terminal, and is even willing to hail a cab for me. I tersely decline and the man retreats, backpedaling and nodding stupidly.

"I hope your bloody resume is up to date, cheeky bugger."

The man's eyes go wide, pleading. I glare at him for another second, forgetting him entirely by the time I sign for my rental car.

I upgrade to an SUV equipped with a GPS, over the economy death trap they held in reserve while I was in the air. I turn up my nose British style at the Fords and Chevys, and opt for a newer Volvo XC90. When the woman at the counter tells me it's reserved, I smack a hundred Euros before her shocked eyes and kindly ask for the keys.

"Reservations get lost all the time," she says with a sneaky smile as she pockets the money.

Once I familiarize myself with the vehicle, I program the Connecticut address into the GPS and follow the clipped voice to the letter. The Volvo's GPS proves accurate beyond my wildest dreams and exercising what's left of my patience, I navigate out of the maze of highways of the Big Apple.

To make things worse, I never recovered the bloody mobile and I have no way to contact Gwen.

I also didn't think to exchange cash and the attendant at the toll booth on the George Washington Bridge gives me a hard time until I convince him that the bill I placed in his grubby little paws will buy him lunch for the entire month. The overworked lad gives in to the angry honking behind me and finally raises the mechanical arm. I've just paid the most expensive toll in history, I'm sure of that. I repeat this same process twice more. By that third time, I didn't care about the 300 Euro I paid in tolls.

I don't recognize myself. These lapses in judgment are uncharacteristic for me, but the only thing in my mind is getting to Quinn.

The GPS has a traffic avoidance feature that comes in handy after I nearly fall asleep at the wheel while waiting for another gridlock to clear up. It makes no bloody sense. It's going on 4:30 A.M. and the bloody traffic is heavy.

The GPS takes me off the busy motorway and guides me through some of the most picturesque roads I've ever seen. Mid-November no longer paints a colorful canvas of vivid oranges, yellows, and dark reds over the normally monochromatic foliage of summer.

I think back on Lorna Matthews telling me about the significance of the fiery colors of Samantha's bouquet.

Change…

I'm a changed man, though I pray the landscape before me is not an accurate representation of my future. Leaves lie brown and dead on the ground around the tree trunks. An early snowstorm has already begun turning them into pasty linoleum. The trees are bare, their probing branches scratching at the low clouds. My surroundings feel barren and desolate just like I've felt without Quinn…

I decide to avoid the Merritt Parkway when I see the bumper to bumper, endless lines of vehicles just as I'm about to take the access ramp. The GPS recalculates and directs me further north before cutting east on a windy road that makes me feel I'm driving in a wintry post card.

When I drive through Weston, my eyes are dangerously heavy and feel full of sand. I see a small pull off facing a body of water identified as the Hemlock Reservoir by the wooden sign staked by the shore of the lake. I recline the seat and let my eyes close and soon I'm fast asleep despite the boiling cauldron of thoughts my mind is at that moment.

***

The roar of a diesel engine rouses me. When I first look around, I feel like I'm back in the wilds of Hoddensdonpark Wood, until the unfamiliar road signs clarify everything in my groggy mind.

Remembering to stay on the right side of the two lane road, I head back towards the main motorways hoping the heavy traffic from earlier saw most of those motorists to their destinations.

I've been in the US for a bit over ten hours now, and my swollen tongue, my bladder and stomach vociferously let me know about it.

After driving through Bridgeport and Stratford, I see a large shopping complex in Milford.

As eager as I am to see Quinn, I can't frighten her by showing up dressed like a bloody vagrant. No sooner I walk through the glass doors into a department store called Target that two security officers fall in step behind me, even as I make my way into the mall.

At the GAP, I quickly pick out new jeans, two shirts, new socks and underwear. When I walk back out onto the main floor, the security officers turn away from me. The GAP sacks have apparently provided me with instant respectability by raising my status.

I stop at a footwear store and quickly settle on a pair of hiking boots. Next stop is the Target store where I quickly select an array of toiletries.

Recalling something from Samantha's observations at malls, I walk to the end of the building and find modern restroom facilities that cater to families. I quickly enter the family room and take full advantage of the private bathroom. I give myself as good a bath as I can, glad to be rid of the musk of two days' worth of sweat. There's a convenient drain on the floor. It's a bit uncomfortable to bathe out of a sink but it works nonetheless. I use an entire roll of paper towels to mop up the wet tiles and my body. After carefully shaving, I dress in my new clothes and emerge a new, respectable, member of the human race.

I approach the AT&T kiosk, but I realize I don't have access to Gwen's number. I don't know it by heart. I don't know her number in Pennsylvania either. There's no point in getting a bloody mobile.

I make another trip to Target and pick up two bottles of Visine after seeing the sad state of affairs of my corneas on a mirror at the sunglasses kiosk.

After attacking four tacos from Taco Bell at the food court, I quickly make my way back to the Volvo, chewing two sticks of spearmint gum at once.

It's nearly four o'clock by the time I take the ramp back onto the motorway I-95 heading for Groton. Traffic steadily grows but I manage to reach Branford without getting trapped in the entanglement of construction and the merging of I-91.

Even as the GPS gives me the next set of instructions, I spot the sign for exit 61, route 79. I follow the state route north then cut northeast on Green Hill Road. I feel the Volvo decelerate as my destination grows nearer. I'm suddenly overwhelmed by a wave of anxiety.

The numbers on the mailboxes increase until I pass by a large, lovely home whose mailbox reads 1000 Grafton's. The property line is marked by a white horse fence that spans down the road about a mile. A tall gate appears on my left, and I wait for two cars driving south to pass before I turn into the drive.

Two wooden posts support a large white wooden sign with the silhouette of a horse striking a dressage pose, its rider smartly dressed in cap and jacket. Under the bowing horse the words McDermont Acres are emblazoned in a large font in black.

I roll down the drive around a trio of large pines that conceal the main house until I make the turn at the dog leg of the drive. It's a gorgeous Tudor style two story with a gambrel roof and wraparound deck. Just beyond the house lies a row of stables adjacent to a large red barn. A silo juts out into the sky, and a weather bane in the shape of a rooster dances in the cold breeze on top of the barn's cupola.

I park the Volvo and step out of the vehicle, mesmerized by the peaceful panorama. Early winter in beautiful New England, the rumors are true.

"Can I help you, young man?"

The voice is low, and it has the same soft diction I heard in Quinn's voice. The woman tentatively approaching has short dark hair and curious brown eyes. She removes a pair of work gloves and glides over to me, something in her eyes flash approval.

"Madame, my name is Lewis Bettford. I'm hoping to see Quinn McDermont."

She looks more amused than intrigued as she brushes her hair to the side with a delicate hand. "Quinn is my daughter. I'm Jane."

"It's lovely to meet you, Mrs. McDermont."

Jane McDermont regards me with interest. "Just Jane. So you are Lewis," she says in a tone that I can't decipher. "Are you the reason she's been crying herself to sleep each night? You came all the way from London, I presume," she adds, not giving me a chance to reply to her question.

"Yes."

"Well, that explains the tired look on your face. That's a dreadful flight, I don't know how you kids do it. Come in, Lewis."

I follow her up the steps onto the porch where a big Golden Retriever turns its blocky head to regard me with soulful dark eyes. The big feathered tail thumps twice on the boards.

"That's Sadie. She really knows how to live life."

Despite my urgency to see Quinn, something makes me crouch down and offer Sadie the back of my hand. The dog sniffs my hand, licks my fingers once, thumps the heavy tail twice more and promptly goes back to sleep.

"Well, some guard dog you are, Sadie," Jane says with an undeniable touch of affection for the family pet. "She normally doesn't care for strangers, particularly foreigners."

I return Jane's warm smile. I see where Quinn got her dazzling grin from.

She removes her boots at the door and I unlace my hikers upon crossing the threshold into an immaculate depiction of country living. Jane removes her quilted coat, but she doesn't indicate for me to remove mine.

"You have a lovely home, Madame."

Jane beams a youthful smile at me. "And you have lovely manners, dear."

"Credit my mum," I say, smiling despite the growing anticipation gnawing at my insides.

Jane invites me to sit at one of the comfortable couches in the den. I take it as a good sign that she didn't lead me to the sterile formal living room I noticed when I came in. The den's walls are covered with photographs of horses and riders elegantly dressed, taken during dressage championships. I see Quinn as a little girl on some of the shots. I'm unable to resist the urge to pace around the den, admiring the photographs, while Jane watches me from the couch.

"Quinn was a star from an early age," she offers.

I notice the same white horse in a lot of the photos. "Andalusian?" I ask, pointing at one of the more prominent portraits. In this one, Quinn looks to be about fifteen.

Jane nods, smiling approvingly, perhaps even properly impressed. "That's Hawthorne."

"He's beautiful."

"He died of a heart malady when Quinn was nineteen, just when she graduated to upper-level competitions. She never recovered and turned to tennis instead."

"Did she not compete again?"

"No. She rides now and again. She might be riding by the pond right now. That's why I didn't holler for her, and why you're still wearing your coat, in case you were wondering."

I was. I scan each window looking for Quinn, wondering if riding is a good idea for a pregnant woman. Suddenly the possibility that she isn't pregnant looms over me with devastating potential.

"Janie, whose car is that? Is it that loudmouth Ellen again?"

"Mind your manners, Harry!" Jane chides the approaching gruff voice.

Harrison McDermont stands at about six foot five, barrel chested and long legged, and one of his arms is thicker than both my legs put together. He peers at me through a familiar hue of gas-flame blue eyes. His thinning blonde hair is pasted to his sunburned scalp. He dries his large hands in a towel as he approaches me with an affable smile.

"Harry," he says, offering his right hand.

"Lewis Bettford, Sir. It's an honor to meet you," I reply, taking his hand which painfully crushes mine with the strength of a man who's worked with his hands his whole life.

"You are Lewis, from London." Harry exchanges a glance with Jane. "I was hoping you'd come, Lewis."

"Yes, Sir," I reply in an even tone resisting the urge to wince over the pulverization of my fingers.

I have to assume that Quinn told her parents about her pregnancy, also that I'm the father. My knees begin to shake.

"You a friend of the girl that just got married?"

I nod. "Samantha. She went to school with Quinn."

He gives me an unreadable smile. "Don't I know it. A wild one, that one. Killed off a fifth of whiskey like nothing when she visited once."

I can only smile. Samantha will be happy to know her drinking is officially legendary. "She's doing much better now."

He nods. "Good thing. Be a shame on a pretty thing like that."

"Harry, I'm in the room," Jane complains with a touch of jealousy.

"Oh, hey, Janie, I didn't say gorgeous, or beautiful, not even ravishing, those are all yours." He gives me an impish grin and a wink.

"Nice save," she says, not entirely mollified.

"So, Lou. Should I venture as to why you're here?" Harry says in a voice that makes me think of distant thunder.

Well, Sir, I'm the father of Quinn's baby. May I call you, Dad?

"He's here to see Quinn."

Harry's expression darkens, like ominous thunderclouds gathering over an unsuspecting village. "You're not associated to Fishface in any way, are you?"

"Fischer!" Jane corrects.

"No Sir. I would never associate with Andrew Fishface."

His tawny eyebrows ride high, wrinkling his forehead before he grins. "Well, son, looks like you get to see your next birthday after all."

At least for now…

"Tell you what, why don't you grab Kahliman out there and ride down to the pond. I think she's over there sitting on the same bench playing the same sad song on her Martin. Maybe you can cheer her up. At least have her get back to the warmth of the house. I don't know what to do anymore."

"Sir," I gather my ebbing courage. "Perhaps I'm the reason she's upset. I'm here in the hopes to do something about that."

Harry shoves his big hands in the pockets of his trousers and rocks on his heels. "Lewis, you have proven quite a bit just by coming here on your own. I can only hope you two figure it out." He turns to his wife. "What about Billy, is he coming or what?"

The name of another man is like a physical blow.

"He just left twenty minutes ago. He'll be here in another hour."

"UConn is not that far," Harry grumbles.

"Pardon me, who's Billy?" I ask, already dreading the answer.

"Our son Billy," Jane replies. "He's good with this type of stuff. He's a senior at UConn, a history major."

"That'd better pan out for him, or I swear I'll—"

"Harrison," Jane warns.

The big man puts up his hands in surrender.

I feel a rush of oxygen replenishing the tissues of my body. I've completely forgotten about Quinn's little brother. "I thought you were going to say he's in school for therapy."

Jane smiles. "When I said, Billy's good with this type of stuff, I meant he's good with Quinn. He's a good kid, very in touch with his feelings."

"What Janie means is, our Billy," his eyes roll skyward, "God helps us, is gay as a songbird."

"Harrison!"

"Hell, Janie, let's start calling apples, apples around here." Jane glares at her husband while he looks me up and down. "Lou, you ought to find Quinnie before Billy gets here and starts telling you how pretty you are. I highly advise you take a dip in the mud to guard off his amorous intentions."

A flying shoe smacks the back of Harry's head and he nearly escapes a second one as he runs down the hallway, but the missile bounces off his broad back.

The moment is so unexpected that I don't know if I imagined it until Jane laughs softly in contrast to Harry's loud guffaws reverberating through the house.

"I'll make sure Billy will be on his best behavior. Why don't you go find Quinn. Do say you'll stay for dinner."

"If Quinn will have me, Madame, it'll be an honor."

When I don't move, Jane frowns at me. "What is it?"

"Madame, I didn't know what to expect once I got here. You see, I—"

"Lewis, before you say another word, go find my daughter and talk to her."

43

There are moments in your life that are so significant you're bound to utter about them on your last day on earth, and relive them in your mind as if it was the first time, before the last of the light of your life extinguishes.

This perilous gallop atop a beast made up of nothing but muscle and attitude, is one of those moments.

Kahliman is a powerfully built Danube Delta, a rare feral breed that is difficult to tame. I only know this because Harrison McDermont typed a description of this horse and pasted it to Kahliman's portrait in the den.

I figured Quinn's father was not worried about giving me his approval through some personality test. He had the bloody beast do it for him. Apparently, he figures if I get dropped, stomped, and killed then I don't deserve to be around his daughter.

The horse becomes slightly docile when I loosen the rein, allowing him to do whatever he wants. Each time I try to steer him in a certain direction he lets me know how displeased he is by thrashing around, threatening to launch me to my death.

I find myself pleading and cajoling with the horse, whose coat is damp and wafting an earthy aroma that reminds me of a wet dog.

When he canters by the barn for the third bloody time, I have no choice but to allow Kahliman to go where he pleases. Thankfully, he finally starts following a trail as the sun vanishes into the horizon.

Up ahead, a lone figure is crouched down on a large boulder, holding a guitar over her crossed legs. A fire crackles beside her.

I can tell it's Quinn just by the length of her hair even though it's a tad longer now.

A chestnut horse half the size of Kahliman, flicks its tail just a few feet from her. It nickers and shudders, shaking its long white mane. The horse sees me and regards me with indifference before putting his mouth to the ground.

Kahliman stops and begins to wander back to the barn. I decide enough is enough. I get my right foot out of the stirrup and kick my leg over the pommel riding sideways for a few steps. Sensing my intent to escape, Kahliman stutters as though he's about to bolt. I jump off his sweaty back but when I land, momentum carries me out of control and sends me flying headlong into the tall grass.

Kahliman's neighing sounds far too similar to human laughter, adding humiliation to the jarring aches assaulting my knees and ribs.

I get to my feet and shoot a dark look at the bloody horse. In response, Kahliman simply shakes his big head before dipping it to the ground for a mouthful of grass.

"I see a jar of glue with your name on it, lad."

I get to my feet and look up the trail some two hundred feet, where Quinn is too engrossed in her playing to notice me.

As I close the distance, I notice trailing wires from her ears. She's listening to music as she plays, practicing a song I can't identify. I hobble along on the flat grass to hide the sound of my approach.

She stops playing and I freeze, but she only shakes her hair off her face and straightens her shoulders. She pulls the ear buds off and taps a count beat on the body of the guitar. Once she's got the beat imprinted in her head, she starts picking a deliberately slow melody, simultaneously strumming a trio of chords and adding a variety of notes.

It's inconceivable to hear so much music out of one instrument. She runs through the progression twice, and I see her shoulder blades rise and her voice comes clear and smooth, right into the depths of my heart. Never in my life have I heard such an angelic sound. It literally brings me to my knees when I'm only ten feet behind her.

The truth of my entire existence is in those poignant lyrics.

Her voice drags over the first part of the verse infusing such emotion into the lyrics that sets my soul ablaze. I know beyond any doubt she's singing to the baby. It's in the promise within the lyrics. She will look after our baby.

When she finishes the song, she puts her head down, as though drained by the effort.

The sun blinks out just to the right of her head, after coloring her hair with a reddish, purplish glow. She cries softly, her cheek resting on the smaller curve of the guitar.

As quietly as I can, I stand and make my way over to her, careful of stepping on loose rocks or a telling brittle branch.

I place my hands gently upon her shoulders and she stiffens but doesn't turn around, she just continues to cry.

"You'll give those blokes from The Fray a run for their money, luv."

She sobs and brings a hand to take mine. I've never been so glad to feel someone's touch.

"Why'd you come? After everything I…"

"I had to see you."

"You saved my foundation…"

I shrug. "It's what you hired me for. Don't give it another thought."

She wipes away the tears with the back of her free hand. "Did you read my note?"

Guilt cuts me down to a bloody stomp. "I…"

"I couldn't call you, Lewis. I didn't know what to say." She turns to me and takes a look down the trail towards the house. "How did you know how to get here?"

"I could've found you anywhere, luv. Anywhere."

She looks into my eyes. "You look… terrible."

I chuckle. "Nothing some beauty sleep won't heal."

She continues to stare at every inch of my face. She only breaks eye contact to place the guitar in a soft case that she leaves unzipped.

"I met your parents. Do they know about me?"

She nods slowly. "They can be infuriatingly intuitive." Her eyes continue to scan my face.

"What is it?"

She shakes her head and shuts her eyes, squeezing a tear that rolls out of the corner of her left eye. "I said things I didn't mean to Gina and Lynn. When they told me how you left, I knew I'd royally screwed up."

Her revelation infuses frustration in my voice. "Why didn't you just call me? Why didn't you talk to me?"

She gives me a helpless shrug that conveys such vulnerability, I inwardly pray for whatever pain she's feeling to be bestowed upon me so she's free of it, just as I did when we were on the boat on the Thames.

She hangs her head and I inhale deeply, fearing I'm only collecting some last mementos.

"You let me go."

I recall the last time I saw her, head down, leaving after we kissed one last time. How could I have been such a coward, turning away from her under the pretense of not wanting to hurt? "But I'm here now."

"In the note I wrote..."

"It doesn't matter," I tell her and gather her to my chest.

"Why did you come?"

"Because I know, Quinn."

She burrows into my chest, crying despondently.

"Look at me, luv."

She shakes her head, continuing to avert her wounded eyes.

"I know, Quinn."

"No, you don't."

I take her chin gently and lose myself in those blue eyes when she forces herself to open them. Something changes in the way she's staring at me as understanding dawns in her gaze.

"How?"

I let go of her pretty face and start emptying my pockets, looking for the one thing that practically has become the reason of my existence.

A gasoline receipt flies away in the cool breeze and the rental car key clatters on the hard stone. I'm breaking into a sweat when it suddenly hits me. I reach back and pull the folded cardboard out of my jeans, unfold it and hand it to her.

Her eyes go wide for a moment, but she looks more defeated than elated.

"You do know…"

"Yes. Quinn I—"

"I'm sorry. I was just so careless and I don't know what to do right now. I didn't do it on purpose. Oh, God, I'm sorry."

She sobs then mumbles something that I don't quite understand.

"What'd you say?"

She takes a shaky breath before replying. "I understand if you don't want this… If you don't… want… me…"

This time I grip her shoulders and roughly prop her up so we are eye to eye. "You're wrong!"

Quinn shakes her head from side to side, the gesture is absolutely maddening.

Some strange current courses through me and the words tumble out. "I love you, Quinn. I'm in love with you. And if you feel the same, the rest is going to be alright."

I can feel her trembling or perhaps it's me as I'm about to ask a question whose answer may alter my life in ways I never thought possible. "Quinn, do you want to have this baby?"

She brings a hand to her pretty mouth to stifle the escaping sobs that seem to shake her entire body. Her eyes pierce me with an incredulous look.

The next words I'm about to say take more courage than I could possibly have.

"Whatever your decision…" I can hear Gwen's words in my head, but the truth is, I want to make good on little Brooke's words and be a father to this baby, even an awesome one. If she decides against it, I don't know that I could possibly bear it. "Whatever choice you make… I'm behind you, all the way."

Quinn continues to cry, and I can almost feel the coming of the devastating answer, like a long black train speeding down the tracks where I lie, helplessly awaiting for it to end me.

"Do you want…" I hesitate for only a second. "…to have our baby?"

A strangled sound of pain distorts her voice and tears well in my eyes, which shut tight, not wanting to face reality ever again.

I actually feel the rumbling of the train in my chest as it gets closer, but just as it's about to tear me to pieces, I feel Quinn nodding.

"Quinn?"

She nods more emphatically, the sobs stealing her voice for a long moment, until something seems to release her from its grip.

"Yes…"

I cradle her head to my chest, praying, hoping she doesn't change her mind and sentence me to an existence without her.

Her arms finally encircle me and I thank God whatever He may be, with every fiber of my being.

I kiss the top of her head, loving the softness of the light strands, deeply inhaling the unique scent of her. When she draws back, I grudgingly release her.

"Yes, I want our baby. I want you. I want everything with you," she says quickly, managing a smile through the tears.

In the flickering light of the fire, her blue eyes are clear pools where I see a man who believes in destiny for the first time in his existence. I see the man I never thought I'd be, a man with a purpose.

Her hands take my face, and I revel in the softness and the warmth of her touch. She kisses my lips once, and she haltingly utters the words that will echo in my heart until the day I die.

"I'm so in love with you…"

Epilogue

Madison, Connecticut July 2012

"Are we forgetting anything?"

"No, I shoved it all in the back of your lorry."

"Truck," Quinn corrects. "Or Chevy, or pickup, but I like truck."

"Of course," I reply.

"Say, okay. It sounds less snobbish."

"I'm a British snob, remember?"

She giggles. "Doctor Rachael said we can go home today."

"Are you sure you don't want to stay one more night?"

She shakes her head. "Doctors' orders."

Dr. Rachael Horowitz and Quinn attended school together when they were kids. The short, stout clinician is one of the most personable people to ever don the white coat. All her patients call her Doctor Rachael.

"It'll be great to sleep in a bed again," I concede as I roll my head, eliciting a loud pop from the vertebrae in my neck.

"Don't get too used to it. We have some sleepless nights ahead of us."

"Looking forward to it, luv." I give her a meaningful grin.

"No Romeo, our little bundle of joy will keep us too busy at night for *that*."

"Pity…" I push the wheelchair down the sterile hall, nodding a hello at the smiling nurse with the Sponge Bob scrubs. "Did you decide on the nursery colors?"

"Oh, Gwen already took care of that."

"She did?"

"Of course she did, she wanted to. She painted while Tony and Billy put the furniture together.

"I'm sure it was a hardship for Billy," I muse, imagining my gay soon-to-be little brother-in-law swooning over our author friend. "Eager to go home?"

Quinn nods. "Eager to be home with you."

"Is Billy still campaigning for the role of godparent?"

"He's just going to have to be content with the role of crazy Uncle Billy."

Quinn's little brother, William "Billy" McDermont is twenty-three. He inherited the thick, strong frame of his father and the dark features of his mother. The lad dresses impeccably well and I've yet to see a single hair out of place. He's very active in the ongoing fight for gay rights at the University of Connecticut, and often consults with me for ideas on peaceful demonstrations for public awareness and calls for tolerance.

Billy and the Alternate Lifestyles League groups from the New England area have been under siege by extremist religious groups who allowed themselves a more direct approach in their condemnation of sinners.

On a rather courageous move, Billy and his group not only joined their local church, but became active members of their congregations, and more importantly, befriended many of the people that had once chanted against them.

There was no hope of changing everyone's mind of course, and it didn't help that other gay groups went on the offensive, shoving their perverted ideal of the lifestyle down people's throats.

Personally, I feel there were larger issues, we as a whole, ought to address, but as the saying goes, a journey of a thousand miles begins with one step, and Billy was taking a good step.

I see much of myself in Billy though he is certain of himself in a way I never was until I fell for Quinn. His partner, Jeremy, is a quiet, decidedly bright young man who may cure cancer one day. I wish them luck.

"Is Sam at the house already?" Quinn asks.

"She would've texted by now."

"So what's the surprise?"

"I'm sure I don't know, luv. She didn't tell me."

"Yeah, right."

"Scout's honor."

"You were never a scout."

"I wanted to be."

"I don't want secrets in our marriage," she lectures.

"We're not married yet."

"If you want to be, you'd better tell me."

I keep from blowing out a frustrated breath. "Quinn, she hasn't told me. I swear on Hawthorne's grave." I purposely bring up her beloved horse's name.

She twists in her seat to look up at me. "Pulling out the big gun, are you?"

"You wish. Not for six weeks. Doctor's orders."

She sighs wistfully. "I don't know if I can wait that long."

I lean down. "I'm counting on it, luv," I growl in her ear, making her hold her breath.

"That was so not cool, Lewis Jonathan. Damn you!"

I laugh. "Hey, refrain from using foul language. Little ears are listening."

Quinn swivels her head to give me a scowl that only makes her even prettier in my book then she sticks her tongue out at me. I'm beginning to realize where Samantha picked up her manners, or lack thereof.

The hospital nursery is surrounded by glass on three sides. Three young nurses in different cartoon-themed scrubs are busily tending to the littlest patients in Madison Medical Center, a brand new affiliate of the prestigious Yale University Hospital.

"Well, here we are, so which one is it?"

Quinn manages to swivel and slap me on my side, hard enough to sting. "I can't believe you don't recognize your own child."

"I'm teasing." Well, partly. Other than the pink and powder blue squares in the small plastic cribs, I have no way of differentiating the eight new little people.

With the exception of one, cute as a button, African American baby girl, the rest look just as fair, just as bald, and just as exhausted. A couple of boys are already stating their grievance of the state of the world they inherit in the form of piercing wails. The Snoopy-clad nurse gently lifts one of the screaming bundles and within seconds, the crying stops and she has one more satisfied customer.

Out of the eight pods, five contain girls, and one of them is ours, but I can't tell which one. Unless I want to test the efficiency of the emergency room in this fine facility, along with Quinn's recuperative powers, I dare not guess the wrong one. I know she'd beat me to a bloody pulp.

"There she is!" Quinn points out to the far pod to our right.

"A mother always knows," I muse.

Quinn gives me a quick glance then points at the pod again. "No, the name is right there, dummy. See? Bettford."

"Oh, how about that?"

"We are so hiring a nanny. You're already proving to be a hopeless male."

The third nurse, a pretty Hispanic middle-age woman, who wears Tweety Bird scrubs, carefully picks up a tiny bundle in her arms. She stares lovingly at the little face, than comes closer to the glass and turns the baby towards us.

It's difficult for me to believe this tiny peanut put Quinn through a distressing period of two weeks of bed rest and nine exhausting hours of labor, but Quinn proved far tougher than me.

And yes, I refuse to give you a glimpse of the inadequacy of the male in a birthing unit here on these pages.

A tiny fist slowly rises as her arm stretches and Quinn and I stare at the movement of that little limb in complete rapture. The tiny head moves slightly and the impossibly tiny lips form a perfect O as our baby girl yawns. Exhausted by the activity, her features relax as slumber claims her once more.

"She's so beautiful…"

"Of course, she takes after me," I tease.

"You wish."

I chuckle.

Once baby Bettford is tucked in, back in her pod, I turn the wheelchair and start back for the room.

Three hours later, an orderly pushes Quinn's wheelchair out the lobby. I have her lorry— Blimey, I mean, truck. I have the truck pulled up, doors open, and the plastic safety contraption tightly cinched in the back seat. After driving the behemoth for a few months, I'm beginning to dislike normal-sized vehicles less and less, especially here in Connecticut where people seem to have their own ever-changing driving rules.

"How about Sidney? It's a lovely name."

Quinn is already shaking her head. "Too close to Sadie, and Samantha will kill me."

I frown quizzically.

"Sidney Crosby? Hockey star? Samantha hates his guts."

I roll my eyes. "You can't possibly be serious."

"It'd be like naming our baby after one of the Manchester United players, which I'd be fine with, of course."

"Oh, bugger me twice!" I say, making a face at the mere mention of Liverpool's most hated rival in the English Premier League.

The quest for the perfect name began as soon as Quinn and I told her family about the pregnancy. I fully expected Harry to do to me what he wanted to do to her ex-husband, but instead, he picked me up in a bear hug and told me several times, "Hey, I'm going to be a grandpa!"

I once asked him if he had any questions for me, but he assured me that as long as he kept seeing a smile on Quinn's face when she spoke of me, he had his questions answered.

Jane, my soon to be mother in law, said to me that my coming after Quinn answered all her questions. I consider this level of acceptance nothing short of a blessing.

And thus began the quest for a name, a quest that's proved to be as daunting as finding the Holy Grail.

"Mia," I suggest, thinking of the American "soccer" sensation, Mia Hamm.

"Forget it. We once had a weiner dog named Mia. She was a terror!"

I silently curse the bloody hound I never met.

The orderly smiles but doesn't contribute to the argument. Instead, he patiently shows me the intricacies of latching the baby carrier. He places the carrier into the base and it locks in place with a resounding clicking that fails to rouse our unnamed baby.

Quinn gingerly climbs into the back seat next to the basket and I shut the door as quietly as I can.

"I recommend you get your baby used to the noise, you guys can't be quiet all the time. They sleep through anything unless you get them used to total silence," the orderly sagely advices.

I file away the information the way I've been doing for the last three months as everyone we've spoken to, insisted on giving us some pearl of wisdom concerning babies. Unlike before, this time I patiently listen, intending to remember everything people tell us.

I read *What to Expect When You're Expecting*, cover to bloody cover, twice. I thought I bloody well knew exactly what to expect. No two parents were as prepared as Quinn and I were.

We shan't revisit the way I froze when the first contraction twisted Quinn's face and made her crush my hand in hers as she rode the wave of pain. I committed the cardinal sin of complaining how much my hand hurt and Quinn screamed at me to do something anatomically impossible to myself.

"Hey, Grandma, I'd like to get home today," Quinn chides.

"I'm doing the bloody limit," I lie.

"You're going twenty in a forty-five zone. Seriously?"

Properly shamed, I invoke my Evil Knievel tendencies and accelerate to twenty-five miles an hour.

"Good grief," Quinn gripes but doesn't say another word about my driving until we pull into the drive of McDermont Acres.

The day is pleasant, the blasted humidity mercifully low for this time of year, according to Quinn.

Out here, the changing of the seasons is a much more palpable event. It allowed me to replace my habit of aimless driving with horseback riding through the expansive grounds of McDermont Acres, along with a chance to bond with my soon-to-be father in law.

Harrison McDermont, the former Texan, served two tours in Vietnam with the 101st Airborne, The Screaming Eagles.

I wondered how he could be so open minded to accept his son's homosexuality, which was something we spoke about at length.

"I don't like the damn fairy ones, you understand. I don't like the transvestite bit. Men shouldn't dress like women, period." He told me during one of our rides. "It's an insult to the fairer sex."

He was surprised that I agreed, but had he seen Carmen Santopietro trying to pass for a woman in his sixties, he wouldn't be so surprised.

There is something disconcerting about seeing a man like Harrison McDermont cry, but he did, over his son. He practically echoed my mother's words from the night she unburdened herself of her feelings towards what I now call my previous life.

I suggested that perhaps one day Billy would change, but Harry proved more grounded on reality than me.

"We are what we are, son. It takes guts to be true to yourself. I'll always respect him for that. He's my boy and I love him, no matter what."

Harrison was also quite fond of expressing his contempt for his former son-in-law by making jokes about the many creative ways he'd use to ensure Andrew Fischer's excruciatingly painful, slow death. He couldn't utter his musings in front of Jane or Quinn, but I got an insight into the mind of a father whose daughter had been hurt. The first time I held my baby girl, I understood his stance very clearly.

Aside of family and tender accounts of Quinn's growing up, told with evident pride, he confided his idea of writing a book about his experiences in Vietnam. He wanted to show a more human side to that bloody conflict in the hopes of lessening the stigma he and his fellow soldiers were forced to carry with them since returning home.

When I suggested he talk to Samantha about it, he doubled over Kahliman, laughing. "I'll call that little cutie if I decide to write smut. Don't tell Janie I said that."

Samantha would be pleased to know that her reputation as a tart is also legendary.

Employing my charming abilities, honed from a lifetime of practice, I won over Jane McDermont, and soon she and my mother held long telephone conversations. Mum and Richard Bergman postponed their nuptials, in order to make themselves available for the birth of our unnamed baby.

Tony Amaya's parents live a short distance from Madison, a wonderful convenience that has allowed Gwen and the girls to be part of this day. Gwen and Quinn have become close friends and we enjoy her visits often. Her kindness was boundless when it came to baby preparations, especially after Jane required a surgical procedure for her back. Gwen did not hesitate to drive the eight hours and brought with her Brooke's helpful disposition and Emily's entertainment prowess.

Gwen was only too happy to have something to do, other than miss her husband, who'd been busy with the television series based on the book Samantha helped him publish. Thankfully, Tony was able to get away for a two week stretch and Gwen immediately put him to work by helping Harry with the preparation of the nursery. The McDermont's and I welcomed them with open arms.

I had offered buying our own home, but Jane and Harry were adamant that the economic climate was less than ideal for buying a house, despite the fact that both, Quinn and I, were in a favorable position to afford the house of our dreams. Quinn, who knew her parents better than me, sensed they wanted her close for just a few more months. The convincing argument was that we could enjoy the help and support of family as we learned the skills required for parenting.

While married to Fischer, Quinn had been forced to miss time with her parents because of Harry's non-hypocritical attitude towards his former son-in-law. The animosity proved to be a bigger wedge than Andrew's blatant infidelity. At one point, she had gone over a year and a half without visiting her family, and seeing how close they are, I knew it had deeply hurt all of them.

Gwen shared a slightly similar situation though in her case, it was her own family doing the damage, but they were making plans to remedy all that. I was so happy to hear about their plans to move to Connecticut.

"We're here, Leslie," Quinn coos to the baby.

"Leslie? Uh uh, perish the thought, luv." I come around and open the door.

"It's a perfect name!" she protests.

"Jacqueline, tell Mum, no way," I tell the sleeping baby.

"Jacqueline? Oh, hell no!"

Sadie, the quiet Golden Retriever, actually picks herself up and bounds down the porch steps to sniff at the new inhabitant of her house.

"Let her smell little Genevieve," Quinn says in a sing song voice.

I lower the carrier, curiously noting for the first time just how big the big dog's mouth really is. "Genevieve? Oh, get real!" I exclaim, deliberately using one of Quinn's favorite phrases.

Sadie gently sniffs the baby's tiny foot, then turns her big soulful eyes at each of us, wags her tail and grins sweetly.

"Glad you approve, mutt," I tell her.

Ever since coming here, I've found myself playing the part of Dr. Doolittle. Even Kahliman, that ornery beast of a horse, shoots the breeze with me every now and then.

The door opens and Harry and the effeminate Billy grin at us. Billy kisses both Quinn and me on the cheek before fixing his eyes on the new addition to his family.

"Oh, Claire, you are beautiful!" he exclaims.

"Claire?" Quinn glares at Billy.

"Just kidding."

"Okay, let me see this little angel," Harry's voice booms. "Oh, will you look at that," he says, crouching down to get a better look at the infant. "She is a Shannon for sure."

"Dad, forget it," Quinn is quick to discourage him.

The entire family has been campaigning to name our child. It's gone on for weeks. Harry, who normally condemned the internet, secretly asked me to show him how to navigate the web.

Quinn discovered the secret when a check of the web browsing history revealed several baby names sites along with others including history articles and horse values. I like to think that had I known my father, he would've been just as excited about his grandchild.

Twin gasps echo from inside the door, then two visions of female prettiness run down the steps.

"I want to hold her!" Gwen tugs at my arm.

"Like hell!" Samantha protests. "I'm the bloody godmother!"

"Momma gets to hold her first." Quinn bends down.

"Are you sure? Are you strong enough?" I say nervously, earning some quizzical scowls from all three of them.

Quinn carefully unclasps the straps before gently plucking the tiny sleeping form.

Samantha and Gwen launch into a full narrative, describing every part of the baby and I hear the words "so cute", and "so little" so often that makes me think they forgot an entire language.

"I'd say, Sophia," Gwen declares.

"I say, Lillian," Samantha says with finality.

"Sophie or Lilly," Quinn mulls the names over. "Not bad ladies."

"Well which one is better?" Samantha demands.

"Oh, Sam, always the competitive lass," I tell her.

Unlike Quinn, Samantha strikes my shoulder with glee.

"How's my mom?"

Gwen smiles at Quinn reassuringly. "She's okay, moving a little more each day. Maddie and Richard are visiting with her."

Inside, the first person to hold our, as yet unnamed, baby is Jane. She and my grinning mother run a much more eloquent commentary of the little features.

"Sherry," Mum says. "Definitely Sherry."

"Rose," Jane offers. "Rosie. What do you think dear?"

Quinn emphatically rolls her eyes. "Don't call us, we'll call you."

The older women laugh.

"Where are the boys?" Quinn asks, looking over Samantha's shoulder, actually trying to. (I wonder how many nights I'll spend on the couch on account of my constant teasing about her height.)

"Oh, they'll be here soon. Can't imagine they'll survive the girls for very long," Gwen says.

Quinn turns to Samantha. "What's this big surprise you mentioned?"

Samantha smiles. "It can wait. You should really check out the nursery. Hell, I want to move in there."

"Let's go."

We leave our baby in the capable hands of our mothers, and follow Gwen and Samantha to the nursery. Since I spent all of fifteen days with Quinn at the hospital, I haven't seen anything other than heavy furniture crammed into the wallpapered chamber.

I see the door has been replaced with a new one, painted white. Gwen opens it and allows Quinn and me to go in first. We stand rooted to the floor as we look around the charming nursery, unable to say a word. Now I know why those people on Quinn's home improvement shows act the way they do when their houses are remodeled.

The walls are a muted pink that the sun coming through the windows lightens to almost white. The whitewashed furniture consists of a well-equipped changing table, a comfortably looking cream-colored rocking recliner, and a very practical dresser with deep drawers. When I point out my concern about it being too tall, Gwen smiles and shows me an anchoring system that will prevent the dresser from ever toppling.

Unlike Quinn, Gwen is not affected by my paranoia. "Tony was the same way, it drove me crazy. So don't worry. I'm pretty sure he thought of every little thing."

A tall mirrored armoire holds an array of classical children's literature and an extensive collection of Dr. Seuss's timeless works, a gift from Jason and Samantha.

All three do the "how little" and "how cute" bits as they inspect every nook and cranny in the nursery. The most important piece is subconsciously saved for last. All four of us huddle around it and stare at the crib, each of us almost moved to tears.

"Tony made it," Gwen says proudly.

"It's round!" I observe, having never seen a round crib.

"Your mom made the bumper," Gwen indicates the soft pink padding around the railings. "Your *mum*," she looks at me, "knitted these blankets."

Quinn smiles in appreciation as she unfolds the hand knitted creation.

"I did the bows," Gwen adds.

"It's so perfect, "Quinn says softly. "Thank you. There's a part of each of you in here."

Samantha looks out the window. "They're here. Come!"

Quinn and I are led back outside where Tony's truck is parked next to Quinn's. I recognize the taller figure as Brooke, but I'm surprised to see two more figures moving in the back seat.

Brooke runs to me with her dimpled smile and hugs me. Emily is not far behind. Tony surprises me by giving me a brotherly embrace with several pats on the back as he offers his congratulations then goes to Gwen, an expectant smile on his face.

Jason is looking down to someone walking beside him. When they round the nose of the truck, I see a little girl of about three. Her hair is long, lustrous black, much darker than Brooke's and several more times straight, framing an oval shaped face of skin so flawless, she seems made of porcelain.

"Who is this pretty vision?" I ask, feeling a flutter inside me.

Jason grins. "Lewis, Quinn, meet our daughter Alainn."

I turn to Samantha, whose smile has never looked so pure in all the time that I've known her. "How did you keep it a secret?"

"It wasn't easy. I couldn't wait for you to meet her." Samantha tucks her chestnut hair behind her ear as she crouches down to talk to her daughter. *Her daughter!*

"Alainn, this is your uncle Lewis. Can you say hullo, luv?"

Alainn gazes at me from her obsidian eyes. They're almond shaped, revealing her Asian lineage.

"Hullo, little luv," I say softly.

"Hullo," she says in a faintly familiar clipped British accent, adding a shy little smile.

"How old is she?"

"The doctors told us almost three," Jason replies.

Quinn, Gwen and Samantha cluster around Alainn, but the little girl only has eyes for Emily and Brooke.

Jason and Tony stand beside me.

"Alainn is originally from China. A small village called Altay."

"Where did you find her, England?" I ask.

Jason shakes his head. "When we were in Madrid, we saw her singing with a chorus from an orphanage. Well, she wasn't doing much singing. She was standing in the front with this pretty smile that made us melt. We made some inquiries about adoption and did it. Nathan and Alicia pulled some strings to speed up the process, and here she is."

"She's a lucky little girl," Tony observes.

"Thanks, Tony. I had my reservations at first, but you both know what this means to Samantha. Now I can't imagine living a life without Alainn."

I feel something warm coursing through me, perhaps the realization that we're all part of this fraternity of parenthood.

Looking back, I never would've dreamed of living this moment. Samantha is a mother, and I'm a father...

...sometimes it's the source of a joy so profound it begets a new life...

Samantha looks over her shoulder, meets my eyes and smiles at me.

You were right, Sam

***

"Aww, she's so cute!" Emily says, one cutie to another.

"Oh, my God, she's so tiny," Brooke says with a voice filled with wonder. "What's her name?" She asks, not taking her gaze away from the crib.

I watch Alainn smiling lovingly at the baby. I still can't get over how precious she is. I'm holding her in one arm and Emily in the other, so they can see over the top railing of the crib.

"We're open for ideas," prompts Quinn.

Brooke frowns in thought. "It has to be something pretty. One of a kind."

"You all have a lot to learn from this young lady," Quinn declares, her short stature enabling her to put an arm around Brooke without crouching.

"Rosetta?" Emily quips. "Or Fawn... how about Tink?" Emily suggests, naming her favorite Disney fairies.

We all laugh and Emily seems to take objection to it so we stop.

"Those are all good ideas, honey. We'll see," Quinn tells her.

Gwen shows Quinn how to set up the monitor and the rest of us walk back downstairs to the living room. Alainn has fallen asleep and Samantha takes her from my arm and lays her down for a nap on the couch. She leaves her with a kiss on her forehead, the same way I saw her mother kiss Samantha when she was little.

"How about you, boys?" Quinn asks, rejoining the group.

Jason and Tony exchange a worried look.

"Don't even think about getting out of this one. Let's have it," Samantha demands.

"You and your friends are just going to shoot us down like ducks in season," Tony says while Jason nods in agreement.

"Oh, come on, Tony!" Quinn urges. "Jason, you first."

Jason looks around uncertainly for a moment. "I'll say, Paige."

"Lorraine," Tony utters hesitantly.

I double over, laughing as Gwen, Quinn, and Samantha, jump all over the two men, vociferously expounding upon the hopeless shortcomings of the male mind.

***

"Lewis?"

"No, it's the bloody Queen of England."

"I've missed that," Samantha says. "What are you doing out here?"

"Thinking. You?"

"Thinking."

We are on the porch watching the sun go down over the western hills.

"It's pretty out here."

"Liar. It's too quiet for you," I counter.

She lightly slaps my shoulder. "You know me too well."

A hawk screams somewhere over the woods far to the north. I love this time of day. I'd like it more out at the boulder where I found Quinn that first time I came here, but I've learned to stick by the citronella candles around twilight after a swarm of mosquitoes feasted on a whole gallon of my blood.

"Not bad for a couple of reprobates, huh?" Samantha says on a chuckle.

"Not bad at all. Except that I've changed my sinful ways. The jury is still out on you."

Samantha laughs. "I limit my sinful ways to my bedroom nowadays, thank you very much."

"It's about bloody time. Does Lancelot know?"

"Ha ha," she mutters sarcastically.

"Sam, did you ever think we'd end up this happy?"

She leans her elbows on the railing, looking off into the distance. The fading light plays on her eyes, coloring them in different hues.

She sighs. "I dreamed about it."

"What's Alainn mean? I know it's one of those Irish words you like so much."

"It means, beautiful."

"Apt."

"Thank you. You know, Quinn is demanding a name by tomorrow. I never thought she'd be this bloody picky."

"Any new names in the lead?"

She shakes her head. "That's a big responsibility, to name a baby."

"How'd you settle on Alainn?"

"As soon as the doctor told me I'd never have a child, I sort of wrote a name just in case that ever changed."

My heart twists. "You were fifteen."

She nods. "I had Alainn for a girl."

"Did you have one for a boy?"

She nods and turns to peer into my eyes. "Lewis Jonathan."

Smiling, I offer her my hand and she laces her fingers with mine. "Are you trying to trick me into naming my baby Samantha?"

"Not at all. You don't want people calling her Sam. Makes me think of a fat, bald man with a mustache."

"Are you kidding?"

"Gwen said that once. Speaking of," she says in a more serious tone. "If you name her Gwen, I'll slaughter you."

I laugh.

"It's going to be an adventure to watch them grow," she adds thoughtfully.

I like the fact that she stated that, implying that we will watch our kids grow, together. I once thought I'd lose her once she got married. Instead, I now have Quinn, my baby girl, another niece in Alainn, and a good friend in Jason Stephen. I've gained so much more than I ever thought possible.

"I bet you Uncle Lewis can do a better job of spoiling Alainn than Aunt Sammie spoiling her niece."

Samantha fixes me with a defiant look and grins. "You are so on."

***

I stand at the doorway listening to Quinn singing as she rocks our baby girl. When she's satisfied our little bundle is deeply asleep, I take her from her arms and gently, ever so slowly, lay her in her crib.

I could stare at this little face forever and I thank God— whom I've been talking to a bit more lately— to have that chance. "I feel like I should thank you for making her," I whisper.

Quinn leans her head on my shoulder. "In that case, I should thank you for helping."

"I'll gladly volunteer my superior services at your request."

"You'd better." She nudges me with her hip. "By the way, I have a name. Actually, Brooke gave me the name."

"Well?"

Quinn whispers it in my ear, the most beautiful name I've ever heard.

We look at each other in the dim light.

And we smile.

AUTHOR'S NOTE

Back in June of 2011 , I wrote a prologue alluding to life being a rollercoaster ride. I included the climbs to triumph, the falls to despair, the twists and turns that are often present in our lives. I even suggested sometimes the entire contraption falls around us, only for us to ride again once the hands of time rebuilt the tracks.

That prologue became the starting point of the stories of two people who have come to mean the world to me, Samantha Reddick, and the incomparable Lewis Bettford.

Somewhere along the way, while writing THE GAZE, I ended up riding this coaster along with them. And when the last line of the epilogue was rewritten more than a few times, I knew I wasn't ready to let go of them.

Where GAZE required ten months of devoted writing, THE NEXT CHAPTER progressed to its first completed version in the span of three months. I didn't develop typing superpowers and I didn't suddenly have all the time in the world. I simply had two characters whom I knew so well, and who still had much to say.

Both stories are meant to honor the unquantifiable power of true friendship and its unique brand of love above all else.

I'm happy to say I didn't come out of this rollercoaster unscathed. I shared into the universe of a special group of people, a universe that runs parallel to my own life, and I imagine, more than a few of yours as well.

I've despaired over their choices, grown angry at their stubbornness, laughed out loud with their antics, cried when they hurt, and cried tears of joy as they found their way.

So, I'd like to thank all these beautiful people, but namely our two lead characters, Samantha and Lewis. I will miss them dearly, though I will visit them often by opening the pages of GAZE and NEXT CHAPTER. It's my sincere hope that you, my dear reader, hold them dear to your heart as I hold you, for joining me on this ride.

Javier A. Robayo
June 19, 2012

Please turn the page for a preview of

My Two Flags

by

Javier A. Robayo

Prologue

Clouds moved in from the north this morning and rain seems imminent. The blazing sun toned down its power and the winds chased the humidity south, revitalizing the tired landscape with cool, clean air. Gray light filters through the picture window on the western wall. I love the rain. I do some of my best writing in the rain.

I turn from the window to glance around the old office. The twin bookcases flanking the fireplace since we moved in seventeen years ago hold my most precious legacies. I heed an impulse to walk over to the left bookcase to grab *The Composition*, my first novel. I thumb through the pages, fondly recalling the endless hours of writing I dedicated to its inception.

The other titles on the shelf, *The Water and The Stone, Leisa's Sin, Archangel,* and *The Andean Connection* evoke a torrent of memories from the past decade and a half. With utmost care, I slide the book and its memories back into place next to its mates. The second shelf bares a collection of works from fellow authors like Bert Carson, John W. Huffman, Elise Stokes, Kaye Vincent, and others, along with a pair of novels, *The Gaze* and *The Next Chapter* written by another bilingual author, given to me by our friend, Samantha McElroy.

I stare at the titles, wondering what to write next. Sometimes it helps to envision the new title on the shelf. Not this time, I guess. With a long, weary sigh I turn away from the books and glance instead at the pictures of my two daughters framed above my desk.

Before allowing my mind to wander into times past, I force myself to sit and bring the computer screen back to life. I make a few attempts to write a witty starting line, but then I change my mind and try instead to uncover a good quote, but the effort only aggravates my frustration. For the first time, I have no idea what to write.

"Coffee, Dad?"

I turn to the voice, my smile already widening. "Oh, you're a life saver. How'd you know?"

I gratefully accept the steaming mug from my daughter, Brooke.

"You always grab a cup of coffee before you write," she says as she shakes her head in disapproval.

Brooke Elizabeth is tall and long limbed, just like her mother. Her dark hair is pulled back into a loose bun, and her glasses are propped on her head as though they're a hair accessory.

"Fuel for the creative juices?" I venture, taking a sip.

"Nice try. Caffeine is bad for you."

Her admonition makes me laugh. "I should listen to the doctor. You'll be prescribing meds before you know it."

Brooke makes that incredulous face that I've seen for twenty-four years. "If I get through this residency, maybe."

Brooke's been working toward a Doctorate in Pediatrics at Yale University. She leans a thin hip on the side of the desk, careful not to rock the flat screen monitor. She reaches for a pen from an old Patriots mug and draws heart-shaped bubbles on my legal pad. She always did that as a child, too.

"Uh oh," she says, noting my expression.

"Uh oh, what?"

"Dad, you always get that look on your face before you break into some story about me when I was little."

I chuckle. She's never liked anyone talking about her, good or bad. "One day, you'll understand."

Her hazel eyes go wide. "No babies for me for a while. You guys will just have to be patient, thank you."

"No rush here." I throw my hands up for emphasis.

Brooke moves off the desk and pulls up a cushioned saucer chair to my left. When she was little, she invariably stood to my right, hampering me from using the computer mouse and forcing me to ask her to move. Maybe she purposefully broke my concentration to force me to address her.

"What are you working on? New novel?"

"Maybe."

"Are you going to write another tear-jerker?"

I frown at her. "I don't set out to make people cry with what I write, you know," I say, feigning indignation.

"Well, thank God it's not intentional. Imagine if it was!" She takes a long sip of tea to hide her smirk.

"Wiseass."

Her grin produces a deep dimple on each cheek. "I learned from the best."

"How many more days before you have to go back?"

"I don't have to be back at school until the tenth. You've got me all to yourself for New Year's too."

"Good. Maybe you should just stay here forever."

"I'd love to."

Me too...

She smiles. "So, I was up in the attic, looking for some old music and I found something."

"You know you can just download music nowadays, right?"

Brooke waves her hand dismissively. "Every once in a while, I like to listen to music without having to stare at a screen. I like those old vinyl records you and Mom keep up there. I love that Beatles album."

"That's actually your grandmother's, but I begged for it long enough."

"That reminds me. I have to call her. I'm taking her shopping on Sunday."

I laugh. "Wear some very comfortable shoes."

"I'm telling," she threatens.

"Grandma's shopping trips are epic. Have fun."

"That's not nice. She's just conscientious about her shopping."

I say nothing, remembering all too well the times when I drove my mother to some department store, whittling away the afternoon while she painstakingly examined each item before simply putting it back.

"While I was up there," Brooke continues. "I found this." She holds a large white book with embossed golden letters up to me.

WELKERTON HIGH SCHOOL 1988-1989

She opens it on her lap and chuckles at the pictures. "Oh my God, holy big hair!" The phone on my desk rings and Brooke lurches to pick it up, leaving the yearbook open on the desk. "What's up, Sis?" Brooke puts the phone against her chest to mute herself and whispers, "It's Em. I need to talk to her. Girl stuff." I nod. "Give her my love and let me talk to her when you're done." Brooke nods and quickly leaves the studio to talk to her sister.

Emily is on her way home from Florida State University with her new boyfriend. *God, help me...*

Her break was delayed due to a volleyball tournament I wish I could've attended. A mouthwatering aroma of hash brown casserole wafting through the open door tickles my nose. God, I love my Gwen.

Maybe I can start writing another love story. I set my hands over the keyboard, willing the words to emanate from my mind, through my fingers, and onto the screen, but nothing comes. Instead I decide to follow the aroma and hunt down a steaming bowl of cheese-covered hash browns. After two steps, my eyes fall upon the old yearbook. Four signatures from my freshman year grace the back cover. A wave of nostalgia crashes through my mind in a deluge of memories I once thought forgotten.

And the years fall away...

ABOUT THE AUTHOR

Javier A. Robayo is the author of THE GAZE. He immigrated to the United States in 1988, and began writing as a way of learning English as a freshman in high school. He studied at Slippery Rock University and lives in Western Pennsylvania, with his wife, and two daughters, where he is currently at work on his next novel.

8362177R00280

Made in the USA
San Bernardino, CA
06 February 2014